COMPUTER GRAPHICS

Volume 24 • Number 4 • August 1990
A publication of ACM SIGGRAPH
Production Editor Richard J. Beach

SIGGRAPH '90 Conference Proceedings
August 6-10, Dallas Texas
Papers Chair Forest Baskett

Sponsored by the Association for Computing Machinery's
Special Interest Group on Computer Graphics

Sample Citation Information:
...Proceedings of SIGGRAPH '90
(Dallas, Texas, August 6-10, 1990)
In *Computer Graphics,* 24, 4 (August
1990) ACM SIGGRAPH, New York, 1990,
pp. xx-yy.

ORDERING INFORMATION

**Orders from nonmembers of ACM
placed within the U.S. should be
directed to:**

Addison-Wesley Publishing
Company
Order Department
Jacob way
Reading, MA 01867
Tel: 1-800-447-2226

Addison-Wesley will pay postage and
handling on orders accompanied by
check. Credit card orders may be placed
by mail or by calling the Addison-Wesley
Order Department at the number above.
Follow-up inquiries should be directed to
the Customer Service Department at the
same number.

Please include the Addison-Wesley
ISBN number with your order:
A-W ISBN 0 201-50933-4

**Orders from nonmembers of ACM
placed from outside the U.S. should be
addressed as noted below.**

Latin America and Asia:
Addison-Wesley Publishing Company Inc.
Reading, MA 01867, U.S.A.
Tel: 617-944-3700;
Cable: ADIWES READING;
Telex: 94-9416

Canada: Addison-Wesley Publishing
(Canada) Ltd.
36 Prince Andrew Place
Don Mills, Ontario M3C2T8
Canada
Tel: 416-447-5101

Australia and New Zealand:
Addison-Wesley Publishing
Company
6 Byfield Street
North Ryde, N.S.W. 2113
Australia
Tel: 888-2733;
Cable: ADIWES SYDNEY;
Telex: AA71919

**United Kingdom, Republic of Ireland,
Africa (excluding North Africa) and
South Africa:**
Addison-Wesley Publishers Ltd.
Finchampstead Road
Workingham
Berkshire RG11 2NZ, England
Cable: ADIWES Workingham;
Telex: 846136

**Continental Europe, the Near East,
Middle East, and North Africa:**
Addison-Wesley Publishing
Company
De Lairesstraat, 90
1071 P J Amsterdam
The Netherlands
Tel: 020 76 40-44
Cable: ADIWES AMSTERDAM
Telex: 844-14046

Orders from ACM Members:

A limited number of copies are available at
the ACM member discount. Send order
with payment to:

ACM Order Department
P.O. Box 64145
Baltimore, MD 21264

ACM will pay postage and handling on
orders accompanied by check.
Credit card orders only:
1-800-342-6626

Customer service, or credit card orders
from Alaska, Maryland, and outside the
US: 301-528-4261

Credit card orders may also be placed
by mail.

**Please include your ACM member
number and the ACM Order number
with your order.**

ACM Order Number: 428900
ACM ISBN 0-89791-344-2
ISSN 0097-8930

Contents

Technical Program, Wednesday, 8 August 1990

9:00-10:30 Opening Session

ACM SIGGRAPH '90 Welcome
David D. Loendorf, Jacqueline M. Wollner

1990 ACM SIGGRAPH Computer Graphics Achievement Award:

10:45-12:30 Dynamics
Chair: Jane Wilhelms

1:45- 3:15 Rendering
Chair: Jim Blinn

3:30- 5:15 Object Space Methods
Chair: Tom Sederberg

Technical Program, Thursday, 9 August 1990

Technical Program, Friday, 10 August 1990

Panel Sessions, Wednesday, 8 August 1990

Panel Sessions, Thursday, 9 August 1990

Panel Sessions, Friday, 10 August 1990

Preface

These proceedings contain the papers presented during the three days of the Technical Program of the 17th annual ACM Conference on Computer Graphics and Interactive Techniques, SIGGRAPH '90. The conference was held August 6, 1990 throught August 10, 1990 in the Dallas Convention Center in Dallas, Texas. These proceedings are being published as a special issue of Computer Graphics. The process that eventually lead to these proceedings began with the Call for Participation, first distributed at aSIGGRAPH '89 in Boston, Massachusetts. The deadline for our receipt of manuscripts was the second Tuesday in January, January 9, 1990. This gave the last minute crowd the opportunity to spend one last weekend on their paper and express mail it on Monday so that we would have it on Tuesday. We received 210 papers before the deadline. A few papers were received after the deadline but were returned to the authors. We felt this was the only fair way to treat the majority who got their papers in on time. Of those 210, 43 were accepted. The quality of the submissions was outstanding. The accepted papers represent, we think, the best of the state of the art of computer graphics today.

The submissions were all scanned by Paul Haeberli, Jim Winget, and me in order to assign each paper to one of the members of the Technical Papers Committee as principal senior reviewer. The Committee consisted of twenty-four of the leading researchers in the field. Each principal senior reviewer was asked to obtain at least two and preferably three reviews from other experts in the field in addition to his or her own review. In addition, each submission was also assigned to a secondary senior reviewer to review.

Thus each paper received four or five reviews, with two being by members of the Technical Papers Committee. The Committee met on March 10th and 11th to make the final selections. We felt that the reviews and the people doing them made for informed as well as lively discussion for almost all submissions. Each submission was individually discussed by the whole Committee with individual members excusing themselves from participation on any paper where there might be or seem to be a conflict of interest.

The Technical Papers Committee deserves to be proud of the results of their considerable efforts and I am indebted to them all. We all learned a lot and I imagine that most of the authors learned as well. The process is not perfect but we expect the past history of some papers being submitted, reviewed, rejected, revised, resubmitted, reviewed, and accepted will continue in the future.

The person who made it all work was Melissa Anderson. She was the real organizer, worker, and task master. She collected, sorted, communicated, and kept all the pieces from unraveling. She made everything easy for me and productive for all of us. She was great.

Jeff Lane, last year's Technical Papers Chair gets special thanks for the coaching and the continuity he provided. Rick Beach continues to support us all with his amazing work in getting it all published. A better editor would be hard to imagine.

The result of all this is a document of lasting value. Use it and care for it.

Forest Baskett
SIGGRAPH '90 Technical Program Chair

Editor's Preface

These proceedings present the state-of-the-art in the field of computer graphics. As such, they contain the best research contributions submitted to SIGGRAPH. To broaden our coverage of accomplishments presented at the SIGGRAPH conference, the proceedings now contain abstracts for the panel sessions, film and video show contributions, the SIGGRAPH courses and the hypermedia exhibits. Of course, the *SIGGRAPH Video Review* continues to publish excerpts of video material and the art show catalog is co-published by SIGGRAPH.

However, the technology used to produce these proceedings lags behind the state-of-the art. At least one good reason is to ensure that they are indeed available at the conference! Depending upon emerging technologies is risky, especially when 22,000 copies of a 400-page full-color document must be produced at the quality levels demanded of the SIGGRAPH proceedings within a 3-month window. SIGGRAPH has undertaken several initiatives to expand our use of computer graphics research in publishing the proceedings. Here are brief descriptions of these initiatives and their current status.

SIGGRAPH Interactive Proceedings

The SIGGRAPH Interactive Proceedings project, initiated by Dick Phillips and Rick Beach, uses hypermedia to present a rich compendium of information from a SIGGRAPH conference. The prototype electronic document that resulted contains formatted text, computable mathematics, line art illustration, color images, audio annotation especially from the panel sessions, animated illustrations and video accompaniments. This project was demonstrated at SIGGRAPH '89 and continues to evolve. However, delays in delivering integrated color and video display hardware has stalled further refinement of the project.

Through these efforts, we have discovered significant challenges for authors who wish to prepare their material for this new medium. Conceivably, an author must combine the roles of technical writer, editor, script writer, animator, graphic designer, illustrator, storyboard writer and publisher. The daunting challenge of doing hypermedia well requires better tools and training for prospective authors. In comparison, the present system of supplying camera-ready copy is much simpler.

Despite these and other difficulties, SIGGRAPH will continue to encourage exploration and utilization of this technology for disseminating computer graphics

research. We believe in the effectiveness of this new form of presentation and will seek to expand involvement by SIGGRAPH, such as introducing hypermedia exhibits at SIGGRAPH '90.

Digital Color Printing Project

The cover of these proceedings, the *Edo Castle*, demonstrates progress in the SIGGRAPH digital color printing project headed by Maureen Stone. SIGGRAPH has funded research into algorithms for faithful color reproduction of synthetic computer graphics images created on displays and printed by photo-offset lithography. Several algorithms are being tested and implemented. The goal is to provide color reproduction tools to SIGGRAPH authors so that they can prepare more authentic color images for printing. Look for more details in future issues of *Computer Graphics*.

SIGGRAPH Course Notes

SIGGRAPH course notes have long served as a wonderful repository of hard-to-find material in computer graphics, conveniently assembled and presented by tutorial speakers. The distribution of "full sets" of course notes to educational and research libraries has further disseminated this information.

However, these notes are not formally published by SIGGRAPH. They are not available at any other time than at the annual conference. We are investigating convenient methods of archiving these notes. Mike Bailey, a SIGGRAPH director and former courses chair for several conferences, has been pursuing the use of CD-ROM for SIGGRAPH course notes. Early experiments will be conducted upon the SIGGRAPH '90 course notes with a view towards full-scale production in following years.

Intellectual Property

SIGGRAPH respects and promotes the intellectual property rights associated with material shown at the conference or published by SIGGRAPH. For example, we have marked copyrighted images as such and we have incorporated disclaimers in the *SIGGRAPH Video Review* about other uses of material submitted by the contributors without permission.

As more material is provided in electronic media, the potential ease of abuse of intellectual property rights increases. We have already experienced a number of concerns raised by copyright holders. The SIGGRAPH Interactive Proceedings project and the course note CD-ROM project represent two challenging

initiatives in this regard. We are working hard to
understand the complexities of the issues involved and
to establish appropriate guidelines and procedures for
SIGGRAPH. Two examples are more complete
copyright assignment forms (when SIGGRAPH needs to
hold the copyright on material we publish) and
publication release forms (when copyright material is
presented at SIGGRAPH).

Production Redesign

A redesign of the SIGGRAPH proceedings and
newsletter is underway. We are looking for a more up-
to-date format to present our complex material in ways
that are more effective and more compatible with
electronic publishing tools. The last design of *Computer
Graphics* was undertaken almost a decade ago. Can you
recall all of the progress since then?

Thanks

These proceedings are testament to the superior
efforts of a team of people who help me produce these
proceedings each year. Foremost is my assistant,
Subhana Menis at Xerox PARC, who has worked with
me to produce each proceedings from SIGGRAPH '87 to
SIGGRAPH '90. Another key ally is Bob Kushner of
Conceptual Litho in New York who has overseen the
printing of the proceedings for the past decade. His
forebearance in recent years as we stressed the
production schedule has been vital to the reliable
delivery of proceedings at each conference. Also, the
production assistance of Leona Caffey at Smith,
Bucklin and Associates has smoothed out rough times
as she coolly handled last minute details for us. I
especially appreciate her assistance with the film and
video show material this year. My colleagues at Xerox
PARC have provided invaluable technical assistance,
including Maureen Stone and the color group at PARC
who have done the digital color reproduction work,
Bridget Tracy who has produced camera-ready copy for
each year and Peter Kessler who has provided technical
assistance with typesetting software. Finally, I
acknowledge the love and support of my family who
have tolerated my perfectionism, my procrastination
and my fanaticism with SIGGRAPH. Thanks, Beth and
Heather, this one's for you!

Richard J. Beach
SIGGRAPH '90 Proceedings Editor
SIGGRAPH Editor-in-Chief

Conference Committee

CONFERENCE CO-CHAIRS

David D. Loendorf
(L&S Computer Technology, Inc.)
Jacqueline M. Wollner
(Convex Computer Corporation)

CONFERENCE COMMITTEE CHAIRS

Forest Baskett, *Papers*
(Silicon Graphics Computer Systems)
Alyce Kaprow, *Panels*
(The New Studio)
Patricia Wenner, *Courses*
(Bucknell University)
Christine A. Barton, *Workshops and Special Interest Groups*
(Morgan Guaranty Trust Company)
Randy Nikel, *Exhibits*
(Regis McKenna, Inc.)
Dave Inglish, *Film and Video Theater*
(Walt Disney Pictures)
Tom Linehan, *Art Show*
(Texas A&M University)
Diana Tuggle, *Slides*
(Los Alamos National Laboratory)
Amie Slate, *Audio/Visual*
Hugh Dubberly, *Creative Directors*
(Apple Computer, Inc./Art Center College of Design)
Thom Marchionna, *Creative Directors*
(Apple Computer, Inc.)
Richard J. Beach, *Hypermedia*
(Xerox PARC)
Lois A. Blankstein, *International Coordinator*
(Association for Computing Machinery)
Laurie A. Windham, *Market Relations*
(Technology Marketing Consultants)
Toni Staffieri, *Merchandise*
(Toni Staffieri & Associates Inc.)
Richard J. Beach, *Proceedings Editor*
(Xerox PARC)
Eric Bosch, *Registration*
(McMaster University)
Martin Streicher, *Student Volunteer Coordinator*
(Convex Computer Corporation)
Raymond L. Elliott, *Treasurer*
(Los Alamos National Laboratory)
Andrew C. Goodrich, *Vice Chair for Conference Planning*
(RasterOps)
Audio Visual Headquarters Corporation, *Audio/Visual Management*
Smith, Bucklin & Associates, Inc., *Conference Accounting*
Smith, Bucklin & Associates, Inc., *Conference Management*
Arta Travel, *Conference Travel Agency*
Andrews-Bartlett & Associates, Inc., *Decorator/Drayage*
Robert T. Kenworthy, Inc., *Exhibition Management*
Smith, Bucklin & Associates, Inc., *Public Relations*

CONFERENCE PLANNING COMMITTEE

Michael J. Bailey (San Diego Supercomputer Center)
Maxine Brown (University of Illinois at Chicago)
Carol Byram (Sony Microsystems Co.)
Branko J. Gerovac (Digital Equipment Corporation)
Andrew C. Goodrich (RasterOps)
Christopher F. Herot (Lotus Development Corporation)
Robert E. Holzman (Jet Propulsion Laboratory)
David D. Loendorf (L&S Computer Technology, Inc.)
Adele Newton (Alias Research)
Jacqueline M. Wollner (Convex Computer Corporation)

PAPERS COMMITTEE

Alan H. Barr (California Institute of Technology)
Richard J. Beach (Xerox PARC)
Jim Blinn (California Institute of Technology)
Ingrid Carlbom (Digital Equipment Corporation, Cambridge)
Loren Carpenter (Pixar)
Edwin E. Catmull (Pixar)
Elaine Cohen (University of Utah)
Robert L. Cook (Light Source Computer Images, Inc.)
Nick England (Sun Microsystems, Inc.)
A. Robin Forrest (University of East Anglia, U.K.)
Henry Fuchs (University of North Carolina, Chapel Hill)
Donald P. Greenberg (Cornell University)
Leo Guibas (MIT and Digital Equipment Corporation, Cambridge)
Satish Gupta (IBM, Yorktown Heights)
Pat Hanrahan (Princeton University)
Paul Heckbert (University of California, Berkeley)
Jeffrey Lane (Digital Equipment Corporation, Palo Alto)
Jock Mackinlay (Xerox PARC)
Tom Sederberg (Brigham Young University)
Robert Sproull (Sutherland, Sproull and Associates)
Turner Whitted (Numerical Design, Ltd.)
Jane Wilhelms (University of California, Santa Cruz)
Jim Winget (Silicon Graphics Computer Systems)

PANELS COMMITTEE

David S. Backer (Fluent Machines, Inc.)
Alka Badshah (Open Software Foundation)
Thomas A. DeFanti (University of Illinois at Chicago)
Masa Inakage (Media Studio)
Delle Maxwell (Consultant)
Vibeke Sorensen (California Institute of the Arts)

COURSES COMMITTEE

Teresa Bleser (The George Washington University)
Frank Bliss (Electronic Data Systems)
Janet Chin (Chin Associates)
Rich Ehlers (Evans and Sutherland)
Mark Henderson (Arizona State University)
Nan Schaller (Rochester Institute of Technology)
Dino Schweitzer (United States Air Force Academy)

ART SHOW COMMITTEE

Paul Brown (Royal Melbourne Institute of Technology, Australia)
Michael Ester (J. Paul Getty Trust)
Isaac Kerlow (Pratt Institute)
Susan Kirchman (Texas A&M University)
Randolph McAusland (National Endowment for the Arts)
Patric Prince (SIGGRAPH Travelling Art Show Chair)
Mark Resch (Computer Curriculum Corporation)
Chris Wedge (Blue Sky Productions)

ART SHOW JURY

Paul Brown (Royal Melbourne Institute of Technology, Australia)
Michael Ester (J. Paul Getty Trust)
Patric Prince (SIGGRAPH Travelling Art Show Chair)
Mark Resch (Computer Curriculum Corporation)
Chris Wedge (Blue Sky Productions)

FILM AND VIDEO CREATIVE DIRECTOR

John Grower (Santa Barbara Studios)

FILM AND VIDEO THEATER JURY

Wayne Carlson (The Ohio State University)
Robert L. Cook (Light Source Computer Images, Inc.)
Doris Kochanek (National Film Board of Canada)
John Lasseter (Pixar)
Frank Thomas (Animator)
Chris Wedge (Blue Sky Productions)

FILM AND VIDEO THEATER COMMITTEE

Janet Doran-Veevers (Santa Barbara International Film Festival)
Scott Johnston (Walt Disney Pictures)
Richard Weinberg (University of Southern California)
Dave Wolf (Walt Disney Pictures)

HYPERMEDIA JURY

Sally Rosenthal (Digital Equipment Corporation)
Bill Buxton (University of Toronto)

TECHNICAL PROGRAM REVIEWERS

Salim Abiezzi
Greg Abram
John Airey
Kurt Akeley
Koji Amakawa
John Amanatides
Tony Apodaca
Dave Arsenault
James Arvo
Russ Athay
Pete Atherton
Norman Badler
Harlyn Baker
Alan Barr
Brian Barsky
Richard Bartels
Ronen Barzel
Dana Batali
Dan Baum
Richard Becker
Thad Beier
Andy Berlin
Marshall Bern
Eric Bier
Gary Bishop
Avi Bleiweiss
Jim Blinn
Jules Bloomenthal
Sara Bly
Jean-Daniel Boissonnat
Alan Borning
John Bradstreet
I.C. Braid
Jack Bresenham
Frederick Brooks
Ken Brooks
Marc H. Brown
Russel Brown
Armin Bruderlin
Bill Buxton
Brian Cabral
Tom Calvert
John Canny
Rikk Carey
Ingrid Carlbom
Wayne Carlson
Loren Carpenter
Ed Catmull

M.J. Chalmers
Rosemary Chang
Bernard Chazelle
Eric Chen
Michael Chen
Hiroaki Chiyokura
Henry Christiansen
Richard Chung
Harvey Cline
Dan Cohen
Michael Cohen
Rob Cook
Frank Crow
Chuck Csuri
Tom DeFanti
Tony DeRose
Mark Dippé
David Dobkin
Julie Dorsey
Bob Drebin
R.L. Drysdale
Scott Drysdale
Tom Duff
Herbert Edelsbrunner
Kells Elmquist
Nick England
David Epstein
Alan Erdahl
John Eyles
Kim Fairchild
Bianca Falcidieno
Steve Feiner
Cindy Ferguson
Dan Field
Dan Filip
Scott Fisher
Ken Fishkin
Eugene Fiume
Kurt Fleischer
Jim Foley
A. Robin Forrest
Alain Fournier
Ed Fox
Randolph Franklin
William Freeman
Henry Fuchs
Don Fussell
Steve Gabriel

Nader Gharachorloo
Ziv Gigus
Andrew Glassner
Ephriam Glinert
Jack Goldfeather
Julian Gomez
Mike Goodrich
James Gosling
Henri Gouraud
Mark Green
Ned Green
Don Greenberg
Leo Guibas
Charlie Gunn
Satish Gupta
Paul Haeberli
Tom Hahn
Eric Haines
Roy Hall
Robert Halstead
Pat Hanrahan
Stephen Harrison
David Haumann
Paul Heckbert
Austin Henderson
Mark Henne
Gary Herron
Bert Herzog
Gary Hodgman
Eric Hoffert
Chris Hoffmann
Scott Hudson
Jeff Hultquist
Kevin Hussey
Dave Immel
Bill Johnston
Christopher Jones
Jim Kajiya
Michael Kaplan
Michael Karasick
Michael Kass
Arie Kaufmann
Tim Kay
Oussama Khatib
David Kirk
Victor Klassen
Lewis Knapp
Gary Knott
Peter Kochevar
David Laidlaw
Jeff Lane
Steve Larky
Jean-Claude Latombe
Jim Lawson
Philip Lee
Sam Leffler
Willima Leier
Marc Levoy
David Levy
Silvio Levy
John Lewis
Andy Lippman
Dani Lishinski
Bill Lorenson
Bruce Lucas
Leon Lumelsky
Dick Lundin
Wendy MacKay
Jock Mackinlay
Nadia Magnenat-Thalmann
Abe Mammen

Nelson Max
John McConnell
Robert McDermott
Eileen McGinnis
Donald Meagher
James Michener
V.J. Milenkovic
G.S.P. Miller
Gavin Miller
Gene Miller
Jim Miller
Larry Miller
Yael Millo
Margaret Minsky
Don Mitchell
Henry Moreton
Chuck Mosher
David Mount
Brad Myers
E. Nakamae
Barry Napier
Bruce Naylor
Ulrich Neumann
Martin Newell
Robin Nicholl
Tina Nicholl
Greg Nielsen
Dan Olsen
Art Olson
Steve Omohundro
Koichi Omura
Peter Oppenheimer
Robert Ornbo
Eben Ostby
Richard Parent
Fred Parke
Nicos Patrikalakis
Darwyn Peachey
Alan Peevers
Q.-S. Peng
Alex Sandy Pentland
Ken Perlin
Dick Phillips
Rob Pike
Steve Pizer
John Platt
Tom Porter
Michael Potmesil
John Poulton
Hartmut Prautzsch
Patrick Prince
Peter Quarendon
Lyle Ramshaw
Ari Raquicha
Rod Recker
Bill Reeves
John Rhoades
Desi Rhoden
Henry Rich
Jeanne Rich
Gary Ridsdale
Igor Rivin
George Robertson
Richard Robb
Todd Rodgers
Alyn Rockwood
John Rokne
Jarek Rossignac
Jaroslaw Rossignac
Nikos Roussopoulos
Steven Rubin

(TECHNICAL PROGRAM REVIEWERS, continued)

Holly Rushmeier
Alan Saalfeld
M.A. Sabin
Hanan Samet
Ray Sarraga
Rick Sayre
Tom Sederberg
Mark Segal
Carlo Sequin
Steve Shafer
Mike Shantz
Mikio Shinya
Peter Shirley
Ken Shoemake
John Sibert
H.B. Siegel
Francois Sillion
Kenneth Sloan
Larry Smarr
Alvy Ray Smith
Diane Souvaine
Rick Speer
Bob Sproull
Larry Stewart
Maureen Stone
Don Stredney
David Sturman
Ivan Sutherland
Richard Szeliski
Filippo Tampieri
Peter Tanner
Brice Tebbs
Demetri Terzopoulos
Daniel Thalmann
Marvin Theimer
James Thomas
Spencer Thomas
Jay Torborg
Ken Torrance

David Tristram
Ben Trumbore
Russ Tuck
Greg Turk
Ken Turkowski
Doug Turner
Craig Upson
Sam Uselton
Mark Vanderwettering
Tim Van Hook
Chris Van Wyk
Brian Von Herzen
Michael Wahrman
John Wallace
Shijie Wan
Jian-Zhong Wang
Greg Ward
Colin Ware
Joe Warren
Wendy Warren
Gary Watkins
Kevin Weiler
Jyuang Weng
Steven Wertheim
Lee Westover
Turner Whitted
Jane Wilhelms
Lance Williams
Jim Winget
Andy Witkin
Andreas Wittenstein
George Wolberg
Henry Wu
Brian Wyvill
Frances Yao
Gary Yost
Polle Zellweger
David Zeltzer
Michael Zyda

PROFESSIONAL SUPPORT

ACM SIGGRAPH '90 Conference Coordinator
Karen Pryor

ACM SIGGRAPH Program Director
Lois Blankstein

Administrative Assistants
Chris Heintzelman, *Courses*
Melissa Anderson, *Papers*
Janice Manning, *Panels*
Robert Lurye, *Art Show*
Subhana Menis, *Hypermedia*
Rozanne Cazian, *Film and Video Theater*
Mary Ann McLeod, *Film and Video Theater*
Jan Sander, *Slides*

Audio/Visual Management
Audio Visual Headquarters Corporation
Jim Bartolomucci
Rich Farnham
Doug Hunt

Conference Accounting
Smith Bucklin and Associates, Inc.
Ruth Kerns
Shelley Johnson

Conference Management
Smith Bucklin and Associates, Inc.
Jackie Groszek
Paul Jay
Deidre Ross
Amy Sandrick
Cynthia Stark

Conference Travel Agency
Arta Travel
Karen Flannery
Karen Lewis

Decorator/Drayage
Andrews-Bartlett and Associates, Inc.
Bob Borsz
Betty Fuller
Ken Gallagher
Tom Gilmore
John Patronski

Exhibition Management
Robert T. Kenworthy, Inc.
Hank Cronan
Barbara Voss

Public Relations
Smith Bucklin and Associates, Inc.
Leona Caffey
Sheila Hoffmeyer
Susan Johnston
Kathleen Nilles

Exhibitors

Abekas Video Systems, Inc.
Academic Press
Addison-Wesley Publishing Company
Advanced Graphics Engineering (AGE)
Advanced Imaging
Advanced Micro Devices (AMD)
Advanced Technology Center
Alias Research, Inc.
Alliant Computer Systems Corporation
American Power Conversion Corporation
Analog Devices, Inc.
Analogic Corporation
Androx Corporation
Apollo
Apple Computer
Applied Visual Technologies Ltd.
Association for Computing Machinery
AT&T Graphics Software Labs
AT&T Pixel Machines
Autodesk
AV Video
Aztek, Inc.
Barco, Inc.
Brooktree Corporation
BTS Broadcast Television Systems
Cahners Publishing Company
Calzone Case Company
Canada, External Affairs & International Trade
Canon USA, Inc.
CELCO
CIS Graphics Inc.
CMP Publications
Commodore Business Machines, Inc.
Computer Graphics Review
Computer Graphics World
Computer Pictures
Convex Computer Corporation
Covid, Inc.
Cubicomp Corporation
Dainippon Screen
Data General Corporation
Digital Arts
Digital Equipment Corporation
Dimension Technologies, Inc.
Display Automation Group, Inc.
Division Limited
Du Pont Company
Dubner Computer Systems, Inc.
Dynair Electronics, Inc.
Eastman Kodak Company
Electronic Display Systems
Electrohome Projection Systems
Electronic Engineering Times
ETAK, Incorporated
Evans & Sutherland
Expert Graphics Systems
Extron Electronics
Folsom Research, Inc.
French Expositions in the U.S., Inc.

Gammadata Computer Inc.
General Electric-PDPO
Gretag Image Systems
GTCO Corporation
Helios Systems
Herstal Automation Ltd.
Hewlett-Packard Company
High-Performance Systems
Howtek, Inc.
IEEE Computer Society
Ikegami Electronics (USA), Inc.
Ilford Photo Corporation
IMAgraph Corporation
Intel Corporation
Intelligent Light
Intelligent Resources
Intergraph Corporation
IRIS Graphics, Inc.
Ithaca Software
JVC Professional Products Company
LAZERUS
Levco Sales
Litton Systems Canada Limited
Lyon Lamb VAS
Macro Data, Inc.
MAGNI Systems, Inc.
Management Graphics, Inc.
Matrox Electronic Systems Ltd.
Maximum Strategy Inc.
McGraw-Hill Publishing Company
Measurement Systems, Inc.
Media Cybernetics
Megatek Corporation
Meiko Scientific Corporation
Mercury Computer Systems, Inc.
Meret, Inc.
Metheus Corporation
Microfield Graphics Inc.
Micrografx, Inc.
Microtime, Inc.
Midwest Communications Corporation
Minolta Corporation
Mitsubishi Electric Sales America
Mitsubishi Electronics America .
Mitsubishi International Corporation
Montage Publishing
Morgan Kaufmann Publishers, Inc.
Motorola Semiconductor Products
National Computer Graphics Association
NEC Technologies, Inc.
NeXT, Inc.
Nikon Inc.
Nissei Sangyo America, Ltd.
Nth Graphics, Ltd.
Number Nine Computer Corporation
Numonics Corporation
Ohio Supercomputer Graphics Project
Omnicomp Graphics Corporation
Oxberry

Panasonic Industrial Company
Pansophic Systems, Inc.
Paragon Imaging
Parallax Graphics
Peritek Corporation
Philips Components-Signetics
Photron Limited
Pixar
Pixel Magazine
Pixelworks, Inc.
Polhemus Limited
Presentation Products Magazine
PRIOR Data Sciences
PTN Publishing
QMS, Inc.
Quantum Data Inc.
Radius, Inc.
Rainbow Technologies
Ramtek Corporation
Raytheon Company, Submarine Signal Division
RGB Spectrum
Ron Scott, Inc.
Sampo Corporation of America
Seiko Instruments USA, Inc.
Seiko Mead Company
SGS-Thomson/INMOS Corporation
Sharp Electronics Corporation
Shima Seiki U.S.A. Inc.
SIGGRAPH '91
Sigma Electronics, Inc.
SigmaSoft and Systems
Silicon Graphics
Softimage Inc.
Software Security
Sony Corporation of America
Spaceward Video Systems Ltd.
Springer-Verlag New York, Inc.
Star Technologies, Inc.

Stardent Computer Inc.
StereoGraphics Corporation
Summagraphics Corporation
Sun Microsystems, Inc.
Supercomputing Review
Supermac Technology
Symbolics, Inc.
TDI-America
TEAC America, Inc.
Team Systems
Tech-Source Inc.
Techexport , Inc.
Tektronix, Inc.
Texas Instruments
Texas Memory Systems, Inc.
Texnai, Inc.
Time Arts Inc.
Toshiba America Electronic Components Inc.
Truevision Inc.
University of Lowell
Univision Technologies, Inc.
UnixWorld Magazine
Van Nostrand Reinhold
Vicom Systems, Inc.
Video Manager
Video Systems
Videomedia S.E.D., Inc.
Videotex Systems Inc.
Viewpoint Technologies
Visual Information Technologies Inc.
VT Inc.
Wacom, Inc.
Waldmann Lighting Company
Wasatch Computer Technology, Inc.
Wavefront Technologies
WaveTracer, Inc.
Winsted Corporation
Yamashita Engineering Manufacture Inc.

1990 ACM SIGGRAPH Awards

Computer Graphics Achievement Award

Richard Shoup

and

Alvy Ray Smith

The 1990 Computer Graphics Achivement Award is awarded jointly to Richard Shoup and Alvy Ray Smith for seminal contributions to computer paint systems. While paint programs have been around as long as frame buffers, Shoup and Smith, through work they did collectively and separately, transformed computer painting from a novelty into a true artistic medium with a richness and range sufficient to attract well-established artists to its use. It is difficult to overstate the pervasiveness of their contributions. Through their work they developed the *definitive* paint system. So well developed were their ideas that they are exemplified, virtually unchanged, by the tens of thousands of paint programs on desktops today. Indeed, some of Shoup's and Smith's algorithms are used today as they were originally elaborated.

The first eight-bit frame buffer paint program ever written is attributed to Dick Shoup. It was developed at Xerox PARC in 1972-73. Soon after, Alvy Ray Smith joined PARC and immediately began making major contributions of his own. Eventually, Smith left PARC to join the Computer Graphics Laboratory at New York Institute of Technology, where he continued paint system development until 1977. In the same time period, Shoup left PARC to form Aurora Imaging Systems, a venture to commercialize his work on paint systems. The NYIT Paint program was eventually sold to CBS and Ampex. It received a showcase national debut when Leroy Nieman used it during halftime at the 1978 Super Bowl.

Shoup obtained his Ph.D. in Computer Science at Carnegie-Mellon University in 1970. Within a year he became one of the first employees at the pioneering laboratories of Xerox PARC, where he spent close to a decade researching projects ranging from computer graphics and animation to digital video and theories of computation. It was there that he conceived and developed the first digital videographics and animation system for graphic artists known as "SuperPaint." This ground-breaking achievement was recognized in 1983 by the National Academy of Television Arts and Sciences in the form of an Emmy for Outstanding Achivement in Engineering Development, and has been included in the permanent collection of the Computer Museum in Boston.

Shoup left Xerox PARC in 1979 to co-found Aurora Systems, a manufacturer of digital videographics and animation systems. In addition to his executive responsibilities, he has continued as designer of two generations of Aurora videographics systems, including PC and workstation-based software packages, user interfaces, and architecture for the real-time hardware of the high-end product.

Smith, a 1970 Ph.D. graduate of Stanford University, was introduced to computer graphics by Dick Shoup at Xerox PARC in 1974. Applying Shoup's 3-bit paint program, Smith invented and contributed the RGB-to-HSV color transform software to the award-winning system. This development served as his passport to the newly formed Computer Graphics Laboratory at the New York Institute of Technology, which Smith joined in 1975. Over the next five years he wrote several paint programs, including Paint3, the first full-color, 24-bit RGB paint program introducing such options as airbrushing, blurring, smearing, soft-edged fill, color-mixing, and matting.

After a brief stint at the Jet Propulsion Laboratory working on Carl Sagan's *Cosmos* television series, Smith joined his former NYIT colleague Ed Catmull in the newly formed Computer Division of Lucasfilm, Ltd. They engaged in a major effort to digitize the filmmaking process with special emphasis on the use of computer graphics in theatrical release motion pictures, including such titles as *Star Trek II* and *Return of the Jedi*. Several hardware advances, including the first RGB laser input and output scanner and the Pixar Image Computer prototype can also be credited to Smith's leadership during his tenure at Lucasfilm.

Drawing on a core group of Lucasfilm talent, Smith co-founded Pixar in 1986. The company created the image computation market by building and selling the first general-purpose image computer, which presently finds application in medicine, remote sensing, design and animation, graphic and photographic arts, and scientific visualization. Pixar is currently devoting full energies to promoting and supporting its 3D rendering standard, RenderMan, and associated products.

Both men have published and spoken extensively on a broad range of computer graphics topics. It is largely through their efforts that paint programs have evolved into a serious artistic medium rather than remaining a demonstration of one use for a frame buffer. By adding a rich set of tools and techniques to digital paint programs, Shoup and Smith have won acceptance from artistic skeptics and set the standards for what has become one of the most widely used applications of computer graphics today.

Previous award winners
1989: John Warnock
1988: Alan H. Barr
1987: Robert Cook
1986: Turner Whitted
1985: Loren Carpenter
1984: James H. Clark
1983: James F. Blinn

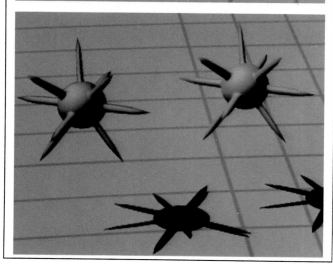

Figure 8: A pair of spike functions before, during, and after a collision.

Each column of M has a separate entry: either a constant for the whole surface, or a function of subregion R. We obtain a tighter set of bounding volumes than with the approach using a single constant.

Perhaps the most general and flexible way to compute constraints on the Jacobian matrix is to create a special function that computes maxima of the derivatives of each parametric function. Frequently we can find analytical expressions of the Jacobian of the parametric function, and the maximum of every component in the Jacobian over some parametric range. In these cases we can produce very tight bounds around a surface. It is frequently possible to find an exact analytic solution to the M function. In other cases we may need to use approximation rules to the various components (Appendix B). We must satisfy only the condition that

$$m_{ij} \geq \max_R |J_{ij}|. \tag{12}$$

In this case, R may be any subregion of the parametric domain of the function. Note that if m_{ij} is much larger than J_{ij}, the algorithm will still work, but will take longer to terminate.

Composition rules such as the triangle inequality in Eqn. 23 can simplify the computation of Jacobian maxima. The rate matrix M for several objects is computed in [Von Herzen 89], along with identities for simplifying the analysis (Appendix B).

6 Potential Application to Physically-Based Simulators

Many physically-based modeling systems need to have an implicit function to tell when a pair of objects come together in a collision. The function should be positive when the two objects do not interfere, negative when the objects overlap, and zero when the objects are just barely in contact. In addition, the function should be continuous.

A simple solution is $h(t) = t_0 - t$, where t_0 is the collision time [Platt 89]. Before the collision, $h(t)$ is positive, and after the collision, $h(t)$ is negative. The function is linear in time, which is very helpful for numerical analysis of physically-based modeling systems. The value of t_0 is computed by the algorithm presented in this paper, whereupon the forces of the collision are computed by the physical simulation system (See, for example [Barzel et al. 88]).

7 Conclusion

We have demonstrated a method to determine collisions between time-dependent parametric functions. The method is guaranteed to find the earliest collision for those functions with computable bounds on parametric derivatives. The collision theory and algorithms developed here may potentially apply to robotics and to ray-tracing problems as in [Kalra et al. 89]. Even for such difficult functions as the spike functions of Figure 8, the method is practical and robust and easily determines potential collisions between objects.

7.1 Advantages of the Method

In summary, the collision algorithm presented here has the following advantages:
- robust method
- works for deforming time-dependent surfaces
- computes to user-specified accuracy
- finds the earliest collision or near-miss

- works with many types of surfaces, including patches
- interfaces to physical modeling systems
- needs analysis only once per surface type, vs. $O(N^2)$ comparisons between all pairs of surface types

7.2 Disadvantages

Disadvantages of the algorithm include:
- must analyze derivatives for each surface type
- can't guarantee collisions for surfaces with unbounded derivatives

Acknowledgments

We would like to thank Carolyn Collins and Pete Wenzel for their assistance. The work presented in this paper was sponsored in part by International Business Machines, Inc., Hewlett-Packard Co., Apple Computer, Inc., and the Fannie and John Hertz Foundation.

References

[Baraff 89] David Baraff, "Analytical Methods for Dynamic Simulation of Non-penetrating Rigid Bodies," *Computer Graphics 23*, 3, July 1989, 223–232.

[Barr 83] Alan H. Barr, *Geometric Modeling and Fluid Dynamic Analysis of Swimming Spermatozoa*, Ph.D. Dissertation, Rensselaer Polytechnic Institute, 1983.

[Barr 84] Alan H. Barr, "Local and Global Deformations of Solid Primitives," *Computer Graphics 18*, 3, July 1984, 21–30.

[Barzel et al. 88] Ronen Barzel and Alan H. Barr, "A Modeling System Based on Dynamic Constraints," *Computer Graphics 22*, 4, August 1988, 179–188.

[Bentley et al. 79] Jon L. Bentley and Jerome H. Friedman, "Data Structures for Range Searching," *ACM Computing Surveys 11*, 4, December 1979, 397–409.

[Besl et al. 88] Paul J. Besl and Ramesh C. Jain, "Segmentation through Variable-Order Surface Fitting," *IEEE Transactions on Pattern Analysis and Machine Intelligence 10*, 2, March 1988, 167–192.

[Bezier 74] Pierre Bezier, "Mathematical and Practical Possibilities of UNISURF," in *Computer-Aided Geometric Design*, edited by Robert E. Barnhill and Richard F. Riesenfeld, Academic Press, New York, 1974, pp. 127–152.

[Blinn 78] Jim Blinn, *Computer Display of Curved Surfaces*, Ph.D. Dissertation, University of Utah, 1978.

[Cameron et al. 86] S. A. Cameron and R. K. Culley, "Determining the Minimum Translational Distance Between Two Convex Polyhedra," *IEEE International Conference on Robotics and Automation*, 1986.

[Canny 84] John Canny, "Collision Detection for Moving Polyhedra," *MIT Artificial Intelligence Lab Memo 806*, October, 1984.

[Catmull 75] Catmull, Ed, "Computer Display of Curved Surfaces," *IEEE Conference Proceedings on Computer Graphics, Pattern Recognition and Data Structures*, May 1975, 11.

[Chadwick et al. 89] John E. Chadwick, David R. Haumann and Richard E. Parent, "Layered Construction for Deformable Animated Characters," *Computer Graphics 23*, 3, July 1989, 243–252.

[Culley et al. 86] R. K. Culley and K. G. Kempf, "A Collision Detection Algorithm Based on Velocity and Distance Bounds," *Proceedings 1986 IEEE International Conference on Robotics and Automation*, Volume 2, pp. 1064–1069.

[Filip et al. 86] Daniel Filip, Robert Magedson and Robert Markot, "Surface Algorithms using Bounds on Derivatives," *Computer Aided Geometric Design 3*, 1986, 295–311.

[Gear 71] C. William Gear, *Numerical Initial Value Problems in Ordinary Differential Equations*, Prentice-Hall, Inc., Englewood Cliffs, New Jersey, 1971, p. 55.

[Going Bananas 88] John Snyder, Jed Lengyel, Devendra Kalra, Ronen Barzel, John C. Platt, Alan H. Barr and Brian Von Herzen, *Going Bananas*, 1988 Siggraph Film Show.

[Hopcroft et al. 83] J. E. Hopcroft, J. T. Schwartz and M. Sharir, "Efficient Detection of Intersections among Spheres," *The International Journal of Robotics Research 2*, 4, Winter 1983, 77–80.

[Kalra et al. 89] Devendra Kalra and Alan H. Barr, "Guaranteed Ray Intersections with Implicit Surfaces," *Computer Graphics 23*, 3, July 1989, 297–306.

[Kaufman 87] Arie Kaufman, "Efficient Algorithms for 3D Scan-Conversion of Parametric Curves, Surfaces, and Volumes," *Computer Graphics 21*, 4, July 1987, 171–180.

[Knuth 69] Donald Knuth, *The Art of Computer Programming; Vol. 1, Fundamental Algorithms*, Addison-Wesley, Menlo Park, CA, 1969, Section 2.2.4.

[Lane et al. 79] Jeff Lane and Loren Carpenter, "A Generalized Scan Line Algorithm for the Computer Display of Parametrically Defined Surfaces," *Computer Graphics and Image Processing 11*, 1979, 290.

[Lane et al. 80] Jeff Lane and Richard F. Riesenfeld, "A Theoretical Development for the Computer Generation and Display of Piecewise Polynomial Surfaces," *IEEE Transactions on Pattern Analysis and Machine Intelligence 2*, 1, January 1980, 35–46.

[Lee et al. 84] D. T. Lee and Franco P. Preparata, "Computational Geometry— A Survey," *IEEE Transactions on Computers C-33*, 12, December 1984, 1072.

[Lin et al. 74] C. C. Lin and L. A. Segel, *Mathematics Applied to Deterministic Problems in the Natural Sciences*, Macmillan Publishing Co., Inc., New York, 1974, pp. 57–58.

[Moore et al. 88] Matthew Moore and Jane Wilhelms, "Collision Detection and Response for Computer Animation," *Computer Graphics 22*, 4, August 1988, 289–298.

[NAG] NAG Fortran Library, Numerical Algorithms Group, 1400 Opus Place, Suite 200, Downers Grove, IL 60515 (312) 971-2337.

[Platt et al. 88] John C. Platt and Alan H. Barr, "Constraint Methods for Flexible Models," *Computer Graphics 22*, 4, August 1988, 279–288.

[Platt 89] John C. Platt, personal communication.

[Samet 84] Hanan Samet, "The Quadtree and Related Hierarchical Data Structures," *Computing Surveys 16*, 2, June 1984, 187–260.

[Samet 90a] Hanan Samet, *The Design and Analysis of Spatial Data Structures*, Addison-Wesley, Menlo Park, CA, 1990, Section 2.4, pp. 66–80.

[Samet 90b] Hanan Samet, *Applications of Spatial Data Structures*, Addison-Wesley, Menlo Park, CA, 1990, Section 1.3, pp. 15–16.

[Schmitt et al. 86] Francis Schmitt, Brian Barsky and Wen-Hui Du. "An Adaptive Subdivision Method for Surface-Fitting from Sampled Data," *Computer Graphics 20*, 4, August 1986, 179–188.

[Schwarz 81] J. T. Schwarz, "Finding the Minimum Distance Between Two Convex Polygons," *Information Processing Letters 13*, 4, 1981, 168–170.

[Schweitzer et al. 82] D. Schweitzer and E. S. Cobb, "Scanline Rendering of Parametric Surfaces," *Computer Graphics 16*, 3, July 1982, 265.

[Sederberg et al. 86] Tom Sederberg and Scott Parry, "Free-Form Deformation of Solid Geometric Models," *Computer Graphics 20*, 4, August 1986, 151–160.

[Snyder 90] John Snyder *Generative Models*, Ph.D. Dissertation, California Institute of Technology, in progress.

[Terzopoulos et al. 88] Demetri Terzopoulos and Kurt Fleischer, "Modeling Inelastic Deformation: Viscoelasticity, Plasticity, Fracture," *Computer Graphics 22*, 4, August 1988, 269–278.

[Uchiki et al. 83] Tetsuya Uchiki, Toshiaki Ohashi and Mario Tokoro, "Collision Detection in Motion Simulation," *Computers and Graphics 7*, 3, 1983, 285–293.

[Von Herzen et al. 87] Brian Von Herzen and Alan H. Barr, "Accurate Triangulations of Deformed, Intersecting Surfaces," *Computer Graphics 21*, 4, July 1987, 103–110.

[Von Herzen 85] Brian Von Herzen, *Sampling Deformed, Intersecting Surfaces with Quadtrees*, Masters Thesis, California Institute of Technology, Computer Science Dept., 5179:TR:85, 1985.

[Von Herzen 89] Brian Von Herzen, *Applications of Surface Networks to Sampling Problems in Computer Graphics*, PhD. Dissertation, California Institute of Technology, Computer Science Dept., Caltech-CS-TR-88-15, 1989.

A   Appendix: Jacobian Bounding Boxes

Here we derive a set of bounding boxes for parametric functions using the Jacobian of the function. These boxes frequently produce tighter bounds on a parametric surface than the Lipschitz bounding spheres. We start with the original definition of the Lipschitz condition for parametric functions ([Gear 71]):

$$\left\| \vec{f}(\vec{u}) - \vec{f}(\vec{u}_c) \right\| \leq L \left\| \vec{u} - \vec{u}_c \right\|. \tag{13}$$

Assume that the condition holds over some parametric subregion $R : u_1 \leq u \leq u_2$, $v_1 \leq v \leq v_2$, and $t_1 \leq t \leq t_2$. We define parametric coordinates $\vec{u}_c = (u_c, v_c, t_c)$ at the center of region R, and modeling space coordinates $(x_c, y_c, z_c) = \vec{f}(\vec{u}_c)$. We choose an L_1 norm for the right side of Eqn. 13, and we apply the condition to each component of $\vec{f}$ separately:

$$\begin{array}{rcl} |x - x_c| & \leq & L_x \left(|u - u_c| + |v - v_c| + |t - t_c| \right), \\ |y - y_c| & \leq & L_y \left(|u - u_c| + |v - v_c| + |t - t_c| \right), \\ |z - z_c| & \leq & L_z \left(|u - u_c| + |v - v_c| + |t - t_c| \right), \end{array} \tag{14}$$

for some suitable values of L_i. We distribute the values L_i and rename them to arrive at a more general inequality:

$$\begin{array}{rcl} |x - x_c| & \leq & M_{xu} |u - u_c| + M_{xv} |v - v_c| + M_{xt} |t - t_c|, \\ |y - y_c| & \leq & M_{yu} |u - u_c| + M_{yv} |v - v_c| + M_{yt} |t - t_c|, \\ |z - z_c| & \leq & M_{zu} |u - u_c| + M_{zv} |v - v_c| + M_{zt} |t - t_c|. \end{array} \tag{15}$$

We can solve for each M_{ij} by choosing appropriate values of (u, v, t). We illustrate with M_{xu}:

$$|x(u, v, t) - x(u_c, v, t)| \leq M_{xu} |u - u_c|, \tag{16}$$

or

$$\left| \frac{x(u, v, t) - x(u_c, v, t)}{u - u_c} \right| \leq M_{xu}, \quad u \neq u_c. \tag{17}$$

Assuming that $x(u, v, t)$ is differentiable, a sufficient value of M_{xu} is

$$M_{xu} \equiv \max_R \left| \frac{\partial x(u, v, t)}{\partial u} \right|. \tag{18}$$

M_{xu} is an upper bound on the parametric derivative over the region R. In general, a sufficient value of the **rate matrix** M is:

$$\mathbf{M} \equiv \begin{pmatrix} \max_R \left| \dfrac{\partial x}{\partial u} \right| & \max_R \left| \dfrac{\partial x}{\partial v} \right| & \max_R \left| \dfrac{\partial x}{\partial t} \right| \\[1.2em] \max_R \left| \dfrac{\partial y}{\partial u} \right| & \max_R \left| \dfrac{\partial y}{\partial v} \right| & \max_R \left| \dfrac{\partial y}{\partial t} \right| \\[1.2em] \max_R \left| \dfrac{\partial z}{\partial u} \right| & \max_R \left| \dfrac{\partial z}{\partial v} \right| & \max_R \left| \dfrac{\partial z}{\partial t} \right| \end{pmatrix}. \tag{19}$$

Just as the Lipschitz value L is a generalization of the derivative, so the rate matrix $\mathbf{M}$ is a generalization of the Jacobian matrix for parametric vector functions of several variables [Lin et al. 74, p. 355]. The matrix $\mathbf{M}$ consists of upper bounds on all the parametric derivatives of all the components of vector function $\vec{f}$.

We define $\Delta u \equiv |u_2 - u_c|$, $\Delta v \equiv |v_2 - v_c|$, and $\Delta t \equiv |t_2 - t_c|$. Since $u_1 \leq u \leq u_2$, we have $|u - u_c| \leq \Delta u$. Similarly, $|v - v_c| \leq \Delta v$, and $|t - t_c| \leq \Delta t$. Substituting into Eqn. 15, we have the **rate condition**:

$$\begin{array}{rcl} |x - x_c| & \leq & M_{xu}\Delta u + M_{xv}\Delta v + M_{xt}\Delta t, \\ |y - y_c| & \leq & M_{yu}\Delta u + M_{yv}\Delta v + M_{yt}\Delta t, \\ |z - z_c| & \leq & M_{zu}\Delta u + M_{zv}\Delta v + M_{zt}\Delta t. \end{array} \tag{20}$$

We define the **bounding box radii** to be

$$\begin{array}{rcl} \Delta x & \equiv & M_{xu}\Delta u + M_{xv}\Delta v + M_{xt}\Delta t, \\ \Delta y & \equiv & M_{yu}\Delta u + M_{yv}\Delta v + M_{yt}\Delta t, \\ \Delta z & \equiv & M_{zu}\Delta u + M_{zv}\Delta v + M_{zt}\Delta t. \end{array} \tag{21}$$

Now we can construct a bounding volume in modeling space from the bounding box radii, based on Δu, Δv, Δt, and the rate matrix. We form a rectangular prism that is aligned with the x,

y, and z axes, centered about modeling coordinates (x_c, y_c, z_c). Combining Eqn. 21 with Eqn. 20, we get the **bounding box inequality**:

$$\begin{array}{rcl} |x - x_c| & \leq & \Delta x \\ |y - y_c| & \leq & \Delta y \\ |z - z_c| & \leq & \Delta z. \end{array} \tag{22}$$

Such a rectangular region is called an *isothetic rectangle*, a rectangle whose sides are parallel to coordinate axes [Lee et al. 84]. The set of points satisfying Eqn. 22 form a bounding box containing the parametric region. We now have an efficient bounding box useful for computing collisions between moving parametric surfaces. We are free to compute the Jacobian maxima over the entire surface, thereby computing with a single-valued constant matrix across the surface. Alternatively, we may compute the Jacobians over subregions in order to tailor the bounding volumes more closely to particular variations in the surface. These boxes frequently produce tighter bounds on the parametric functions than does the Lipschitz condition of Eqn. 3.

B   Appendix: Bounds on Parametric Derivatives

Here we describe how to compute the entries in the matrix $\mathbf{M}$ from Eqn. 19. In addition to the differentiable surfaces, some non-differentiable surfaces also have computable Lipschitz values from which to derive rate matrices ([Von Herzen 89, Appendix B.3]). In this section we will focus our attention on differentiable parametric surfaces.

B.1   Maxima of scalars

We frequently have a closed-form description of $x(u, v, t)$ that permits us to compute the derivative $x'(u, v, t)$ directly. Then we can use the following identities to compute the maxima of functions:

Eqn. 23 is known as the triangle inequality. It is equivalent to the law that the length of the longest side of a triangle must be less than the lengths of the two shorter sides added together:

$$\max_R |\vec{f}(R) + \vec{g}(R)| \leq \max_R |\vec{f}(R)| + \max_R |\vec{g}(R)|. \tag{23}$$

Similar laws hold for the operations of subtraction, multiplication, and division of functions.

$$\max_R |\vec{f}(R) - \vec{g}(R)| \leq \max_R |\vec{f}(R)| + \max_R |\vec{g}(R)|, \tag{24}$$

$$\max_R |\vec{f}(R)\vec{g}(R)| \leq \max_R |\vec{f}(R)| \max_R |\vec{g}(R)|, \tag{25}$$

$$\max_R |\vec{f}(R)/\vec{g}(R)| \leq \frac{\max_R |\vec{f}(R)|}{\min_R |\vec{g}(R)|}, \tag{26}$$

for all $\vec{f}(R)$ and $\vec{g}(R)$.

B.2   Maxima of polynomials

Given $h(t)$, a polynomial function of degree $n = 2, 3$, or more, we want to maximize its value over a range $t_a \leq t \leq t_b$. The polynomial $h(t)$ is assumed to be of the form $h(t) = a_0 + a_1 t + a_2 t^2 + a_3 t^3 + a_4 t^4 + \ldots$. The maximum in $h(t)$ occurs either at 0, t_0, or at the points of solution to $h'(t) = 0$.

We take the derivative analytically and then solve the resulting polynomial equation using any one of a variety of numerical analysis programs (see [NAG]) for t, to get a set of values $t = t_1, \ldots, t_N$. Add 0 and t_0 to the set to get $0, t_1, \ldots, t_N, t_0$.

Then we substitute these values into the definition for $h(t)$. and pick the maximum value of $h(0)$ or $h(t_i)$, for $0 \leq i \leq N$. This is the maximum value for the whole interval, $0 \leq t \leq t_b$.

For any interval $t_a \leq t \leq t_b$ we only need to evaluate $h(t)$ at the endpoints t_a and t_b and any values in the solution set between t_a and t_b. This recalculation will reduce the magnitude of the Lipschitz value as the interval decreases with further iterations.

Similar solutions are possible for polynomial patches that use a rational cubic representation in one parametric direction ([Filip et al. 86, p. 307]). It is straightforward to extend these results to several dimensions.

B.3 Product surfaces

Product surfaces include superquadrics, spheres, profile surfaces, translational sweeps, and spherical products [Barr 83]. These surfaces take the mathematical form:

$$x_i(u,v) = k(v)c_i(u) + d_i(v), \qquad (27)$$

where $i = 1, 2, 3$, and subscripts 1,2 and 3 correspond to components x, y, and z.

The partial derivative of this surface with respect to u is:

$$\frac{\partial x_i(u,v)}{\partial u} = k(v)\frac{\partial c_i(u)}{\partial u} + d_i(v). \qquad (28)$$

Sufficient values of the entries of the rate matrix $\mathbf{M}$ are:

$$m_{iu} = \max_R |k(v)| \max_R \left| \frac{\partial c_i(u)}{\partial u} \right| + \max_R |d_i(v)|, \qquad (29)$$

$i = 1, 2, 3$. The rate matrix entries with respect to parameter v are given by:

$$m_{iv} = \max_R \left| \frac{\partial k(v)}{\partial v} \right| \max_R |c_i(u)| + \max_R \left| \frac{\partial d_i(v)}{\partial v} \right|. \qquad (30)$$

Finally, all the time derivatives are zero: $m_{it} = 0$. Given differentiable scalar functions for $k(v)$, $c_i(u)$, and $d_i(v)$, we can find the rate matrix for the product surface.

B.4 Surfaces with Translational Motion

Assuming that we can compute the rate matrix for a stationary surface $\vec{f}(u,v)$, how can we compute the rate matrix for the same surface that is translating as a function of time? ([Von Herzen 89, Appendix B.2]). We define the translation function to be $\vec{s}(t)$. The translating surface is given by function $\vec{g}(u,v,t) = \vec{f}(u,v) + \vec{s}(t)$. If the value m_{ij} represents the rate matrix for $\vec{f}$, then the new rate matrix $\mathbf{Mg}$ for the moving surface $\vec{g}(u,v,t)$ is

$$\mathbf{Mg} = \begin{pmatrix} m_{xu} & m_{xv} & \max_R \left| \frac{\partial s_x(t)}{\partial t} \right| \\ m_{yu} & m_{yv} & \max_R \left| \frac{\partial s_y(t)}{\partial t} \right| \\ m_{zu} & m_{zv} & \max_R \left| \frac{\partial s_z(t)}{\partial t} \right| \end{pmatrix}. \qquad (31)$$

B.5 Surfaces with Rotational Motion

We now examine rotational motion for rigid objects. Given a function $\vec{f}(u,v)$, and a rotation matrix $\mathbf{R}(t)$ as a function of time, we have $\vec{g}(u,v,t) = \mathbf{R}(t)\vec{f}(u,v)$. The parametric derivatives of $\vec{g}$ are given by

$$\frac{\partial \vec{g}(u,v,t)}{\partial u} = \mathbf{R}(t)\frac{\partial \vec{f}(u,v)}{\partial u}, \qquad (32)$$

$$\frac{\partial \vec{g}(u,v,t)}{\partial v} = \mathbf{R}(t)\frac{\partial \vec{f}(u,v)}{\partial v}, \qquad (33)$$

$$\frac{\partial \vec{g}(u,v,t)}{\partial t} = \frac{\partial \mathbf{R}(t)}{\partial t}\vec{f}(u,v). \qquad (34)$$

B.6 Example of a deformation

As an example of computing the rate matrix for a deforming function, we illustrate how to compute the rate matrix for an object with a variable taper as given in [Barr 84], assuming we have the rate matrix for the undeformed object. Let $\vec{f}(u,v)$ be the undeformed object with components (x,y,z). The deformed coordinates are given by $X = r(z,t)x$ for the x component, $Y = r(z,t)y$ for the y component, and $Z = z$ for the z component,

where $r(z,t)$ is the tapering function that varies over time. Then the derivatives for the deformed coordinates are:

$$\frac{\partial X}{\partial u} = \frac{\partial r}{\partial z}\frac{\partial z}{\partial u}x + \frac{\partial x}{\partial u}r(z,t), \qquad (35)$$

$$\frac{\partial X}{\partial v} = \frac{\partial r}{\partial z}\frac{\partial z}{\partial v}x + \frac{\partial x}{\partial v}r(z,t), \qquad (36)$$

$$\frac{\partial X}{\partial t} = \frac{\partial r}{\partial t}x + \frac{\partial x}{\partial t}r(z,t). \qquad (37)$$

The equations are analogous for the Y component. All of the derivatives for Z are equal to the derivatives for z.

A typical taper function $r(z,t)$ is a piecewise linear function that tapers from r_1 to r_2 starting at z_1 and ending at z_2. We can make the ending values of the taper vary as a function of time, $r_1(t)$ and $r_2(t)$. The function $r(z,t)$ is given by

$$r(z,t) = \begin{cases} r_1(t) & z < z_1, \\ \dfrac{(z-z_1)r_2 + (z_2-z)r_1}{z_2-z_1} & z_1 \le z \le z_2, \\ r_2(t) & z > z_2. \end{cases} \qquad (38)$$

The derivatives of $r(z,t)$ are given by

$$\frac{\partial r}{\partial z} = \begin{cases} 0 & z < z_1, \\ \dfrac{r_2-r_1}{z_2-z_1} & z_1 \le z \le z_2, \\ 0 & z > z_2. \end{cases} \qquad (39)$$

The temporal derivative is given by

$$\frac{\partial r}{\partial t} = \begin{cases} \dfrac{\partial r_1(t)}{\partial t} & z < z_1, \\ \dfrac{(z-z_1)\dfrac{\partial r_2}{\partial t} + (z_2-z)\dfrac{\partial r_1}{\partial t}}{z_2-z_1} & z_1 \le z \le z_2, \\ \dfrac{\partial r_2(t)}{\partial t} & z > z_2. \end{cases} \qquad (40)$$

Eqn. 40 is valid for dynamic tapers of static objects. The differentiation rule for products leads to the equation for tapers of distorting objects. These equations may be substituted directly into Eqn. 19 for the rate matrix to obtain derivative bounds on parametric surfaces tapering as a function of time.

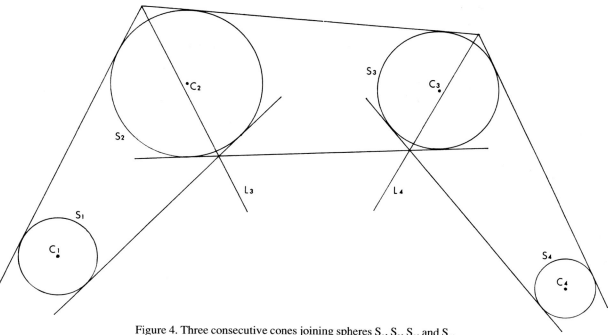

Figure 4. Three consecutive cones joining spheres S_1, S_2, S_3, and S_4.

and shade them appropriately. Instead, the shading for an infinite cone is used within the outline mask of each cone sphere, and the blending smooths the shading across the spherical elbow.

The width of the linear strip to the right of L_4 where the blending function decreases from 1 to zero must be set at a compromise value, wide enough to give a reasonably smooth transition, but not so wide that the anti-aliasing mask along the profile of S_3 causes an abrupt jump to zero.

One problem with the "$2\frac{1}{2}$-D" compositing method is that the sorting order may change from frame to frame as the object and/or camera motions change the distance relationships. For example, the center cone-sphere in Figure 4 may be in front of the right-hand one in one frame, and behind it in the next, causing the region of blending between the two to "pop" from the right side of line L_4 to the left side. We tried to alleviate this problem by changing the shading computations linearly across each cone-sphere, so that successive ones matched more closely across their common sphere. We also found this popping less noticeable when texture and bump mapping were added.

Shading

We wanted to develop shading and texture mapping computations for the conical surfaces, which could be vectorized across horizontal scan lines so as to run efficiently on our vector supercomputer, the Fujitsu VP 200. Both shading and texture require the angular coordinate around the circular cross section of the cone.

For simplicity, we computed the shading as if the projection were orthogonal. Figure 5 shows the projection of a circular section E perpendicular to the axis CF of a cone, with P a point on E. Let BC and PD be lines in the plane of E, which are also parallel to the picture plane. Then BC is the radius of E, and PD is this radius times $\sin\theta$, where θ is an angular measure around E, starting from the point closest to the viewer. Therefore, $\theta = \arcsin(PD/BC)$. The length PD is a linear function of the projected (x,y) coordinates of P, as is the length QD. Therefore we approximated BC by QD, and took $\theta = \arcsin(t)$, where $t = PD/QD$, the quotient of two linear functions in x

and y. The angle θ is the first texture coordinate, and the distance v of the circular cross section along the axis is the second. This second coordinate can be computed as $G + Hu$, where G and H are also linear in x and y, and $u = \cos\theta = \sqrt{1 - t^2}$. The term Hu adds the appropriate curvature to the sections of constant v.

To find the unit normal N to the cone at P, let N_1 be a unit vector along the axis, let N_2 be a unit vector perpendicular to N_1 and parallel to the picture plane, and let N_3 be a unit vector perpendicular to both N_1 and N_2, chosen to face towards the viewer. Then

$$N = N_1 \sin\beta + N_2 \cos\beta \sin\theta + N_3 \cos\beta \cos\theta,$$

where β is the angle of opening of the cone, positive if the cone is closing down in the direction N_1, and negative if the cone is opening out.

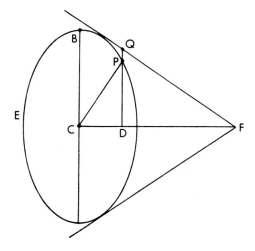

Figure 5. The orthogonal projection of a cross section circle E of radius CB of a cone with axis CF. In this figure, the same letters refer both to 3-D points and their projections, but since the projection is orthogonal and the lengths under discussion are along lines parallel to the picture plane, this makes no difference.

In order to make the shading match as closely as possible along the spheres where adjacent cone shadings overlap, we made the functions N_1, N_2, and N_3 vary linearly across the projected cone sphere, between values defined at the end spheres.

For texture mapping, the angle θ is measured relative to the N_3 direction toward the eye, but this direction may change during animation. Therefore, an extra phase must added, which varies from frame to frame, to account for the angle between N_3 and some standard fixed reference direction. The phase may be constant for each cone sphere, or vary linearly in order to match the N_3 phase at each end sphere, or to introduce a spiral twist to the texture.

Results

Figure 1, reprinted from [10], shows a motion-blurred chromatin fiber represented by 14,050 cylindrical cone-sphere analogs, twisting into a chromosome shape. The motion blur is most visible at the top, where the twirling is fastest. Given the positions of the generating spheres for two successive frames, it took the scalar Fujitsu M380 34 seconds to render, blur, and composite.

Figure 2 shows a branching root, represented by 13,000 bump-mapped cone spheres surrounded by water molecules. It took 116 seconds to render with motion blur at 2048 x 1500 pixel resolution on our vector supercomputer, the VP200.

Figure 6 shows 24 cone spheres joined together into a torus. Note that while the highlights have straight sections, these join together smoothly due to the blending. It took less than one second on the VP200, at 640 x 480 resolution.

Figure 7 shows a Christmas tree, made up of 1770 cone spheres and 1000 semi transparent colored spheres. It took 20 seconds on the VP200, at 640 x 480 resolution.

Acknowledgments

Figure 2 was designed by Takayuki Ohguchi, and implemented by Shinji Satoh, who also made figure7. Takayuki Ohguchi also suggested implementing cone spheres, for the purpose of designing and rendering these scenes, and, in addition, drew figures 3, 4, and 5. The sorting and compositing system used was developed by Keiichi Kameda. The motion blur algorithm was coded by Douglas Lerner, who also reviewed and typed this paper. This work was supported by Fujitsu Ltd., during the computer animated film production for its World's Fair pavilions. Typesetting services were provided by Lawrence Livermore National Laboratory, where Gerri Braswell typed improvements suggested by the reviewers.

References

[1] Kakimoto, M., Hayashi, N., Ohguchi, T., Santoh, S. and Max, N., "Methods for modeling and mapping branched surfaces using generalized cylinders," (in Japanese) Information Processing Society of Japan, Computer Graphics and CAD technical report 89-CG-39, Vol. 89, No. 64 (1989) pp 1-8.

[2] Blinn, J. F., "Optimal tubes," IEEE Computer Graphics and Applications Vol. 6 No. 5 (1989) pp 8-13.

[3] Wijk, J. J. van, "Ray tracing objects defined by sweeping a sphere," Proceedings of the Eurographics '84 Conference, North Holland, Amsterdam (1984) pp 73-82. See also Van Wijk, "On new types of Solid Models and their Visualization with Ray tracing," Delft University Press (1986).

[4] Bronsvoort, W., and Klok, F. "Ray tracing generalized cylinders," ACM Transactions on Graphics Vol. 4 No. 4 (1985) pp 291-303 and Corrigendum Vol. 6 No. 3 (1987) pp 238-239.

[5] Smith, A. R., "Paint" in "Tutorial: Computer Graphics " (Beatty, J., and Booth, K., editors) IEEE Computer Society catalog no. EH0194-1 (1982) pp 501-515.

[6] Whitted, T., "Anti-aliased line drawing using brush extrusions," Computer Graphics Vol. 17 No. 3 (1983) (Siggraph '83 proceedings) pp 151-156.

[7] Max, N., "Siggraph '84 Call for Omnimax Films," Computer Graphics Vol. 17, No. 1 (1983) pp 73-76.

[8] Max, N., "ATOMLLL: ATOMS with shading and highlights," Computer Graphics Vol. 13 No. 2 (1979) (Siggraph '79 Proceedings) pp 165-173.

[9] Porter, T., and Duff, T., "Compositing digital images," Computer Graphics Vol. 14 No. 3 (1984) (Siggraph '84 Proceedings) pp 253-259.

[10] Max, N., and Lerner, D., "A two-and-a-half D motion blur algorithm," Computer Graphics Vol. 19 No. 3 (1985) (Siggraph '85 Proceedings) pp 85-93.

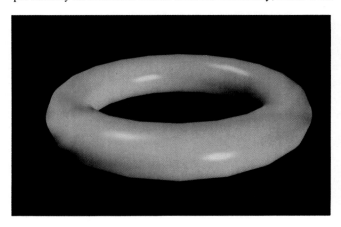

Figure 6. A torus formed from 24 cone spheres.

Figure7. A Christmas tree, formed from 1700 bump mapped cone spheres and 1000 semi-transparent colored spheres.

Rendering CSG Models with a ZZ-Buffer

David Salesin* and Jorge Stolfi†

*Computer Science Department
Stanford University
Stanford, CA 94305

†DEC Systems Research Center
130 Lytton Avenue
Palo Alto, CA 94301

ABSTRACT

The ZZ-buffer is a simple acceleration scheme for ray tracing that can be applied to a wide variety of scenes, including those with small features, textured and transparent surfaces, shadows and penumbrae, and depth-of-field effects. In this paper, we describe how the ZZ-buffer algorithm can be adapted to the rendering of scenes defined by constructive solid geometry operations.

CR Categories and Subject Descriptors: I.3.3 [Computer Graphics]: Picture/Image Generation. I.3.7 [Computer Graphics]: Three-dimensional graphics and realism.

Additional keywords and phrases: ray tracing, antialiasing, constructive solid geometry, transparent surfaces, display buffers, visible-surface algorithms, rendering algorithms.

1 INTRODUCTION

The ZZ-buffer algorithm [35, 36] is a simple acceleration scheme for ray tracing that can be applied to a wide variety of scenes, including those with small features, textured and transparent surfaces, shadows and penumbrae, and depth-of-field effects.

The ZZ-buffer improves on the performance of naive ray tracing by three major strategies. First, it uses an efficient indexing scheme, similar to the "item buffer" of Weghorst *et al.* [40], for locating the objects intersected by primary rays and by rays to the light sources. Second, it uses symbolic manipulation of the scene description to perform the visibility computations for many rays at once. Finally, it uses rough estimates of the depths of objects at each pixel in order to eliminate invisible objects, without ever computing their exact depths.

Unlike most other optimization schemes for ray tracing, such as octrees [14], hierarchical subdivision [22], and ray classification [2], the ZZ-buffer algorithm puts all its effort into optimizing only the tracing of "initial" and "final" rays; that is, those rays traced from the camera to the visible objects, and from the visible objects to the light sources. For most scenes, including those with many inter-object reflections, such rays constitute the majority of all rays that are traced, since a new ray must be traced back to each light source at every ray–object intersection. By limiting its scope to

initial and final rays, the ZZ-buffer achieves substantial speed-ups in a very simple fashion.

The ZZ-buffer algorithm superficially resembles the A-buffer [6] and Z-buffer [7, 13] algorithms, in that it uses an image-space buffer to aid in determining visibility. However, unlike the Z-buffer and A-buffer, the ZZ-buffer is used only as an acceleration scheme for stochastic ray tracing [9, 11, 23, 24], and is therefore free of the aliasing artifacts that plague these other methods.

In this paper we show how the ZZ-buffer algorithm can also be used to speed up the ray tracing of models built with constructive solid geometry (CSG) operations. Several schemes have been proposed for accelerating this computation, exploiting, for example, scan-line coherence [3] and the notion of "active zones" [33]. Our use of the ZZ-buffer for CSG models most closely approximates the depth buffer techniques of Rossignac and Requicha [32], Okino, Kakazu, and Morimoto [30], and Goldfeather, Hultquist, and Fuchs [15]. Compared to these methods, the ZZ-buffer algorithm has several advantages: it produces antialiased shadow edges, avoids the shading of invisible objects, and does not require computing exact z-coordinates for every object at every pixel.

The major drawback of the ZZ-buffer algorithm is the large size of its data structures. For instance, our current (unoptimized) implementation typically uses from 10 to 20 megabytes of virtual memory to render simple scenes such as the ones shown in this paper. Fortunately, computers and workstations with address spaces of this size are becoming increasingly common. Furthermore, the ZZ-buffer algorithm can be easily tuned to use less memory, at the cost of increased rendering time.

2 CONSTRUCTIVE SOLID GEOMETRY

The CSG solid modeling paradigm is very popular because of its power and its compatibility with the standard ray-tracing algorithms [34]. CSG models are built from a set of primitive objects (such as half-spaces and quadrics), combined with Boolean-like operations such as union, intersection, and set difference.

While the meaning of these operations for point sets is well-established, their meaning for the kind of objects normally used in solid modeling is not entirely obvious. The difficulty lies in specifying the effect of those operations on the various geometric and optical properties normally attached to these objects, such as surface normals, textures, and shading attributes. Since the ZZ-buffer algorithm relies heavily on symbolic manipulation of CSG expressions, it is important that we define these operations with some care.

2.1 Shapes

In our model, the shape of an object A can be described by its *characteristic function* $C_A(p)$, which associates to each point of space p a *class*, either *exterior* (E), *surface* (S), or *interior* (I). We assume that characteristic functions are reasonably well-behaved. In particular, we require that any ray in general position contain only a finite number of surface points in any finite interval. Furthermore, we require that along each ray there exist at least one surface point between any interior point and any exterior point. The CSG operations defined below preserve these requirements. Note that a surface may have interior points on both sides, or exterior points on both sides.

A CSG operation combines the characteristic functions of its operands in a point-wise fashion: the class of a point p in the resulting object depends only on the classes of p in each operand. In particular, for the union operation $\cup$, the class $C_{A \cup B}(p)$ is the stronger of the two classes $C_A(p)$ and $C_B(p)$, where interior is stronger than surface, and surface is stronger than exterior. For the unary complement operation $\neg$, the class $C_{\neg A}(p)$ is interior if $C_A(p)$ is exterior, and vice versa, while surface points are left unchanged.

The operations of intersection and difference are defined by the formulas $A \cap B = \neg((\neg A) \cup (\neg B))$ and $A \setminus B = A \cap (\neg B)$.

The CSG operations defined here enjoy many of the properties of their Boolean counterparts. In particular, for any objects A, B, and C, we have $A \cup B = B \cup A$, $(A \cup B) \cup C = A \cup (B \cup C)$, $A \cup A = A$, and $\neg(\neg A) = A$. The CSG equivalent of the empty set is the *vacuum* object $\mathbf{0}$, which is everywhere exterior. Its complement is the *plenum* $\mathbf{1} = \neg\mathbf{0}$, an object that is everywhere interior. These objects satisfy the relations $A \cup \mathbf{0} = A$ and $A \cup \mathbf{1} = \mathbf{1}$, for any A. These properties also hold for intersection and union distribute over each other. As we shall see, the ZZ-buffer algorithm relies heavily on these properties when constructing and simplifying CSG expressions.

Note that the CSG operations fail to satisfy some properties of the corresponding Boolean functions. For example, $A \cap (\neg A)$ is not $\mathbf{0}$, since all the surface points of A survive in the result; dually, $A \cup (\neg A)$ is not $\mathbf{1}$.

2.2 Shading parameters

For rendering purposes, we also associate with each object a *shading function* $S_A(p)$, which maps each point of space p to a collection of shading parameters, such as color, transparency, normal direction (for surface points), and so on. Note that the shading function is defined not only for interior and surface points of each object, but also for exterior points, which are typically (but not necessarily) invisible.

A CSG operation must combine not only the characteristic functions of its operands, but their shading parameters as well. For the union operation, at every point p where $C_A(p) \neq C_B(p)$, the shading parameters $S_{A \cup B}(p)$ of the result are copied from those of the object with the stronger class at p. At any point p where $C_A(p) = C_B(p)$, the shading parameters of A and B must be combined with an appropriate union-like operation $\dot{\cup}$, that is, $S_{A \cup B}(p) = S_A(p) \dot{\cup} S_B(p)$.

Similarly, when taking the CSG complement of an object A, we need to transform its shading parameters by a suitable complement-like operation $\dot{\neg}$, that is, $S_{\neg A}(p) = \dot{\neg} S_A(p)$.

The operations $\dot{\cup}$ and $\dot{\neg}$ can be chosen arbitrarily, provided that they satisfy the basic properties of union and complement listed in the previous section. In particular, we must arrange things so that the shading parameters of the vacuum $S_\mathbf{0}$ and of the plenum $S_\mathbf{1}$ are respectively minimal and maximal, in the sense that $S_A(p) \dot{\cup} S_\mathbf{0}(p) = S_A(p)$, and $S_A(p) \dot{\cup} S_\mathbf{1}(p) = S_\mathbf{1}(p)$.

For example, we can define the complement of a color (r, g, b) to be the color $(1 - r, 1 - g, 1 - b)$, and define the union of two colors to be their component-wise maximum. In this case, vacuum should be black, and plenum, white. Other shading parameters, such as transparency coefficients and highlight colors, can be handled in the same way.

Note that these definitions provide a reasonable behavior in most typical situations. For example, intersecting an object with a clipping half-space—a flat surface with vacuum on one side and plenum on the other—gives a cut-away view of the object, without affecting the colors of the surviving parts.

2.3 CSG expression trees

For the purposes of this paper, we assume that the scene to be rendered is represented by a *CSG tree*, a data structure built from three kinds of nodes: *Substance*, *Primitive*, and *Union*.

A *Substance* node describes a shading function divorced from any shape information. Its detailed representation does not concern us here. A *Primitive* node describes a basic CSG building block and contains two fields: a characteristic function *shape*, which describes a partition of space into exterior, surface, and interior points; and pointers to the three *Substance* nodes, *subst*[E], *subst*[S], *subst*[I], which specify the shading parameters to be used for each point class. Finally, a *Union* node represents the union of two CSG models, and contains pointers to the two corresponding subtrees.

type *PointClass* $= \{$E, S, I$\}$

type *Substance* = **record** ... **end record**

type *Primitive* = **record**
  shape: Shape
  subst: **array** *PointClass* **of** *Substance*
end record

type *Union* = **record** *a, b: CSGTree* **end record**

Instead of using explicit *Complement* nodes to denote complement operations, we always refer to a CSG tree or subtree by means of a "tagged pointer," a pair consisting of a pointer to the tree's root node and a one-bit *negate* flag. Besides saving some space, this encoding allows us to quickly complement any CSG expression, without incurring any allocation or garbage collection overhead:

type *CSGTree* = **record**
  node: **pointer to** (*Union* **or** *Primitive* **or** *Substance*)
  negate: **boolean**
end record

5.1 Computing ray–tile intersections

The intersections between a ray and the scene are represented as a list of *hits*. Each hit is a segment of the ray whose points all have the same class, and whose shading parameters all come from a single *Substance* node or from a CSG combination of *Substance* nodes:

type *Hit* = **record**
  expr: CSGTree
  zz: Interval
  class: PointClass
  color: ColorFlag
  trans: TransFlag
end record

Note that a *Hit* record is essentially equivalent to a *Tile* record whose ZZ-buffer cell has been contracted to a single point, and whose z-range is small enough that every point in the hit belongs to a single point class.

The computation of hit lists is entirely similar to that of tile lists, except that the *ComputeHits* routine always returns hits whose objects are *Substance* nodes or unions of *Substance* nodes. These computations are the same as those of ordinary ray tracing.

5.2 Shading and filtering

Once we have determined the visible hits—i.e., the objects visible along a sample ray, and their z-coordinates—we compute the contribution of each hit to the image sample, based on the amount of light reaching the hit and the shading parameters of *hit.expr*. Note that we need not prefilter the textures to avoid aliasing artifacts, since (as observed by Cook, Porter, and Carpenter [10]) the stochastic sampling of the camera rays used to antialias object edges will antialias textures as well.

The output of the rendering phase is an array of samples, with $S \times S$ samples for each pixel of the final image. We combine these samples using standard convolution filtering [25, 29]. Each sample contributes to a 3×3 square of pixels in the final image, with weights that depend on the distance between the unjittered sample position and the centers of those pixels.

6 SHADOWS

The ZZ-buffer can also be used to compute shadows, in a manner similar to the "light buffer" of Haines and Greenberg [17]. To implement shadows, we modify the ZZ-buffer algorithm in two ways. In the tiling phase, we construct an additional ZZ-buffer from the point of view of each light source. In the rendering phase, when computing the illumination at each visible point of the scene, we use the ZZ-buffer of each light source to test whether the point is shadowed by other objects.

More precisely, to compute the light reaching a point p from a given source, we cast a ray from the source through p and locate the cell of the source's ZZ-buffer that is hit by this ray. We extract the list of tiles from that cell, and for each tile t we compute the intersections between the ray and the object *t.expr*, clipped to the tile's *zz* range. The intersections are computed by the same algorithm used for

camera rays. If we find an opaque object that intersects the ray, we conclude that p is in shadow with respect to that light source. If we find any semitransparent objects, we filter the light by their transmission coefficients.

For computing shadows, the ZZ-buffer has many advantages over methods based on ordinary Z-buffers, such as William's algorithm [41] or "percentage-closer filtering" [31]. First, the ZZ-buffer allows us to correctly antialias sharp shadow boundaries and shadows cast by small objects and fine textures, independently of the size and resolution of the light's ZZ-buffer. Our algorithm also handles colored transparent surfaces that filter light, an effect that cannot be reproduced by Z-buffers, which can keep track of only one shadowing object at each point.

7 PENUMBRAE AND CAMERA BLUR

The ZZ-buffer can also be used to compute the penumbrae (soft shadow edges) produced by extended light sources, as shown in Figure 6. To obtain this effect, we imagine that the light source is a disk of some fixed size, oriented parallel to the projection plane of its ZZ-buffer. When computing the illumination of some point p of the scene, we cast a ray from a random point on this disk towards the point p, as in distributed ray tracing [10].

In the light source's screen space, each of these rays will consist of points of the form $(x_p + m_x z, y_p + m_y z, z)$, where (x_p, y_p) is the point where the ray hits the screen plane, and m_x, m_y are numbers that measure how far the ray deviates from the z-axis direction. See Figure 5.

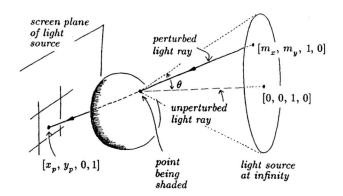

Figure 5: Ray tracing penumbrae.

In the light's screen space, the light source itself is a disk at infinity centered at the point $(0, 0, -\infty)$. If θ is the angular radius of the light source, as seen from the light's screen plane, then $\sqrt{m_x^2 + m_y^2}$ is at most $\tan \theta$. Note that this bound on m_x and m_y is independent of the screen coordinates x_p and y_p.

In order to quickly find the objects that could be intersected by the perturbed ray, we have to modify the computation of tiles somewhat. When computing the tile lists for a primitive object A in a given ZZ-buffer cell, we need to estimate the z-coordinates of the intersections between A and the rays from all points in the light source to all points in the given cell.

Figure 6: Penumbrae.

Figure 8: Limited depth of field.

In general, computing the the z-range information for such slope-perturbed rays is not much harder than for parallel rays. In particular, for planes we can use the same algorithm described in Section 4.3, except that the long prism considered there must be replaced by the double truncated pyramid shown in Figure 7, whose "waist" is the ZZ-buffer cell, and whose walls flare out with angle θ relative to the z-axis. We handle quadric surfaces in a similar manner, using an extension of the interval arithmetic method described in Section 4.3.

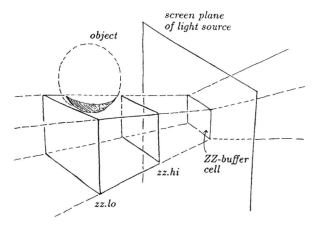

Figure 7: Computing tiles for penumbrae.

By using these same tiling techniques when computing the camera's ZZ-buffer, we can also simulate the image blurring effects of lenses with limited depth of field, as shown in Figure 8.

8   OPTIMIZATIONS

There are many optimizations that can be applied to the basic algorithm described above, some of which are essential to bringing its time and memory requirements down to a reasonable level.

Caching tile lists. Since the same CSG subexpression may occur many times in the data structures associated with a given cell, it is important that we compute the tile list for that expression only once. To achieve this goal, we use a hash table that maps CSG node addresses to the corresponding tile lists. Note that this table needs to be reinitialized every time we start computing the scene's tile list for a new cell.

Caching CSG nodes. While computing the union of two tile lists, whenever we need to create a new *Union* node, we should check whether a *Union* node with the same operands has already been created; if so, we can reuse that node. For this purpose, we use a hash table indexed by the node's operands. (This technique was also used by Séquin and Smyrl in a similar context [37].) Note that this optimization saves more than just the cost of creating the *Union* node itself: combined with the caching of tile lists described above, it also prevents us from recomputing the tile lists for this node and for all of its descendants. Note also that this hash table can be shared among all cells and all ZZ-buffers.

Successive refinement of tile lists. A third optimization involves exploiting the coherence between the contents of the coarse ZZ-buffers and their refined versions. Suppose that we are computing the tile list l for a *Union* node A in ZZ-buffer cell C, which is part of a larger ZZ-buffer cell C'. Instead of calling *ComputeTiles* for the smaller cell C right away, we can check whether we have already computed a tile list l' for A in the larger cell C'. If so, we can reuse much of this work by applying *RefineTileList* to l'. (However, this optimization can only be applied if none of the tiles in l' has $expr = A$.)

Pruning of tile lists. If the tile list for a node A is too long, we can always shorten it by coalescing two or more consecutive tiles into a single tile whose $expr$ field points to the node A itself. This optimization is particularly important since the basic algorithm for computing the union of two tile lists, described in Section 4.4, produces a resulting list with about as many tiles as the two child lists combined. Thus, for n primitive objects, the basic algorithm may produce up to $\Omega(n \log n)$ tiles. However, if we systematically prune every tile list by coalescing some constant fraction of its elements, then the overall number of tiles generated will be at most

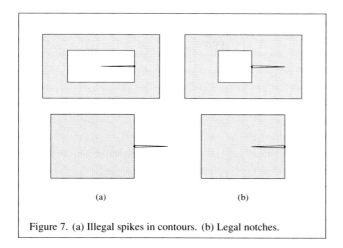

(a)   (b)

Figure 7. (a) Illegal spikes in contours. (b) Legal notches.

are unique; there can be no more than one edge between any pair of vertices.

Faces

A face's flat is described by an implicit plane equation given by a point on and a unit normal to the plane. Its boundary is described by one or more pairwise disjoint contours, some of which may be holes. Each contour is a list of edges that form a non-self-intersecting loop.

A contour must bound an open planar set so that the local orientation of the contour is defined at each vertex (Figure 7). This restriction ensures that a contour does not contain zero-width "spikes," although zero-width notches are allowed (the algorithm may insert such notches into faces as partitioning proceeds).

Solid Boundaries

The boundary of a solid is simply a list of faces that make it up.

Tolerances and Related Quantities

Three quantities are kept with each feature f in addition to the coordinates that specify its flat's position. The first of these is a tolerance describing the accuracy of these coordinates. The second, kept for edges and faces only, is an *extent*, denoted $ext(f)$. This value gives the maximum deviation of the feature's tolerance region from its specified flat. The third quantity is called the *near* value, denoted $near(f)$. This value is initialized to a large positive number when the modeler starts. Whenever the distance between a feature and some other feature is computed, and the pair of features are deemed not to intersect, the near value is updated so that it is the minimum distance to all features found to not intersect the feature so far. The use of the extent and near values will become apparent as the algorithm is described.

If objects are presented to the algorithm without edge or plane equations or feature tolerances, the equations and tolerances are computed. Each vertex in the input is assigned an arbitrary small tolerance, typically 10^{-10} for an object centered about the origin whose longest edges have approximate length 1. This makes the ratio of the tolerance to the vertex coordinates a few times the machine precision when using IEEE double-precision floating-point, guaranteeing that round-off error will generally not affect tolerances. An edge's equation is found by finding the line that

passes through its two endpoints. The tolerance assigned to such a computed edge equation is zero, because the line must intersect the vertices' tolerance regions. The extent for the edge is the larger of the two endpoints' tolerances. A face's equation is computed by applying Newell's algorithm[15] to each of the faces contours and averaging the results. The tolerance is found by substituting the coordinates of each vertex in the face's boundary into the computed equation and recording the maximum deviation from zero. The extent is this deviation added to the maximum of the vertices tolerances.

4.3 Topological Modifications

As the algorithm proceeds, it modifies the topology of the input to incorporate computed intersections. These modifications are:

1. Breaking an edge into two edges at a new vertex where the edge crosses a face.

2. Inserting new edges into a face along an intersection line.

3. Merging coplanar faces, coincident edges, and coincident vertices.

Of these operations, (1) and (2) are purely topological in that they do not require alteration of metric data or tolerances. The operations in (3), however, require the selection of new coordinates and a new tolerance for the merged feature. Further, merging a pair of features may require topological changes beyond the merge itself.

Vertex Merging

If there is an edge between two merged vertices, it must be eliminated. This means excising the corresponding pointer from every contour that uses the edge. Further, there may be an edge from each of the merged vertices to a third vertex; such edges must be merged into a single edge.

Edge Merging and Edge Breaking

If two distinct edges are bounded by the same two vertices (as may happen after a vertex merge), then the edges must be merged. Every reference to the either of the original edges must be replaced with a reference to a single new edge. If the two merged edges belong to a contour with three edges that is not a hole (Figure 8a), then merging the edges would create an illegal two-edged contour. In this case the vertices at the ends of this illegal contour are merged, eliminating the contour. Further, merging edges may create a spike in a contour that has more than three edges (Figure 8b). This possibility is detected by checking if the angle made by the unmerged edges in the contour is less than $180°$. If so, the spike is removed from the contour.

Two edges that have no boundary vertices in common *overlap* if one approximately aligns with the other and they approximately intersect. They also overlap if they violate the restriction illustrated in Figure 6b. Two overlapping edges e_1 and e_2 must be broken into a series of two or three non-overlapping ones. This breaking creates two edges with identical bounding vertices that must be merged. Figure 8c shows how a merged edge resulting from an edge break can create a spike. This spike is eliminated when the edges are merged.

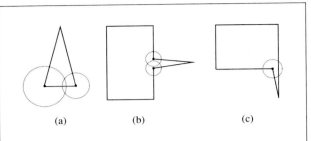

Figure 8. (a) A triangular non-hole must be merged when two of its vertices are. (b) A spike can be created when two vertices are merged. (c) Breaking an edge may create a spike.

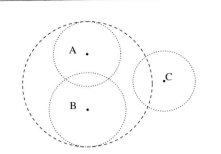

Figure 9. Revision of a coincidence determination. Vertex C becomes coincident with vertices A and B only after A and B are found coincident.

Coplanar Faces

Two faces that approximately align and intersect must be merged into a set of non-overlapping contours just as edges are. In general, this would require using an algorithm to partition intersecting polygons in the plane, but no such action is taken. Instead, we rely on there being two contours on either side of an edge. For an edge that lies in the plane of the coplanar faces, one of these contours belongs to one of the coplanar faces. The other contour belongs to a face that does not lie in the coplanar faces' plane. This third face will induce partitions in each of the coplanar faces. Eventaully (after all such edge-sharing faces have been considered), the coplanar contours will be partitioned into non-overlapping parts.

Perturbation of Merged Features

Merging two features f_1 and f_2 into a single new feature f requires finding coordinates and a tolerance for that feature. To maintain consistency, we must have $tol(f_1) \cup tol(f_2) \subseteq tol(f)$. As much as possible, the coordinates of f's flat are selected so as to minimize f's tolerance subject to this inclusion condition. For a pair of vertices, this amounts to finding the sphere of minimum radius that encloses two intersecting spheres. For a pair of edges, an attempt is made to find the bounded cylinder that encloses two intersecting bounded cylinders. For a pair of faces, a less than optimal approach is taken for the sake of simplicity. Newell's algorithm is applied to each of the contours in the coplanar pair and the results are averaged to find a new plane equation. The coordinates of each of the vertices of the edges in $B(f)$ are substituted into the new plane equation and the maximum deviation recorded. Then for each $e \in B(f)$ with vertices v_1 and v_2, the coordinates of $P_e(v_1)$ and $P_e(v_2)$ are substituted into the plane equation and the maximum deviation found. The largest of these two maximum deviations becomes f's tolerance. The procedure ensures that f approximately contains its boundary.

Both $ext(f)$ and $near(f)$ must also be assigned a value. $ext(f)$ must be recomputed from f's boundary features (this is done during the computation of its new coordinates and tolerance), while $near(f) = \min\{near(f_1), near(f_2)\}$. If f_1 and f_2 are vertices or edges, they may be contained in a feature of higher dimension. The extent of this feature may be affected when f_1 and f_2 are merged, so every feature that includes f_1 or f_2 must be located and a test made to see if its extent needs updating.

Backtracking

A merged feature f may be assigned a tolerance that is larger than either of the tolerances of the original features f_1 and f_2. This may create an inconsistency, because a third feature f_3 may have previously been determined not to intersect f_1 or f_2 individually, but f, with its larger tolerance region, may now approximately intersect f_3. Figure 9 shows the situation with vertices. If vertex C is considered against vertices A and B individually, vertex C will be found not coincident with either one. However, if vertex A is then considered against vertex B, these will be deemed coincident. A new tolerance region will be constructed that encloses those of A and B, contradicting the previous conclusion that C did not coincide with either A or B.

This situation is accomodated by maintaining the near value for each feature. If a feature f's tolerance is increased (i.e. by merging two features) and the new tolerance exceeds $near(f)$, an inconsistency may have been created. If this occurs, $near(f)$ is reset to a large positive value, and the algorithm is rerun from the beginning. While this *backtracking* is certainly expensive, it is essential to ensure that no inconsistencies are introduced. The cost of backtracking could be reduced by employing a spatial subdivision to limit those features that are reconsidered, but this has not been implemented.

Backtracking may lead to further backtracking, but any recursion must eventually terminate. The reason is that when backtracking occurs, all intersections between features considered so far will have been accounted for. Thus, any modifications made during a backtracking phase can only reduce the number of features (by merging them). At worst the process ends when all features that had been considered when backtracking started are merged into a single feature with a large tolerance.

4.4 Algorithm Operation

The first step in partitioning a pair of faces f_1 and f_2 is to compute the line of intersection between their planes a_1 and a_2. The direction of this line is given by $\mathbf{u} = \mathbf{n}_1 \times \mathbf{n}_2$ where $\mathbf{n}_i$ is the normal to a_i. A third plane is introduced with normal $\mathbf{u}$ and passing through a point in one of the faces boundaries. The intersection point of the three planes gives a point $\mathbf{v}$ on the intersection line. The intersection line tolerance is made large enough so that the tolerance region about the intersection line encloses $tol(a_1) \cap tol(a_2)$. If the face's tolerances are ϵ_1 and ϵ_2, respectively, the tolerance turns out to be

$$\epsilon = \left(\frac{\epsilon_1^2 + \epsilon_2^2 + 2\epsilon_1\epsilon_2 \cos\alpha}{\sin^2\alpha} \right)^{1/2}$$

where $\sin\alpha = \|\mathbf{n}_1 \times \mathbf{n}_2\|$.

4.5 Coplanarity

If $\frac{\epsilon}{\max\{\epsilon_1,\epsilon_2\}} > n$, where n is a user-specifiable *coplanarity factor*, the faces are tested for coplanarity. n is typically between 100 and 1000. Small values force the algorithm to deem pairs of faces that intersect in a relatively large dihedral angle to be coplanar.

If the ratio exceeds n, the faces are deemed coplanar if two vertices in one face's boundary lie on opposite sides of the other's plane, or if any vertex of one face lies within a distance equal to the extent of the other. This second condition ensures that two faces whose tolerance regions intersect in more than one connected component are found to be coplanar (see Figure 5).

4.6 Finding Edge-Face Intersections

If the ratio of the edge tolerance to the maximum of the two face tolerances is not too large, then the intersections of one of the face's edges with the other face's plane are found. For each edge, there are four possibilities: (1) the edge does not intersect the plane, (2) the edge intersects the plane in one boundary vertex, (3) the edge lies entirely in the plane, or (4) the edge crosses the plane.

These possibilities are distinguished by computing the signed distance of each of the edge's endpoints to the plane. The signed distance is deemed to be zero if the vertex lies within tolerance of the computed intersection line. If the line's equation is $\mathbf{v} + t\mathbf{u}$ and the vertex's coordinates are $\mathbf{p}$, then the vertex lies on the intersection line if

$$\|\mathbf{p} - \mathbf{v}\|^2 - [\mathbf{u} \cdot (\mathbf{p} - \mathbf{v})]^2 \leq (\epsilon + \epsilon_p)^2$$

where ϵ is the intersection line tolerance and ϵ_p is the vertex's tolerance.

If the vertex v does not lie on the intersection line its signed distance d_v to the plane is obtained by substituting its coordinates into the plane equation $d = \mathbf{n} \cdot (\mathbf{p} - \mathbf{o})$ where $\mathbf{n}$ is the plane unit normal and $\mathbf{o}$ is the point in the plane. $|d_v|$ is compared with both the vertex's and other face's near value; each value, if less than $|d_v|$, is replaced with $|d_v|$.

Even if the vertex does not lie on the intersection line, it may still intersect one of the other face f's boundary features. If $|d_v| < ext(f)$, then each of the other face's boundary features is checked to see if it intersects the v. If so, the v's distance from the plane is zero.

If $\text{sign}(d_{v_1}) = \text{sign}(d_{v_2})$ for the edge e's vertices v_1 and v_2, then e does not cross the other face's plane. If one sign is positive and the other is negative, e crosses the plane and the intersection point x between e and the plane is computed. The tolerance for x is ϵ. This guarantees that x approximately intersects both faces' planes as well as the computed intersection line. $near(x)$ is $\min\{near(e), dist(x, v_1), dist(x, v_2)\}$. The computed intersection point, along with auxilliary information indicating the edge and contour from which it came, are added to the list of intersection points.

If one of an edges' vertices lies in the other face's plane, the vertex is entered into the list of intersection points. Information about edge adjacency and local orientation of the contour at the vertex is also recorded.

Figure 10. One face completely contained in another's tolerance region. Some vertices must be merged and some edges broken because they violate the constraint illustrated in Figure 6.

If it turns out that all the edges of one face lie in the other's plane, the faces are deemed coplanar. This may happen in spite of the intersection line having a relatively small tolerance if one face's edges are all about the same length as the other face's tolerance. Even if this is the case, the vertices are still recorded in the intersection point list. Some of the vertices may have to be merged (Figure 10); such merging is done after sorting the points.

Finally, it may happen that one or both of an edges' endpoints lie off of the other face's plane, but the edge itself is approximately contained in the plane. This can occur if an edge e's tolerance is large compared to those of its endpoints. This situation is detected by determining if $P_e(v_1)$ and $P_e(v_2)$ (v_1 and v_2 are e's vertices) are both approximately contained in the other face's plane. If so, then the plane's tolerance is made large enough so that both of the original vertices approximately intersect the plane. If the new tolerance exceeds the face's near value, backtracking occurs. Otherwise, the current face pair is rerun with the increased face tolerance.

4.7 Feature Merging

After finding the intersection points of each face's edges with the other's plane, the points are sorted into order along the intersection line. This is accomplished by computing the value $t = (\mathbf{x} - \mathbf{v}) \cdot \mathbf{u}$ for each intersection point $\mathbf{x}$ (this effectively projects the point onto the calculated intersection line). and sorting in order of increasing t. Points that appear more than once are sorted secondarily using orientation information.

With the points ordered, a search is made for points that lie close enough together that they must be merged. Each point in the sorted list is checked against the next point. If they approximately intersect, the vertices defining the points are merged into a single vertex. This process may be repeated, eventually coalescing several vertices. In addition to vertex merging, edges that lie on the intersection line must be broken at intersection points that fall between their endpoints. Performing this operation ensures that pairs of edges that overlap are broken into a sequence of non-overlapping segments.

Vertex and edge merging may invalidate some of the data about orientation and incident edges stored with the intersection points. Sometimes it is difficult to determine how to update these data. In these cases the current face pair is simply rerun.

4.8 Cutting

The list of sorted and merged intersection points is used to determine where to slice contours to partition the pair of faces. Figure 11 shows some examples of cuts that are inserted into pairs of simple faces.

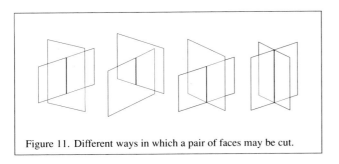

Figure 11. Different ways in which a pair of faces may be cut.

Either or both endpoints of a cut may correspond to newly calculated intersection points. Therefore an edge giving rise to such a point must be broken at that point before the cut is made. The edge is not broken when the intersection is computed because it is not known at that time whether or not the point lies in the interior of the face that the edge intersects. The point at which the edge is to be broken may approximately intersect one of the edges endpoints. If this is the case, the cut is made, after which the vertices are merged.

5   Results

Figure 12 shows the results of a union of two cubes centered at the origin where one cube is rotated through a small angle about a line through the origin with direction $(1, 2, 3)^T$ and the other is aligned with the coordinate axes. All computations were carried out in double-precision IEEE floating-point on a Silicon Graphics IRIS 4D/210VGX workstation. To make the results of this test easier to see, the face coplanarity factor was set to the rather low value of 20. The figure on the left was obtained with an angle of 9.59863838340879299° while that on the right was produced with an angle of 9.59863838340879300°. The entries in the corresponding rotation matrices differed by no more than one significant bit in their mantissas. The algorithm was also tested for many values of the rotation angle slightly above and below these two values. For all higher values, the object produced was similar to the one at right; for all lower values, the object was similar to the one at left. Further transitions occur as the angle is decreased even more until the object finally becomes a cube (but with non-planar faces) at an angle of about 1.5°. Figure 13 shows the object in Figure 12 in terms of its feature's tolerance regions.

If the coplanarity factor is increased to a more reasonable factor of 500, the angle at which the transition occurs is approximately 0.2°. In this example, even high coplanarity factors (10^5) with tiny angles (about 0.001°) produce a boundary of something other than a cube (but with some very short edges). This is because starting face and edge tolerances are zero, so computed vertex tolerances are set to the minimum value (10^{-10}). If face tolerances are initialized to about 10^{-6}, however, such high coplanarity factors and small angles cause computed vertex tolerances to become so large as to engulf the original vertices, eventually collapsing the cubes into a single vertex. Higher coplanarity factors can be used to achieve reasonable results if the input tolerances are reduced, but a vertex's tolerance may not be reduced so far that its ratio to the coordinates whose inaccuracy it quantifies approaches the machine precision.

Figure 14 shows the union of a pair of more complex objects, and Figure 15 shows the same union computed with a small coplanarity

factor and with the final tolerances displayed.

Figure 16 shows that the modeler can be used to generate complex objects without the tolerances causing any feature merging. This object was generated by starting with two congruent cubes in different orientations and computing their intersection. Then the resulting objects were rotated with respect to one another and the union taken and so on until, after eight iterations, the final result was obtained. In this object tolerances remain imperceptibly small because features are not merged (with the default tolerances and a coplanarity factor of 1000). If the process is carried out for another iteration, however, some features are near enough to one another that they are merged, and tolerances increase. Continued iteration causes tolerances to grow; features are rapidly collapsed so that after 11 iterations, the object is reduced to a single vertex.

6   Conclusions

We have presented a tolerance scheme that accounts for the consistent definition of boundary representations whose specification may be numerically uncertain. This scheme has been applied to a polyhedral modeler computing CSG operations on boundary representations. The modeler always succeeds in producing a result that is a consistent polyhedral boundary. Doing so may entail the localized collapse of several features into a single feature with a large tolerance.

Achieving this behavior has its costs; the algorithm runs 5-10 times slower, even when backtracking is not required, than an earlier version that performed only cursory tolerance checking. If n is the number of faces, the algorithm runs in time $O(n^2)$ without backtracking, although the average time can be made $O(n)$ by employing a spatial subdivision. Careful attention to making certain checks only when absolutely necessary, and replacing often called functions (such as the distance of a vertex to a plane) with in-line code would certainly reduce the required time. Even so, the resulting algorithm would likely be at least a factor of two slower than a similar algorithm that is not guaranteed to work in all cases.

With backtracking, the worst case behavior is $O(e^f)$ where f is the number of features. In practice, it is difficult to construct a case that achieves this behavior, although if backtracking occurs once it typically occurs several times. For most object constellations no backtracking occurs; it is only necessary when features approximately coincide and then only if there are other features near the coincident ones.

If the input to the algorithm has numerical uncertainties, there may be no other solution than to occasionally collapse features. In normal situations, such as computing the union of two imperfectly abutting objects, this collapsing leads to modest tolerance increases that have only local effect. Only in unusual situations, such as those designed to stress the algorithm shown in Figures 12-16, are the tolerance increases compounded enough to be objectionable. In any case, it makes sense to report large tolerances so that a user or higher-level program equipped with heuristics can be alerted to regions where unexpected behavior may occur. Perhaps tolerances can be decreased or features slightly perturbed to remove such behavior. In some cases the algorithm is too conservative in assigning tolerances to computed features because it has no access to global relationships among these features. It may be possible to design a post-processor that decreases tolerances while maintaining consistency. One possibility is to use a relaxation algorithm that perturbs feature coordinates in an attempt to reduce an objective function made up of a weighted sum of all the features' tolerances.

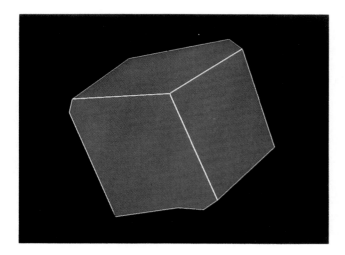
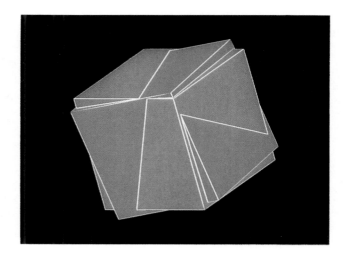

Figure 12. Union of two cubes.

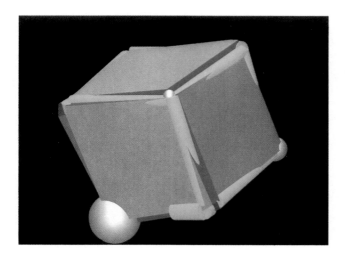

Figure 13. Union of two cubes with tolerance regions.

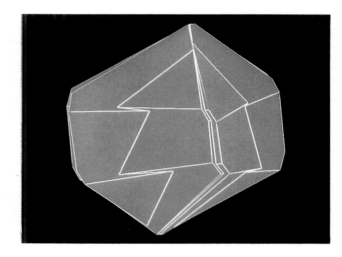

Figure 14. Union of two objects

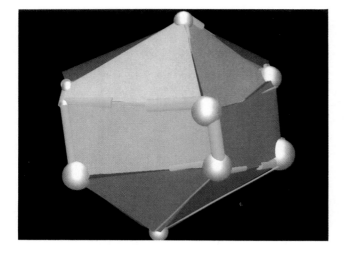

Figure 15. Union of two objects with tolerance regions.

Figure 16. A complex object formed by a series of CSG operations

The tolerance scheme can, in principle, be applied to other algorithms in geometric modeling. As already noted, polyhedral modelers other than the one described here can be modified to incorporate tolerances. Further, there is nothing inherently three-dimensional about a system of tolerances, so that the same techniques can be applied to geometric algorithms that operate in higher dimensions. Finally, it should be possible to extend the tolerance scheme to accomodate curved objects. The topological features of such objects are the same: vertices, edges, and faces. In this case the tolerances would not only reflect how accurately a feature is specified but also the accuracy of the computation used to evaluate points that lie on it. The challenge for this application is to extend the notions of approximate containment and coincidence to features that may intersect in several connected components or in isolated regions of tangency.

Acknowledgements

Many thanks to Carlo Séquin for his continued encouragement and support. Thanks also to Dan Baum, Derrick Burns, and Bob Drebin for helpful comments and criticisms.

References

[1] Dennis S. Arnon. Topologically reliable display of algebraic curves. Proceedings of SIGGRAPH'83 (Detroit, Michigan, July 25–29, 1983). In *Computer Graphics 17*,3 (July 1983), 219–227.

[2] John Francis Canny. *The Complexity of Robot Motion Planning*. PhD thesis, MIT, 1987.

[3] David Dobkin and Deborah Silver. Recipes for geometry & numerical analysis—part I: An empirical study. In *Proceedings of the Fourth ACM Symposium on Computational Geometry*, pages 93–105, Urbana, Illinois, 1988.

[4] A. Robin Forrest. Computational geometry and software engineering: Towards a geometric computing environment. In David F. Rogers and Rae A. Earnshaw, editors, *Techniques for Computer Graphics*, pages 23–37. Springer-Verlag, New York, 1987.

[5] W. Randolph Franklin, Peter Y.F. Wu, and Sumitro Samaddar. Prolog and geometry projects. *IEEE CG & A 6*,11 (November 1986), 46–55.

[6] Leonidas Guibas, David Salesin, and Jorge Stolfi. Epsilon geometry: Building robust algorithms from imprecise computations. In *Proceedings of the Fifth ACM Symposium on Computational Geometry*, pages 208–217, 1989.

[7] Cristoph M. Hoffmann, John E. Hopcroft, and Michael E. Karasick. Robust set operations on polyhedral solids. *IEEE CG & A 9*,6 (November 1989), 50–59.

[8] Cristoph M. Hoffmann, John E. Hopcroft, and Michael S. Karasick. Towards implementing robust geometric computations. In *Proceedings of the Fourth ACM Symposium on Computational Geometry*, pages 106–117, Urbana, Illinois, 1988.

[9] John E. Hopcroft and Peter J. Kahn. A paradigm for robust geometric algorithms. Technical Report TR 89-1044, Department of Computer Science, Cornell University, October 1989.

[10] David H. Laidlaw, W. Benjamin Trumbore, and John F. Hughes. Constructive solid geometry for polyhedral objects. Proceedings of SIGGRAPH'86 (Dallas, Texas, August 18–22, 1986). In *Computer Graphics 20*,4 (August 1986), 161–170.

[11] Martti Mäntylä. Boolean operations of 2-manifolds through vertex neighborhood classification. *ACM Transactions on Graphics 5*,1 (January 1986), 1–29.

[12] Victor Milenkovic. Verifiable implementations of geometric algorithms using finite precision arithmetic. *Artificial Intelligence 37* (1988), 377–401.

[13] Victor Milenkovic. Calculating approximate curve arrangements using rounded arithmetic. In *Proceedings of the Fifth ACM Symposium on Computational Geometry*, pages 197–207, 1989.

[14] S.P. Mudur and P.A. Koparkar. Interval methods for processing geometric objects. *IEEE CG & A 4*,2 (February 1984), 7–17.

[15] I.E. Sutherland, R.F. Sproull, and R.A. Schumacker. A Characterization of Ten Hidden-Surface Removal Algorithms. *Computing Surveys 6*,1 (March 1974), 1–55.

[16] Thomas Ottmann, Gerald Thiemt, and Christian Ullrich. Numerical stability of geometric algorithms. In *Proceedings of the Third ACM Symposium on Computational Geometry*, pages 119–125, Waterloo, Ontario, 1987.

[17] Aristides A. G. Requicha. Toward a theory of geometric tolerancing. *International Journal of Robotics Research 2*,4 (Winter 1983), 45–60.

[18] Mark Segal and Carlo H. Séquin. Consistent calculations for solid modeling. In *Proceedings of the First ACM Symposium on Computational Geometry*, pages 29–38, 1985.

[19] Mark Segal and Carlo H. Séquin. Partitioning polyhedral objects into non-intersecting parts. *IEEE CG & A 8*,1 (January 1988), 53–67.

[20] J. Stoer and R. Bulirsch. *Introduction to Numerical Analysis*. Springer-Verlag, New York, 1980.

[21] Chee-Keng Yap. A geometric consistency theorem for a symbolic perturbation scheme. In *Proceedings of the Fourth ACM Symposium on Computational Geometry*, pages 134–142, Urbana, Illinois, 1988.

small random perturbations of the discriminators (the program may fail as well). While a number of schemes have been devised to ameliorate the problem, the simplest and most common is the use of ε−intervals. For example, a discrimination based on whether a real value X is less than, greater than, or equal to 0 can be replaced with one that determines whether a X < -ε, X > +ε, or in [−ε +ε] respectively. More sophisticated methods enforce the intended semantics through a variety of schemes (see e.g. [Karasick 89]).

The only numerical computation in this work is the partitioning of a polygon by a plane. Its primitive operation is the dot product of a point and a plane to determine the location of that point with respect to the plane. The specific algorithm we use assumes the semantics of *planar*, *convex* polygons, and we rely on the epsilon method just described to attain robustness (to dampen the noise). Thus, the hyperplanes are in effect slabs 2ε thick. Any failure of this technique is detected, but no correction strategy is evident other than using larger epsilons (this has been in use since [Naylor 81]).

Unfortunately, this approach is insufficient to achieve a robust bi-partitioning operation. In fact, larger epsilon exacerbate the problem. Recall that there is a correlation between the location of the two bps: P1's location = InBoth ⇔ P2's location = InBoth, and similarly On ⇔ On, and NotInBoth ⇔ NotInBoth . Numerically this does not always hold. Our approach is to detect inconsistencies and induce a mapping to one of the consistent result. When one location is InBoth and the other is InNegHs or InPosHs, we can force the the former to be either InNegHs or InPosHs by selecting the "half" which contain vertices farthest from the partitioning plane, or we can force the second to the InBoth condition by extracting "on" vertices. If only one bp is On, we force it to a value consistent with the other bp. While we believe that forcing semantic consistency is essential, our current choices for enforcing this are at this point only tentative.

Numerical problems also affect attaining the semantics of the neighborhood operation. The method used for constructing bsp trees, defined in the continuum, implies that any sets lying in T.root_region.bp.shp will not be On any sub-hp in either of T's subtrees; however, numerically this does not always hold. We employ the following defense.When a face fragment from node V is classified as On during the neighborhood operation at a descendant node U, we essentially treat that node as if it were contained in the face's sub-hp, i.e. as if it did not exist. We then choose the subtree of U that is "not adjacent" to V, and continue the search.

The combination of these techniques has led to a robust set operation algorithm is the sense that the program will not fail and its output is in the neighborhood of the ideal output over a large numerical range. For example, the standard test in which a set operation is performed between a cube and a second cube that has been rotated successively about each of its three principal axes by an angle α has been executed successfully with α = 10^{-9} with ε < 10^{-11}, including ε = 0, using 64-bit floating point numbers. For 10^{-9} > α > 10^{-14}, union continued to give the same results, while intersection and difference found some sides to be equivalent. As the value of ε approaches α, more equivalences are produced until the two objects are computationally considered identical.

While using a small epsilon is interesting for testing the numerical limits, large epsilons are much more desirable (thicker hyperplanes) since they limit the size of the smallest fragments and so avoid representing features far below any viewing resolution. An upper bound to the thickness is the point at which the affect of treating faces as being co-planar, when in fact they are not, becomes visible to a viewer.

VIII. Complexity

A simple worst case lower bound of $\Omega(n^2)$ is obtained by noting that a checker board can be constructed from the symmetric difference of two trees, the first composed of n horizontal strips with alternating boolean values and the second composed of n similiar vertical strips.

As for an upper bound, the binary partitioner of each node of one tree is compared with the bp of each node of the second tree at most once, giving $O(|T1| * |T2|)$ or more simply $O(n^2)$. This analysis would be sufficient if each comparison was guaranteed to be $O(1)$. However, it is possible for a sub-hp to be of size $O(n)$, e.g. the base of an n sided cone. If this were true for every sub-hp, Partition_Bspt could take $O(n^2)$ per call, giving a total time of $O(n^3)$.

To show that this is not the case, we first observe that each sub-hp vertex is compared to a hyperplane of the other tree at most once per node. So if we can show that the total number of sub-hp vertices is $O(n)$, we will have $O(n^2)$ total work. To prove this we use arrangements of hyperplanes. An arrangement comprised of n d-cells can be represented by a bsp tree with an isomorphism from arrangement cells to bsp tree cells (leaf nodes) [Naylor 81]. Since it is known that the number of vertices of an arrangement is $O(n)$ and the sub-hp vertices are a subset of these, it can be shown that despite the fact that there are multiple instances of some vertices, the number of sub-hp vertices of an arrangement is also $O(n)$. Any bsp tree can be converted to its corresponding arrangement by replacing each cell/leaf with a tree representing the partitioning of that cell by all hyperplanes of the tree that intersect it. If we now remove any sub-hp separating two of the newly created cells, the new number of vertices will be:

$$n * O(1) - \Omega(1) < (n-1) * O(1).$$

If this is repeated , one node at a time, until the original tree is recreated, we will have $O(|T|)$ vertices. We then have that merging bsp trees is worst case optimal $\Theta(n^2)$.

Of even greater interest is the expected case. This requires a definition of "good" trees, which we have developed but do not have space here to explore. If, for now, we simply take good to mean balanced, then merging two balanced trees of size n can produce, at worst, a tree with maximum depth of *2 log n*. Or more generally speaking, merging two good trees should yield a reasonably good tree. Note that the use of a bounding simplex as in figure 3.4 can lead to $O(d)$ time to merge two trees whose bounding simplices are disjoint and the interior of one simplex is not intersected by a sub-hp of the other.

Concluding remarks

It is worth comparing this algorithm to the method in [Thibault and Naylor 87]. One of the two methods in that work performs a set operation between a bsp tree represented polyhedron and a b-rep represented polyhedron. The inserted entity is the b-rep polyhedron, represented as a list of polygons. In this work, we have instead a bsp tree, clearly a more complex structure than a list, although not necessarily more complex than the more general b-rep structure as a hierarchy of lists (not used in [Thibault and Naylor 87]). However, there are at least two ways in which one gains from the using a bsp tree.

The first advantage arises from the efficiency of a hierarchical search structure: entire subtrees can be classified without examining their contents. In the average case, this can lead to $O(\log n)$ behavior instead of $O(n)$. The second is algorithmic simplicity. Besides the obvious advantage of having only the bsp tree data type to deal with, it is difficult to determine with a b-rep the relative spatial classification of some other entity. The algorithms in [Thibault and Naylor 87] require, when the faces of the b-rep object are entirely to one side of a partitioning hyperplane, the determination of whether the corresponding sub-hp is inside or outside of the polyhedron. While [Thibault and Naylor 87] gives the simplest solutions for this in 2D and 3D, the method is cumbersome and does not easily generalize to arbitrary dimensions (so much so that we have not seriously attempted to do so). In our new setting, while we still need this classification of the sub-hp with respect to the inserted object, its spatial structure being a bsp tree makes this straightforward, and in fact occurs as part of the partitioning operation itself, thereby necessitating no additional consideration and so solves the problem for arbitrary dimensions.

This work remains a hybrid approach, since b-reps are used for polygons, both as sub-hps and faces. However, prior to implementing this scheme, we devised an "all bsp tree" representation which dispenses with b-reps entirely (see [Naylor 90b] for a brief description). Thus, the sub-hps and the faces of a d-dimensional tree are represented by d-1 dimensional trees, and so on recursing in dimension until d = 0. This representation has many advantages including dimension independence as well as obviating the problem encountered here with b-reps not being able to represent unbounded sets. We chose to implement the hybrid approach described here to provide a more easily attainable intermediate step, since many techniques have been developed using polygons as b-reps that must be provided in the new scheme. Nonetheless, the routines Merge_Bspts and Partition_Bspt are essentially the same in both schemes, the difference being limited primarily to Bi-Partition_Bps; and forming the boundary requires only the capabilities already provided by these routines.

References

[Bloomberg 86]
Sandra H. Bloomberg,"A Representation of Solid Objects for Performing Boolean Operations", U.N.C. Computer Science Technical Report 86-006 (1986).

[Chin and Feiner 89]
N. Chin and S. Feiner,"Near Real-Time Shadow Generation Using BSP Trees", **Computer Graphics** Vol. 23(3), pp. 99-106, (Aug. 1989).

[Fuchs, Kedem, and Naylor 80]
H. Fuchs, Z. Kedem, and B. Naylor, "On Visible Surface Generation by a Priori Tree Structures," **Computer Graphics** Vol. 14(3), pp. 124-133, (June 1980).

[Fussell and Campbell 90]
Donald Fussell and A.T. Campbell, "Adaptive Mesh Generation for Global Diffuse Illumination," **Computer Graphics** Vol. 24(3), (Aug. 1990).

[Hoffmann 89]
Christoph M. Hoffmann, **Geometric and Solid Modeling**, Morgan Kaufmann, 1989.

[Karasick 89]
Michael Karasick, "On the Representation and Manipulation of Rigid Solids," Ph.D. Thesis, Cornell University (March 1989).

[Mantyla 88]
Martti Mantyla, **Solid Modeling**, Computer Science Press, 1988.

[Naylor 81]
Bruce F. Naylor, "A Priori Based Techniques for Determining Visibility Priority for 3-D Scenes," Ph.D. Thesis, University of Texas at Dallas (May 1981).

[Naylor 90a]
Bruce F. Naylor, "SCULPT : An Interactive Solid Modeling Tool", Proc. of Graphics Interface, (May 1990).

[Naylor 90b]
Bruce F. Naylor, "Binary Space Partitioning Trees as an Alternative Representation of Polytopes", **Computer Aided Design**, Vol 22(4), (May 1990).

[Naylor and Thibault 86]
Bruce F. Naylor and William C. Thibault, "Application of BSP Trees to Ray-Tracing and CSG Evaluation," Technical Report GIT-ICS 86/03, School of Information and Computer Science, Georgia Institute of Technology, Atlanta, Georgia 30332 (February 1986).

[Paterson and Yao 89]
M.S. Paterson and F.F. Yao, "Binary partitions with applications to hidden-surface removal and solid modeling", Proceedings of Fifth Symp. on Computational Geometry, pp. 23-32, (1989).

[Paterson and Yao 90]
M.S. Paterson and F.F. Yao, "Optimal Binary Space Partitions for Orthogonal Objects", Proceedings of 1st Symp. on Discrete Algorithms, pp. 100-106, (Jan. 1990).

[Schumaker et al 69]
R. A. Schumacker, R. Brand, M. Gilliland, and W. Sharp, "Study for Applying Computer-Generated Images to Visual Simulation," AFHRL-TR-69-14, U.S. Air Force Human Resources Laboratory (1969).

[Sutherland, Sproull and Schumaker 74]
I.E. Sutherland, R.F. Sproull and R. A. Schumacker, "A Characterization of Ten hidden Surface Algorithms," **ACM Computing Surveys** Vol 6(1), (1974).

[Thibault and Naylor 87]
W. Thibault and B. Naylor, "Set Operations On Polyhedra Using Binary Space Partitioning Trees," **Computer Graphics** Vol. 21(4), (July 1987).

[Thibault 87]
William C. Thibault, "Application of Binary Space Partitioning Trees to Geometric Modeling and Ray-Tracing", Ph.D. Dissertation, Georgia Institute of Technology, Atlanta, Georgia, (1987).

[Torres 90]
Enric Torres, "Optimization of the Binary Space Partition Algorithm (BSP) for the Visualization of Dynamic Scenes" Eurographics '90 (Sept. 1990).

An Efficient Radiosity Solution for Bump Texture Generation

Hong Chen and En-Hua Wu

Institute of Software, Academia Sinica
P. O. Box 8718, Beijing 100080, China

Abstract

The development of global illumination and texture generation makes it possible to produce the most realistic images. However, it is still difficult or deficient so far to simulate bump texture effects while the interreflection of light being modeled by the present ray tracing or radiosity methods. A method of bump texture generation, being incorporated into the process of radiosity solution, is presented in the paper. The method is characterized by introduction of a *perturbed radiosity map*, established in the context of either progressive radiosity or standard radiosity solution. To calculate the perturbed radiosity, a concept of *perturbed form-factors* is proposed, and the algorithms for evaluating the perturbed form-factors are also given. As a result, a bilinear-interpolation shading scheme for perturbed surfaces is provided, and the texturing method is easily added to a newly improved solution of progressive refinement radiosity for non-diffuse environment.

CR Categories and Subject Descriptors: I.3.3 [Computer Graphics]: Picture/Image Generation; Display Algorithm; I.3.7 [Computer Graphics]: Three-Dimentional Graphics and Realism.

General Terms: Algorithms.

Additional Key Words and Phrases: perturbed radiosity map, perturbed form-factor, perturbed hemi-cube, bumpy texture, radiosity, interreflection, progressive refinement.

1. Introduction

The most realistic and attractive computer generated images are those that contain a large amount of visual complexity and detail. Ray tracing and radiosity methods are able to produce highly realistic images by faithful simulation of light energy exchange between surfaces. However, if an image is rendered only by taking illumination model into account, it will look artificial due to the extreme smoothness of surfaces. To overcome this shortage, the surface complexity should be increased. Comparatively, texturing is an acceptable method that can increase the surface detail by a relatively low cost. Generally speaking, the surface texture mapping approaches come into two main categories: color mapping and bump mapping.

The conventional ray tracing method simulates light reflection and refraction for specular and transparent surfaces, and produces direct illumination and shadow effects[23]. The diffuse interreflection in the ray tracing is simply treated as a constant "ambient" term, which makes images obviously computer-generated, as the interreflection has significant effect on the lighting of a scene.

There have been many approaches[2][3][4][5][6][14] which incorporate the texture generation process directly into reflection calculation. These approaches are suitable for rendering pictures via standard ray tracing method. But within the standard ray tracing methodology, the texture solution for diffuse interreflection is by no means viable due to the inherent nature of standard ray tracing.

In 1988, Ward et al. introduced a new ray tracing method of modeling (diffuse) interreflection[22]. By their method, indirect illuminance is averaged over surfaces from a small set S of computed values to avoid calculation at each pixel. The members of the set S are determined by the split sphere model which estimates the illuminance gradient on each surface using the illuminance coherence. But such split sphere model only relates the illumninance gradient to the scene geometry without considering the lighting distribution. To maintain accuracy, when the orientation of a surface, such as a wrinkled surface, changes rapidly, the computation of indirect illuminance increases at a very high rate. Therefore, this method is not efficient for simulating textures, in particular the bumpy texture[3], with diffuse interrflection effect.

The radiosity method, based on the principle of heat transfer[19], is well suited to calculating diffuse interreflection[12]. In 1985 and 1986, Cohen, Greenberg et al. developed the standard radiosity method, in a diffuse environment[8][9]. Various radiosity methods were developed in the following years for rendering pictures in a non-diffuse environment[20][16][17][18]. The progressive refinement radiosity method proposed by Cohen et al. in 1988[10] has made it possible for radiosity to be employed interactively for image synthesis in a complex environment.

A diffuse interreflectional texture algorithm based on a reformed colour texture mapping technique was realized in Cohen's standard radiosity approach[9]. However, no efficient technique available so far for simulating the bump mapping texture[3] in an interreflectional environment within the framework of radiosity or ray tracing methods.

In the following part of the paper, we will present a radiosity solution for bump mapping texture rendering, based on illuminance coherence. The technique has been realized without significant degradation of the radiosity methods utilized. Efficiency is obtained with an introduction of so called *perturbed radiosity map* and *perturbed form-factor*. Combined with an adapted progressive refinement radiosity method for non-diffuse environment[7], a general rendering method, which has a highly practical value, is established.

2. Bumpy Mapping Texture by Perturbed Radiosity Map

The slight change of a surface normal direction will result in variation in the intensity distribution of the reflected light. Based on this principle, Blinn first made a proposal for simulating wrinkled surfaces by perturbing surface normals. This is popularly known as "bumpy mapping"[3]. He developed a method for generating the direction and value of the normal perturbations from a bump function $F(u,v)$ of the surface parameters. $F(u,v)$ is stored as a two-directional lookup table indexed by u and v. By moving the parameterized surface $\vec{P}(u,v)$ a small value $F(u,v)$ in the direction of the surface normal $\vec{N}$, new normal $\vec{N}'$ is calculated and the bumpy surface is produced in terms of $\vec{N}'$.

By the shading scheme of radiosity method, the radiosity at a point within a patch is calculated by bilinear interpolation from the radiosities at the patch vertices, and thus the true surface normal at the visible point has not been utilized directly during the rendering process. Therefore, the traditional bump mapping technique is unable to be added into radiosity solution.

We notice that within a relatively small range, the surfaces which have the same normal will have their illuminance more or less the same. Based on this phenomenon of *illuminance coherence*, we are able to design a shading scheme to calculate the perturbed radiosity on a perturbed patch. Briefly speaking, if the radiosity $B(\vec{N}', \vec{P}_v)$ at a patch vertex P_v can be calculated and recorded in a *perturbed radiosity map* for different perturbed directions of $\vec{N}'$, then The perturbed radiosity $B(\vec{N}', \vec{P})$ at any point $\vec{P}$ on the patch can be derived from the traditional method of bilinear interpolation of the radiosities $B(\vec{N}', \vec{P}_v)$ at vertices.

If the patch is not perturbed, $\vec{N}'$ is identical to $\vec{N}$, $B(\vec{N}, \vec{P})$ can be determined just as in the standard radiosity method.

Next, in Section 2.1, before going through the detailed discussion of texture generation, we first review an implementation of two-pass method for non-diffuse environments combining an adapted progressive radiosity and ray tracing methods. It was taken to be the bed for our texture generation. A description is given in Section 2.2 on how to evaluate the perturbed diffuse radiosity, which is followed in Section 2.3 by derivation of a method for the evaluation of perturbed form-factors.

2.1 Progressive Refinement Radiosity for Non-diffuse Environment

Within a diffuse environment, the radiosity of a patch, say i, is given by:

$$B_i = E_i + \rho_i \sum_{j=1}^{N} B_j F_{ji} A_j / A_i \qquad <1>$$

where B_i is radiosity of patch i (*watts/m²*),

E_i is emission of patch i (*watts/m²*),

ρ_i is reflectance of patch i,

A_i is area of patch i (*m²*),

F_{ji} is form-factor from patch j to patch i,

N is number of discrete patches in the environment.

The equation <1> suggests that the energy on patch i is the result of gathering those from the environment. In this standard radiosity method, energy distribution in the environment may be simply obtained by solving the set of simultaneous equations derived from equation <1>. However, establishment of the coefficient matrix requires calculating and saving form-factors between all patch pairs so that a computation and storage expense of $O(N^2)$ is required.

The method of progressive refinement radiosity has overcome the shortcoming above. The solution proceeds in a series of refinement steps by shooting radiosities from a shooting patch with greatest energy at each step. It is efficient since only one hemi-cube on the shooting patch need to be established at each iterative step, so that the time and space trade-off is only $O(N)$.

When the progressive refinement radiosity method[10] was proposed in 1988, it was constrained to diffuse environment. In 1989, an extended two-pass method for non-diffuse environment, capable of being adapted into a progressive process, was provided by Sillion and Puech[18]. In their method, the extended form-factors accounting for specular reflections are determined in terms of ray tracing.

We have designed a different two-pass method[7] into which the texture generation is incorporated. The method and the related derivation are briefly introduced here to give a view of radiosity solution environment with which the texture generation is involved.

Within a non-diffuse environment, surfaces are no longer perfectly diffuse reflectors and emitters, therefore, all interreflections of light between diffuse and non-diffuse surfaces should be taken into consideration. For a non-diffuse surface, the bidirectional reflectance function is approximated as a sum of a diffuse portion ρ_d and a specular portion ρ_s [17][20]:

$$\rho''(\theta_{out}, \theta_{in}) = k_s \rho_s(\theta_{out}, \theta_{in}) + k_d \rho_d$$

where k_s, k_d are specular and diffuse reflectance of the surface respectively. $k_s + k_d \leq 1$.

In order to facilitate the incorporation of specular reflectance into the process of progressive refinement radiosity in our method, the irradiation(H), a counterpart of radiation(B), is defined and utilized. For instance, the irradiation H_{ji} is defined as the irradiative amount incident on patch i due to the radiation from patch j. Thus, the radiosity equation in non-diffuse environments can be reformulated as

$$B_i = E_i + k_{di}\rho_{di}\pi\sum_{j=1}^{N} H_{ji} \qquad <2>$$

For a non-diffuse patch j, H_{ji} consists of a diffuse term, H_{ji}^d, and a specular term, H_{ji}^s, reflected onto patch i via patch j, or:

$$H_{ji} = H_{ji}^d + H_{ji}^s$$

here

$$H_{ji}^d = A_j B_j F_{ji}/A_i \qquad <3>$$

$$H_{ji}^s = \sum_{k=1}^{N} A_j H_{kj} F_{kji} k_{sj}/A_i \qquad <4>$$

where F_{kji} represents the fraction of energy shooting out from patch k to patch j and finally landing on patch i via specular reflection of patch j[17]:

$$F_{kji} = \frac{1}{\pi F_{jk}} \int\int_{A_k A_i} \rho_{sj}(\theta_{out}, \theta_{in})\frac{\cos\theta_k \cos\theta_j'}{r_{jk}^2}\frac{\cos\theta_j \cos\theta_i}{r_{ji}^2}dA_i\,dA_k$$

Using the hemi-cube over patch j, F_{kji} is evaluated by

$$F_{kji} = \frac{\pi}{F_{jk}}(\sum_{p\in P}\sum_{q\in Q}\rho_{sj}(\theta_q, \theta_p)\Delta F_q \Delta F_p) \qquad <5>$$

where P, Q are the set of hemi-cube pixels covered by projection of patch k, i onto the hemi-cube, and ΔF_p and ΔF_q are delta form-factors related to pixel p and q respectively.

Given k in <4>, H_{ji}^s is increased by

$$\frac{A_j K_{sj}\pi}{A_i}\sum_{q\in Q}\Delta F_q\sum_{p\in P}\rho_{sj}(\theta_q, \theta_p)\frac{H_{kj}\Delta F_p}{F_{jk}}$$

Denote $H_p = \dfrac{H_{kj}\Delta F_p}{F_{jk}}$, is the delta irradiation related to pixel p. Since the non-diffuse patch j satisfies the "phong-like" bidirectional reflectance[13][17][20], the specular reflective energy leaving patch j through hemi-cube pixel q is approximated by the weighted summation of energy which reaches the patch j through the area $P(q)$ on the hemi-cube (Fig. 1). Therefore,

$$H_{ji}^s = \frac{A_j k_{sj}\pi}{A_i}\sum_{q\in Q}\Delta F_q\sum_{p\in P(q)}\rho_s(\theta_q, \theta_p)H_p \qquad <6>$$

$\rho_s(\theta_q, \theta_p)$ is employed as a weighted factor and is presented by an array of weights during implementation.

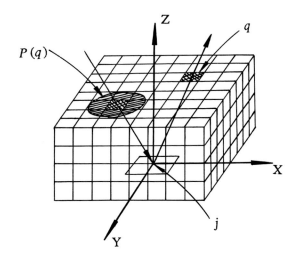

Fig. 1   Relationship between Outgoing and Incoming Energy Distribution

Based on the linear equations <2><3><6>, by also equally assigning non-diffuse patches the shooting candidacy, a two-pass progressive solution for non-diffuse environments is established, with a progressive preprocess iteratively refining the distribution of radiosities including specular reflections, followed by a postprocess of ray tracing for adding view-dependent effects such as highlight and mirrors.

The solution of the first pass proceeds as follows:

Do until convergence

    Select patch with greatest unshot energy as shooting patch;

    Compute form-factors from shooting patch to all other elements by hemi-cube algorithm;

    If shooting patch is non-diffuse, compute delta irradiations;

    Based on form-factors and delta irradiations, add contribution of the shooting patch to radiosity of all elements and irradiation of none-diffuse elements.

Instead of directly using the specular form-factors or extended form-factors like in methods in [16][17][18][21], in our method, when a selected shooting patch is non-diffuse, apart from calculating the standard form-factors by the newly constructed hemi-cube, delta irradiations are evaluated from the increment of irradiation which has been recorded in a queue from previous calculations. The delta irradiations are then utilized for calculating the specular portion of the shooting to other patches.

When the number of non-diffuse patches is relatively small compared to the number of diffuse patches, and the technique of subdivision[9][10] is employed, the storage cost of irradiation queues is low.

The method above is based on hemi-cube algorithm, so it is readily implemented in terms of hardware Z-buffer. In contrast, the method of ray tracing is now hardly implemented by hardware, particularly when a complex reflectance function and an advanced ray tracing algorithm such as distributed ray tracing are utilized. Therefore, our method, with the hemi-cube algorithm assisted by hardware on the workstation such as SGI IRIS 4D/20, is more efficient than the methods like that described in [18].

2.2 Perturbed Radiosity

As shown in Fig. 2, the plane $PL(i, \vec{N}')$ is through the center O_i of the patch i and its normal vector is the perturbed normal $\vec{N}'$. Because the value of the perturbation function $F(u,v)$ upon the patch i is small, we can assume that the solid angle $d\omega_{ji}$ is not affected by the perturbation. The Radiant flux Φ_{ji} is shooting out from patch j to patch i within the solid angle $d\omega_{ji}$. The area on the plane $PL(i, \vec{N}')$ which is subtended by the solid angle $d\omega_{ji}$ forms a new patch i', referred to as perturbed patch i', or P-patch i'. Note that P-patch i' and its area A_i' is affected by the perturbed normal vector $\vec{N}'$.

The form-factors between patch i and j have a reciprocity relationship[8]:

$$A_i F_{ij} = A_j F_{ji} \qquad <7>$$

where A_i is the area of patch i and A_j is the area of patch j;

    F_{ij} is the form-factor from patch i to patch j;

    F_{ji} is the form-factor from patch j to patch i.

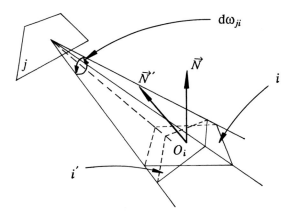

Fig. 2   Assumptive Perturbed Patch

Define the form-factor from P-patch i' to patch j , F_{ij}', a function of $\vec{N}'$, as perturbed form-factor. Since the solid angle $d\omega_{ji}$ is constant, the form-factor from patch j to P-patch i' is equal to F_{ji} . So

$$A_i' F_{ij}' = A_j F_{ji} \qquad <8>$$

From <7> <8>, we have

$$\frac{A_i'}{A_i} = \frac{F_{ij}}{F_{ij}'}$$

The irradiance $H_{ji}'(\vec{N}')$ of P-patch i' from patch j is :

$$H_{ji}' = \frac{\Phi_{ji}}{A_i'} = \frac{\Phi_{ji}}{A_i} \frac{F_{ij}'}{F_{ij}} = H_{ji} \frac{F_{ij}'}{F_{ij}} \qquad <9>$$

Similar to equation <2>, the diffuse radiosity $B_i'(\vec{N}')$ of P-patch i' is

$$B_i' = E_i + k_i \rho_i \pi \sum_{j=1}^{N} H_{ji}'$$

$$= E_i + k_i \rho_i \pi \sum_{j=1}^{N} H_{ji} \frac{F_{ij}'}{F_{ij}} \qquad <10>$$

It is clear from <10> that, to obtain the perturbed radiosity (B_i') of patch i, we have to know, for each patch j, the irradiation H_{ji}, and the form-factors F_{ij}', F_{ij}. In other words, the perturbed radiosity on one patch is *gathered* from all other patches in the environment. Therefore, the task of perturbed radiosity evaluation has to be taken by a postprocess while the formula <10> is utilized. Latter on in the paper, we will derive another method to allow the evaluation of perturbed radiosity being performed at each iterative step in the process of progressive refinement solution with a *shooting* way.

In sum, a bump mapping technique, by the perturbed radiosity map has been proposed in radiosity solution for texture generation in non-diffuse environment. Separate algorithms have been provided for evaluation of the perturbed form-factors to fit different radiosity methods. Consequently, the texture processing is taken either as a postprocess or as a refinement step, incorporated into the procedure of progressive radiosity solution.

The shading scheme based on the perturbed radiosity map is view-independent, and the perturbed radiosity map is also independent of the texturing perturbation function adopted. The bump mapping technique has improved the visual realism of radiosity image and promoted the practical value of radiosity solution.

Acknowledgements

Thanks are given to Yun-Mei Dong and Kei-De Li for providing Apollo-DN580 on which the software was developed during the first stage, and for providing printing facilities. Acknowledgements are also due to Kong-Shi Xu, You-La Zhang and Yu-Guo Wang for their support and various help during the working period. We are grateful to You-Dong Liang and Qun-Sheng Peng of Zhejiang University for their generous help in providing related theses for references long before their papers appeared at conferences. Thanks are also given to SIGGRAPH reviewers for their helpful comments.

The work has been supported by the National Natural Science Foundation.

References

1. Baum, D. R., Rushmeier, H. E. and Winget, J. M., *Improving Radiosity Solutions through the Use of Analytically Determined Form-Factors,* Computer Graphics, Vol 23(3), 1989, pp.325-334

2. Blinn, J. F. and Newell, M. E., *Texture and Reflection in Computer Generated Images,* Comm. ACM, Vol 19(10), 1976, pp.542-547

3. Blinn, J. F., *Simulation of Wrinkled Surfaces,* Computer Graphics, Vol 12(3), 1978, pp.286-292

4. Cabral, B., Max, N. and Springmeye R., *Bidirectional Reflection Functions from Surface Bump Maps,* Computer graphics, Vol 19(4), 1987, pp.273-281

5. Carey, R. J. and Greenberg, D. P., *Texture for Realistic Image Synthesis,* Computer & Graphics, vol 9(2), 1985, pp.125-138

6. Catmull, E., *A Subdivision Algorithm for Computer Display of Curved Surfaces,* Ph.d Dissertation, Univ. of Uta, Salt Lake City, 1974

7. Chen, H. and Wu, E. H., *An Adapted Solution of Progressive Radiosity and Ray Tracing Methods for Non-diffuse Environment,* Proceedings of CGI'90, June 26-30, 1990

8. Cohen, M. F. and Greenberg, D. P., *The Hemi-cube: A Radiosity Solution for Complex Environment,* Computer Graphics, Vol 19(3), 1985, pp.31-40

9. Cohen, M. F., Greenberg, D. P., Immel, D. S. and Brack, P. J., *An Efficient Radiosity Approach for Realistic Image Synthesis,* IEEE CG&A, Vol 6(2), 1986, pp.26-35

10. Cohen, M. F., Chen, S. E., Wallace, J. K. and Greenberg, D. P., *A Progressive Refinement Approach to Fast Radiosity Image Generation,* Computer Graphics, Vol 22(4), 1988, pp.75-84

11. Cook, R. L., *Shade Trees,* Computer Graphics, Vol 18(3), 1984, pp.223-231

12. Goral, C. M., Torrance, K. E. and Greenberg, D. P., *Modelling the Interaction of Light between Diffuse Surfaces,* Computer Graphics, Vol 18(3), 1984, pp.213-222

13. Immel, D. S., Cohen, M. F. and Greenberg, D. P., *A Radiosity Method for Non-diffuse Environment,* Computer Graphics, Vol 20(4), 1986, 133-142

14. Max, N. L., *Shadows for Bump-mapped Surfaces,* Advanced Computer Graphics, Kunii T.L. Ed. Springer Verlag, Tokyo, 1986, pp.145-156

15. Perlin, K., *An Image Synthesizer,* Computer Graphics, Vol 19(3), 1985, pp.287-296

16. Shao, M. Z., Peng, Q. S. and Liang, Y. D., *A New Radiosity Approach by Procedural Refinements for Realistic Image Synthesis,* Computer Graphics, Vol 22(4), 1988, pp.93-101

17. Shao, P. P., Peng, Q. S. and Liang, Y. D., *Form-factors for General Environments,* Proc. Eurographics'88, Nice, 1988, pp.499-510

18. Sillion, F. and Puech, C., *A General Two-pass Method Integrating Specular and Diffuse Reflection,* Computer Graphics, Vol 23(3), 1989, pp.335-344

19. Sparrow, E. M. and Cess, R. D., *Radiation Heat Transfer,* McGraw-Hill, New York, 1978

20. Wallace, J. R., Cohen, M. F. and Greenberg, D. P., *A Two-pass Solution to the Rendering Equation: A Synthesis of Ray Tracing and Radiosity Methods,* Computer Graphics, Vol 21(4), 1987, pp.311-320

21. Wallace, J. R., Elmquist, K. A. and Haines, E. A., *A Ray Tracing Algorithm for Progressive Radiosity,* Computer Graphics, Vol 23(3), 1989, pp.315-324

22. Ward, G. J., Rubinstein, F. M. and Clear, R. D., *A Ray Tracing Solution for Diffuse Interreflection,*

Computer Graphics, Vol 22(4), 1988, pp.85-92

23. Whitted, T., *An Improved Illumination Model for Shaded Display,*   Comm. ACM, Vol 23(6), 1980, pp.343-349

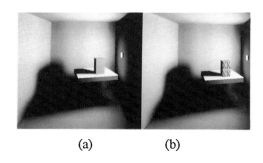

(a)   (b)

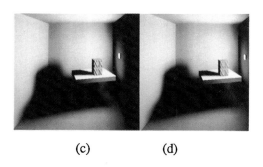

(c)   (d)

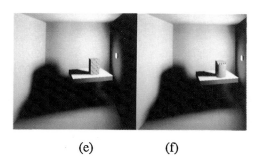

(e)   (f)

Figure 4

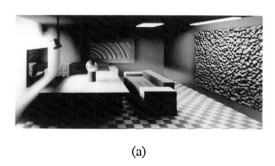

(a)

Figure 8

(b)

Figure 7

Incremental Radiosity: An Extension of Progressive Radiosity to an Interactive Image Synthesis System

Shenchang Eric Chen

Advanced Technology Group
Apple Computer, Inc.

ABSTRACT

Traditional radiosity methods can compute the illumination for a scene independent of the view position. However, if any part of the scene geometry is changed, the radiosity process will need to be repeated from scratch. Since the radiosity methods are generally expensive computationally, the traditional methods do not lend themselves to interactive uses where the geometry is constantly changing. This paper presents a new radiosity algorithm to incrementally render scenes with changing geometry and surface attributes. In other words, the question to be asked is *"What is the minimum recomputation I need to do if I turn off a light source, change the color of a surface, add or move an object?"* Because a modeling change generally exhibits some coherence and affects only parts of an image, the proposed method may drastically reduce the rendering time and therefore allow interactive manipulation. In addition, since the method is conducted incrementally and view-independently, the rendering process can start before the modeling process is completed. The traditional paradigm of *modeling-then-rendering* is changed to *rendering-while-modeling*. This approach not only gives the user better visual feedback but also effectively utilizes CPU time otherwise wasted in the modeling process.

CR Categories and Subject Descriptors: I.3.3 [Computer Graphics]: Picture/Image Generation - Display Algorithms. I.3.7 [Computer Graphics]: Three-Dimensional Graphics and Realism

General Terms: Algorithms

Additional Key Words and Phrases: Radiosity, Incremental Rendering, Incremental Radiosity, Global Illumination, Lighting Design, Progressive Radiosity.

* Author's address: Apple Computer Inc., MS-60W, 20705 Valley Green Dr. Cupertino, CA 95014. E-mail: chense@apple.com

INTRODUCTION

Recent introduction of the progressive radiosity method has opened the door for using the technique in an interactive image synthesis system [1]. This new method applied the approach of rendering by progressive refinement to speed up the radiosity computation. In this approach, the image quality is continuously improved over time and intermediate results are displayed throughout the rendering process. However, as with the other radiosity methods, [2], [3], [4], this technique requires the rendered scene to be static. Whenever there is a change of the scene geometry, the entire radiosity process needs to be repeated from scratch. Although the progressive method has greatly reduced the rendering time, it is still too expensive to be used in an interactive environment where the scene descriptions are constantly changing.

Our primary goal is to use the radiosity method in an environment where we can interactively modify the viewing positions, geometry and surface attributes. Because the radiosity method is view-independent, it allows view positions to be changed freely once the radiosity computation is completed. In addition, the radiosity method can accurately simulate the diffuse interreflection between surfaces. In many applications such as lighting, or interior space design, this degree of realism is necessary and could not be obtained from other commonly used fast rendering techniques like Gouraud [5] or Phong shading [6]. The method introduced in this paper performs the radiosity computations incrementally based on the scene changes. This method is in the spirit of progressive refinement, i.e. image quality is constantly improved with time. When a scene change is made, the proposed method will attempt to update only the areas affected by the change directly. The change will later be propagated throughout the whole scene to account for diffuse interreflection. Since the change tends to be local and affects only a small portion of the image, the incremental method may drastically reduce the rendering time and therefore allow interactive manipulation.

This approach also bridges the gap between modeling and rendering, which are traditionally regarded as two separate processes performed sequentially. Because of the view-independence and incremental nature of the proposed method, the rendering process can start before modeling is finished. This approach offers several advantages over the conventional modeling-then-rendering approach. It provides a great degree of realism during modeling and reduces the turnaround time. It also effectively utilizes the wasted CPU cycles in a modeling session.

Early work in radiosity has shown that surface reflectance can be altered independently without affecting form-factors, which are purely geometrical relationships between surface patches [3]. Once the form-factors are pre-computed and stored, radiosity images can be generated quickly with different color variations. However, the cost of storing the form-factors is $O(n^2)$, where n is the number of surface patches. Even though the form-factors are normally quite sparse, the overwhelming storage cost still makes it impractical for rendering complex scenes. This method also requires the geometry to be static and needs very long preprocessing time.

A method presented by Baum et al. [7] attempts to lift the restriction of static geometry imposed on the radiosity methods. This method is primarily directed toward computing an animation sequence and requires the path of object movement to be known in advance. Therefore, it is not suitable for our purpose. A ray-tracing method presented in [8] shows the possibilities of updating the geometry and color changes incrementally if all the *illumination links* connecting the surfaces are pre-computed and stored. These approaches face the same storage and preprocessing problems as the previous one.

Our algorithm is an extension of the progressive radiosity method. Therefore, it has the same advantages as the progressive method in that it only requires $O(n)$ storage cost and does not need long preprocessing time. The new algorithm allows both the surface attributes and scene geometry to be changed during the rendering process. As with progressive radiosity, this method currently is limited to rendering diffuse surfaces only.

The following section presents a brief review of progressive radiosity, since it is the basis of the proposed method. This is followed by the introduction of the incremental radiosity method and its implementation. Results are also shown to illustrate the usefulness of the new method.

PROGRESSIVE RADIOSITY

The progressive radiosity algorithm is a reformulation of the original radiosity method [3]. The original method proceeds by evaluating the following equation on some discrete surface areas or patches iteratively until the differences of radiosities between iterations are within some given tolerance.

$$B_i = E_i + [B_1 B_2 \ldots B_n] \begin{bmatrix} \rho_i F_{i1} \\ \rho_i F_{i2} \\ \vdots \\ \rho_i F_{in} \end{bmatrix} \qquad (1)$$

where

B_i = the radiosity of patch i (energy/unit area/unit time),

E_i = the emission of patch i (energy/unit area/unit time),

ρ_i = the reflectance of patch i, and

F_{ij} = the form-factor from patch i to patch j (fraction of energy arrives at patch j from patch i).

The above equation effectively computes the radiosity of a patch by *gathering* the energy from some other patches. The progressive method reverses the process by *shooting* the energy out from a patch. In each solution cycle, a patch that potentially contributes the most energy to the whole scene is chosen as the *shooting patch* and its *unshot radiosity* (the radiosity that has not been distributed previously) is distributed to every other patch. This process updates the radiosity of every patch in the scene instead of just one patch as in the gathering case. In each shooting, the radiosity of

every patch is updated by:

$$\begin{bmatrix} B_1 \\ B_2 \\ \vdots \\ B_n \end{bmatrix}^{new} = \begin{bmatrix} B_1 \\ B_2 \\ \vdots \\ B_n \end{bmatrix}^{old} + B_i^u \begin{bmatrix} \rho_1 F_{1i} \\ \rho_2 F_{2i} \\ \vdots \\ \rho_n F_{ni} \end{bmatrix} \qquad (2)$$

where B_i^u is the unshot radiosity of patch i.

The form-factors in Equation (2) are obtained from the reciprocity relationship [9]:

$$F_{ji} = F_{ij} A_i / A_j \qquad (3)$$

where A_i is the surface area of patch i.

Since only the form-factors from the shooting patches are needed, the form-factors can be computed on-the-fly after each shooting patch is found.

Fig. 1 shows one solution cycle of the progressive method. The cycle is iterated continuously until the solution converges to some threshold.

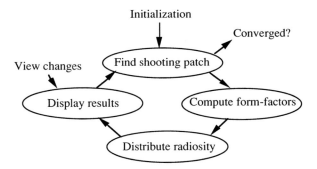

Fig. 1 *One solution cycle of the progressive radiosity method. The view position can be changed freely during the solution.*

INCREMENTAL RADIOSITY

The incremental radiosity method is an extension of the progressive radiosity algorithm. The proposed algorithm proceeds with the normal progressive solution. In the beginning of each solution cycle, though, the new method will monitor any requests from the user for scene changes. When a change is requested, the solution will be interrupted temporarily to process the request and resume when the processing is completed. The allowable changes currently include changing surface attributes, such as reflectance and emission, and scene geometry. Fig. 2 shows a solution cycle of the incremental method.

The proposed extensions to the progressive method include algorithms to incrementally adjust the radiosity values after an attribute or a geometry change. We also introduce a method to buffer the geometry changes in a queue so that multiple changes can be made in succession, without waiting for the incremental method to converge. Methods to provide fast feedback during an interactive seession are also discussed.

Adaptive Radiosity Textures for Bidirectional Ray Tracing

Adaptive Radiosity Textures for Bidirectional Ray Tracing

Paul S. Heckbert

Dept. of Electrical Engineering and Computer Science
University of California, Berkeley, CA 94720

Abstract

We present a rendering method designed to provide accurate, general simulation of global illumination for realistic image synthesis. Separating surface interaction into diffuse plus specular, we compute the specular component on the fly, as in ray tracing, and store the diffuse component (the radiosity) for later-reuse, similar to a radiosity algorithm. Radiosities are stored in *adaptive radiosity textures* (*rexes*) that record the pattern of light and shadow on every diffuse surface in the scene. They adaptively subdivide themselves to the appropriate level of detail for the picture being made, resolving sharp shadow edges automatically.

We use a three-pass, bidirectional ray tracing algorithm that traces rays from both the lights and the eye. The "size pass" records visibility information on diffuse surfaces; the "light pass" progressively traces rays from lights and bright surfaces to deposit photons on diffuse surfaces to construct the radiosity textures; and the "eye pass" traces rays from the eye, collecting light from diffuse surfaces to make a picture.

CR Categories: I.3.3 [**Computer Graphics**]: Picture/Image Generation - *display algorithms;* I.3.7 [**Computer Graphics**]: Three-Dimensional Graphics and Realism - *visible line/surface algorithms.*

General Terms: algorithms.

Additional Key Words and Phrases: global illumination, density estimation, texture mapping, quadtree, adaptive subdivision, sampling.

1 Introduction

The presentation is divided into four sections. We first discuss previous work on the global illumination problem. Then we outline our bidirectional ray tracing approach in an intuitive way. Next we describe our implementation and some early results. We conclude with a summary of the method and of our experiences to date.

2 The Global Illumination Problem

The primary goal of realistic image synthesis is the development of methods for modeling and realistically rendering three-dimensional scenes. One of the most challenging tasks of realistic image synthesis is the accurate and efficient simulation of *global illumination* effects: the illumination of surfaces in a scene by other surfaces. Early rendering programs treated the visibility (hidden surface) and shading tasks independently, employing a *local illumination* model which assumed that the shading of each surface is independent of the shading of every other surface. Local illumination typically assumes that light comes from a finite set of point light sources only. Global illumination models, on the other hand, recognize that the visibility and shading are interrelated: the shade of a surface point is determined by the shades of all of the surfaces visible from that point.

The intensity of light traveling in a given outgoing direction $\vec{out}$ from a surface point is the integral of the incident intensity times the *bidirectional distribution function* (BDF) over all possible incoming directions $\vec{in}$:

$$\text{intensity}(\vec{out}) = \int_{sphere} \text{intensity}(\vec{in})\,\text{BDF}(\vec{in}, \vec{out})\, d(\vec{in})$$

The bidirectional distribution function is the fraction of energy reflected or transmitted from the incoming direction $\vec{in} = (\phi_i, \theta_i)$ to the outgoing direction $\vec{out} = (\phi_o, \theta_o)$; it is the sum of the bidirectional reflectance distribution function (BRDF) and the bidirectional transmittance distribution function (BTDF). See [Hall89] for a more detailed discussion of the physics of illumination. We will characterize previous global illumination algorithms by the approximations they make to the above integral.

Because of the superposition properties of electromagnetic radiation, we can segregate surface reflectance into two types: diffuse and specular. We define *diffuse interaction* (both reflection and transmission) to be the portion of interaction that scatters light equally in all directions, and *specular interaction* to be the remaining portion. BDF = $\text{BDF}_{diff} + \text{BDF}_{spec}$. For many materials, specular interaction scatters light in only a small cone of directions. When this cone includes just a finite number of directions, each a cone with solid angle zero, we call the interaction *ideal specular*, otherwise, when the cone(s) have a positive finite angle, we call it *rough specular*. Two examples of ideal specular surfaces are: (1) a perfect mirror that reflects in one direction, and (2) a perfect transmitter that refracts in one direction and reflects in another. An ideal specular surface with micro-bumps behaves statistically like a rough specular surface. Our three classes of interaction are diagrammed in figure 1.

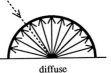

diffuse   rough specular   ideal specular

Figure 1: *Three classes of reflectance: diffuse, rough specular, and ideal specular; showing a polar plot of the reflectance coefficient for fixed incoming direction and varying outgoing direction. Transmittance is similar.*

A diffuse surface appears equally bright from all viewing directions, but a specular surface's brightness varies with viewing direction, so we say that diffuse interaction is *view-independent* while specular interaction is *view-dependent*. The simplest materials have a position-invariant, isotropic BDF consisting of a linear combination of diffuse and ideal specular interaction, but a fully-general BDF can simulate textured, anisotropic, diffuse and rough specular surfaces.

2.1 Ray Tracing vs. Radiosity

The two most popular algorithms for global illumination are ray tracing and radiosity. Ray tracing is both a visibility algorithm and a shading algorithm, but radiosity is just a shading algorithm.

2.1.1 Ray Tracing

Classic ray tracing generates a picture by tracing rays from the eye into the scene, recursively exploring specularly reflected and transmitted directions, and tracing rays toward point light sources to simulate shadowing [Whitted80]. It assumes that the BDF contains no rough specular, and that the incident light relevant to the diffuse computation is a sum of delta functions in the direction of each light source. This latter assumption implies a local illumination model for diffuse.

A more realistic illumination model includes rough specular BDF's and computes diffuse interaction globally. Exact simulation of these effects requires the integration of incident light over cones of finite solid angle. Ray tracing can be generalized to approximate such computations using *distribution ray tracing* [Cook84], [Lee85], [Dippe85], [Cook86], [Kajiya86]. (We propose the name "distribution ray tracing" as an alternative to the current name, "distributed ray tracing", which is confusing because of its parallel hardware connotations.) In distribution ray tracing, rays are distributed, either uniformly or stochastically, throughout any distributions needing integration. Many rays must be traced to accurately integrate the broad reflectance distributions of rough specular and diffuse surfaces: often hundreds or thousands per surface intersection.

2.1.2 Radiosity

The term *radiosity* is used in two senses. First, radiosity is a physical quantity equal to power per unit area, which determines the intensity of light diffusely reflected by a surface, and second, radiosity is a shading algorithm. The meaning of each use should be clear by context.

The *Classic radiosity* algorithm subdivides each surface into polygons and determines the fraction of energy diffusely radiated from each polygon to every other polygon: the pair's *form factor*. From the form factors, a large system of equations is constructed whose solution is the radiosities of each polygon [Siegel81], [Goral84], [Nishita85]. This system can be solved either with Gauss-Seidel iteration or, most conveniently, with progressive techniques that compute the matrix and solve the system a piece at a time [Cohen88]. Form factors can be determined analytically for simple geometries [Siegel81], [Baum89], but for complex geometries a numerical approach employing a visibility algorithm is necessary. The most popular visibility method for this purpose is a *hemicube* computed using a z-buffer [Cohen85], but ray tracing has recently been promoted as an alternative [Wallace89], [Sillion89]. Classic radiosity assumes an entirely diffuse reflectance, so it does not simulate specular interaction at all.

The output of the radiosity algorithm is one radiosity value per polygon. Since diffuse interaction is by definition view-independent, these radiosities are valid from any viewpoint. The radiosity computation must be followed by a visibility algorithm to generate a picture.

The radiosity method can be generalized to simulate specular interaction by storing not just a single radiosity value with each polygon, but a two-dimensional array [Immel86], [Shao88], [Buckalew89]. The resulting algorithm, which we call *directional radiosity*, simulates both diffuse and specular interaction globally, but the memory requirements are so excessive as to be impractical.

2.1.3 Hybrid Methods

Ray tracing is best at specular and radiosity is best at diffuse, and the above attempts to generalize ray tracing to diffuse and to generalize radiosity to specular stretch the algorithms beyond the reflectance realms for which each is best suited, making them less accurate and less efficient. Another class of algorithms is formed by hybridizing the methods, using a two-pass algorithm that applies a radiosity pass followed by the ray tracing pass. This is the approach used by [Wallace87] and [Sillion89].

The first pass of Wallace's algorithm consists of classic radiosity extended to include diffuse-to-diffuse interactions that bounce off planar mirrors. He follows this with a classic ray tracing pass (implemented using a z-buffer). Unfortunately, the method is limited to planar surfaces (because of the polygonization involved in the radiosity algorithm) and to perfect planar mirrors.

Sillion's algorithm is like Wallace's but it computes its form factors using ray tracing instead of hemicubes. This eliminates the restriction to planar mirrors. The method still suffers from the polygonization inherent in the radiosity step, however.

2.2 Sampling Radiosities

Many of the sampling problems of ray tracing have been solved by recent adaptive algorithms [Whitted80], [Cook86], [Lee85], [Dippe85], [Mitchell87], [Painter89], particularly for the simulation of specular interaction. The sampling problems of the radiosity algorithm are less well studied, probably because its sampling process is less explicit than that of ray tracing.

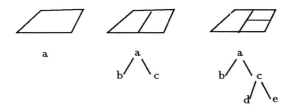

Figure 5: Polygon Substructuring

routine for that node. Thus the exact order of traversal is determined by the viewing position, and it is guaranteed that this order will output polygons in front to back order relative to the viewing position. Further details can be obtained in [7]. Figure 4(c) shows the output order using this algorithm on the viewing position and scene shown in Figure 4(a).

The BSP tree calculated in the initialization step, which we call a polygon BSP tree (pBSP tree) is used to sort surface elements in front to back order from the point of view of the centroid of each emitting element in turn. This ordering is used to speed up shadow calculations.

Some other operations are also enhanced through the use of the pBSP tree. In the processing of a source polygon, before all the other polygons are sorted in front to back order, backfacing polygons are removed from consideration and polygons in the back halfspace of the emitting surface's plane are also removed. The pBSP tree can also be used for visible surface determination for progressive rendering when the energy transfer computations at each step are complete using the technique of [7].

In processing a source element, all polygons that are in the front halfspace of this element and are not backfacing are sorted in front to back order using a pBSP tree traversal from the point of view of the centroid of the emitter. We call a node of the pBSP tree a *pnode*. It contains the equation of the plane passing through a set of coplanar input mesh polygons, the boundary representations of those polygons, and a representation of the surface elements into which each of these polygons has been subdivided. The collection of elements for each polygon in the pnode forms a BSP tree in two rather than three dimensions, which we call an element BSP tree (eBSP tree). This eBSP tree initially consists of a single *enode* representing the input polygon for that element tree. Surfaces in an eBSP tree are always found at the leaves, with internal enodes representing splitting lines. When an element at one of these leaves is split, its enode is replaced by a tree whose root represents the splitting line, with left and right children being the new leaves representing the two new elements formed by the split. This process is illustrated in Figure 5.

3.2. LIGHT SOURCE SUBDIVISION

For each iteration of the illumination process, we use the polygon with most untransmitted energy as the light source.

After the source polygon, S, is chosen, we use the pBSP tree to determine R, the nearest frontfacing receiver polygon. Then we calculate A, the solid angle subtended by S in the viewing hemisphere centered at R's midpoint. If A is small enough, then S may be approximated as a point light source for shadowing computations. We have experimentally determined that .005 steradians is an effective size tolerance. The average color of the source polygon is used as the light color in illumination calculations.

If the light source exceeds our size criterion, we first check if it has already been subdivided by previous calculations. If so, the the size check is recursively applied to elements successively deeper in the subdivision hierarchy until either we find small enough pieces or the substructure can be traversed no further. If bottom level subpolygons are too large, they are subdivided across their long axes until the size criterion is met.

3.3. SHADOW BOUNDARY COMPUTATIONS

The first step in processing a receiving polygon for any given emitting element is to determine whether any of the polygons closer to the emitter casts a shadow on the current receiving polygon. This is done by testing the receiving polygon against the merged shadow volume generated by the emitter centroid and closer polygons. This volume consists of a collection of semi-infinite pyramids, one pyramid emanating from each shadowing polygon. The merged structure is maintained as a second BSP tree, called a shadow volume BSP tree (sBSP tree), similar to the SVBSP trees of [2], whose nodes we refer to as *snodes*,

The sBSP tree is made up of the shadow volume planes cast by each of the previously-processed polygons. Internal snodes represent clipping planes, and leaf snodes represent regions which are classified as either totally lit or totally in shadow with respect to the current light source. Elements are filtered down this tree to determine which of their regions are lit or in shadow.

Our algorithm is similar to that of [2], but features important improvements in the shadow testing algorithm. We use the pBSP tree to generate a front-to-back ordering from the light source position. Polygons are tested for shadows in this order, which guarantees that no polygon will be processed before any that can shadow it. After shadow testing, the processed polygons are added to the sBSP tree.

For the illumination step, we start out with the light source position, the pBSP tree of input polygons, and an empty merged shadow volume. Each polygon is filtered down the sBSP tree. If the entire polygon is completely lit or shadowed, the polygon does not need to be subdivided. If, however, the polygon crosses a shadow boundary, the polygon is split across this edge.

When a polygon is split, we must refine its eBSP. Each split adds a level to the sBSP tree. We maintain the elements in this structure for efficiency in future illumination passes. This differs from [2], who maintain a simple linked list of fragments.

After the first illumination pass, many of the original polygons may have been split multiple times by previous shadow planes. As a polygon is tested for shadows, we first check if the original polygon boundary is totally lit or in shadow. If so, we are done with this polygon. If not, we recursively descend the eBSP tree, each time checking if the current element is totally lit or shadowed. In this way we are potentially able to avoid testing all the leaf enodes individually. When we finally do have to process a leaf enode, we know that it definitely falls across a shadow edge and must be split.

Pseudocode is provided in Figure 6.

A straightforward implementation of the described algorithm produces a mesh which is indeed fine and coarse in all the right places. However, the continuous splitting of elements across shadow boundaries throughout all illumination calculation leads to excessive mesh refinement at shadow boundaries. In addition to the general undesirability of too fine a mesh, the memory costs can soar dramatically.

Since shadow boundaries become less important after the brighter light sources are processed, at some point we can terminate splitting across shadow boundaries to prevent large numbers of unnecessary small elements from being created. The polygon can still be split for form factor computation as usual, but its pieces may be merged back after illumination computations have been made. We have found that stopping the shadow clipping after half of the light has been dissipated is effective. Using this optimization, light leaks may occur, but if a proper clipping termination threshold is used, the energy levels of the light sources are low enough to make this effect negligible.

3.4. INTENSITY CALCULATIONS

Once shadow calculations are done for a particular source-receiver pair, the next step tests the quality of the resulting receiving mesh against our criterion of balanced energy distribution across mesh elements. This is of course done only for elements which have previously been determined to be completely visible to the light source. The form factor for the receiving element is first estimated. This is done by computing the point to point form factors between the centroid of the emitter and each of the receiver's vertices. These vertex form factors are averaged and multiplied by the receiver's area to provide a form factor approximation for the entire element.

Note that in the event that the receiver has a large aspect ratio, there can be significant differences in the form factors at its vertices. In such cases, the two longest edges of the receiver can be bisected to form a pair of elements of lower aspect ratio, and the vertex form factors for each

```
(* Use sBSP tree for shadowing *)
Procedure SbspShadow(Src, NumRcv, Rcv)
Begin
    ShadTree := SbspInit();
    For i := 1 To NumRcv Do Begin
        ShadowCalc(Src, ShadTree, Rcv[i]);
        ShadTree := SbspUpdate(Src, ShadTree,
                                Rcv[i])
    End;
    SbspDestroy(ShadTree)
End;


(* Traverse nested polygons *)
(* LeafShadowCalc() does single-level
   sBSP shadowing, as in [2]. *)
Procedure ShadowCalc(Src, Tree, Rcv)
Begin
    DivOnSrcPlane(Src, Rcv, Front, Back);
    If Front = NIL Then
        SetIllum(Rcv, NONE);
    Else If HasChildren(Rcv) Then Begin
        If (Back <> NIL) Then Begin
            ShadowCalc(Src, Tree, Rcv.Pos);
            ShadowCalc(Src, Tree, Rcv.Neg)
        End;
        Else Begin
            PolyCopy(Rcv, Rcv1);
            LeafShadowCalc(S, Tree, Rcv1);
            If (HasIllum(Rcv1, NONE)) Then
                SetIllum(Rcv, NONE)
            Else If (HasIllum(Rcv1,TOTAL))
                SetIllum(Rcv, TOTAL)
            Else Begin
                SetIllum(Rcv, PARTIAL);
                LeafShadowCalc(S, Tree, Rcv.Pos);
                LeafShadowCalc(S, Tree, Rcv.Neg)
            End
        End
    End
    Else Begin
        If (Back <> NIL) Then Begin
            SetIllum(Rcv, PARTIAL);
            AddChildren(Rcv, Front, Back);
            ShadowCalc(Src, Tree, Front)
        End
        Else
            LeafShadowCalc(Src, Tree, Rcv);
    End
End;
```

Figure 6: Shadow Testing

resulting element calculated. Once the differences in vertex form factors fall within a specified tolerance, this subdivision is terminated and the averages calculated. This process can be done efficiently since all points on the original receiver are known to be illuminated by the source and therefore no visibility calculations are involved in determining form factors at the bisection points.

The sum of all element form factors, R, is computed. In theory, this sum should be 1, but as with other radiosity techniques, errors resulting from the approximate calculation of form factors can cause this to vary. Thus we scale form factors, both for elements and vertices, by $1/R$ to conserve energy balance. These normalized vertex form factors are used to calculate the vertex intensity contributions from the current light source. If these intensity contributions make the element intensity gradient exceed the intensity tolerance, the element must be subdivided as for large form-factor variations. The intensities at the newly-created vertices are computed and intensity variations determined for each new element. This process continues until the variation of each piece is within the specified bound.

Once the intensities of the vertices have been determined, an image can be displayed by Gouraud shading the receiving elements. If this rendering technique is used, however, care must be taken to ensure that the T-vertices created by our mesh generation algorithm do not cause shading anomalies. One way to handle this problem is to make a T-vertex a three-way vertex, with two collinear edges instead of a single edge orthogonal to the remaining edge. The element with the two collinear edges is then triangulated before shading is done.

4. RESULTS

We have implemented our algorithm in the C programming language. Mesh generation and illumination computation is performed on a SUN 4/260, which is rated at ten VAX 11/780 mips. Polygon scan-conversion and smooth shading are done separately on an HP 9000 series 300. All timing figures are given for the SUN machine. Rendering time on the HP is only a few seconds. Times were measured using the UNIX *time* facility.

Figures 8 through 15 show the progress of our algorithm on a domestic scene. The input data consists of 211 polygons. Timing data is given in Figure 7.

Notice how fine detail is prominent in bright areas and near shadow boundaries, but not anywhere else. The algorithm has successfully pinpointed the areas of high gradation in the scene. Note that the meshes are not triangulated at T-vertices as described above.

Iterations	1	2	5	9
Mesh Polygons	9711	17958	20718	21073
pBSP Build (s)	3.7	3.7	3.7	3.7
sBSP Build (s)	26.0	46.0	60.7	72.8
Shadow Testing (s)	339.8	806.7	1036.2	1300.5
Illumination (s)	24.1	57.8	71.7	94.0
Total Time (s)	393.6	914.2	1172.3	1471.0

Figure 7: Timing Statistics

Figure 8: Mesh for 1 Iteration

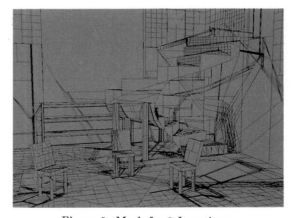

Figure 9: Mesh for 2 Iterations

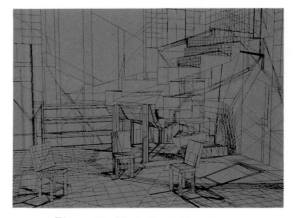

Figure 10: Mesh For 5 Iterations

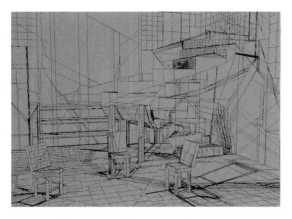

Figure 11: Mesh For 9 Iterations

Figure 12: Rendering For 1 Iteration

Figure 13: Rendering For 2 Iterations

Figure 14: Rendering For 5 Iterations

Figure 15: Rendering For 9 Iterations

$P3$ are merged together, as well as $t0$, $t1$, $t2$, $t'2$ and $t'0$, $t'1$, $t3$, $t'3$.

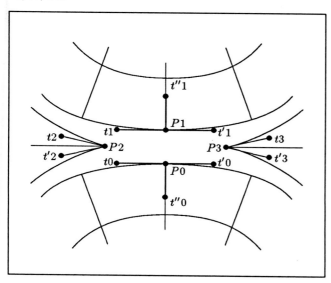

Figure 4: Merging four points

When several points are merged together, such as the center of a disc, some continuity problems may occur. These problems are discussed in paragraph 3.1.5. While the implemented welding method is very simple, some more sophisticated ones such as the one presented in [9], could be implemented as well. In the "8" example (see Figure 9a), the 3D EFFD lattice is defined from a composite two-dimensional lattice made from 3 elementary two-dimensional lattices, two discs and an exterior lattice.

In the future, more specific two-dimensional lattice design methods will be developed. An example of these methods is to automatically compute the 2D lattice from either the skeleton of the shape or from its boundaries.

3.1.5 Continuity versus complexity

Continuity is one of the most important problems to consider when working with piecewise surfaces or volumes. Before examining continuity constraints for volumes, let us recall some results on piecewise surfaces continuity; see [6] for a complete survey. Assuming non-degenerate 4-sided cubic patches, known results are as follows:

- C^1 and G^1 smooth connection between patches defined over a topologically rectangular network can be guaranteed.
- C^1 continuity cannot be guaranteed if more than 4 patches meet at a point.
- For G^1 continuity around an n-patch corner (n>4), constraints intertwining often requires either to subdivide patches or to increase their degree (cf. [6]).

With degenerate patches constraints propagation is even more important. With volumes the problem is more tricky.

Surface continuity property can easily be extended to prismatic volumes but general non-prismatic volumes can lead to unsolved continuity problems. Even when a solution to the continuity problem exists, maintaining this continuity may be penalizing for the EFFD technique. For example, as continuity constraints require the increase of the degree or of the subdivision level of chunks, editing points have to be added automatically. This is not convenient for the user and allowing only lattices for which continuity problems are easily solved (without adding points) is too restrictive. Our choice is thus not to restrain volume complexity but rather to insure lattice continuity only for the simplest cases. What is important for the user is the surface continuity but not the lattice continuity. Depending on the surface type, it is often possible to guarantee the surface continuity even if lattice continuity is not assured (for example with spline surfaces). Thus, from our point of view, lattice continuity is not a primary concern.

3.2 Associating a lattice with the surface

The next step consists in taking an EFFD lattice out of the library and associating it with the desired surface. A list of EFFD lattices may be associated with the surface. Associating an EFFD lattice with a surface consists of adding the lattice to the list. While an EFFD lattice is associated with a surface, one can still edit it without deforming the surface. At this time, an attractive capability is the positioning command which allows moving the EFFD lattice to a user specified point on the surface.

3.3 Freezing a lattice

Everything is now ready to deform the surface. Assuming that several lattices are associated with the surface, the user must first select one of the EFFD lattices and "freeze" it. Freezing a lattice consists in computing the u_s, v_s and w_s coordinates of each point of the surface in the EFFD lattice parameter space. For each surface only one EFFD lattice can be frozen at a time. With arbitrarily shaped lattices, finding the (u_s, v_s, w_s) coordinates of the surface points is decomposed into two steps. First, the chunk where the point is supposed to lie is determined by using the convex hull property of Bézier volumes. The (u, v, w) coordinates inside the chunk are then computed using Newton approximation. Two problems have to be considered: the technique convergence and the degenerated chunks treatment.

- The convergence and consequently the determination of the starting point of Newton iteration is usually considered as a delicate problem. However, for our problem, experience has proved that choosing $u = 0.5$, $v = 0.5$ and $w = 0.5$ as a starting point leads to very good convergence. No divergent cases have been so far noted. A simple solution has thus been chosen. It consists of subdividing the chunk in order to get a better starting point when no convergence is detected.

- With degenerated chunks, matrix inversion required by the Newton technique may not be possible because of differential vanishing. In this case, as proposed by Lukács in [11], the pseudo-inverse matrix method is used.

3.4 Deforming the surface

When an EFFD lattice is frozen, all the transformations applied by the user to the lattice are passed to the surface when the user selects the update command. Only moving transformations are valid for frozen lattices. The C^1 continuity along the intersection of an exterior face of the lattice with the object can be assured either by keeping the two planes of control points adjacent to the lattice border fixed or by guaranteeing the surface continuity as suggested in 3.1.5. The computation of the X_{ffd} coordinate points of the deformed surface is equivalent to the FFD one.

The presented method has been implemented with polygonal surfaces but, as FFD, it also works with other surfaces, such as spline surfaces, and it should work with hierarchical surfaces [8] as well. Whatever surface is used, a subdivision technique such as that of Griessmair et al. [10] is recommended in order to maintain an acceptable resolution of the surface. The technique of Griessmair et al. is valid for polygonal surfaces. Each polygon is subdivided into triangles that are again subdivided according to a given accuracy threshold.

Considering a surface with several lattices positioned on it, the deformation process can be described as follows:

    Loop 1:

        Deform the unfrozen lattices (move, insert, remove and merge control points)

        Freeze one of the surface EFFD lattices

        Loop 2:

            Deform the frozen EFFD lattice (move points)

            Update the surface

        End loop 2

        Unfreeze the EFFD lattice

    End loop 1

The ability to work with several EFFD lattices associated with the same surface is very important; it allows the user to apply successively different shaped deformations.

In order to allow for an exact repetition of the same deformation on several surfaces, a recording operator has to be implemented.

4 Examples and concluding remarks

Some simple examples of surfaces deformed using the EFFD technique are illustrated in Figures 6 to 11. Figures 6a to 11a present the initial surfaces with the EFFD lattices positioned on them. In Figures 6b to 11b, the EFFD lattices have been frozen, some of their points have been moved, and the surfaces updated. Both the deformed lattices and the deformed surfaces are shown. In Figures 6c to 11c, shaded pictures of the resulting surfaces or objects are shown.

In Figures 6 and 7, the same EFFD lattice (see Figure 7a) is used to define two different deformations. In Figure 6, the axis and the intermediate cylinders of points are translated whereas in Figure 7, the axis and every second column of points of the intermediate cylinder have been moved back. As shown in Figures 6c and 7c, sandpies are easily modeled with EFFD. In Figures 8 and 9 two characters are impressed onto a surface. The "8" is sculptured into a piece of marble by "pulling" some of the lattice points whereas the granite "S" is sculptured by "pushing" the points.

Sculpturing and moulding are accurately simulated by EFFD. Other types of deformations can also be reproduced with this technique. The shape of cloth-like surfaces can also be simulated. Figures 10 and 11 are two examples where folds are modeled with EFFD. In Figure 10c, a leather-like cushion is shown. Starting with a surface of revolution embedded into a cylindrical EFFD lattice, the points of the lattice axis are first moved in order to create a hull at the center of the cushion, then the folds are designed by moving some of the intermediate points of the lattice (see Figure 10b). In Figure 11, an oilcloth on a round table has been modeled. Starting with a planar surface embedded into a cylindrical lattice, the outermost points of the EFFD lattice are moved as shown in Figure 11b to create the folding effect. The resulting textured picture is shown in Figure 11c.

EFFD is an easy to use and efficient method for modeling cloth-like surfaces. Shapes cannot, of course, be as natural as with physical methods [20] [18] but it can be an interesting alternative when other methods are computationally prohibitive or when naturalness is not the main objective.

Deforming a surface with EFFD technique is very efficient. Only a few minutes were needed to design most of the previous examples. It is very easy to implement EFFD on a system including the FFD capability. This deformation technique is part of ACTION3D, a general interactive modeling system developed jointly by SOGITEC and INRIA.

5 Acknowledgements

I would like to thank Laurent Alt, Wen-Hui Du, Michel Gangnet, Tony Kasvand, and Marie-Luce Viaud for helpful discussions and for reviewing early drafts of this paper. I am grateful to INRIA's audiovisual department for their assistance with color images and video demonstrations. I would also like to thank the reviewers for their helpful comments.

References

[1] A. H. Barr. Global and Local Deformations of Solid Primitives. In *SIGGRAPH'84*, volume 18, pages 21–30. ACM, July 1984.

[2] W.E. Carlson. *Techniques for the Generation of Three Dimensional Data for Use in Complex Image Synthesis*. PhD thesis, Ohio State University, 1982.

[3] J.E. Chadwick, D.R. Haumann, and R.E. Parent. Layered Construction for Deformable Animated Characters. In *SIGGRAPH'89*, volume 23, pages 243–252. ACM, 1989.

[4] J.H. Clark. Parametric curves, surfaces and volumes in computer graphics and computer-aided geometric design. Technical Report 221, Stanford University, 1981.

[5] B.S. Cobb. *Design of Sculptured Surfaces Using the B-Spline Representation*. PhD thesis, University of Utah, June 1984.

[6] W.H. Du and F.J.M. Schmitt. Free-Form Surface Modelling using Tensor Product Bézier Patches: A Review with New Solutions. Technical Report Télécom Paris 89 D 014, Ecole Nationale Supérieure des Télécommunications, 1989.

[7] J.P. Duncan and G.W. Vickers. Simplified Method for Interactive Adjustment of Surfaces. *Computer Aided Design*, 12(6):305–308, November 1980.

[8] D.R. Forsey and R.H. Bartels. Hierarchical B-Spline Refinement. In *SIGGRAPH'88*, volume 22, pages 205–212. ACM, August 1988.

[9] M.P. Gascuel. Welding and Pinching Spline Surfaces: New Methods for Interactive Creation of Complex Objects and Automatic Fleshing of Skeletons. In *Graphics Interface'89*, pages 20–27, 1989.

[10] J. Griessmair and W. Purgathofer. Deformation of Solids with Trivariate B-Splines. In *EUROGRAPHICS'89*, pages 137–148. North-Holland, 1989.

[11] G. Lukács. The Generalized Inverse Matrix and the Surface-Surface Intersection Problem. In *Theory and Practice of Geometric Modeling*, pages 167–185. Springer-Verlag.

[12] R. E. Parent. A System for Sculpting 3-D Data. In *SIGGRAPH'77*, volume 11, pages 138–147. ACM, July 1977.

[13] S.R. Parry. *Free-Form Deformations in a Constructive Solid Geometry Modeling System*. PhD thesis, Brigham Young University, 1986.

[14] L. Piegl. Modifying the Shape of Rational B-Splines. Part 1 : Curves. *Computer Aided Design*, 21(8):509–518, October 1989.

[15] L. Piegl. Modifying the Shape of Rational B-Splines. Part 2 : Surfaces. *Computer Aided Design*, 21(9):538–546, November 1989.

[16] T.W. Sederberg and S.R. Parry. Free-Form Deformation of Polygonal Data. In *Second Image Symposium*, pages 633–639. CESTA, April 1986.

[17] T.W. Sederberg and S.R. Parry. Free-Form Deformation of Solid Geometric Models. In *SIGGRAPH'86*, volume 20, pages 151–160. ACM, August 1986.

[18] D. Terzopoulos and K. Fleischer. Modeling Inelastic Deformation: Viscoelasticity, Plasticity, Fracture. In *SIGGRAPH'88*, volume 22, pages 269–278. ACM, August 1988.

[19] G.W. Vickers, J.P. Duncan, and V. Lee. Interactive Surface Adjustment of Marine Propellers. *Computer Aided Design*, 10(6):375–379, November 1978.

[20] J. Weil. The Synthesis of Cloth Objects. In *SIGGRAPH'86*, volume 20, pages 49–54. ACM, August 1986.

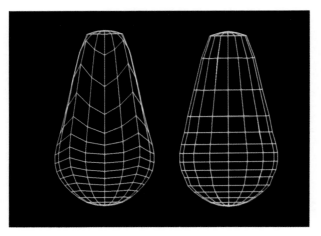

Figure 5a: A sphere deformed with a parallelepipedical lattice

b: A sphere deformed with a cylindrical lattice

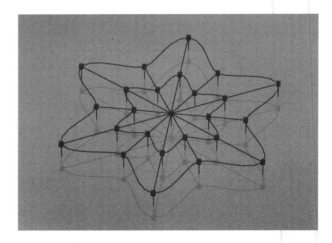

Figure 6a: A lattice positioned on a planar surface

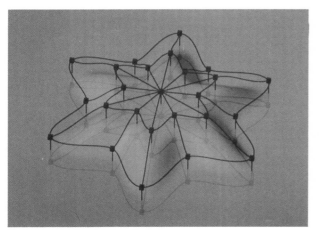

Figure 6b: The deformed lattice and the deformed surface

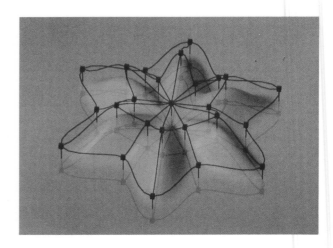

Figure 7b: Another lattice transformation and the deformed surface

Figure 6c: A sandpie

Figure 7c: Another sandpie

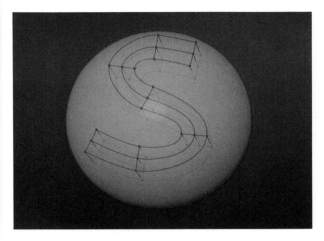

Figure 8a: An "S" lattice positioned on a sphere

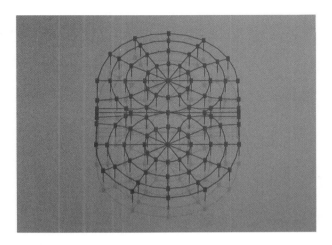

Figure 9a: An "8" lattice positioned on a planar surface

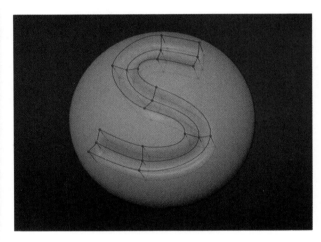

Figure 8b: The deformed lattice and the deformed surface

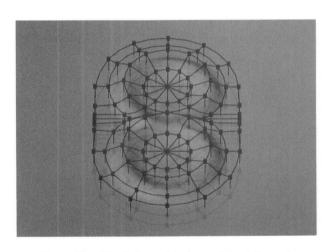

Figure 9b: The deformed lattice and the deformed surface

Figure 8c: An "S" sculpted into a granit sphere

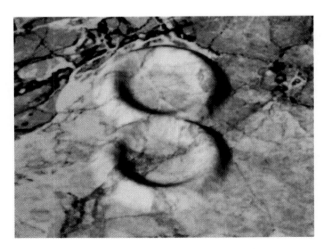

Figure 9c: An "8" sculpted into a piece of marble

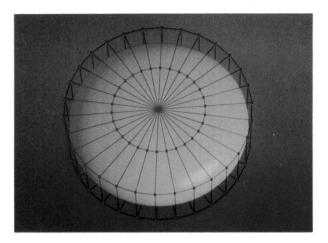

Figure 10a: A cylindrical lattice positioned on a surface of revolution

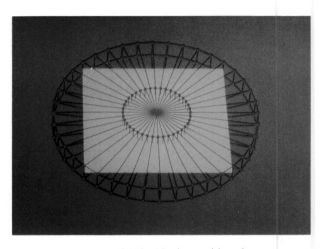

Figure 11a: A cylindrical lattice positioned on a planar surface

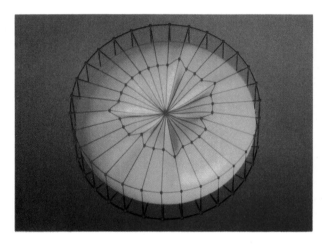

Figure 10b: The deformed lattice and the deformed surface

Figure 11b: The deformed lattice and the deformed surface

Figure 10c: A leather like cushion

Figure 11c: An oilcloth

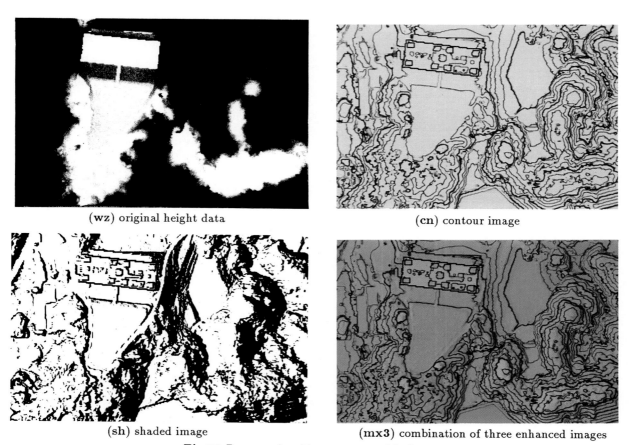

(wz) original height data

(cn) contour image

(sh) shaded image

(mx3) combination of three enhanced images

Fig.11 Process of making a topographical map.

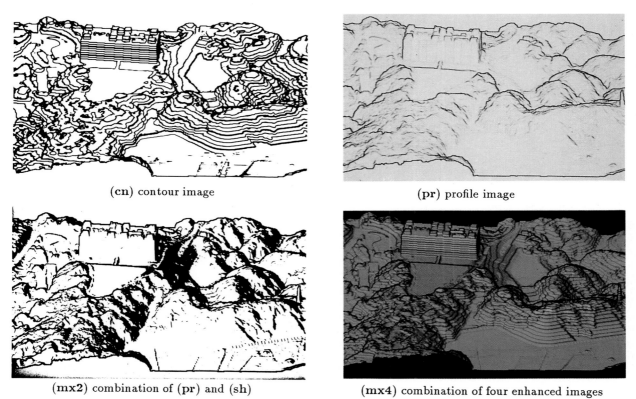

(cn) contour image

(pr) profile image

(mx2) combination of (pr) and (sh)

(mx4) combination of four enhanced images

Fig.12 Bird's eye maps.

Fig.13 A sumi-e.

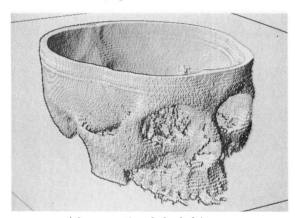

(a) conventional shaded image

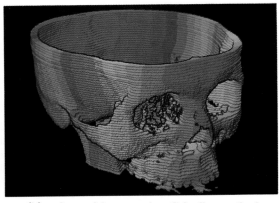

(b) enhanced image using G-buffer method

Fig.14 Medical imaging from CT data.
Data courtesy of Dr. Jin Tamai, Department of Radiology,
Nippon Medical School.

 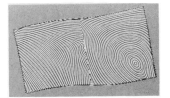

(a) contour lines   (b) pseudo-highlight pattern

Fig.15 An example of surface analysis.

Two bicubic patches are connected with C^1 continuity.

4.3 Topographical Maps

A topographical map can be drawn with a combination of multiple techniques in order to effectively visualize the height data. For example, the following basic techniques are very familiar:

- contour lines — Usually they are drawn at regular intervals. Often two contour thicknesses are used: thick contours for large intervals such as 100m and thin contours for small intervals such as 20m.

- color bands — To present absolute height, several discrete color bands are used. Continuous color change is also available.

- relief — To visualize the direction of slopes, shading is applied.

These techniques can be easily simulated with the proposed method if the height value is prepared for each pixel.

Figure 11 shows the process of making an enhancement map of the region around NTT's Yokosuka R&D Center. Image (**wz**) is the original height data. In the contour line image (**cn**), two contour thicknesses were used for $20m$ and $5m$ intervals. The constant c_{dense} of Eq.(15) was set to the line color (black) for $20m$ contours. On the other hand, it was set to background color (white) for $5m$ contours. With this technique, the combined contour image (**cn**) can present both large and small gradient regions. When the gradient becomes large and $5m$ contours become too dense, they are thinned out and only $20m$ contours are displayed. Image (**sh**) is the relief (shaded image), which was obtained from the gradient images of the (**wz**) image. Image (**mx3**) is the combination of (**cn**), (**sh**), and color bands.

The above processes for normal (cartesian) maps can be also applied to draw bird's-eye maps, which is but one advantage of our method. Example bird's-eye maps are shown in Fig.12, which shows the same region as in Fig.11. Four G-buffers (**sz**, **wx**, **wy**, **wz**) were generated from the original height data. The contour image (**cn**) and the relief image (**sh**) were obtained from (**wz**) and (**wx**, **wy**, **wz**) respectively. For bird's-eye maps, the profile image (**pr**) is also effective; it shows the shape of mountains clearly. In Fig.12, four images (**cn**, **pr**, **mx2**, **mx4**) are presented, where (**mx2**) is the combination of (**pr**) and (**sh**), and (**mx4**) is the combination of (**pr**), (**cn**), (**sh**), and color bands.

An artistic example — Japanese sumi-e (Indian-ink drawing) — is shown in Fig.13. This picture was easily obtained from (**cn**) and (**sz**).

4.4 Medical Imaging

Recently, a lot of research has been done for visualizing volume data from CT images [6,12,21]. Many techniques for shading, coloring, and transparent drawing have been developed to generate comprehensible images. These techniques are effective to present an overview of the data. However, medical doctors usually require the information about a more specific part; how the shape of the object has been deformed by the disease or injury, or what is the exact place of the diseased part. For this requirement, we can make the image more comprehensible with G-buffers and 2-D image processing techniques. It is easy to draw profiles and contour lines that show us some useful geometric information of the 3-D shapes. These line drawings can be combined interactively with a conventional shaded or colored image.

Example images are shown in Fig.14. The original voxel data had 50 slices of CT data. After separating the bone part [6], seven G-buffers (**wx, wy, wz, sz, nx, ny, nz**) were generated by ray-tracing the voxel data. The enhanced image (b) is the combination of four techniques: the profiles, shading, the contour lines of (**wz**), and the color bands for (**wy**). The conventional shaded image (a) is more realistic, however, the enhanced image (b) gives us much more information about the bone shapes.

4.5   Surface Analysis

Free form surfaces such as Bezier or spline surfaces are widely used in geometric modeling. A shape with these parametric surfaces can be controlled flexibly, and their continuity is mathematically well known. However, it is difficult to evaluate the *quality* of surfaces; because the quality depends on a lot of geometric properties, and photorealistic rendering is insufficient. For this purpose, it is important to visualize and analyze the geometric properties. For example, contour lines, pseudo-highlight patterns, and curvature maps are effective to describe the features of a curved surface [1,5,9,10]. In conventional methods, line drawings are calculated by tracking, which requires a lot of consideration about numerical analysis.

Some of the surface analysis techniques are easily realized with our method. For example, a pseudo-highlight pattern can be obtained as follows. A pseudo-highlight pattern is the reflected image on a curved surface of parallel lines that are assumed to lie at an infinite distance [10]. Assume the cylindrical coordinate whose z-axis is parallel to the parallel lines. Then, each line has a constant θ value. For each pixel, the θ value in the reflected image on the visible surface is easily calculated from the normal vector and the position of the surface, and the eye position. By drawing contour lines or curved hatching for the image of θ value, the pseudo-highlight pattern is generated.

In Fig.15, contour lines (a), and a pseudo-highlight pattern (b) of a curved surface are presented. The curved surface consists of two bicubic patches that connect with C^1 (not C^2) continuity. The overview of the shape is comprehensibly presented with the contour lines. The discontinuity is clearly shown in the pseudo-highlight pattern.

5   Discussions

5.1   Antialiasing and Reflective/Transparent Objects

A G-buffer contains the property of only one surface per pixel. This restriction leads the following problems:

- aliasing artifacts occur on surface borders;
- reflected or transparent images cannot be enhanced.

Some simple solutions are possible. For example, edges can be anti-aliased by calculating the sz image as the average depth value in each pixel. Edges in reflected images can be drawn with the method in Subsection 4.1. However, these are not fundamental solutions.

These problems can be solved by preserving the properties of all surfaces visible in each pixel. This can be realized with *Extended G-Buffers*. In Extended G-buffers, each G-buffer has an extra memory area; the main area has the property of the primary visible surface at each pixel, and the extended area has the property of the other visible surfaces. A couple of additional G-buffers are preserved to retain pixel coverage information and the pointer to the next area for each pixel. This method can be considered as an extension of the A-buffer method [2], and reflection/refraction and antialiasing can be achieved with duplicated operations on the appropriate Extended G-buffers. Extended G-buffers have not been implemented yet; it requires more investigation.

5.2   Local Enhancement

To draw a picture more comprehensibly, local enhancement is often required for some specific regions. This can be provided with conventional 2-D paint systems. Various interactive paint systems have been developed and effectively used. A system with useful enhancement tools for technical illustration has also been developed [11]. Using such a paint system to enhance computer generated images, a designer can draw an image with any enhancement as he likes. However, it requires a great deal of effort to apply the same enhancement technique globally, *i.e.* apply it to a whole image, or a set of similar images such as an animation sequence. Furthermore, it is difficult to apply the enhancement uniformly.

Our method is mainly for global enhancement. However, it is also possible to realize local enhancement by applying operations only where some condition is satisfied. The object/patch identifier (the **id** image) can be effectively used for this condition.

5.3   Errors and Artifacts

To implement G-buffers, the data type for each property should be carefully considered. In our experimentations shown in Section 4, all images including G-buffers are preserved as floating point data in order to avoid digitization errors. However, it is rather inefficient in both execution time and memory space. Though it is difficult to generally discuss the required precision of images, the following expectation is usually true. The required precision of an image depends on the subsequent operations. If the image is just used for linear operations, 1 byte integers are usually sufficient. Normal vectors (the **nx, ny, nz** images) are an example if they are used for the calculation of diffuse reflection only. On the other hand, if the image is used for a differential operation, 2 or 4 byte integers or floating point numbers are needed. Since the process of drawing edges has differential operations, the sz image must have higher precision.

It is also necessary to maintain the precision in the geometric processes. If a G-buffer is generated with an approximation and is used for a differential operation, undesirable artifacts sometimes occur. Such artifacts are shown in Fig.3; thin lines shown on smooth curved surfaces are the border of tessellated polygon patches. Linear interpolation of normal vectors can make the shaded image smooth, however, the interpolation of depth values leads artifacts in the internal edge image.

6 Conclusion

We have proposed a new technique for rendering 3-D shapes comprehensibly. Enhancement techniques — drawing discontinuities, contour lines, and curved hatching — are developed with 2-D image processing operations, so that these line drawing algorithms can be easily combined with conventional surface rendering algorithms. By preserving geometric properties in G-buffers and visualizing the properties in postprocesses, various combinations of enhancement techniques can be rapidly examined and a user can efficiently select the best enhancement technique. Furthermore, G-buffers are also useful for photorealistic rendering. Example images of edge enhancement, line drawing illustrations, topographical maps, medical imaging, and surface analysis confirm that our method can be flexibly and efficiently applied in various fields.

Acknowledgements

We would like to thank Dr. Hiroshi Yasuda, Kei Takikawa, Dr. Rikuo Takano, and Dr. Masashi Okudaira for their continuous support. We also wish to thank Prof. Tomoyuki Nishita of Fukuyama University, Mikio Shinya, Toshimitsu Tanaka, and other colleagues in our section for helpful discussions. We are very grateful to Dr. Jin Tamai of Nippon Medical School for providing us the original CT image data of Fig.14, and Atsushi Kajiyama for his assistance to generate the G-buffers of Fig.14. Special thanks to Michael Blackburn for his useful comments.

References

[1] Beck, J. M., Farouki, R. T., and Hinds, J. K. Surface Analysis Methods. *IEEE Computer Graphics and Applications 6*, 12 (1986), 18–36.

[2] Carpenter, L. The A-buffer, an Antialiased Hidden Surface Method. *Computer Graphics 18*, 3 (*Proc. SIGGRAPH '84*) (1984), 103–108.

[3] Cook, R. L. Shade Trees. *Computer Graphics 18*, 3 (*Proc. SIGGRAPH '84*) (1984), 223–231.

[4] Crow, F. C. A More Flexible Image Generation Environment. *Computer Graphics 16*, 3 (*Proc. SIGGRAPH '82*) (1982), 9–18.

[5] Dickinson, R. R., Bartels, R. H., and Vermeulen, A. H. The Interactive Editing and Contouring of Empirical Fields. *IEEE Computer Graphics and Applications 9*, 3 (1989), 34–43.

[6] Drebin, R. A., Carpenter, L., and Hanrahan, P. Volume Rendering. *Computer Graphics 22*, 4 (*Proc. SIGGRAPH '88*) (1988), 65–74.

[7] Duff, T. Compositing 3-D Rendering Images. *Computer Graphics 19*, 3 (*Proc. SIGGRAPH '85*) (1985), 41–44.

[8] Ghazanfarpour, D., and Peroche, B. A Fast Antialiasing Method with A-Buffer. In *Proc. Eurographics '87* (1987), 503–512.

[9] Higashi, M., Kohzen, I. and Nagasaka, J. An Interactive CAD System for Construction of Shapes with High-quality Surface. In *Computer Applications in Production and Engineering* (*Proc. CAPE '83*) (1983), 371–390.

[10] Higashi, M., Kushimoto, T. and Hosaka, M. On Formulation and Display for Visualizing Features and Evaluating Quality of Free-form Surfaces. In *Proc. Eurographics '90* (to appear).

[11] Kondo, K., Kimura, F., and Tajima, T. An Interactive Rendering System with Shading. In *Japan Annual Reviews in Electronics, Computers & Telecommunications 18, Computer Science and Technologies*, Kitagawa, T. (Ed.), Ohmsha and North-Holland, Tokyo, 1988, pp. 255–271.

[12] Lorensen, W. E., and Cline, H. E. Marching Cubes: A High Resolution 3D Surface Construction Algorithms. *Computer Graphics 21*, 4 (*Proc. SIGGRAPH '87*) (1987), 163–169.

[13] Mammem, A. Transparency and Antialiasing Algorithms Implemented with the Virtual Pixel Maps Techniques. *IEEE Computer Graphics and Applications 9*, 4 (1989), 43–55.

[14] Nadas, T. and Fournier, A. GRAPE: An Environment to Build Display Processes. *Computer Graphics 21*, 4 (*Proc. SIGGRAPH '87*) (1987), 75–83.

[15] Nakamae, E., Ishizaki, T., Nishita, T., and Takita, S. Compositing 3D Images with Antialiasing and Various Shading Effects. *IEEE Computer Graphics and Applications 9*, 2 (1989), 21–29.

[16] Newman, W. M. and Sproull, R. F. Principles of Interactive Computer Graphics, 2nd Ed., McGraw-Hill, 1979.

[17] Perlin, K. An Image Synthesizer. *Computer Graphics 19*, 3 (*Proc. SIGGRAPH '85*) (1985), 287–296.

[18] Porter, T. and Duff, T. Compositing Digital Images. *Computer Graphics 18*, 3 (*Proc. SIGGRAPH '84*) (1984), 253–259.

[19] Rosenfeld, A. and Kak, A. C. Digital Picture Processing, 2nd Ed., Academic Press, 1982.

[20] Saito, T., Shinya, M., and Takahashi, T. Highlighting Rounded Edges. In *New Advances in Computer Graphics* (*Proc. CG International '89*) (1989), 613–629.

[21] Udupa, J. K. Display of Medical Objects and their Interactive Manipulation. In *Proc. Graphics Interface '89*, (1989), 40–46.

[22] Whitted, T. and Weimer, D, M. A Software Testbed for the Development of 3D Raster Graphics Systems. *ACM Trans. Graphics 1*, 1 (1982), 43–58.

Paint By Numbers: Abstract Image Representations

Paul Haeberli

Silicon Graphics Computer Systems

ABSTRACT

Computer graphics research has concentrated on creating photo-realistic images of synthetic objects. These images communicate surface shading and curvature, as well as the depth relationships of objects in a scene. These renderings are traditionally represented by a rectangular array of pixels that tile the image plane.

As an alternative to photo-realism, it is possible to create abstract images using an ordered collection of brush strokes. These abstract images filter and refine visual information before it is presented to the viewer. By controlling the color, shape, size, and orientation of individual brush strokes, impressionistic paintings of computer generated or photographic images can easily be created.

CR Categories and Subject Descriptors: I.3.2 [**Computer Graphics**]: Picture/Image Generation - Display algorithms; I.3.6 [**Computer Graphics**]: Methodology and Techniques - Interaction techniques;

Additional Key Words and Phrases: Painting, image processing, abstract images.

Introduction

This paper is not about radiosity, anti-aliasing, or motion blur. Its not about making pictures more realistic. It is about creating interesting abstract representations of natural and synthetic scenes.

Graphic designers are experts at visual communication. In their work, graphic designers use photographic images when they are appropriate, but often chose to use more abstract images such as drawings or paintings. In many cases the designer must balance realism and effectiveness. Sometimes a realistic photographic image may be less effective than a stylized image.

In a panel discussion at Siggraph 1988 [Phillips 88] on the design of effective images Margret Hagen described the goal of the visual artist:

> "The goal of effective representational image
> making, whether you paint in oil or in numbers,
> is to select and manipulate visual information
> in order to direct the viewer's attention and
> determine the viewer's perception."

Impressionist painters use brush strokes to control light to simulate objects without modelling object detail explicitly. Only a few brush strokes are needed to represent a standing figure, a person's face at a distance, or a tree. By carefully selecting the location, color, size and direction of brush strokes, they control visual information to communicate abstract images to the viewer.

A Simple Painting Technique

Our goal is to take a synthetic or natural scene, and convert it into abstract impressionistic image. We want to make it easy for a user to interactively select and manipulate visual information to explore many different representations of a single source image. To do this we will point sample the source image at some set of brush stroke locations, and draw a synthetic brush stroke with the appropriate color.

A simple interactive program allows the user to operate on a source image. The basic interactive technique

Figure 1. Creating a painting.

is to follow the cursor across the canvas, point sample the color of a stored image at the location of the cursor, and then paint a brush stroke of that color. Figure 1. shows a painting being created. The image that drives the painting is shown as an inset. The final painting is on the right. Using this process a user can easily explore different abstract representations of the source image.

In the work described here, a painting is an ordered list of brush strokes. Each stroke of the brush is described by a collection of attributes as shown in Figure 2.

Location - Position of the brush stroke.

Color - The RGB and Alpha color of the stroke.

Size - How big the stroke is.

Direction - Angle of the stroke in the painting.

Shape - The look of the brush stroke.

Figure 2. Brush stroke attributes

We will use the location, color, size, direction, and shape of brush strokes to communicate visual information to the viewer. The kinds of information we want to communicate are surface color, surface curvature, center of focus, and location of edges.

The program follows the position of the cursor across the canvas and point samples the source image to obtain a color. If a mouse button is down, an image of a brush stroke is drawn at a particular size and direction. In this way, visual information is selectively transferred from the source image to the canvas. By changing the size, direction and shape of brush strokes, many different representations of a single photographic image may easily be created.

One limitation in conventional paint programs is the time needed to pick a new color to paint with. [Lewis 84] described this as the "put-that-color-there" procedure that most paint programs use. Since the overhead in chosing a new color is high, it is very difficult to create a painting with a large number of different colors. The simple technique described escapes this problem by continuously sampling the color of the input image as painting proceeds.

Brush stroke locations are created in a stochastic distribution in the neighborhood of the cursor. This generates a scattering of brush stokes instead of a line of strokes when the cursor is moved in a straight line. This is an example of a simple interactive particle system [Reeves 85].

The size of brush strokes can be controlled in two ways. One technique uses the average speed of the cursor to control the brush size. If the user is painting quickly, the brush strokes will be made larger. When the user slows down, the brush size gets smaller. This makes it easy to first create a rough representation of the image with large bush strokes before adding finer detail with smaller brush strokes. Another technique allows the user to control the size of brush strokes using up and down arrow keys.

The orientation of brush strokes is controlled in several ways. One technique orients brush strokes with respect to the direction that the user moves the cursor. This is the tracking brush described in [Smith 79]. An alternative is to use a gesture of the mouse to set the current direction for brush strokes. To do this the user clicks down with the middle mouse button, moves in the direction brush strokes should flow, and releases the button. Other input devices could be used to interactively change the brush stoke size and orientation, as described in [Smith 79].

The shape of brush stokes can significantly influence the character of the final painting. The geometry of brush

208

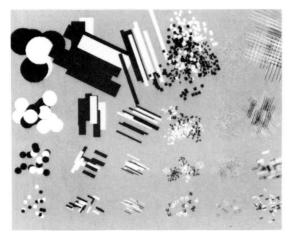

Figure 3. Several brush shapes.

strokes can be selected using a pop-up menu. The user can select among circles, rectangles, lines or scatterings of points and polygons for brush strokes, or they draw their own stroke if they want. In this implementation, all brush strokes are drawn using geometry instead of bitmaps - this makes scaling and rotating the brush very efficient on our hardware. Figure 3 shows several possible brush stroke shapes.

Three paintings of the same image are shown in Figure 4. The original image is shown inset. Diagonal brush strokes were used to create the painting on the left. In these paintings the amount of detail across the painting was modulated to direct the viewer. Noise was added to the original image to create a distribution of paint colors.

One interesting brush stroke geometry is a cone. When a group of cones are z-buffered onto the canvas, they create domains of color that share the image plane. The result is a pattern of color that has a cellular characteristic. These domains of color are Dirichlet domains [Preparata 85] derived from the location of the brush strokes. A paint-

ing made with z-buffered cones is shown in the center of Figure 4. By lingering with the cursor more detail can be exposed on any part of the canvas. A pointillist representation is shown on the right of Figure 4.

A description of the painting can be saved by interacting with a menu. A complete painting is an ordered set of brush stokes. A binary file format is used to store a stroke by stoke description of the painting. Figure 5 shows what a textual representation of a painting looks like.

```
painting with 9298 strokes
position        RGBA color              siz dir brush
0.447 0.541   241 128 173 255  attr:   30   89    5
0.444 0.531   220  57  35 255  attr:   30   89    5
0.441 0.524   172  29   1 255  attr:   30   89    5
0.444 0.553   230 100  75 255  attr:   30   89    5
0.447 0.526   220 112 162 255  attr:   30   93    5
0.456 0.554   245 189 137 255  attr:   30   93    5
0.503 0.522   245 183 237 255  attr:   31  107    5
0.479 0.545   228 141  92 255  attr:   31  101    5
0.498 0.517   246 181 230 255  attr:   31  103    5
```

Figure 5. A textual representation of a painting

Operations on Paintings

After a painting is saved, we can transform it using several paint processing programs. A painting renderer transforms a description of a painting into an RGB image. This can be used to create an extremely high resolution image of a painting.

A set of unary operators modify a single painting. All the brush strokes in a stored painting can be scaled up or down. Paintings can be altered by adding noise to brush stroke locations, color, size or direction. If wanted, each

Figure 4. Three paintings of one image.

brush stroke can be rotated by adding a constant to its direction. The order of brush strokes in a Painting can be sorted by color, direction, position, or size.

Binary painting operators use two paintings as input. It is easy to interpolate between or extrapolate beyond two paintings that have the same number of brush strokes. Paintings may be animated in this way. The brush strokes in two paintings can also be concatenated to overlay one painting on top of another.

Another tool lets us use an RGB image to modify the color, size, or direction of brush strokes in a stored painting.

The tools described above can be used to automatically roto-scope live action. To do this, we generate a rectangular array of brush locations, then add noise to their positions. Finally, RGB colors are assigned to each brush stroke in the painting by sampling one frame of live action.

Advanced Painting Techniques

Interesting effects can be created by using arbitrary images to control the brush direction across the canvas. Figure 6. shows a painting that was created by using a second image to control the brush direction. This painting consists of 9298 brush strokes.

When sampling a natural image, we start with only RGB information. Sometimes when painting, we might want to make brush strokes become aligned automatically with edges in the image. This can be done by generating an image that contains information about direction of the luminance gradient in the image [Kass 87]. Figure 7. shows a painting that was created using this technique. First the original image was converted to black and white and low pass filtered. Then the direction of the gradient of this image was used to control the brush stroke direction while painting. Notice how the brush strokes outline the shape of the head and flow along the collar of the shirt.

Another interesting technique is to blend the brush strokes onto the canvas. In Figure 8, a scanned in image of a real brush stroke is used. This brush stroke image was texture mapped onto the canvas to create the final painting.

Spice for images: Video-Sodium Glutamate

Before painting a synthetic or natural image it may be good to use a little spice (VSG) to accentuate the features we consider most important. These enhancements can be applied globally or locally to draw attention to particular parts of the painting.

When traditional artists make illustrations or paintings, many techniques are used. Often important edges in the scene are exaggerated. Where a dark area meets a light area the dark area is drawn slightly darker, and the light area is drawn slightly lighter. Some artists call this tech-

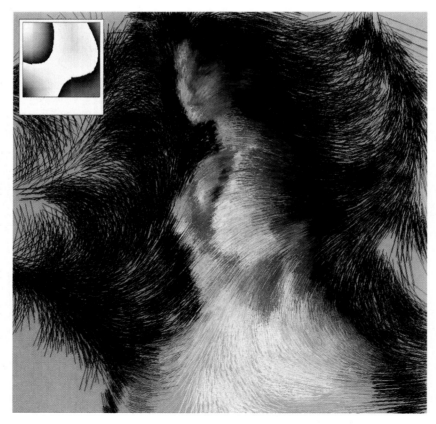

Figure 6. Using a second image to control brush stroke direction.

Figure 7. Using the gradient direction to control brush strokes.

Figure 8. A texture mapped brush stroke.

nique "pushing" an edge. This technique can be used to make depth relationships between objects in the scene more explicit where they overlap [Porter 88].

To simulate "pushing edges" we can high pass filter the original image. High frequencies are enhanced by using unsharp masking. This is done as a two step process. First the original image is blurred by convolution. Next we create an enhanced image by extrapolating from the blurry image out beyond the original image.

To do this we define a linear interpolation operation on these two images such that a parameter of 1.0 gives us the blurred image and 0.0 gives the original image. To create an image with pushed edges, we make the parameter negative. As a result of this flat fields in the original image will remain unchanged, but edges are accentuated.

This process has two important variables; how blurry the image is made in the first step, and how much we extrapolate in the second step. Convolving with a 3 by 3 kernel, and making the parameter -0.5 will accentuate very high frequency detail and change the shading only very near edges. To make the shading change within 10 pixels of edges, a kernel with a width of more than 20 should be used. Some interesting effects can be created when the kernel is made very large - approaching 20% of the image diameter.

An artist may chose to enhance the richness of some colors in a scene. Sometimes the color is uniformly saturated throughout the scene, or only particular parts of the image are enhanced in this way.

If we want to increase the saturation of the image first we create a luminance image using a formula like this:

```
lum = 0.3*r + 0.59*g + 0.11*b.
```

Next, we extrapolate from the luminance image out beyond the original image. Achromatic parts of the image will remain unchanged, but all the colored parts of the image will be even more colorful, while preserving the same luminance. It is important that the original image be properly color balanced before this is done, otherwise improper colors for skin tones will become obvious.

When painting solid colored areas, artists may use a wide range of colors to communicate the color of a surface. This helps the viewer see a range of component colors in a surface that may be a single, flat color.

To add detail to regions of flat color, noise may be added to the image. When this is done, the final painting will have brush stokes with an interesting distribution of colors. This can make the final painting much more lively and interesting.

Most books on painting recommend sticking to a fairly limited palette of colors so as to achieve an overall

harmony of color across the painting. The palettes used by the impressionists usually contained fewer than 12 colors [Callen 82]. These raw colors were mixed to create additional intermediate colors. Many beautiful paintings use remarkably few colors. With a restricted set of colors some brush strokes in the sky will closely match the color of brush strokes used to represent water. Restricting the number of different colors in a painting has the effect of unifying the painted image as a whole.

By quantifying colors in the source image, we can reduce the number of different colors in a scene without restricting the color gamut. If a sufficient amount of noise was added as discussed above, then no contouring will be visible.

Artists often cover the entire canvas with a wash of color before painting the image. The color of this background image can affect how the colors are perceived by the viewer if it is left exposed in some areas of the final painting. It has been noted by Michel-Eugene Chevreul [Smith 87] that having some proximity to gray makes all primary colors gain in brilliance and purity. Allowing the background wash color to be exposed throughout an image gives it a kind of unity and integrity.

Colors are sometimes used to provide depth cues. Colors in the range green (grass), cyan, and blue (sky) recede, while yellow, orange, red and magenta move to the foreground.

We can use many of the techniques above to enhance digital images before painting begins.

Sampling Geometry using Ray-Painting

These painting techniques can be used to create painted representations of synthetic 3D scenes as well. When sampling geometry, we have direct access to the color of each surface, its normal, and its depth. We can use the surface normal to control the direction of the brush strokes. This provides the viewer with valuable information about the orientation of surfaces. Figure 9. shows a raytraced scene, and a painting that uses surface normals to control the direction of brush strokes. To make these illustrations, the user interface of the paint program was attached to a raytracer, letting the user reveal the geometry by sampling it in real-time. Notice how the brush strokes appear to wrap around the sphere, the cone and the cylinder.

Approximating Images by Relaxation

An iterative relaxation technique may be used to create interesting paintings with remarkably brush strokes. The left side of Figure 10 shows a painting of 100 rectangular brush strokes that approximates an image of a seated man. The right side of Figure 10 shows a painting

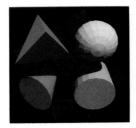

Figure 9. Sampling geometry using raytracing.

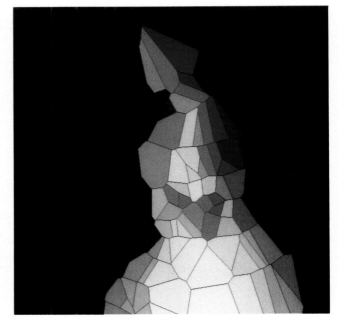

Figure 10. Using relaxation to create paintings automatically.

of 100 Dirichlet domains. These two paintings were created by stochastically perturbing the attributes of the brush strokes, while minimizing the root mean squared difference between the original image and the painted representation. This process ran for several hours before these images were saved.

Conclusions

We present several techniques for creating static and animated abstract images of photographed and synthetic scenes.

In this work, the goal is not to make photo-realistic images, but rather effective, interesting images that communicate. By interactively processing an image we can select and manipulate visual information to eliminate distracting detail, provide cues about surface orientation, and influence the viewer's perception of the subject.

It is natural that we want to continue to explore new painting techniques. A logical extension of this work would incorporate the texture synthesis work of [Lewis 84] and the brush modelling work of [Strassman 86].

Acknowledgements

I would like to thank Seth Teller for creating software to support rendering Dirichlet domains. I also appreciate the many helpful comments provided by the reviewers.

Some aspects of this work are patent pending.

References

[Callen 82] Anthea Callen, "Techniques of the Impressionists", 1982.

[Heckbert 87] Paul S. Heckbert, "Ray Tracing Brand Gelatin", Computer Graphics, 1987.

[Kass 87] Michael Kass and Andrew Witkin, "Analyzing Oriented Patterns", Computer Vision, Graphics, and Image Processing, 37, 1987.

[Lewis 84] John-Peter Lewis, "Texture Synthesis for Digital Painting", Computer Graphics, 1984.

[Phillips 88] Dick Phillips, "Siggraph '88 Panels Proceedings", 1988.

[Porter 88] Tom Porter and Sue Goodman, "Designer Primer", Charlse Scribner's Sons, 1988.

[Preparata 85] Franco P. Preparata and Michael Ian Shamos, "Computational Geometry", Springer-Verlag, 1985.

[Reeves 85] William T. Reeves and Ricki Blau, "Approximate and Probabilistic Algorithms for Shading and Rendering Structured Particle Systems", Computer Graphics, 1985.

[Smith 79] Alvy Ray Smith, "Table Paint", SIGGRAPH tutorial notes for "Two Dimensional Computer Animation, 1981.

[Smith 87] Ray Smith, "The Artists Handbook", Alfred A. Knopf, 1987.

[Strassman 86] Steve Strassman, "Hairy Brushes", Computer Graphics, 1986.

Direct WYSIWYG Painting and Texturing on 3D Shapes

Pat Hanrahan* and Paul Haeberli†

*Princeton University

†Silicon Graphics Computer Systems

Abstract

This paper describes a 3D object-space paint program. This program allows the user to directly manipulate the parameters used to shade the surface of the 3D shape by applying pigment to its surface. The pigment has all the properties normally associated with material shading models. This includes, but is not limited to, the diffuse color, the specular color, and the surface roughness. The pigment also can have thickness, which is modeled by simultaneously creating a bump map attached to the shape. The output of the paint program is a 3D model with associated texture maps. This information can be used with any rendering program with texture mapping capabilities. Almost all traditional techniques of 2D computer image painting have analogues in 3D object painting, but there are also many new techniques unique to 3D. One example is the use of solid textures to pattern the surface.

CR Categories: I.3.5 [Computer Graphics] Three-Dimensional Graphics and Realism - Color, shading, shadowing and texture; Visible line/surface algorithms. I.3.6 [Computer Graphics] Methodology - Interaction Techniques

Additional Keywords and Phrases: Painting, direct manipulation, user-interface

1. Introduction

In recent years the technology of 3D computer graphics is finding application in a large number of different disciplines. In the near future, it is likely that the typical personal computer or workstation will be fast enough to produce 3D models, animations, and high quality computer generated imagery just as easily as the typical personal computer of today produces 2D paintings, illustrations, and documents. The key to the widespread use of 3D computer graphics, however, is not just dependent on advances in hardware, but requires similar advances in interactive techniques that make 3D concepts easy to use and accessible to large numbers of people.

There is no reason to think this is an impossible task. Almost all the design principles that have been successfully applied to designing current user interfaces are likely to apply to 3D applications as well. One such principle is to use *common metaphors*. Users can then rely on their everyday experience to infer how a program works by analogy with how everyday things work[1, 22]. This principle is easy to apply in 3D computer graphics because the 3D world provides so many concrete metaphors. Another general principle in designing user interfaces is *direct manipulation*[27]. A pointing device such as a mouse can be used to move, drag, or manipulate graphics representations on the screen. The act of moving the mouse is directly associated with some action to be performed, and feedback is given immediately to reinforce the action. Ideally, the results of the interactive action should be a faithful reproduction of the final product, or WYSIWYG (What You See Is What You Get).

Unfortunately, most applications involving 3D computer graphics are still indirect and not WYSIWYG. The most progress has been in positioning and creating geometric models[3, 21]. One example is the *virtual sphere* where the user rotates an object by manipulating a hypothetical crystal ball containing the object[9]. Another example is to fix a 3D plane and use the same direct manipulation techniques used by 2D illustration programs to create and modify geometry on the plane. This 2D geometry can be converted to 3D models using sweep operations. More recently, Williams has described how a ordinary paint program can be used to sculpt height fields[33]. However, the models needed for computer generated imagery involve not only geometric attributes, but also optical attributes that define the properties of materials and light sources. One technique for interactively modifying the optical properties of a single surface illuminated by distant lights is to display an image of quantized surface normals (sometimes referred to as an *orientation coded image*) using a colormap whose entries have been set to the calculated shades[2, 7, 15, 28]. This type of table is often referred to as a *reflectance map*. Since the reflectance map is small it can be recomputed quickly so the properties of the lights or of a single surface can be adjusted in real-time. Warn describes a program for interactively manipulating the position and properties of spotlights[31]. Some commercial modelers contain material editors that allow the user to adjust the various coefficients that go into the standard shading models by using sliders. These editors normally shade a single simple shape such as a sphere and not the objects being built by the modeler.

The visual appearance of materials is strongly influenced by their spatial textures and patterns, not only their local reflectance properties. The above methods for directly manipulating materials and lights only work with surfaces made of materials with uniform properties. In computer graphics the most expedient way to model local variations in material properties involves using texture maps[16]. Texture maps are images mapped onto a surface. The value of the texture map at a point on the surface is used to control parameters in the local shading formula. Texture maps can be used to modulate surface color[8] and transparency[13], ambient, diffuse and specular coefficients, and the roughness or shininess (specular exponent) of the surface. Texture maps can also be used to select between different types of materials; this allows a simple shape to contain inlays or be constructed from composite materials[10]. Finally, texture maps can be used to modulate small-scale geometric properties. Normals can be perturbed using bump maps[6], positions can be displaced using a height field or displacement map[10], and a preferred tangential direction (for use with anisotropic shading models) can be defined using tangent bundle mapping[17, 20]. Because of their versatility, texture maps are a key component of a high quality rendering system.

Texture maps are typically created by scanning in existing artwork, painting them with a 2D paint program, or synthesizing them from procedural image models. However, because the creation of the texture and the mapping of it to the surface are separated, setting up a model involving texture mapping is an indirect process. This makes using texture maps to modulate material properties tedious and error prone. First, it is difficult to place the texture map on the surface in the desired position and orientation. This is made more complicated if several surfaces share the same texture map, because it is important that no seams be visible at their boundaries. Second, the texture map is often indexed by the surface parameters, so this requires the user to know about the mathematics of the surface parameterization when creating the texture map. Another problem is caused because when a curved surface is uniformly subdivided in parameter space, the surface area of each piece can vary greatly. This causes the texture map to be locally compressed or expanded in different parts of the surface, and results in undesirable distortions which must be undone when creating the texture map.

This paper describes an interactive paint program that allows the user to directly paint with different types of pigments and materials onto 3D shapes. The user controls the position of a brush using a tablet; the brush contains paint that is applied to the shape being painted on. Rather than creating a final 2D image like most paint programs, this paint program creates an object description that describes the composite material properties everywhere on the surface of the object. The material properties are stored as a set of associated texture maps. An image is created of this object using conventional rendering techniques (optimized for this application) as the user paints. These material properties interact with the illumination environment to create the appearance of the object. Almost all the conventional computer painting modes can be used with this program. Examples include

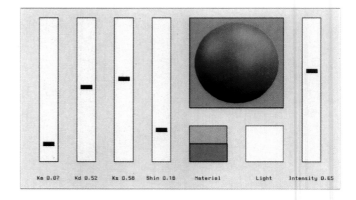

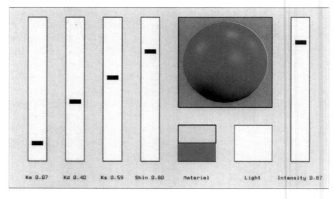

Figure 1. The material editor *medit*. Above, a metallic bronze; below, a green plastic.

airbrushing or alpha blending, smearing, patterning, table painting, etc[29, 30]. However, some computer painting effects, such as z-paint[30, 32], are just simulations of things that can be directly done in 3D, in this case using bump mapping. In fact, conventional 2D painting can be interpreted as a special case of this program, where a painting is made by laying down pigment on a 3D flat rectangular polygonal canvas. Other painting effects, similar to how a pottery maker or sculptor might work rather than a traditional painter, are also possible with this program. Once the model has been painted the geometry and the texture maps can be saved and used with traditional batch rendering programs.

2. Material and Geometric Representations

The pigments used as paint have the same properties as materials used in shading calculations. The properties are defined by the following shading formula:

$$C = (Ka*Ca)*La + (Kd*Cd)*Ld(P,N) + (Ks*Cs)*Ls(P,N,r)$$

Ka – *ambient coefficient*
Ca – *ambient color*
La – *ambient light color*

Kd – *diffuse coefficient*
Cd – *diffuse color*
Ld – *diffuse light color*

r – *roughness*
Ks – *specular coefficient*
Cs – *specular color*
Ls – *specular light color*

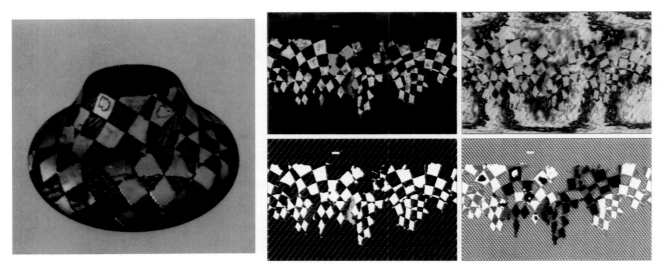

Figure 2. A painted pot and its associated texture maps: (upper left) the diffuse color, (upper right) the specular color, (lower left) the roughness, (lower right) the displacement.

The local properties of a material are modeled as an ambient color ($Ka*Ca$), a diffuse color ($Kd*Cd$), and a specular color ($Ks*Cs$). For simplicity the ambient coefficient and color are set equal to the diffuse values. The roughness or shininess is also a material property. Rough materials ($r=1$) have fuzzy highlights while smooth or shiny materials ($r=0$) have sharp highlights. The various light colors (La, Ld, and Ls) are given by sums over all the lights illuminating the object times the bidirectional reflection function for that type of light transport. The diffuse transport is given by Lambert's law and is a function of the surface position and normal; the specular transport is given by a simplified version of the Torrance-Sparrow model described by Blinn[5] and is a function of the position, normal and roughness. The choice of this shading model was motivated by what is commonly available in real-time rendering systems, but other shading models could also be used.

Material pigments are created using an interactive pigment editor shown in Figure 1. Sliders control the relative contributions of ambient, diffuse and specular light. The diffuse and specular colors can be set by picking colors on the screen from color editors and palettes running as separate processes. The properties of light sources can also be controlled by this editor. Lights are positioned by interactively dragging their highlights on a sphere, and calculating the position of the light that would cause a highlight at the new location.

The paint program internally stores geometric objects as rectangular meshes. Meshes are a common surface representation in computer graphics and can be created in a variety of ways: (i) from mathematically defined parametric surfaces such as spheres or tori, (ii) from procedurally defined models such as surfaces of revolution formed from arbitrary curves, or (iii) from a 3D input device such as a Cyberware scanner or Polhemus digitizer. A mesh defines a discrete parametric surface. The independent parameters of the surface are the 2D integer indices of the mesh, and the dependent data is a vertex containing the position, normal, diffuse and specular color, the roughness, and the bump height. The mesh data structure is organized so that only the vertex data that is needed is allocated, and so that it is easy to add additional fields to experiment with new material properties. The optional appearance attributes are organized as 2D arrays, and are really just texture maps embedded in the mesh structure. It is easy to extract them from the mesh data structure and store them as image files or directly as texture maps depending on the requirements of the final rendering system. The size of the mesh is related to the size of the texture maps created and is under user control. The mesh structure also stores whether the mesh wraps around in either the u or v direction, or both, and this information is used when painting. Figure 2 shows a shaded image of a pot and the set of four associated texture maps.

The material and geometric data structures were chosen so that the object could be drawn quickly. Since most existing graphics hardware does not support the use of texture maps, we choose to draw the mesh as many small 4-sided micropolygons.

```
bgnpolygon();
    material(Cd[u][v],Cs[u][v],r[u][v]);
    normal(N[u][v]);
    vertex(P[u][v]);
    vertex(P[u+1][v]);
    vertex(P[u+1][v+1]);
    vertex(P[u][v+1]);
endpolygon();
```

The material procedure outputs the parameters for the current material, and the remainder of the procedures output the geometric information. The graphics system handles the transformation and shading of each micropolygon. Hidden surfaces are removed using a z-buffer.

The workstation we are using, a Silicon Graphics 4D220 GTX, which is typical of a high-performance 3D workstation, is capable of drawing approximately 100,000 shaded quadrilaterals per second. (Although this number depends on the size of the polygons, the number of light sources, and is particularly sensitive to how often the surface roughness changes.) This means that a mesh with a 512 by 512 texture map can be drawn in about 2 1/2 seconds. Since this is not fast enough to redraw the entire object in real-time, it is useful to optimize drawing for two cases: when moving the object or camera, and when painting on the object. When the position of the object changes, the mesh is subsampled to a resolution that can be drawn in real-time, and then redrawn in its entirety when the movement ends. The next frame is always drawn into the back-buffer while the current frame is being displayed in the front-buffer. Double-buffering insures that the

the normal. This is a reasonable approximation to what might happen if a real 3D brush was being used to paint on a solid object, since the brush bends to conform to the surface.

Since parameter space brushes can be implemented much like 2D brushes in a 2D paint program, that method is used at the lowest levels to implement the actual painting into texture maps. The other two methods could be implemented by first distorting the brush pattern to form a parameter space brush, and then using the distorted brush to perform the painting. In general, the distortion of the brush is a complicated non-linear mapping to parameter-space and cannot be easily approximated. Fortunately, the mapping from screen-space to parameter-space is stored in the object id buffer. At each xy screen location is the uv parameter that is visible at that location and this information can be used to reconstruct the functions $u(x,y)$ and $v(x,y)$. This reconstruction of the distortion is valid as long as all micropolygons contain at least one sample, or, are magnified and not minified. Unfortunately, this technique does not work for tangent-space brushes. Another approach to simulating screen-space brushes is to simulate spray painting by randomly picking points within the brush and applying dabs of paint at these locations. This technique has the nice effect of varying the density of the applied paint with the cosine of the angle between the normal and the viewing direction. Inclined surfaces receive less paint per unit area than surfaces normal to the direction of view.

Resampling brushes allows the paint program to undo any distortions due to the surface parameterization, and makes the system feel more natural. Unfortunately, resampling brushes is expensive and involves making simplifying assumptions; also, since these brush distortions are done in the innermost loops, they can slow the system down.

Paint is usually applied to a surface using *strokes*. A stroke begins when the tablet stylus or mouse button is pressed and continues until the pressure is released. Most paint programs allow different types of strokes. For example, a *rubberstamp* only samples the initial position, a *rubberband* stroke allows for perfectly straight lines, and an interpolated strokes fills in intermediate brush positions between sampled cursor positions. All these methods can be used with this paint program. However, there are some subtleties in 3D painting that don't come up in 2D painting. One issue is when to terminate a stroke. A stroke should always end when there is no object underneath the brush. A stroke should normally end whenever a silhouette is crossed, since that would cause the brush to leave the surface momentarily as it jumps to its new position. It is reasonable, however, to think that silhouettes should be handled differently for screen-space vs. object-space brushes, since a screen-space brush tends to behave like spray can. It is also unclear whether paint should be applied to portions of the surface which are back-facing even though the center of the brush is on a front-facing surface. Another issue unique to 3D is the fact that there may be multiple objects (this would be like having multiple canvases in 2D). A parameter-space brush naturally paints on only one object; a tangent-space or screen-space brush, however, might feel more natural if it were allowed to paint on multiple objects if positioned near a point of intersection or contact between objects. A similar issue comes up when surface patches are pieced together, or joined to themselves. Connectivity information is important, otherwise seams might be visible when painting across a boundary. Ideally these details about the structure of the model should not be known by the user. Surfaces also have two sides, so it is reasonable to require a complete set of materials properties for the inside and outside surface.

4. Paint Modes and the Paint Equation

The mathematics of painting is controlled by the *paint equation*[26, 30].

```
surface = blend( paint op surface, surface, brush )
```

This equation governs how the *brush* controls the application of *paint* to the *surface*. The brush shape is represented by a *matte* image; the brush is present where the matte image is 1, and not present where the values are 0. The matte is continuous so that it can represent the partial coverage of the brush over a matte sample[32]. The function *blend*, also sometimes referred to as *lerp*, linearly interpolates the first two arguments under the control of the third argument.

```
blend(c0,c1,a) = (1-a)*c0 + a*c1 = c0 + a*(c1-c0)
```

This blend in the paint equation combines the original values on the surface with the new computed values resulting from the interaction of the paint with the surface.

There are many different possible paint operators. Those based on compositing are described in Salesin and Barzel[26]. The most common of which are *copy* and *over*. Other possibilities include *max* to implement z-paint[30, 32], filtering or blurring under the brush to simulate smearing or mixing, and sliding the surface values in a certain direction to simulate another form of smearing. All these painting modes can, in principle, be used when painting in 3D.

Normally the paint on the brush is a constant material, but it is possible to allow the paint to vary as a function of position so that the paint has texture or is patterned. We will refer to this as *pattern paint*. The value of the paint applied at a given position is a function of a constant *pigment* and the *pattern*.

```
paint = pigment in pattern(P)
```

Ordinary painting can be considered a special case of pattern paint, if we use a pattern that is constant. The pattern function can be generated procedurally (see, for example, Lewis)[18], or from stored 1D tables, 2D images, or 3D voxel arrays. The pattern is combined with the pigment using the in compositing operator[25] which says the pigment is present only where the pattern matte alpha values are non-zero. Since patterns don't always contain a matte, we provide two built-in methods for automatically generating mattes. *Self-matting* sets the matte to the value of the pattern, and *opaque-matting* sets the matte to 1.

In most 2D paint programs, patterns are indexed by the coordinates of the canvas. In our 3D paint program, there is a much richer set of pattern coordinate transformations. First, there is a question as to what set of variables to use to index the pattern. These can be either (i) the surface parameters or texture coordinates (u,v), (ii) the screen or raster coordinates (x,y), or (iii) the position of points on the surface P. The default method used is texture coordinates, since this seems to be most like ordinary pattern paint. Using raster coordinates is useful if the brush is in screen space and the pattern is designed to simulate a frisket. Finally, using the surface position allows solid textures[19, 23, 24] to be used as patterns and leads to many new painting styles. When using solid textures as patterns it is also useful to transform points before indexing the solid texture. The same solid texture can then be overlaid multiple times with different orientations and phases. This is done by positioning the object with respect to a reference cube defining the texture coordinate system (by default this cube is aligned with the viewing pyramid) and issuing a command which sets transformation to texture coordinates.

An operator exists to apply a *wash* to the geometric object. This is equivalent to painting everywhere on the object and is used to set the initial material properties and to apply patterns and

Figure 3. A pot and its object identifiers: (upper) shaded image, (lower left) the u parameter, (lower right) the v parameter.

motion is smooth. When painting on the object so only the part of the surface whose appearance changes needs to be redrawn. Since painting is usually localized to a small region, this involves redrawing many fewer polygons and can easily be done in real-time. These incremental changes are drawn using *z-equal mode* into the front-buffer and no buffer swaps are done. Z-equal mode is a variation of z-buffering where the screen is updated only if what is being drawn has the *same* depth as what has been drawn previously. This usually is enough to insure that polygons are only drawn on top of themselves and hence where they are visible.

3. Brush-Surface Geometry

A 2D pointing device such as a mouse or tablet is used to move a cursor around the screen. The hot spot of the cursor specifies a unique point on the screen; in a typical 2D paint program this specifies the position of the brush. In 3D things are more complicated. First, the brush needs to be positioned on a surface being painted on. Second, there are more possible interpretations for brush orientation that must be taken into consideration.

The most natural interpretation for the brush position is on the frontmost surface underneath the brush. To paint on back surfaces involves reorienting the object so those surfaces are now frontfacing. One way to find the point under the brush is to find where the line of sight through the 2D brush position intersects the surface, and if multiple intersections occur, return the closest one. This is what a ray tracer does, and several ray tracers can in fact be controlled in this way[3]. Most graphics hardware systems, however, implement selection using picking or hit detection. This involves setting a pick window and then drawing the entire scene. A list of objects that intersect the pick window is returned, and the application still must determine which one was picked, if more than one is returned. A disadvantage of this approach for

this application is that because of the large size of the mesh it takes too long to redraw. Also, typically many paint strokes are laid down between changes of the view or object position so it would be worthwhile to only redraw when the object position changes. An easy way to find the brush position that takes advantage of the graphics hardware is to draw object identifiers (id's) into an auxiliary framebuffer (sometimes called an object tag buffer or an item buffer). The object id is a integer that uniquely specifies what part of the object is visible at a given screen position. Given the position of the cursor on the screen and an object id buffer, the brush position on the surface can be found by just reading the pixel in the object id buffer under the cursor, This id encodes the mesh and the texture coordinates of that mesh's micropolygon. Because the meshes must be divided into large numbers of micropolygons, the object id buffer must have quite a bit of precision. For example, drawing an object with a 512 by 512 texture map, requires at least an 18-bit id buffer.

As mentioned in the last section, when painting, the object is stationary, and the paint strokes are drawn into the front-buffer. This means that the back-buffer is available for object ids. When an object is being moved, the object ids are not drawn, but when the movement stops, a shaded version of the object is drawn at high resolution, the buffers are swapped, and then the object ids are drawn into the back-buffer. When movement begins again the normal buffer swap is initially disabled and the object is drawn into the back-buffer containing the object ids. Subsequent frames are double-buffered in the normal way. Although our current implementation takes advantage of the double-buffering capabilities of the hardware, object ids could also be stored in any available memory since they are never displayed. Figure 3 shows the two types of buffers, the color image buffer and the object id buffer (for illustrative purposes this is shown as separate *u* and *v* images).

Another complication with the brush geometry is how to orient the brush with respect to the surface and its texture maps. In 2D painting the brush pattern remains aligned with the 2D image. In 3D there are more possibilities:

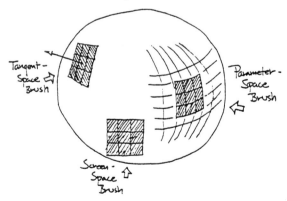

- *Parameter-space brushes*. This is the simplest and most direct method to index a brush. The 2D brush paints directly into the 2D texture maps at the texture coordinates of the brush position on the surface. Brush samples and texture samples are mapped one-to-one.

- *Screen-space brushes*. A screen space brush is projected onto the surface using the inverse viewing transformation. This gives the effect of spray painting on the surface.

- *Tangent-space* brushes. A tangent space brush is mapped onto the surface by first placing the brush in the plane tangent to the surface at the brush position, and then projecting the brush onto the surface in the direction parallel to

Figure 4. A marble sphere with applied paint strokes.

textures globally. A variation of a wash is a *dip* where another 3D texture acts a 3D brush or matte which controls where the wash is applied. A dip simulates dipping the object is a bath made of the material coating.

5. Material Paint

As mentioned previously, a pigment is modeled as a material with the following properties: diffuse color, specular color and roughness. The paint equation combines each of these properties with the corresponding texture channels on the surface of the object. Combining colors with the surface is just like a 2D paint program. The paint program has separate weights, or alphas, for each channel that can be used to modulate the blending of pigment with the surface. A channel alpha of 0, prevents painting from changing that channel's properties on the surface.

```
color.Cd = paint.Cd op surface.Cd
color.Cs = paint.Cs op surface.Cs

surface.Cd = blend(color.Cd,surface.Cd,alphad*brush)
surface.Cs = blend(color.Cs,surface.Cs,alphas*brush)
```

Note that even though roughness is not a color, it is bounded between 0 and 1 and reasonable behavior results if it treated as a single component color.

```
surface.r = blend(paint.r,surface.r,alphar*brush)
```

Various special effects can be produced by painting channels selectively. Some of these are:

- *Full Material Paint*. Changes all the material properties of the surface. It is just like applying a coating of that material onto the surface.

- *Paint Remover*. This removes paint previously applied to the surface and sets its properties to those of the underlying object.

- *Dye Paint*. Changes just the diffuse and specular colors of the surface. Dye paint could also change the saturation of a color to simulate bleaching the surface.

- *Polish or Varnish Paint*. Changes the surface roughness and the specular coefficient. This makes the surface shinier and causes highlights to appear more focussed, but leaves the underlying color of the material the same.

- *Sandpaper Paint*. This is the opposite of polishing. The surface is made rougher and its shininess is reduced.

To reduce the amount of storage devoted to texture maps the various material coefficients and colors are premultiplied and stored as a single color. For the painting modes that modulate the coefficient and not the color of the material, the coefficient is extracted from the premultiplied color by finding the maximum of the three components.

6. Geometry Paint

In addition to having the brush apply a pigment to the surface, the brush can also be used to alter the small-scale geometry of the surface. Associated with the surface is a height or displacement map consisting of a signed floating point number indicating how far the surface is displaced along the geometric (or true normal) from its original position.

```
P = surface.P + surface.h * surface.N
```

From a mesh of displaced positions P, a new perturbed normal for shading can be computed.

Figure 5. Two batch renderings.

Figure 6. A screen dump of the paint program in use.

The displacement is painted just like the roughness channel.

```
surface.h = blend(paint.h,surface.h,alphah*brush)
```

The weight controlling displacement mapping can be either positive or negative; a positive value adds gloppy thick material to the surface, whereas a negative value dents the surface inward. It is possible to associate different thicknesses or viscosities with different pigments and simultaneously displace and paint on the surface. Another nice effect is to use the current displacement as a pattern matte. This can be used to simulate pastels or charcoal sticking on the tops of bumps[4].

Other types of geometry paint are also possible. For example, averaging or filtering within a brush will locally smooth the surface. Smearing and sliding also can be used to move the surface. Another type of geometry paint could simulate a blowtorch, and be used to cut holes or windows in the surface.

7. Results

Figure 4 shows a sphere with several types of painting. Originally the sphere is carved from a marble solid texture similar to that used by Perlin[24]. The marble texture is also used to perturb normals to simulate corrosion of the softer layers. After this a thick goopy blue diffuse pigment is applied which fills in the corroded areas. Next to this a watery shiny red pigment is applied next to the blue. Since this pigment has negligible thickness the the geometry of the bumps on the surface is unchanged but they stand out more because the paint is shiny. After this several strokes of a gold pigment are applied while simultaneously gouging the surface. And finally, the whole sphere is coated with a soft translucent turbulent pattern to simulate dust. This is done several times with the sphere in different orientations so that each turbulence function is added with a different "phase."

Figure 5 shows two pots that were painted and then converted to separate texture maps and geometry and finally rendered using a conventional rendering system.

Figure 6 is a screen dump showing the paint program, the color chooser, and the material editor. Notice the user interface to the paint program. Finally, Figure 7 shows the process of painting on a digitized head input with a Cyberware™ 3D digitizer. With a Cyberware model, the original object is typically composed of various materials. Unfortunately, when the model is digitized this information is lost and it is normally difficult to reassign these material properties. Direct painting on the 3D shape is a natural solution to this problem. The geometry paint modes can also be used to clean up problems with the input data.

Figure 7. Four snapshots during painting on a Cyberware model of a face.

8. Discussion

One effect that is conspicuously absent from the initial implementation is transparency. We imagine two ways to see through an object, either by making it fully or partially transparent, or by cutting holes in its surfaces. Transparent objects still have a front surface that can be painted on, whereas holes allow the paint brush to pass through to a back surface. Transparency is problematic, because redrawing the object requires redrawing the polygons in sorted order. And even if the sorted order is known, to incrementally redraw the object under the brush requires knowing not only the frontmost surface, but also what surface (or surfaces) are immediately behind it. We are continuing to investigate ways to implement transparency in connection with the graphics hardware the workstation provides.

Although we have implemented the paint program on a high-powered 3D workstation, we think similar techniques can be used on personal computers without special 3D hardware. When beginning the project we thought the computationally intensive part of the program would be painting. However, in the current implementation the rate limiting step is the high resolution redraw after the object has been moved. The process of painting is fast because it is localized to the area under the brush. A less demanding implementation might be possible by fixing the number of views, in effect, eliminating the high resolution redraw.

The painting techniques discussed in this paper are just some of many possibilities. More and more realism could be added by simulating the physics of paint and painting in more detail. For example, more accurate models exist for the physics of pigment mixtures[11]. Wet paint could gradually dry or be absorbed differentially across a textured surface, or paint could drip under the influence of gravity or spread due to centrifugal forces when the object rotates. Other interactive techniques could be based on duplicating techniques artists use. For example, it should be possible to put masking tape on the object, paint over it, and then peel it off to form a perfectly straight edge. Texture maps could act as real decals, and be slid over the surface conforming to its local shape. A pressure sensitive stylus would allow pressure to directly control the depth of the brush's impression on the surface. Of course, the goal of incorporating physical simulation into computer-assisted painting is not just the simulation of reality, but rather, to drive the development of a flexible procedural modeling environment that artists and designers can use to implement the abstractions they are interested in. Related work along these lines is described in another paper by one of the authors (Haeberli)[14].

9. Acknowledgements

This project was inspired by George Francis's "Topological Picture Book,"[12] where it became clear to the authors that there is an art to drawing even simple, pure 3D shapes. Thanks to Al Marden and Charlie Gunn and the Geometry Supercomputer Project, and to Silicon Graphics Computer Systems for supporting this work. David Addleman provided the Cyberware data. A special thanks to Delle Maxwell for experimenting with the program, providing feedback, and painting Figures 2, 6 and 7. Larry Aupperle wrote the software which created RenderMan™ input from the data structures used by this program.

222

References

1. APPLE,, *Human Interface Guideline: The Apple Desktop Interface,* Addison-Wesley, Menlo Park (1987).

2. BASS, DANIEL H., "Using the Video Lookup Table for Reflectivity Calculations: Specific Techniques and Graphics Results," *Computer Graphics and Image Processing* **17**(3) pp. 249-261 (1981).

3. BIER, ERIC A., "Skitters and Jacks: Interactive 3-D Positioning Tools," *Proceedings 1986 Workshop on Interactive 3-D Graphics,* pp. 183-196 (October 1986).

4. BLESER, TERESA W., JOHN L. SIBERT, AND J. PATRICK MCGEE, "Charcoal Sketching: Returning Control to the Artist," *ACM Transactions on Graphics* **7**(1) pp. 76-81 (January 1988).

5. BLINN, JAMES F., "Models of Light Reflection for Computer Synthesized Pictures," *Computer Graphics* **11**(2) pp. 192-198 (1977).

6. BLINN, JAMES F., "Simulation of Wrinkled Surfaces," *Computer Graphics* **12**(3) pp. 286-292 (August 1978).

7. BLINN, JAMES F., "Raster Graphics," pp. 150-156 in *Tutorial: Computer Graphics,* ed. K. S. Booth,IEEE Press (1982).

8. CATMULL, EDWIN, "A Subdivision Algorithm for Computer Display of Curved Surfaces," Phd dissertation, University of Utah, Salt Lake City (1974).

9. CHEN, MICHAEL, S. JOY MUMFORD, AND ABIGAIL SELLEN, "A Study of Interactive 3-D Rotation Using 2-D Control Devices," *Computer Graphics* **22**(4) pp. 121-129 (August 1988).

10. COOK, ROBERT L., "Shade Trees," *Computer Graphics* **18**(3) pp. 223-231 (July 1984).

11. FISHKIN, KENNETH, "An Application of Color Science to Computer Graphics," Master's Thesis, University of California, Berkeley, CA (1985).

12. FRANCIS, GEORGE K., *A Topological Picturebook,* Springer-Verlag, New York (1987).

13. GARDNER, GEOFFREY Y., "Visual Simulation of Clouds," *Computer Graphics* **19**(3) pp. 297-303 (July 1985).

14. HAEBERLI, PAUL E., "Paint By Numbers: Abstract Image Representations," *Computer Graphics,* (24)(1990).

15. HECKBERT, PAUL S., "Techniques for Real-time Frame Buffer Animation," in *Computer FX '84,* , London (October 1984).

16. HECKBERT, PAUL S., "Survey of Texture Mapping," *IEEE Computer Graphics and Applications* **6**(11) pp. 56-67 (November 1986).

17. KAJIYA, JAMES T., "Anisotropic Reflection Models," *Computer Graphics* **19**(3) pp. 15-22 (July 1985).

18. LEWIS, JOHN PETER, "Texture Synthesis for Digital Painting," *Computer Graphics* **18**(3) pp. 245-252 (July 1984).

19. LEWIS, JOHN P., "Algorithms for Solid Noise Synthesis," *Computer Graphics* **23**(3) pp. 263-270 (July 1989).

20. MILLER, GAVIN S. P., "From Wire-Frames to Furry Animals," *Graphics Interface '88,* pp. 138-145 (1988).

21. NIELSON, GREGORY M. AND DAN R. OLSEN, JR., "Direct Manipulation Techniques for 3-D Objects Using 2-D Locator Devices," *Proceedings 1986 Workshop on Interactive 3-D Graphics,* pp. 175-182 (October 1986).

22. NORMAN, DONALD A., *The Psychology of Everyday Things,* Basic Books, New York (1988).

23. PEACHEY, DARWYN, "Solid Texturing of Complex Surfaces," *Computer Graphics* **19**(3) pp. 279-286 (1985).

24. PERLIN, KEN, "An Image Synthesizer," *Computer Graphics* **19**(3) pp. 287-296 (July 1985).

25. PORTER, THOMAS AND TOM DUFF, "Compositing Digital Images," *Computer Graphics* **18**(3) pp. 253-260 (July 1984).

26. SALESIN, DAVID AND RONEN BARZEL, "Two-Bit Graphics," *IEEE Computer Graphics and Applications,* pp. 36-42 (June 1986).

27. SCHNEIDERMAN, BEN, "Direct Manipulation: A Step Beyond Programming Languages," *IEEE Computer* **16**(8) pp. 57-69 (1983).

28. SLOAN, KENNETH R. AND CHRISTOPHER M. BROWN, "Color Map Techniques," *Computer Graphics and Image Processing* **13**(4) pp. 297-317 (August 1979).

29. SMITH, ALVY RAY, "Table Paint," in *Siggaph '81 Tutorial Notes: Two-Dimensional Computer Animation,* (August 1981).

30. SMITH, ALVY RAY, "Paint," pp. 501-512 in *Tutorial: Computer Graphics,* ed. K. S. Booth,IEEE Press (1982).

31. WARN, DAVID R., "Lighting Controls for Synthetic Images," *Computer Graphics* **17**(3) pp. 13-21 (July 1983).

32. WHITTED, TURNER, "Anti-aliased Line Drawing Using Brush Extrusion," *Computer Graphics* **17**(3) pp. 151-156 (July 1983).

33. WILLIAMS, LANCE, "3D Paint," *Computer Graphics (Proceedings 1990 Symposium on Interactive 3D Techniques)* **24**(2) pp. 225-233 (March 1990).

Reusable Motion Synthesis Using State-Space Controllers

Michiel van de Panne*, Eugene Fiume** and Zvonko Vranesic*

Department of *Electrical Engineering/**Computer Science
University of Toronto
Toronto, Canada M5S 1A4

Abstract

The use of physically-based techniques for computer animation can result in realistic object motion. The price paid for physically-based motion synthesis lies in increased computation and information requirements. We introduce a new approach to realistic motion specification based on state-space controllers. A user specifies a motion by defining a goal in terms of a set of destination states. A state-space controller is then constructed, which provides an optimal-control solution that guides the object from an arbitrary starting configuration to a goal. Motions are optimized with respect to time and control energy. Because controllers are specified in terms of destination states only, it is easy to reuse the same controller to produce different motions (from different starting states), or to create a complex sequence of motions by concatenating several controllers. An implementation of state-space controllers is presented, in which realistic motions can be produced in real time. Several examples will be considered.

CR Categories: I.3.7 [Computer Graphics]: Three Dimensional Graphics and Realism – animation; I.6.3 [Simulation and Modelling]: Applications; G.1.6 [Constrained Optimization].

1 Introduction

Computer-assisted animation embodies a wide variety of motion-synthesis techniques. Kinematic approaches still predominate and are likely to do so, but physically-based techniques are gaining in popularity. The cost of greater physical realism has been increased computational cost and information requirements. Moreover, it is not usually possible to reuse a previously-computed motion in other contexts.

The physical modelling of natural phenomena or motions requires physical *simulation*. In such cases, one typically defines some initial conditions and then invokes a physical simulation of the model. In a general animation system, some notion of motion *control* is also required. In this case, a desired goal is specified, and the system attempts to generate a suitable series of forces and torques on a moving object in order to reach the goal from some initial configuration. The control problem is difficult, and it is the focus of this paper. We propose the use of encapsulated optimal control laws in the form of *state-space controllers*. The same controller can be used in many different situations, and it can be concatenated with other controllers to produce seamless composite motions. The next section gives an overview of motion specification techniques. We then describe our approach, some examples of its use, and future work.

2 Previous Work

2.1 Kinematic Motion Synthesis

Complex motion synthesis has traditionally been performed kinematically using interpolation mechanisms such as keyframing [9-11,18,21,23,27,33]. Approaches to simplifying the specification of key positions include inverse kinematic solutions [5,14,19], and procedural position specification [10,14,31,41]. Keyframes can also be obtained from real moving objects with the use of rotoscoping. Techniques for the kinematic specification of cyclic motions such as walking or hopping have also been investigated [14,41].

2.2 Physically-Based Motion Synthesis

To satisfy the physical constraints of motion, animators have turned to physical simulation [3,7,16,38]. Simulation guarantees realistic, but not necessarily desirable, motion. Achieving the desired motion is a difficult control problem. Objects such as articulated figures (AFs) are controlled by internal torques applied at the joints. The *control problem* is to find the function of the torques over time that produces the desired motion.

Several methods of generating the required torque functions have been suggested. One method requires the user to specify torques directly [3,13,37,38]. It is in general difficult to come up with the necessary torques to perform desired motions through a process of trial and error. One need only observe a backhoe operator to see that this is true. An alternative is to use inverse dynamics to solve for the torques required to produce a known acceleration [6,8,16,17]. This approach is useful when it is desired to have a portion of an object follow a particular path, or to have an initial guess of the torques needed to perform a motion. One can also obtain the

[0]The financial assistance of the Natural Sciences and Engineering Research Council of Canada, and of the Information Technology Research Centre of Ontario, is gratefully acknowledged.

required torques by using the desired joint positions as set-points for closed-loop controllers [3,20]. This models robots controlled by position-servos, permitting kinematic control while still utilizing the equations of motion.

A solution to a specific inverse-dynamics problem can be encapsulated in a dedicated *controller* or *control procedure*. This method cleanly partitions the control from the dynamics equations. Although the concept has often been suggested in the literature, the construction of the required controller or control procedure has always been left to the animator or is constructed using *a priori* information, such as clinical data [8,16,41]. Many controllers have been carefully hand-engineered to solve specific problems. These include mechanical bipeds [26,28,35], human walking [8], six-legged robots [24], snakes [25], and one-legged hopping robots [30].

Existing controllers have thus far been carefully tuned to solve a specific problem. Consequently, they are not likely to be flexible, reusable, or optimal with respect to time and energy constraints. The state-controllers proposed in this paper seek to overcome these shortcomings.

2.3 Optimal Control Methods

Good solutions to the motion control problem have been achieved by viewing it as a problem in optimization. A motion can be formulated as a two-point boundary problem with the start and end points of the motion sequence being constraints in state space that must be met. An optimization function reflecting the control energy expended and time taken for the motion [1,7,40] is then minimized to produce the optimal solution (see Figure 1).

The method of *space-time constraints* by Witkin and Kass uses a variant of sequential quadratic programming to solve the optimization problem, and generates convincing motion [40]. The user provides expressions for the total kinetic energy of the object and must express all other constraints in a mathematical form. This is something that animators are unlikely to be adept in doing. The solution is also costly to compute. Brotman and Natravali [7] present a similar approach to solving the control problem, but make use of a different mathematical formulation. The same problems exist as for the method of space-time constraints. Neither paper suggests the possibility of saving a motion for future reuse. A generalization of these approaches would be to define a large set of optimal-control solutions in the form of a general control law.

3 State-Space Controllers

3.1 Overview

We now introduce the main contribution of this paper. A *state-space controller* (SSC) defines a set of control torques that guides an object to a specified goal from a large domain of initial configurations, in a fashion that optimizes time taken and energy expended. A goal is characterized by a set of destination states, and depending on the nature of this set, several classes of motion are possible. Simple motions include those with a stationary destination state. A non-stationary destination state will result in periodic motions such as hopping or walking. One can also define motions with goals consisting of many destination states. This captures motions in which the terminal velocities or positions of parts of the object are irrelevant. For example, in a race, it is irrelevant which part of the body crosses the finish line first. Lastly, "conditional" motion can be defined: given more than one destination state, perform the easiest motion.

While individual SSCs may define interesting motions in themselves, the real power of the approach lies in the ability to concatenate SSCs to create a composite motion. SSCs can also be concatenated with other motion-generation techniques such as motor programs and key-framing, as we shall see later. Consider the following example. Suppose Luxo (the jumping lamp, Figure 2) is to hop forward several times, take a long forward jump to miss a ditch, and then do a backflip out of elation of surviving. Given an appropriate set of controllers, a user can build (and view) an animation sequence by writing a script consisting of the desired sequence of controllers. Figure 3 depicts the interaction of controllers with an animation system.

The concatenation of SSCs may be specified in two ways. One way is to run each SSC to its conclusion or for a specified duration. The terminal state of this SSC will then become the starting state of the next SSC, as in the Luxo example above. An alternative approach is to specify *state-space breakpoints*, in which an SSC is associated with particular regions of state space. An object may thus have a complex interleaving of SSCs attached to it.

3.2 Motion through State-Space

The *state* of an object represents all the information required to specify the position and velocity of every point on the object. The *state space* of the object is the set of all possible states that the object can assume. The state of a moving ob-

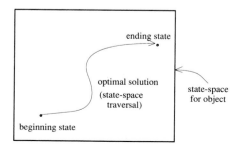

Figure 1: *Optimal-control motion synthesis.*

Figure 2: *The jumping lamp.*

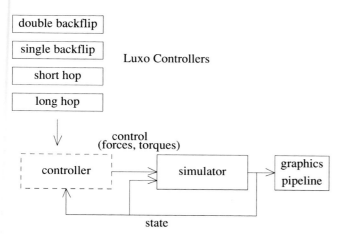

Figure 3: *Using state-space controllers.*

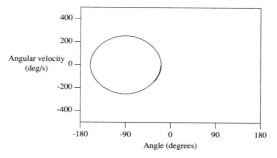

Figure 5: *Pendulum swing as represented in state space.*

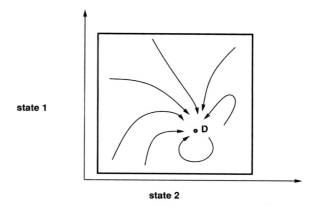

Figure 6: *A one boundary-point state-space controller.*

ject changes with respect to time. Consider a swinging pendulum, a simple articulated object (Figure 4). The state of a freely-swinging pendulum continuously changes with time under the force of gravity. Its angular velocity plotted with respect to time is a near-sinusoid, and likewise for the pendulum angle. When these two functions are combined to obtain the state, the resulting path through the state-space of the pendulum is the almost circular path shown in Figure 5. By exerting control torques, it is possible to influence the state-space trajectory taken by an articulated object. We can use this technique to guide an object toward a goal. This is the central principle underlying state-space controllers.

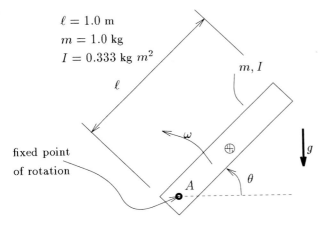

Figure 4: *The pendulum has mass m, length l, moment of inertia I, angular velocity ω; θ is the CCW angle from the positive x-axis, and g is the force of gravity.*

3.3 Specification and Concatenation

The motion to be executed by a controller is expressed in terms of a set of destination states for the object. The state transitions from an arbitrary start state to a destination state are optimized with respect to the time and energy taken to perform the motion, and can only use the internal torques that fall within the range of torques capable of being exerted by the object. The controller thus functions as a control law, which defines the optimal-control solutions to a one

boundary-point problem (the destination state), as shown in Figure 6. In this case, point D represents a destination state in a two-dimensional state-space. The arrows show some possible state-space paths that will be followed by the object for various initial states.

A controller is defined over a user-specified, bounded region of state-space called its *domain*. Figure 7 shows the regions of state space over which controllers A, B, and C are defined, as well as three respective destination states, D_a, D_b, and D_c. Let S_0 represent the initial state of the object. Suppose that while controller A guides the object toward D_a, it is desired to invoke controller B. Similarly, assume that it is next desired to change to controller C. The solid line in Figure 7 indicates one such set of changes, where S_1 and S_2 are the states at which the new controllers are invoked. The only constraints on S_1 and S_2 are that $S_1 \in \text{Domain}(A) \cap \text{Domain}(B)$ and $S_2 \in \text{Domain}(B) \cap \text{Domain}(C)$. Clearly, concatenation of controllers need not occur only at destination states.

3.4 Structure of Controllers

A controller is defined in a local co-ordinate system, and defines relative motions. Formally, a controller denotes a vector function $f : \mathcal{S} \to \mathcal{T}$, where $\mathcal{S}$ is a state space and $\mathcal{T}$ is a set of torque tuples. It is entirely possible to define procedural controllers based on motor programs or kinematic interpolation (see below). We shall focus our discussion on the automatic generation of controllers that solve one-point optimal-control problems.

In our current scheme, a continuous state-controller f is synthesized from a discrete table of torques in state space. An n-

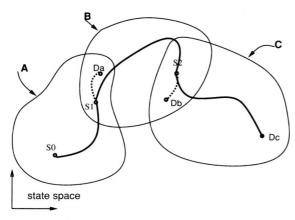

Figure 7: *Valid domains for exchanging controllers.*

dimensional volume forming the controller's domain is regularly subdivided into small n-dimensional cubes. Here n represents the number of dimensions of the object's state space, or alternatively how many numbers are required to specify the object's state. Table elements correspond to the corners of the small hypercubes. The torques provided by the tables are made continuous through n-linear interpolation in all dimensions of the object's state space (e.g., bilinear interpolation in two dimensions). Hierarchical or non-uniform sampling is advisable, and is planned. We expect to use better-quality reconstruction filters when we move to non-uniform sampling.

3.5 The Generation of Controllers

It is infeasible (and inefficient) to solve a one-point optimization problem by solving many instances of two-point problems. We instead employ a divide-and-conquer technique called *dynamic programming*. The principle of dynamic programming is illustrated in Figure 8. Suppose path AC is optimal. Then the optimal path from any state P on AC to state C is given by the subpath PC of AC. If a better alternative path had existed (as shown by the dashed line), the optimal path from A to C would contain this subpath. This property is true of any monotonically-increasing optimization function of object motion, such as time or expended energy.

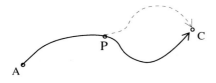

Figure 8: *The principle of dynamic programming.*

Figure 9 illustrates how dynamic programming can be applied to the generation of state-space controllers. Suppose optimal solutions are known for states located in region 1, which contains destination state D. To calculate the optimal solutions for states located in region 2, we solve a local optimization problem to get from the current state to the edge of region 1. This provides a composite optimal solution for both regions. Clearly, then, an appropriate strategy for controller generation is to work backward from D, radiating the solutions outward.

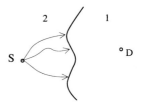

Figure 9: *Dynamic programming applied to an SSC.*

A more detailed picture of the local optimization problem to be solved is shown in Figure 10. θ_n and ω_n are the angular position and angular velocity of a link of an articulated figure. The quantization intervals of the table entries are given by q1 and q2. The figure shows the possible state-space trajectories as projected onto the $\theta_n \omega_n$ plane of state space. The trajectory taken from state **S** depends on the angular acceleration α_n, which in turn depends on the control value (torque vector) contained in the table element corresponding to point **S**. The *local optimization problem* is to find the control value at **S** that minimizes the optimization function.

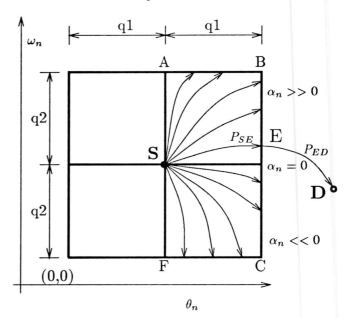

Figure 10: *The effect of various torques applied at* **S**.

The optimization function we use is given by two terms:

$$f_{opt}(P_{SD}) = t_{P_{SD}} + \int_0^{t_{P_{SD}}} KT(t) \, dt. \qquad (1)$$

The first term represents the time taken to perform the motion, while the second term measures the energy expended [1,40]. P_{SD} represents a path through state space from an initial state S to a destination D, and $t_{P_{SD}}$ represents the time taken to traverse this path. K is a user-defined vector of constants that specifies the time/energy tradeoff, and $T(t)$ represents the applied torques (control values). A small value of K will minimize the *time* taken to perform the motion. A large value minimizes the *energy* used to perform the motion. Typical values for K depend on the magnitude of the forces and torques capable of being exerted by the object. For our pendulum example, a value of $K = 1$ implies we are willing to exchange one second of time taken in reaching the destination state for the "energy" expended to exert a torque of 1 Newton-metre for one second. Our "energy" term is more properly a measure of the effort required to perform a motion. Other objective functions are possible.

It is required to find the torque vector at S that produces a state-space path P_{SD} such that $f_{opt}(P_{SD})$ is minimized. The solution we currently employ consists of calculating $f_{opt}(P_{SD})$ from a set of samples of torque vectors and then choosing the vector that results in the minimal value of the optimization function. The samples are chosen by uniformly sampling the space of torque vectors (since this space is bounded). This is admittedly a slow, brute-force approach whose sole virtue is that it works. For each sample torque vector, the state-space trajectory is calculated by simulating the motion of the object. The trajectory is followed until the object enters a region of state space in which the value of the optimization function is already known. For the path P_{SD} this is indicated as point E in Figure 10.

Once the exit state is known, the value of the optimization function can be determined from the equation

$$f_{opt}(P_{SD}) = t_{P_{SE}} + \int_0^{t_{P_{SE}}} KT(t)\, dt + f_{opt}(P_{ED}). \quad (2)$$

For the local optimization problem, the values of the optimization function are assumed to be known at neighbouring points (points A, B, C, and F in Figure 10) and are linearly interpolated between the points. The first two terms in Eq. 2 are simply $f_{opt}(P_{SE})$ (Eq. 1), while the last term represents the value interpolated between the values of the optimization function at B and C. Several iterations of controller computation are required, because the values of the optimization function at neighbouring points may be unknown for the first iteration. In Figure 10, this means that the computation of a control value for state **S** is only accurate if the values of the optimization function are accurately known at points A, B, C, and F. It is difficult to sequence local optimizations such that each local optimization always uses accurate information. It is simpler to approximate this order and repeat this for several iterations. For each iteration, the value of the optimization function will decrease. When the maximum such change is less than a user-specified value, the solution is assumed to be complete. An upper limit can also be placed on the number of iterations to use. Technically, this approach only yields a local minimum, but the local minimum found has always been satisfactory.

3.6   The Size of State Space

While generating controllers for objects with few degrees of freedom is feasible, in our current implementation the number of state-space dimensions becomes a problem for more complex articulated figures. Both the time-complexity of the algorithm and the size of the state-space control table are exponentially dependent on the number of state-space dimensions. The size of the table is given by $n_s^{d_s}$, where d_s is the number of state-space dimensions (typically twice the number of degrees of freedom since each degree of freedom has a position and velocity), and n_s is the number of samples per state-space dimension. The time-complexity of the algorithm is given by $O(n_s^{d_s} n_t^{d_t})$, where d_t is the number of torques or forces to be applied, and n_t is the number of samples per torque or force. The problem arises because state space is defined as a large bounding hypercube that is uniformly sampled. There are two main aspects to the problem. First, the bounding hypercube is almost always far too large. A user should be allowed to eliminate irrelevant areas of state space. Second, uniform sampling is far from optimal. The sampling rate close to the destination should be high, but the rate should fall off dramatically with "distance" from the destination. Sampling artifacts do not seem to affect the stability of the controller significantly. If the interpolation of control values between table entries causes the object to drift from the optimal path to the destination state, the controller corrects itself because the control values being applied are always computed based on the current state. This allows the controller to function properly, even if the object's state changes suddenly as a result of a collision involving the object. There is a considerable amount of interesting research to be performed in studying the placement and frequency of control-table values in state space.

4   Dynamics Formulation

To embed state-space controllers effectively in our animation system (see below) it is necessary to perform physical simulations quickly. To date, we have focused our formulation on the planar forward dynamics of articulated figures (AFs). The extension to fully three-dimensional articulation is straightforward. (It involves adding a Coriolis-force term and changing moments of inertia from scalars to tensors so that the moment of inertia for a link becomes dependent on the current axis of rotation.) We assume that AFs have joints and links that can be represented as a tree, with one link serving as the root link. A link can have any number of child links, which are connected by a rotating joint.

The recursive Newtonian dynamics formulation we use is well known [4], and is based on two fundamental equations that balance the forces and moments exerted on each link. Ultimately, we solve for the linear acceleration of the root link and the angular acceleration for all the links with respect to the root link. The accelerations are then numerically integrated with an adaptive time step to determine the new velocity and position of the links. What is important about our approach is that, unlike most previous implementations of dynamics formulations, the equations of motion are formed symbolically, directly from the basic masses, forces, and inertial properties of the object. This is very useful representation. We have written a *dynamics compiler* which can compile a brief physical description of the AF into the desired equations of motion. The equations generated are of the form $Ax = b$ where A and b are dependent on the physical properties and configuration of the links, and x represents the vector of unknown accelerations. The output of the dynamics compiler gives the symbolic value of each of the elements of the matrix A and the vector b. In the implementation the values of A and b are output as lines of 'C' code so that the equations of motion can be compiled and placed in a library. This makes our system more portable, and it allows us to separate the equations of motion from the remainder of the system.

Special-purpose motions could also be compiled and placed into this library. A symbolic representation of the equations of motion also allows a programmer or a compiler to simplify the expressions to be computed.

For objects containing about 12 joints or fewer [36], the equations of motion are best solved using LU-decomposition with back-substitution [29] once the values of A and b are calculated. This solution has a complexity of $O(n^3)$ for an AF with n links. $O(n)$ methods do exist, but in practice they are only useful for AFs with many degrees of freedom [2,12].

Almost all interesting animations of objects involve collisions with the environment and have other constraints on the motion of the object, such as joint limits and friction. We use springs and dampers to implement collisions and joint limits [13,16,39].

We have developed an animation system that incorporates the above dynamics formulation, and in which controllers can be generated offline and subsequently scripted for use in realtime animation. Figure 11 depicts our animation system, called *Mosys*.

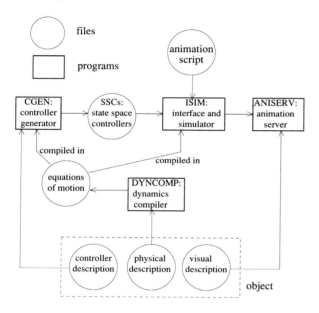

Figure 11: *Mosys implementation.*

5 Examples

We now consider several examples of the generation of state-space controllers using Mosys. The generation of controllers is entirely separate from their use, and are usually computed offline. Once computed, they allow realtime animation of the objects for which they were constructed.

5.1 Periodic Motions

A periodic motion, such as a link swinging or Luxo-lamp hopping corresponds to a cycle in the object's state-space. A controller that produces a periodic motion is created by specifying a destination state with non-zero velocities. As the controller guides the object along the state-space cycle, the object performs a periodic motion corresponding to the states

passed through along the way. One of the many possible periodic, swinging motions of a frictionless, free-swinging pendulum is shown by the state-space cycle in Figure 5.

Motions such as walking or repeated hopping can be produced by making the object follow a cyclic path through state space. In this case the state representing the horizontal distance denotes the distance to complete one cycle. The value of this state increases until the object lands, at which point the state wraps back to the starting position. This allows a repeated motion to be described in terms of a state-space cycle, which can be modelled by a state-space controller. This idea was motivated by the fact that the spinal cord of animals can produce a periodic sequence of control signals resulting in periodic walking motions [15,32].

5.2 Pendulum

The pendulum has only one degree of freedom and therefore has a two-dimensional state space consisting of the angle and the angular speed (see Figure 4). The link is free to rotate in both directions (without friction) and has the force of gravity acting on it. The pendulum also has a motor or muscle located at the point of rotation that can exert a control torque on the pendulum. It is easy to represent the state-space path of a pendulum using a plot, which helps to illustrate how general SSCs guide objects to a destination.

SSCs with various destinations have been generated to control the motion of a pendulum. Figure 12 describes an SSC with a destination state of $\theta = 0$ deg, $\omega = 0$ deg/s. Applied torques are constrained to the range -10 to 10 Nm, and pendulums cannot rotate at absolute angular speeds of more than 500 degrees per second. The state-space dimensions of θ and ω are divided into 36 and 21 discrete intervals respectively, yielding SSCs with a total of 756 entries. Figure 13 summarizes the pendulum SSCs that were generated.

```
# controller for a single link
# controller description commands:
#      ssd <name> <min> <max> <steps>
#      torq <name> <tmin> <tmax> <tsteps> <Ktorq>
#      dest <state>

dyn link1              # dynamics equations

ssd omega -500.0 500.0 21
ssd angle -180 170 36
wrap angle
torq torque -10.0 10.0 11 0.1
dest angle=0 omega=0
```

Figure 12: *Specification for pendulum SSCs*

name	destination state		generation
	θ (deg)	ω (deg/s)	time (s)
A	0	0	381
B	120	0	452
C	-120	0	341
D	0	300	460
E	-120	-300	459
F	160	250	454

Figure 13: *Six pendulum controllers. Controllers were computed on a Sun 3/60 workstation.*

Figures 14 and 16 depict some state-space plots of pendulum motion under control of the SSCs. The scales used for the state-space plots in are as in Figure 5. The curve connecting each starting state and the destination state represents the state-space path that the pendulum takes when guided by the SSC. The right and left boundaries of the state-space plots are connected, giving each plot a cylindrical topology.

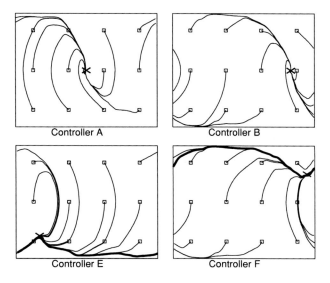

Controller A   Controller B

Controller E   Controller F

Figure 14: *State-space trajectories followed using various SSCs (C and D omitted). The destination state is given by an encircled X, while some sample start states are given by the small squares.*

Controllers D, E, and F define periodic motions because their destination states specify non-zero angular velocities (see above). As seen in Figure 14, these controllers eventually drive the pendulum toward their respective state-space cycles, from all initial states. The state-space cycles are indicated in the figure with a thick line.

The six different SSCs form a library of motion commands for the pendulum. Figure 15 shows an animation script used to 'animate' the pendulum, assuming that one would want to endow a pendulum with a 'muscle' that can exert a torque at the joint. Figure 16 depicts the resulting motion.

The animation begins with controller B being used to drive the pendulum to the destination state for controller B. The point 'sB' in Figure 16 shows the point at which controller B is invoked, and point 'dB' denotes the destination state for controller B. After 0.4 seconds of proceeding toward dB, controller A is invoked for 0.7 seconds. Before it reaches dA (the destination state for controller A), controller D is invoked for 0.6 seconds. The remainder of the animation script consists of similar exchanges of controllers.

While the state of the pendulum is continuous over time, torques (and hence accelerations) are discontinuous at the point of controller exchange. Such discontinuities might detract from the realism of the resulting motion because real actuators (muscles or motors) cannot instantaneously change their applied torque or force. A simple solution to this problem is to apply a slew limitation to the control values. This would limit the absolute rate of change of the control value,

```
state   link -135,350     # starting state
swapcon link conB.ctab    # invoke controller B
sim 0.4                   # simulate 0.4 seconds
swapcon link conA.ctab    # invoke controller A
sim 0.7                   # simulate 0.7 seconds
swapcon link conD.ctab    # invoke controller D
sim 0.6                   # simulate 0.6 seconds
swapcon link conE.ctab    # invoke controller E
sim 0.4                   # simulate 0.4 seconds
swapcon link conC.ctab    # invoke controller C
sim 0.4                   # simulate 0.4 seconds
swapcon link conF.ctab    # invoke controller F
sim 0.7                   # simulate 0.7 seconds
```

Figure 15: *A pendulum animation script.*

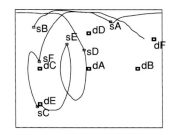

Figure 16: *State-space trajectory of pendulum.*

resulting in $C^{(2)}$ continuous motion.

6   The Self-Parking Car

We now consider the design of an SSC that is to parallel-park a car on the street as shown in Figure 17. The car has five state-space dimensions shown in Figure 18. The destination state for the car is given by the dotted line in Figure 17, with the car being at rest. The domain of the controller is marked with a dashed line. The reference point of the car, located between the front wheels, must remain within this region. The animator can place the car anywhere within the domain of the SSC and have it park in a fashion similar to people(!). The walls in Figure 17 are additional obstacles to be avoided.

The car has two control variables: ω_{st}, the rate at which the steering wheel turns, and α_w, the angular acceleration or deceleration of the front wheels of the car.

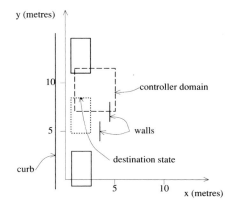

Figure 17: *The street (non-contact parking only).*

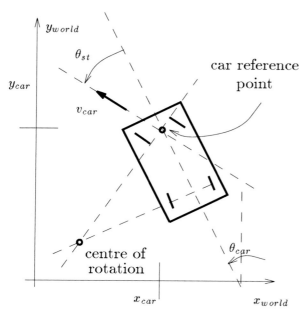

Figure 18: *State-space dimensions for a car.*

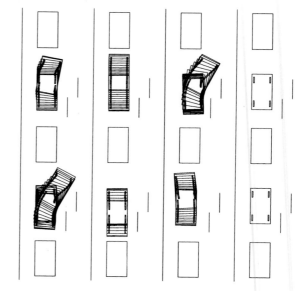

Figure 19: *Animation using the car-parking SSC.*

The final SSC for the car has 13250 states. All table entries that correspond to collision states are removed while the state-space is being generated; thus the SSC algorithm knows these states are out of the controller domain. Some results of the car SSC in operation are shown in a sequence of frames in Figure 19. The position of the car is shown every 0.3 seconds. The parked cars on the right are used to provide a reference showing the destination state for the car. In all six cases shown, the car is placed in the initial state at rest, but the wheels are oriented differently. The car SSC is then invoked to park the car. The bottom-left and top-right cars are especially interesting. In these cases the cars back up past the desired destination and then drive forward to straighten the wheels.

7 Luxo

In our next example, Luxo will perform a sequence of interesting motions, such as jumps and flips. Because we use uniform sampling of the state space to generate a continuous controller, two practical problems arise in trying to create a jump or flip controller for Luxo. The first is the size of the state space. As illustrated in Figure 20, Luxo has 5 degrees of freedom when in the air, and thus has a 10-dimensional state space. The second is that many of the most important states during a jump occur during takeoff and landing, when only one edge of the lamp's base is in contact with the ground. Since the state space is sampled uniformly without paying special attention to interactions with the environment (like the floor), collisions may not be properly sampled. The problem is illustrated in Figure 21, which shows the states of successive table entries. The second state has its base protruding through the floor, and would therefore be discarded from the SSC table (removing it from the controller's domain). The state that is really of interest is the third one, with the left side of the base touching the ground. Both of the above problems serve to show that our choice of uniform sampling is some-

what crude. Fortunately, the remedy for the case of Luxo is not difficult.

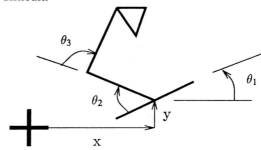

Figure 20: *Degrees of freedom for a jumping lamp.*

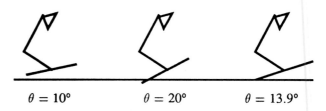

$\theta = 10°$ $\theta = 20°$ $\theta = 13.9°$

Figure 21: *The collision sampling problem.*

The problem of state-space size can be solved by breaking up canonical Luxo motions into two pieces: airborne motion, and motion on the ground (i.e., takeoff/landing motion). It is easy to write motor programs (i.e., procedural functions of torques over time) to make Luxo perform a flip or jump. It is very much more difficult to do a correct landing. We thus use motor programs for the airborne motions, and a controller to guide Luxo to a safe landing and to prepare it for the next motion. All airborne motions begin from a distinguished starting state, which coincides with the destination state of the "landing" controller. Thus motions based on motor programs can be easily concatenated with motions based on SSCs. The "landing" controller only has to deal with 2 degrees of freedom, or a four-dimensional state space, which is quite feasible.

The dynamics compiler was used to generate the equations of motion for Luxo. Some code was added to the resulting dynamics procedure in order to model collisions with the environment, consisting of the floor and a set of stairs. Four motions were created for the Luxo animation: a forward jump, a single back flip, a double backflip, and a single backflip down a step. Once controllers and motor programs for the individual motions have been generated, scripting various animations is a simple exercise. Figure 22 is a sample back-flip from the animation. See also the photographs at the end of this paper.

Figure 22: *A Luxo back-flip*

A brief comparison with previous animations of Luxo is informative. The *Luxo Jr.* video [22] by Pixar was produced entirely using keyframing. The motion was synthesized manually and succeeds in looking realistic because of the formidable artistic talent of the animators. The repertoire of motions that Luxo performs in the video is not large or complex; most motions are performed with the base on the ground. Witkin and Kass obtain a jumping motion for Luxo by formulating it as a two-boundary-point optimization problem [40]. The results produced are impressive, but their formulation appears to have a problem with the takeoff and landing occurring with only one edge of the base in contact with the ground. Their Luxo jump sequence has a takeoff and landing with a flat base. From our experience with the torques necessary to make Luxo perform a jump, we are convinced that a jump with a flat base on takeoff and landing is very difficult to perform and would therefore not be a natural mode of locomotion for a lamp!

8 Conclusions

We have introduced a new approach to reusable motion synthesis based on state-space controllers. The controllers produced are unique in that they are used to control the simulation of the object with no *a priori* knowledge of the object or how it should move, apart from a destination goal. The forward dynamics of articulated figures is automatically generated from a basic physical description of the object.

While the use of controllers in physically-based motion synthesis is very encouraging, there are several aspects that require more thought. First, we wish to carefully compare controller response to the actual optimal solution. This may allow us to develop error-control mechanisms for controller generation. Second, we would like to create hierarchical or distributed controller structures, in which more "abstract" controllers actually manage lower-level controllers in response to events in the system. Third, a controller is cur-

rently quite dependent on the specific physical parameters of an object. To what extent can controllers themselves be parameterized by, for example, interpolating between similar controllers? Fourth, faster controller-generation techniques are required. Fifth, better controller sampling and reconstruction techniques are needed. Sixth, we wish to develop a better user interface for scripting controllers into significant animations.

References

[1] R. Alexander. The gaits of bipedal and quadrupedal animals. *Int. Journal of Robotics Research*, Summer 1984.

[2] W. W. Armstrong. Recursive solution to the equations of motion of an n-link manipulator. *Proc. 5th World Congress Theory Mach. Mechanisms*, volume 2, 1343–1346, 1979.

[3] W.W. Armstrong, M. Green, and R. Lake. Near-real-time control of human figure models. *IEEE Computer Graphics and Applications*, 7(6):52–61, June 1987.

[4] H. Asada and J.-J.E. Slotine. *Robot Analysis and Control*. John Wiley and Sons, 1986.

[5] N.I. Badler, K.H. Manoocherhri, and G. Walters. Articulated figure positioning by multiple constraints. *IEEE Computer Graphics and Applications*, 7(6):28–38, June 1987.

[6] R. Barzel and A.H. Barr. A modeling system based on dynamic constraints. *Proc. of SIGGRAPH'88 (Aug. 1988). ACM Computer Graphics 22,4*, 179–188.

[7] L.S. Brotman and A.N. Netravali. Motion interpolation by optimal control. *Proc. of SIGGRAPH'88 (Aug. 1988). ACM Computer Graphics 22,4*, 309–315.

[8] A. Bruderlin. Goal-directed, dynamic animation of bipedal locomotion. Technical report, Simon Fraser University, 1988.

[9] N. Burtnyk and M. Wein. Computer generated keyframe animation. *Journal of the Society of Motion Picture and Television Engineers*, 80(3):149–53, March 1971.

[10] T. Calvert, J. Chapman, and A. Patla. Aspects of the kinematic simulation of human movement. *IEEE Computer Graphics and Applications*, 41–50, Nov. 1982.

[11] C. Csuri. Real time film animation. *IEEE Convention Digest*, 42–3, March 1971.

[12] R. Featherstone. The calculation of robot dynamics using articulated body inertias. *Int. Journal of Robotics Research*, 2(1):13–30, Spring 1983.

[13] D.R. Forsey and J. Wilhelms. Techniques for interactive manipulation of articulated bodies using dynamic analysis. *Proc. of Graphics Interface*, 8–15, 1988.

[14] M. Girard. Interactive design of computer-animated legged animal motion. *IEEE Computer Graphics and Applications*, 7(6):39–51, June 1987.

[15] S. Grillner. Locomotion in vertebrates: Central mechanisms and reflex interaction. *Physiological Reviews*, 55:247–304, 1975.

[16] Paul M. Isaacs and Michael F. Cohen. Controlling dynamic simulation with kinematic constraints, behaviour functions and inverse dynamics. *Proc. of SIGGRAPH '87. ACM Computer Graphics 21,4*, 215–224.

[17] P.M. Isaacs and M.F. Cohen. Mixed methods for complex kinematic constraints in dynamic figure animation. *The Visual Computer*, 4:296–305, 1988.

[18] D.H. Kochanek and R.H. Bartels. Interpolating splines for keyframe animation. *Graphics Interface*, 41–42, 1984.

[19] J. U. Korein and N. I. Badler. Techniques for generating the goal-directed motion of articulated structures. *IEEE Computer Graphics and Applications*, 71–81, Nov. 1982.

[20] B.C. Kuo. *Automatic Control Systems*. Prentice-Hall, Inc., 1987.

[21] J. Lasseter. Principles of traditional animation applied to 3-d computer animation. *Proc. of SIGGRAPH'87 (July 1987). ACM Computer Graphics 21,4.*, 35–44.

[22] J. Lasseter and W. Reeves. Luxo jr. Pixar Video, 1986.

[23] N. Magnenat-Thalmann and D. Thalmann. *Computer Animation: Theory and Practice*. Springer-Verlag, 1985.

[24] R. B. McGhee and G. I. Iswandhi. Adaptive locomotion of a multilegged robot over rough terrain. *IEEE Transactions on System, Man, and Cybernetics*, 176–182, April 1979.

[25] G.S.P. Miller. The motion dynamics of snakes and worms. *Proc. of SIGGRAPH'88 (Aug. 1988). ACM Computer Graphics 22,4*, 169–178.

[26] H. Miura and I. Shimoyama. Dynamic walk of a biped. *Int. Journal of Robotics Research*, 60–74, Summer 1984.

[27] T. J. O'Donnel and Arthur J. Olsen. Gramps - a graphical interpreter for real-time interactive three-dimensional picture editing and animation. 1981.

[28] K. Ogo, A. Ganse, and I. Kato. Quasi dynamic walking of biped walking machine aiming at completion of steady walking. *Third Symposium on Theory and Practice of Robots and Manipulators*, 340–356, Sept. 1978.

[29] W.H. Press, B.P. Flannery, Saul A. Teukolsky, and William T. Vetterling. *Numerical Recipes*. Cambridge University Press, 1986.

[30] M.H. Raibert. *Legged robots that balance*. Artificial Intelligence series. MIT Press, Cambridge MA, 1985.

[31] C. Reynolds. Computer animation with scripts and actors. *Proc. of SIGGRAPH'81.*, 1981.

[32] M. L. Shik and G. N. Orlovskii. Neurophysiology of a locomotor automatism. *Physiological Reviews*, 56:465–501, 1976.

[33] S. Steketee and N.I. Badler. Parametric keyframe interpolation incorporating kinetic adjustment and phrasing control. *Proc. of SIGGRAPH'85 (July 1985). ACM Computer Graphics 19,3.*

[34] D. Sturman. Interactive keyframe animation of 3-d articulated models. *Graphics Interface*, 35–40, 1984.

[35] M. Townsend and A. Seirig. Effect of model complexity and gait criteria on the synthesis of bipedal locomotion. *IEEE Transactions on Biomedical Engineering*, 433–444, November 1973.

[36] M. W. Walker and D. E. Orin. Efficient dynamic computer simulation of robotic mechanisms. *Journal of Dynamic Systems, Measurement, and Control*, 205–211, Sept. 1982.

[37] J. Wilhelms. Virya: A motion control editor for kinematic and dynamic animation. *Proc. Graphics Interface 86*, 141–146. Morgan Kaufman, May 1986.

[38] J. Wilhelms, M. Moore, and R. Skinner. Dynamic animation: interaction and control. *The Visual Computer*, 4(6):283–295, 1988.

[39] J. Wilhelms. Using dynamic analysis for realistic animation of articulated bodies. *IEEE Computer Graphics and Applications*, 7(6):12–27, June 1987.

[40] A. Witkin and M. Kass. Spacetime constraints. *Proc. of SIGGRAPH'88 (Aug. 1988). ACM Computer Graphics 22,4*, 159–168, 1988.

[41] D. Zeltzer. Motor control techniques for figure animation. *IEEE Computer Graphics and Applications*, 53–60, Nov. 1982.

Performance-Driven Facial Animation

Lance Williams

Advanced Technology Group
Apple Computer, Inc.
20705 Valley Green Drive
Cupertino, CA 95014

ABSTRACT

As computer graphics technique rises to the challenge of rendering lifelike performers, more lifelike performance is required. The techniques used to animate robots, arthropods, and suits of armor, have been extended to flexible surfaces of fur and flesh. Physical models of muscle and skin have been devised.   But more complex databases and sophisticated physical modeling do not directly address the performance problem. The gestures and expressions of a human actor are not the solution to a dynamic system. This paper describes a means of acquiring the expressions of real faces, and applying them to computer-generated faces. Such an "electronic mask" offers a means for the traditional talents of actors to be flexibly incorporated in digital animations. Efforts in a similar spirit have resulted in servo-controlled "animatrons," high-technology puppets, and CG puppetry [1].   The manner in which the skills of actors and puppeteers as well as animators are accommodated in such systems may point the way for a more general incorporation of human nuance into our emerging computer media.

The ensuing description is divided into two major subjects: the construction of a highly-resolved human head model with photographic texture mapping, and the concept demonstration of a system to animate this model by tracking and applying the expressions of a human performer.

Cr Categories and Subject Descriptors: I.3.7 [Computer Graphics]:   Three Dimensional Graphics and Realism--Animation. I.3.5 [Computer Graphics]: Computational Geometry and Object Modeling -- Curve, surface, solid, and object representations. J.5 [Computer Applications]: Arts and Humanities--Arts, fine and performing.

General Terms: Algorithms, Design.

Additional Keywords and Phrases: Animation, Facial Expression, Texture Mapping, Motion Tracking, 3D Digitization.

BACKGROUND

The seminal work of Parke [2] involved the photogrammetric digitization of human faces and expressions, and the creation of a parametric model that used local interpolations, geometric transformations, and mapping techniques to drive the features of a computer-animated face. Demonstrations of the face in action included lip-synchronized speech.

Platt and Badler [3],[4] applied physical modeling techniques to the parametric face problem. Once again, the goal was to drive the face at a higher level of control. Simulation of muscles in this paper established the use of deformation functions, rather than interpolation, to animate a face.

Brennan [5], working with hand-digitized 2D vector faces, implemented a kind of automatic caricature by exaggerating the differences of individual subjects from a prestored "norm."

Burson and Schneider [6] established a mapping correspondence between facial features in different photographs, a mapping defined by hand-digitizing key points of correspondence. Changes in shape and texture between one pair of photographs could then be used to map changes in shape and texture to a third. This process has been used to artificially "age" the photographs of missing children (that is, to estimate an image of the same child some years hence). Similar mappings have been used by Burson and Kramlich (Face Software, Inc., NY., NY.) to interpolate faces and create composites.

Concurrently, experiments at New York Institute of Technology involved mapping 2D animated features onto 3D characters (James Blinn and the author, 1976), and mapping of live-action video faces onto 3D "masks" (3D face surface models in which the eye and mouth regions have been smoothed over, so as not to interfere with the moving lips and blinking eyes of the mapped video). Live-action mapping was first essayed by Duane Palyka and the author in 1977, and was applied by Paul Heckbert in the NYIT videos, "Adventures in Success," and "3DV" (1984).   At the same time, NYIT researcher Tom Brigham was doing extensive work with screen-space (2D) interpolation of texture and form. Brigham's "shape interpolation" was applied to faces, among other subjects, and must be considered an influence on this work. One conclusion of these experiments was that much of the detail and realism of the faces depicted was simple surface texture.   A face model like Parke's would be much more powerful and convincing with photographic mapping, and perhaps more individual and personable, as well.   The photographic mapping of [7] illustrates the power of texture alone, without surface shading of any kind.

An extended, expressive facial animation was essayed by Phillipe Bergeron, Pierre LaChapelle, and Daniel Langlois in 1985, in their short, "Tony de Peltrie"[8]. Photogrammetrics as in [2] were used to digitize both human expressions and the neutral features of a stylized model. Then, scaled differences of the various human expressions from the "neutral" human expression, were applied to the neutral stylized model. This basic cross-mapping scheme, as in [5], requires a norm to apply the mapping. Since the mapped differences are scaled, "caricature" (this time in 3D) is straightforward.

The most recent wrinkle in facial animation is Keith Waters' application of tailored local deformation functions analogous to musculature in animating a neutral face definition [9]. This technique was adopted by the Pixar animation team to control the patch-defined baby face of "Tin Toy" [10].

The formulations described in this paper are an attempt to extend the mapping of texture and expression to continuous motion mapping. Using current technologies, both human features and human performance can, in the opinion of the author, be acquired, edited, and abstracted with sufficient detail and precision to serve dramatic purposes.

Figure 1. Processed model with mosaic texture map

CONSTRUCTING THE MODEL

Dancer Annette White, a personal friend of the author, was a featured performer in Patrice Regnier's RUSH dance company which performed at SIGGRAPH in 1985. Her head was cast in plaster by Long Island sculptor Val Kupris, and the surface of the plaster head digitized at Cyberware, Inc. [11]. A number of conventional color 35mm photos of Annette were taken at this time by Nancy Burson of Face Software, Inc., with the intent of creating a complete composite photograph (in cylindrical projection) of Annette's head to match the scanned relief data of the plaster cast. Face Software shared an interest in developing electronic mask technology, and cooperated in the initial test of the model. They were able to apply their mapping techniques to warp sections of the multiple photos to the range data acquired from scanning the plaster head. To facilitate this process, the 16-bit range data was compressed to eight bits, and a Sobel filter applied. This "edge enhancement" filtering brought out the important features (edges of the lips, corners of the eyes) from

the otherwise ghostly range image. The mapping, based on a triangular mesh, is shown applied to the model in figure 1. Below the two projections of the model in the photo are the composite texture map, produced by Face Software, and an eight-bit compression of the range image after Sobel filtering, to the right. (The black regions in the filtered range image are the result of a color map artifact; they should be white.) A kerchief is worn about the head in this texture map. A shading discontinuity between photographic sections is visible in the composite map on the left.

Cyberware had been sent a plaster cast of Annette's head, and sent back a tape with the digitized surface data, scanned four times. Data were in the form of 16-bit integers defining a mesh surface in a cylindrical coordinate system, each entry a radius indexed by phi (azimuth) and Y. The mesh consisted of 512 columns of samples in phi, by 256 rows in Y. The mesh was in fine shape to serve as a map with which to register the photographic texture, but in the meantime, required some additional work to serve as a satisfactory 3D model.

The usual fashion in which Cyberware displayed digitized data, at the time this work was undertaken, was as a faceted model. Missing data -- data obscured from the sensor by occlusion of the projected laser line -- was mapped to the center of the Y axis, and was in most cases invisible. If the data were Gouraud shaded in a straightforward fashion, the missing samples would severely impact the visible ones, by clobbering the computed surface normals. In order to make smooth shading and texture mapping possible, it was necessary to refine the model: to "heal shut" the missing data, by interpolating the surface across neighboring samples. It was moreover desirable to apply a certain amount of data smoothing to suppress spurious texture, and to use larger local neighborhoods of samples to estimate surface normals. Such processing of the digitized surface, very similar to image processing, proved essential for subsequent mapping and shading. An outline of the surface processing steps follows.

Healing Shut the Missing Data

Missing data is marked, in the Cyberware format, by a reserved "Z" value. The first step in surface processing is to restore surface continuity, a prerequisite for many subsequent operations. The scanner data is copied into a floating point array with missing values set to 0.0, and a second floating point array, a matte, is set to 1.0 where valid data exists, and 0.0 elsewhere. In the vicinity of 0.0 matte values, a small blurring kernel is applied to both the matte and the surface. Where the matte value increases (due to the blur) above a threshold, the surface sample is replaced by the blurred surface divided by the blurred matte. Filtering is recursively applied until no matte values are below threshold. Thus, the missing data are replaced by smooth neighborhood estimates, that gradually grow together. An implementation of this basic general scheme was coded so that the smooth replacement regions could "grow outward" slightly, smoothing the correctly-acquired data at the boundaries. All iterations of the "healing" process were visible, and the matte threshold, outward creep, and blur kernel could be varied for different results. Practically speaking, the process worked well for the small regions of missing data on the digitized face. It could not be expected to perform well for missing regions much larger than the blur kernels used. For this reason, a more detailed discussion of the filtering algorithm would not be justified. For future work, the methods of [12] are preferred.

Hysteresis Filtering

In many types of data acquisition, noise at the scale of the sampling interval is particularly bothersome. Special

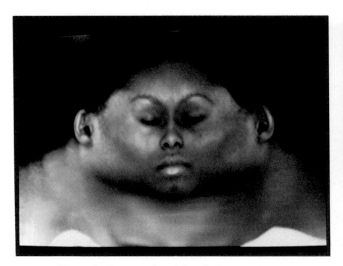

Figure 2. Processed peripheral photograph.

Figure 3. Sobel-filtered range image warped into a rage.

techniques for removing "salt and pepper" noise from imagery have been adopted for many purposes. A typical model will dampen high-amplitude sample-frequency noise in a nonlinear way. For the filtering used in the head model, a smooth estimate of the surface at a point was computed by a 3x3 blur kernel with unity gain and 0.0 as the center sample coefficient. If the estimate differed from the center sample by greater than a threshold amount, the center sample was replaced by the estimate. Such a filter is occasionally called a Tukey filter, or a "hysteresis" filter (because it modifies the data only when the threshold is exceeded).

Subjectively, this filtering process smoothed out a number of glitches and spurious details in the surface of the face. It performed equally well on small bubbles in the plaster cast and on data that, for whatever reason, seemed somewhat rougher than the plaster.

Low-Pass Filtering

By filtering and downsampling data, it is possible to trade precision for resolution directly. This tradeoff occurs in a continuous way as data are low-pass filtered. The reduced bandwidth of the surface is accompanied by an increase in precision for each of the samples. Where the data to be estimated are more bandlimited than sources of noise in the system (where the signal is pink, and the noise is white), low-pass filtering will increase the signal-to-noise ratio.

A weak low-pass filter was applied to the cylindrical R (range) coordinates of the data, before conversion of the surface from $R(\emptyset,Y)$ to $X(u,v)$, $Y(u,v)$, and $Z(u,v)$. The skin seemed smoother after filtering, and faint striations visible in the surface normals (assumed to be scanner artifacts) diminished.

Filtering the Normals

In fact, surface normals are extremely sensitive indicators of perturbations in the digitized surface, including all noise and artifacts. The usual methods of computing surface normals from polygon meshes are too local for imperfect data so closely spaced. It is reasonable to smooth such local normal estimates, or to use normals of a surface somewhat smoother than the one actually displayed. In this way, satisfactory shading can be achieved without smoothing features from the surface.

When filtering is applied to the range data in the cylindrical mesh, artifacts occur at the poles, where sample aliasing is greatest (because the laser line may project very steeply). Because the spacing of the samples is far from uniform in 3D space, such filtering is very anisotropic. On the other hand, filtering the components of the derived normals is much more expensive, and requires special care. Some normals may vanish (magnitudes go to zero) after filtering; all normals require re-unitization.

Some polar artifacts were tolerated in the range-filtering stage, with the intent of completing the top of the head with a "scalp mesh." This makes sense because the texture, as well as the model, would otherwise be very poorly resolved on top of the head. Despite the difficulties imposed by the "singularity," the polar map is a very convenient representation for interacting with the head model. It provided the basis for interactive texture mapping, and interactive setup of expressions.

Registering Cylindrical Texture

Most of the model processing steps described could be performed automatically. The most tedious process described so far was that performed by Face Software: taking the photographs necessary to completely record the subject's head, and then painstakingly registering the mosaic of photos to the model range data. Ideally, this step, too, would be automatic. A scanner which simultaneously captured R, G, B, and range, would simplify "mask" acquisition greatly. Such a scanner has only recently become commercially available[11].

In order to generalize the texturing process, as well as to exercise the "virtual muscles" expected to drive the face, an alternate method was devised. The first step was to capture the head texture completely in a single photo. Traditional photographic methods exist, based on slit-scan cameras. A camera which exposes its film by moving it continuously past a vertical slit, while the camera and lens rotate horizontally, is termed a "panoramic" camera. If the camera is stationary while the subject rotates on a turntable, the device is termed a "peripheral" camera. Panoramic cameras are commercially available, and adapting one for peripheral photography should be straightforward. The peripheral camera used in this work was built by Prof. Andrew Davidhazy of the Rochester Institute of Technology. Prof. Davidhazy was kind enough to photograph Annette's head while she stood on a rotating turntable; her dance experience proved very useful in maintaining a vertical and unwavering posture during the spin. The resulting photograph, like the Cyberware scan, is a cylindrical projection.

The peripheral photograph was scanned and digitized. An interactive texture-warping program was written for an SGI Iris workstation. Using the 12-bit double-buffered display mode, the user could ping-pong back and forth between a Sobel-filtered range image and the peripheral photo. Standard digital "painting" functions were provided by the program, but its key feature was a "coordinate airbrush." This is simply a deformation function in the style of [7] and [9], described in digital painting terms. In fact, the "coordinate airbrush" implements an inverse, rather than a forward, mapping. For many purposes this is equally convenient, and much more rapid to compute. The idea is that an X, Y coordinate offset is supplied for the center of the brush (so the center pixel is replaced by the pixel value in the image at the offset X, Y), and the airbrush kernel tapers the blend of the coordinate offsets away from the center of the brush. If the offset is larger than the span of the airbrush kernel, a singularity results, like a dimple in a specular surface. In fact, these

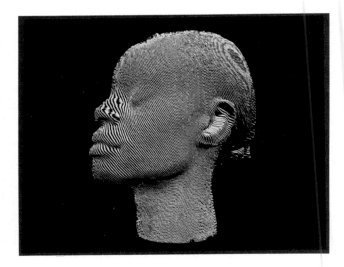

Figure 5. "Zebra" triangulation.

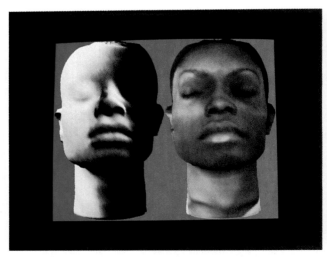

Figure 4. Final model, with and without texture.

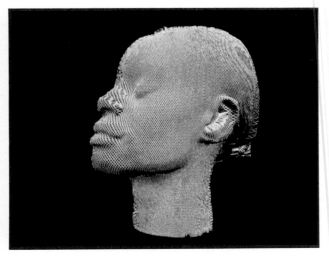

Figure 6. "Serpentine" triangulation.

inverse mappings resemble nothing so much as reflections from curved mirrors. If the offset is smaller than the span of the brush kernel, then the mapping behaves much like the "forward" mapping, like a rubber sheet that can be stretched to fit points of correspondence together. Figure 2 shows the final texture after remapping. The general technique was to use large kernels first, and then use smaller and smaller warps to register the details. Registering the texture with the filtered range image took about three hours of interaction. Figure 3 shows a Sobel-filtered range image which has been interactively warped to change its neutral expression to one of profound annoyance (the contouring in the image is a result of the compression to 8 bits). This illustrates the primary motivation for development of this "warpware": to apply similar deformation functions to animation of the 3D model.

Figure 4 shows the model with and without texture. Rendering was performed using the SGI Iris graphics pipeline, and supporting rendering software by G. W. Hannaway & Associates. With a generation of graphics hardware that does not handle texture explicitly, many users effect "texture

mapping" by rendering large meshes of polygons, with texture multiplying intensities at each mesh vertex. A mesh of vertices with the same resolution as the texture map essentially reproduces the map, warped to shape, with bilinear interpolation (Gouraud shading). To compress the map, filtering is necessary. In approaching texture this way, which is certainly a practical expedient on today's Z-buffer polygon engines, mesh tesselation is an issue. Figure 5 shows the head model textured with a pixel-scale checkerboard. The striping of the texture is due to triangulation. To avoid sending twisted quadrilaterals, all mesh elements are first divided into triangles. In figure 5, the triangulation diagonals cut across the mesh in parallel, and become stripes. In figure 6, the same texture is rendered with a "herringbone" or "serpentine" triangulation. Alternate mesh quads are divided on alternate, criss-crossing diagonals. Note that the texture still does not look like a checkerboard (we could hardly expect it to at this scale), but is much more isotropic.

After the mapping was corrected, an animation of the head rotating about the Y axis was taped, and the result examined

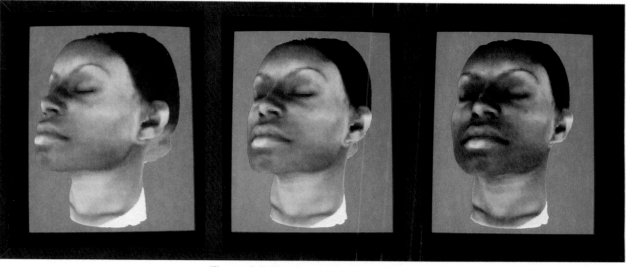

Figures 7-9. Rotations of the mapped 3D model.

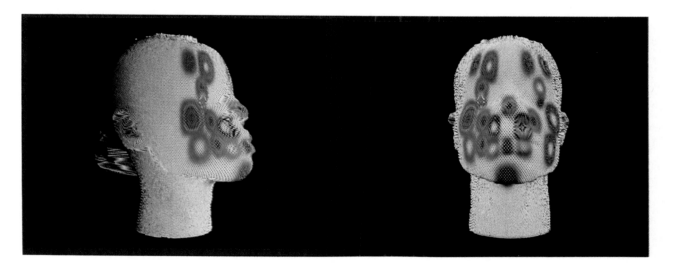

Figures 10-11. Basis functions on the model face.

for registration (which looked good!). Figures 7-9 show the model rotating, exhibiting the mapped texture in 3D.

MODIFYING EXPRESSION

The next step is applying our warpware to animation of the model. First, a set of warping kernels is distributed about the face. The factors that govern this distribution include physiology (the placement of muscles in the face, and the location of the most motile areas) as well as various practical considerations relating to the planned use of spot-tracking on an actor's face to ultimately drive the model. The "bas-ketweave" texture of figure 6 has been applied to the faces of figures 10 and 11, and the set of basis functions driving the face has been slightly offset. The resulting interpolations display the centers and relative sizes of the control kernels. The kernels are larger than they appear, but they are radially symmetric (like the basis functions of [7], rather than the more

elaborate bases used by [9]). Each is a Hanning (cosine) window, scaled to 1.0 in the center, and diminishing smoothly to 0.0 at the edge, with no negative values.

Like the enraged expression applied to the range image of figure 3, the expressions of figures 12 and 13 were created by hand-warping (with the "coordinate airbrush") the polar representation of the model. The realistic model can be stretched in a completely unrealistic way, and actually resembles a latex mask in some respects.

Tracking Expressions of Live Performers

The final link in our proof-of-concept demonstration is to increase realism by deriving the basis-function control offsets from the expressions of a live actor. Video-based tracking was the method of choice, although various mechanical schemes were considered. Video offers the most leverage

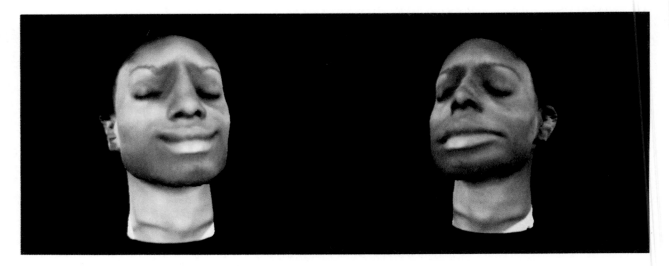

Figure 12. "Comedy"   Figure 13. "Tragedy"

Hand-animated exaggerated expressions.

because it does not restrict the performer, it is a simple, widely-available technology, and promises ultimately to permit motion-tracking without special makeup or fiducial marks.

The "special makeup" in this case was Scotchlite®, a retroreflective material manufactured by 3M. Scotchlite uses a layer of tiny spheroids to behave much like a surface of tiny corner-reflectors; reflection efficiency is very high within a small angle from the incident light. A beam-splitter setup was employed to record the performer, which for budgetary reasons turned out to be the author. The beam-splitter is simply a sheet of window glass, between the camera and the performer, at 45° from the camera's optical axis. At right angles to the camera, aimed at the performer's side of the glass, was a slide projector, used as a light source. The setup is adjusted so that the light reflected from the glass illuminates the performer's face. The point of the apparatus is, that the light source and camera are coaxial. Since the light comes "from the camera's point of view," the efficiency of retroreflectors in the camera's field of view is very high. When properly set up, contrast and brightness can be adjusted so that the camera can see retroreflectors in its field of view, and little else.

A paper punch was used to make little round adhesive spots from Scotchlite tape; figure 14 shows the author applying spots to his face (the brightness of the image has been scaled so that the face is visible; originally, only the spots could be seen). A typical frame (once again, brightened) is illustrated in figure 15.

The problem of digitizing the actor's performance now becomes one of tracking a set of bright spots in a dark field. The special case of tracking spots on a face which faces the camera is particularly favorable; the spots (if placed wisely) will never actually touch one another, and can never be obscured by another part of the face. For the test animation, the head was held relatively still, and only the facial expression changed. The algorithm used was to have a human operator indicate the position of each spot in the initial frame of a digitized sequence. This takes care of the correspondence between each spot and the basis function on the face that it controls. Spots are tracked automatically in subsequent frames. The spot tracking routine outputs the X, Y

coordinates of the spot centers in each frame.

When the operator selects a spot, it is a matter of touching the spot, or the spot's near vicinity. A window about the point indicated is scanned, and the X, Y coordinates of each pixel are multiplied by the intensity of the pixel; running sums of the X and Y pixel intensity products are saved. A running sum is also kept of the pixel intensities. When the window is completely scanned, the summed X, Y's are each divided by the summed intensities. This supplies the window's "center of gravity" or first moment, a fairly robust estimate of the center of light intensity in the window, which has fractional pixel precision if the spot falls across a reasonable number of pixels. A new window is then scanned from the computed center, and the process iterated a few times. The window size should be slightly larger than the spots, so that the iterated result will be the first moment of the spot itself. In figure 16, tracking crosses have been superimposed on the spots. Note that crosses appear even where the spots they mark are very dim; the spot tracker proved robust, and the motion of the tracking crosses is quite convincing even for spots of marginal

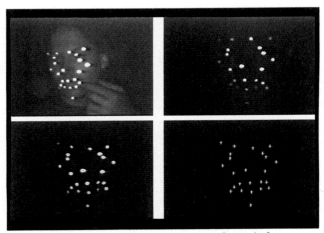

Figures 14-17. Tracking spots on performer's face.

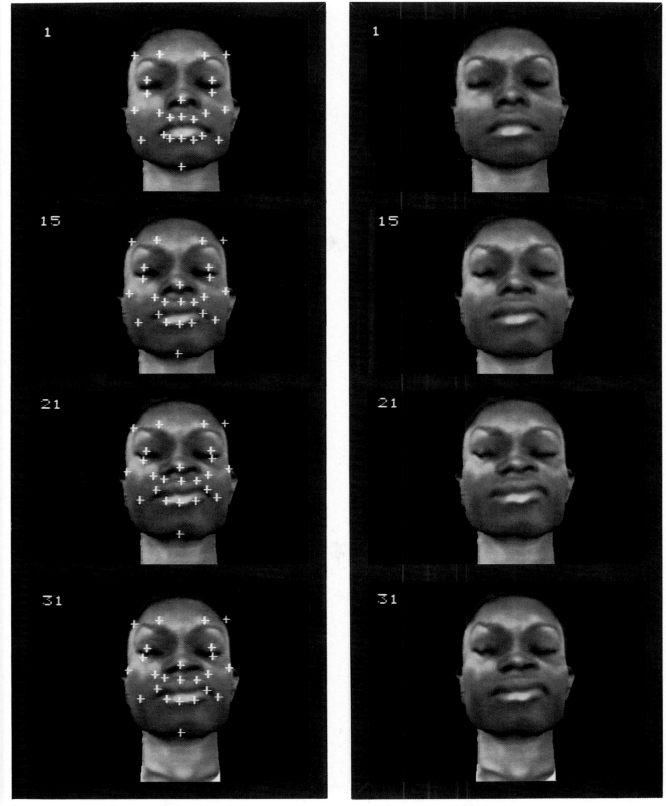

Figures 18-25. Tracked expressions applied to the model face.

visibility. Figure 17 shows the tracking crosses without the spots. Figures 18-25 show the model face being driven by the tracked spots, marked by the tracking crosses in one of each pair of images.

CONCLUSIONS AND FUTURE WORK

The appearance of the model head is quite realistic, and the test animation is very striking. Although short, the sequence exhibits some lifelike twitches and secondary motions which would be unlikely to arise in pure animation. The fundamental idea of mapping the motions of a live performer to a computer animated character promises to be a rich one. Previous efforts to animate faces by interpolating between various canonical expressions can now be supplemented by interpolation of canonical motion sequences. Driving a face or head of very different proportions or physiognomy should be attempted soon.

The animation of the face is very much a "proof of concept," not a completely realized system. At present, the face cannot open its eyes or mouth, and this portion of the model will demand a great deal of time. Some ripples on the eyes (visible in the last two figures) result from the fact that the performer could blink his eyes (in fact, found it hard not to) and the model could not. The test did establish that eyeblinks are quite trackable!

For reasons of efficiency, and to test the validity of the simplifications, the performer's face was tracked in 2D, and the result "projected" to the model, which was animated in the cylindrical coordinates of the range data before being converted into X, Y, Z meshes with normals. The changes in the performer's expressions were transferred to the model with appropriate scaling of the offsets, and a straight projection onto the face approximates projection onto a cylinder. A test setup with angled mirrors at the sides of the actor's head showed that 3D coordinates could be acquired with a single camera. A more fully-realized system would track expressions in 3D and apply them in Cartesian, rather than cylindrical, coordinates.

ACKNOWLEDGEMENTS

My profuse thanks go to Annette White, the model; to Nancy Burson and David Kramlich, my initial collaborators; to Ariel Shaw and Andrew Davidhazy, for extraordinary photographic assistance; to Wyndham Hannaway and Bill Bishop of G.W. Hannaway & Associates, who made available much of the computer time, utility software, and exotic paraphernalia this research required; to my manager, Mark Cutter, and to Ned Greene, Pete Litwinowicz, and Libby Patterson of Apple's Advanced Technology Animation Group, for constant support, advice, and inspiration.

REFERENCES

[1] Walters, Graham, The Story of Waldo C. Graphic. ACM SIGGRAPH '89 Course Notes, *3D Character Animation by Computer*, August 1989.

[2] Parke, Frederick I., A Parametric Model for Human Faces. Ph.D. dissertation, Department of Computer Science, University of Utah, 1974.

[3] Badler, Norman, and Platt, Stephen, Animating Facial Expressions. Proceedings of SIGGRAPH '81 (Dallas, Texas, August 3-7, 1981). In *Computer Graphics 15*, 3, (August 1981), 245-252.

[4] Platt, Stephen Michael, A Structural Model of the Human Face. Ph.D. Department of Computer and Information Science, School of Engineering and Applied Science, University of Pennsylvania, Philadelphia, PA., 1986.

[5] Brennan, Susan Elise, Caricature Generator. M.S. Visual Studies, Dept. of Architecture, Massachusetts Institute of Technology, Cambridge, MA. Sept. 1982.

[6] Burson, Nancy, and Schneider, Thomas, "Method and Apparatus for Producing an Image of a Person's Face at a Different Age," U.S. Patent #4276570, June 30, 1981.

[7] Oka, Masaaki, Tsutsui, Kyoya, Ohba, Akio, Kurauchi, Yoshitaka, Tago, Takashi, Real-Time Manipulation of Texture-Mapped Surfaces. Proceedings of SIGGRAPH '87 (Anaheim, California, July 27-31, 1987). In *Computer Graphics 21*, 4, (July 1987), 181-188.

[8] Lachapelle, Pierre, Bergeron, Philippe, Robidoux, P., and Langlois, Daniel, *Tony de Peltrie*. [film] 1985.

[9] Waters, Keith , A Muscle Model for Animating Three-Dimensional Facial Expression. Proceedings of SIGGRAPH '87 (Anaheim, California, July 27-31, 1987). In *Computer Graphics 21*, 4 (July 1987), 17-24.

[10] Lasseter, John, Ostby, Eben, Reeves, William, Good, Craig, Rydstrom, Gary. *Tin Toy*. [film] Pixar, 1988.

[11] Cyberware Laboratory, Inc.: 4020/PS 3D Scanner, 4020/RGB 3D Scanner with color digitizer. 8 Harris Court 3D, Monterey, California 93940.

[12] Burt, P.J., Ogden, J.M., Adelson, E.H., and Bergen, J.R., Pyramid-Based Computer Graphics. *RCA Engineer*, Vol. 30, 5, Sept.-Oct. 1985.

where only the constraint force C is unknown. Equation 7 gives a set of linear conditions that C must satisfy, but in general there are fewer equations than unknowns. This deficiency is rectified by requiring that the constraint force does not add or remove energy from the system, which leads to the requirement, known as the *principle of virtual work,* that the constraint force be a linear combination of the constraint gradients. This in turn means that C must satisfy

$$C_j = \lambda_i \frac{\partial c_i}{\partial q_j},$$

for some vector λ. The λ's are known as *Lagrange multipliers.* Substituting for C in equation 7, after some rearrangement, gives

$$-\left[\frac{\partial c_i}{\partial q_j} W_{jk} \frac{\partial c_r}{\partial q_k}\right]\lambda_r = \frac{\partial c_i}{\partial q_j} W_{jk} Q_k + \frac{\partial \dot{c}_i}{\partial q_j}\dot{q}_j + \frac{\partial^2 c_i}{\partial t^2},$$

(8)

in which the matrix on the left hand side is square, with dimensions of the constraints, and only λ is unknown. The constraints are enforced by solving equation 8 for λ, using λ to compute C, adding C to the applied force, and computing the constrained acceleration $\ddot{q}$. In practice, an additional feedback term must be added to the force to inhibit drift, and also to bring the system to a legal state initially. Including the damped feedback term, the total force becomes

$$Q_j + (\lambda_i + \alpha c_i + \beta \dot{c}_i)\frac{\partial c_i}{\partial q_j},$$

where α and β are constants.

Equation 8 refers to the entire constrained system. In a system comprising a number of distinct objects, the global state vector q is formed by concatenating those of the original objects, and the constraint vector c is formed by concatenating the constraints. The inverse mass matrix W is block diagonal, receiving a block from each object. The constraint Jacobian receives a non-zero block for each constraint/object pair for which the constraint depends on the object.

Although we have written the constraints as direct functions of state, in practice there is usually an intermediate quantity to which constraints are applied. For example, a constraint that nails a pair of points together depends on the points, and the points' coordinates depend in turn on the respective objects' state. See [19] for a general partitioning scheme that exploits this kind of structure. In brief, if c is a constraint on one or more points, x is a point on which c depends, and q is the state of the object to which x is attached, then the chain rule gives

$$\frac{\partial c_i}{\partial q_j} = \frac{\partial c_i}{\partial x_k}\frac{\partial x_k}{\partial q_j},$$

as the Jacobian block representing c's dependence on q through the point x.

3.2 Impulses

When very large forces act for very short times, producing large transient accelerations, it is often useful to describe the behavior of the system in terms of the integral over the short time interval, neglecting the internal dynamics of the event, and to treat the duration of the event as zero. The force integral is known as an *impulse.* Instead of accelerations, impulses produce instantaneous changes in velocity. The calculation of an impulse response closely resembles that of an acceleration. The equation $\ddot{q}_i = w_{ij}Q_j$ becomes $\Delta\dot{q}_i = w_{ij}I_j$ where I is the impulse, and $\Delta\dot{q}$ is the change in velocity. In computing an impulse all non-impulsive forces, such as gravity, are neglected.

Impulses are most frequently encountered in the analysis of collisions. Here, we are interested in impulses in connection with motion control, where we may wish to allow the prescribed velocity of a controlled point to undergo a discontinuous change. The desired discontinuity appears in the direct derivative of the constraint with respect to time, leading to an equation similar to equation 8:

$$-\left[\frac{\partial c_i}{\partial q_j} W_{jk} \frac{\partial c_r}{\partial q_k}\right]\lambda_r = \Delta\frac{\partial c_i}{\partial t},$$

(9)

where the right hand side gives the constraint discontinuities. Once λ is obtained, the constraint impulse is

$$I = \lambda_i \frac{\partial c_i}{\partial q_j}.$$

3.3 Linearly deformable bodies

Now we recast equation 8 for the special case of a system of linearly deformable bodies, subject to constraints each of which depends linearly on one or more points on the bodies. This restricted class of constraints includes point-to-point attachments, and constraints that nail points in place or require them to follow arbitrary known trajectories. This set is thus sufficient for building models by attaching deformable pieces together, and controlling the models by controlling the motions of specified points. The benefit of imposing this restriction is a large one: the constraint matrix on the left hand side of equation 8 remains constant, except when constraints are added or deleted. The matrix is inverted whenever the constraint structure changes, after which evaluating the constraint force requires only a matrix multiply rather than the solution of a linear system. Figure 2 illustrates the behavior of linearly deformable bodies subjected to attachment constraints.

If x is a point on a linearly deformable body then its derivative with respect to the body's state is

$$\frac{\partial x_i}{\partial R_{rs}} = \frac{\partial}{\partial R_{rs}}\left(R_{ij}p_j\right) = \delta_{ir}p_s,$$

which is a constant. Because each constraint is a linear function of one or more points, the derivative of any constraint c with respect to a point x is a constant as well. Hence the global constraint Jacobian is composed of constant blocks each having the form $\delta_{ir}p_s$, possibly times a constant. For example, a two-point attachment constraint of the form $a_i - b_i = 0$ yields two such blocks, one positive and the other negative.

Because x is a vector and R is a matrix, the derivative has rank 3. In practice, though, the R's are flattened and concatenated to form the global state, so that in an expression like $\delta_{ir}p_s$, the r and s are combined to form a linearized state index, and the quantity may then be viewed as a block in the global matrix. The bookkeeping involved in performing these index calculations is greatly simplified by the use of a block-sparse matrix data structure, in which a matrix is composed of a collection of rectangular blocks. Operations such as matrix-times-vector and matrix-times-matrix are readily implemented in terms of this structure.

Once the constant Jacobian matrix has been computed, the left-hand-side matrix of equation 8 can be calculated and inverted. Because $\dot{c}$ does not depend on q, one term of the equation vanishes, giving

$$\lambda_r = -Y_{ri}\left(\frac{\partial c_i}{\partial q_j}W_{jk}Q_k + \frac{\partial^2 c_i}{\partial t^2}\right), \qquad (10)$$

where Y is the inverted constraint matrix.

4 Motion Control

The preceeding sections provide the machinery required to animate a collection of connected objects—a puppet, for example—by moving control points on the puppet as arbitrary functions of time. As the control points follow their assigned paths, the rest of the puppet moves with correct passive dynamics. We begin this section by considering the generic problem of constraining a point to follow a known trajectory. Given this capability, we proceed to treat the issue of generating motion paths both by interactive keyframing and by the specification of motion goals.

A constraint that nails a point p at a fixed location n may be written $R_{ij}p_j - n_i = 0$. Such a nail constraint depends on time only indirectly, through R, so that the constraint's contribution to the direct time derivative term of equation 10 is zero. Suppose that the nail position n is not constant, but is instead a known, twice-differentiable function of time, $n(t)$.[2] By saying that $n(t)$ is known, we mean that we have a way to evaluate n, $\dot{n}$, and $\ddot{n}$ at the current time. We need not know anything further about

---

[2]We may relax this requirement to piecewise differentiability by inserting impulses at velocity discontinuities.

the form of n or the manner in which it is computed. The control constraint then becomes

$$R_{ij}p_j - n_i(t) = 0,$$

with direct second time derivative

$$\frac{\partial^2 c}{\partial t^2} = -\frac{\partial^2 n}{\partial t^2}.$$

Inserting this term into equation 10 induces a constraint force that causes point p to move with the desired acceleration. The feedback term

$$(\alpha c_i + \beta \dot{c}_i)\frac{\partial c_i}{\partial q_j}$$

inhibits drift from the desired trajectory. Note that

$$\dot{c}_i = \dot{R}_{ij}p_j - \frac{\partial n_i}{\partial t},$$

so that the feedback term as well as the constraint force take account of the desired motion.

Depending on the acceleration supplied at each instant in time, the control point can be made to accurately follow any piecewise twice-differentiable trajectory. This form of control is analogous to attaching a jet engine at the control point and continuously adjusting its thrust to drive the point along the desired path. Note that it is not necessary that the path be completely specified in advance—only values at the current time need be known.

Having the general ability to control the motion of points on an object makes it possible to separate the problem of motion specification from that of enforcing the specified motion. We now consider two approaches to motion specification: keyframing, and goal-directed motion.

4.1 Keyframed Motion Paths

A direct extension of standard animation techniques is to specify control point trajectories by interpolating between keyframes. If a user is allowed to interactively position control points on arbitrary frames, piecewise cubic splines passing through the keyframed points suffice to provide the required values for n, $\dot{n}$, and $\ddot{n}$ at each instant in time. Provided that position and velocity are matched at the beginning of a keyframed motion, our models are able to track the keyframed paths accurately and stably at interactive speeds.

Experiments quickly showed us that physical keyframe control differs fundamentally from standard direct control of object parameters. First, the quantities that we are able to control are more likely to be the ones that we *want* to control. Second, we are permitted to employ far fewer degrees of control than degrees of freedom, the rest of the motion being determined by physics. This is a property with no counterpart in conventional keyframing, where nothing moves unless we move it.

To fully exploit the ability to *refrain* from controlling all aspects of the motion, control points ought not to be regarded as persistent entities whose keyframed trajectories span an entire scene. The style of keyframe control that we believe will be most effective is based on the ability to freely turn control points on and off during an animation, establishing and relinquishing control as required. For example, in animating a walk it is necessary to control heel, toe, knees, hips, shoulders, etc., but not all at the same time. The heel position must be accurately controlled just before and during the support phase, but during the swing the heel can simply be allowed to follow the toe. It would be an unnecessary burden to specify the heel's position all the time.

The ability to turn control points on and off raises technical issues. Turning a path constraint off is simply a matter of letting the point "go ballistic," eliminating the relevant blocks from the constraint matrix, and turning off the restoring forces. Turning a path constraint on in the midst of an ongoing motion is more difficult: at the moment that control is initiated, the position and velocity of the point being controlled must match those specified by the splined trajectory. However, the point's state cannot generally be predicted in advance. We handle this problem using what we call *constraint preroll,* by analogy to the video term. A short time before the nominal onset of control we dynamically compute a spline segment that smoothly joins the point's current position and velocity to those at the start of the pre-specified path. During the preroll interval, this segment serves to bring the point smoothly from its uncontrolled state to the required initial state.

Impulses provide additional keyframing possibilities by allowing control points to undergo arbitrary velocity discontinuities. For example, at the end of a motion path, it is possible to insert an impulse that makes the control point stop dead or "bounce," simulating collisions. Although not generally physical, starting a motion impulsively may also produce interesting effects. We also use impulses as a graceful way to start and stop animation runs. Before starting the run, we use an impulse to install the initial control point velocities, and at the end, an impulse is used to bring them to an instant but well behaved halt.

4.2 Goal-Directed Motion

Keyframing of point trajectories, though offering real advantages over object-parameter keyframing, can still be a frustrating process, primarily because motion must be specified in such a literal way. For instance, the fact that a reaching motion is intended to bring the hand into contact with an object to be grasped is entirely lost in the translation to spline curves. If the object's position is changed, the hand will happily grab the empty space where it used to be, unless the hand's motion is manually changed as well.

An alternative to keyframing is to specify the goals of actions directly, dynamically calculating the motion required to satisfy them. In contrast to the first-principles approach to motion synthesis described in [20], our objective here is to develop a minimal vocabulary of simple behaviors that are chained to produce motion. With the ability to control the motions of individual object points already in hand, it is comparatively simple to develop a variety of useful atomic actions. To implement an action that governs the behavior of one or more points, we must provide a way to compute the desired positions, velocities, and accelerations, as a function of state and of time.

An example will illustrate the approach. Suppose we want to make one point chase another, making contact at a specified time, and with specified final velocity. If the target point is stationary, then a cubic spline segment can be constructed, taking the chaser's current position and velocity as initial conditions, and the position and velocity of the target point as final conditions. As the motion progresses, the spline and its derivatives are evaluated to supply the desired position, velocity, and acceleration. This is equivalent to the "preroll" segment described earlier. To chase a moving target, we use its current position and velocity to make a linear prediction of its position at the desired time of contact, build a spline to that point, and continuously update the estimate as things change. The action is complete when the appointed contact time is reached.

Figure 3 shows some frames of a very simple animation in which a sky hook swoops down, grabs a pyramid, flies off with it, then hangs itself up, leaving the pyramid dangling. It was created using two primitive behaviors, "Chase," as described above, and "Connect," which applies a velocity-matching impulse, then creates an attachment constraint. For convenience, we define a behavior "Grab" which performs a Chase followed by a Connect. Having first created the geometry and defined some named control points at strategic locations, we used the following script to produce the motion:

```
Grab(hook_tip,pyr_tip, dt1, vx1, vy1)
Grab(hook_eye,sky_point, dt2, vx2, vy2)
```

where the dt's and v's are durations and final velocities for the chase segments.

Figure 4 shows a more complex sequence in which a hinge-horned monster skewers and ingests a small humanoid. The fine grained action is as follows: the monster waits until a humanoid comes in range, skewers it, moves its "elbow" to a suitable spot, and accelerates the humanoid to a point just outside its mouth. At just that moment, the monster lets go, simultaneously stopping its claw, and the humanoid pops neatly into the gaping jaws. Here is the script, including interactively chosen values for timing and velocity:

```
Wait_For_Humanoid()
Grab(claw_tip,humanoid, 1.0)
Grab(elbow,feeding_position, 1.0, 0, 0)
Grab(claw_tip,mouth_point, 1.0, -1.5,
    -1.5)
Disconnect(claw_tip,humanoid)
Grab(humanoid,gullett, .5, -.07, -.07)
```

When no final velocity is specified, "Grab" computes a default based on the current position and velocity, duration and distance to the target. The predicate "Wait_For_Humanoid" serves to trigger the action when suitable prey comes within range. Unlike a conventional animation script, this sequence defines what amounts to a reflex. The monster responds to its environment, successfully capturing its prey over a wide range of initial conditions.

References

[1] William W. Armstrong and Mark W. Green. The dynamics of articulated rigid bodies for purposes of animation. In *Visual Computer*, pages 231–240. Springer-Verlag, 1985.

[2] Alan H. Barr. Global and local deformations of solid primitives. *Computer Graphics*, 18:21–29, 1984. Proc. SIGGRAPH 1984.

[3] Ronen Barzel and Alan H. Barr. *Topics in Physically Based Modeling, Course Notes*, volume 16, chapter Dynamic Constraints. SIGGRAPH, 1987.

[4] Ronen Barzel and Alan H. Barr. A modeling system based on dynamic constaints. *Computer Graphics*, 22:179–188, 1988.

[5] John E. Chadwick, David R. Haumann, and Richard E. Parent. Layered construction for deformable animated characters. *Computer Graphics*, 23(3):243–252, 1989. Proc. SIGGRAPH 1989.

[6] Kurt Fleischer and Andrew Witkin. A modeling testbed. In *Proc .Graphics Interface*, pages 127–137, 1988.

[7] Michael Girard and Anthony A. Maciejewski. Computational Modeling for the Computer Animation of Legged Figures. *Proc. SIGGRAPH*, pages 263–270, 1985.

[8] Herbert Goldstein. *Classical Mechanics*. Addision Wesley, Reading, MA, 1950.

[9] Paul Issacs and Michael Cohen. Controlling dynamic simulation with kinematic constraints, behavior functions and inverse dynamics. *Computer Graphics*, 21(4):215–224, July 1987. Proc. SIGGRAPH '87.

[10] Alex Pentland and John Williams. Good vibrations: Modal dynamics for graphics and animation. *Computer Graphics*, 23(3):215–222, 1989. Proc. SIGGRAPH 1989.

[11] John Platt. *Constraint Methods for Neural Networks and Computer Graphics*. PhD thesis, Caltech, 1989.

[12] John Platt and Alan Barr. Constraint methods for flexible models. *Computer Graphics*, 22:279–288, 1988.

[13] Peter Schroeder and David Zeltzer. Dynamic simulation with linear recurive constraint propogation. *Computer Graphics*, 24(2):23–32, March 1990.

[14] Thomas Sederberg and Scott Parry. Free-form deformation of solid geometric models. *Computer Graphics*, 20(4):151–160, 1986. Proc. SIGGRAPH 1986.

[15] Demetri Terzopoulos, John Platt, Alan Barr, and Kurt Fleischer. Elastically deformable models. *Computer Graphics*, 21(4), July 1987. Proc. SIGGRAPH '87.

[16] Demetri Terzopoulos and Andrew Witkin. Physically based models with rigid and deformable components. In *Proc. Graphics Interface*, pages 146–154, Edmonton, Alberta, Canada, June 1988.

[17] Jane Wilhelms and Brian Barsky. Using dynamic analysis to animate articulated bodies such as humans and robots. *Graphics Interface*, 1985.

[18] Andrew Witkin, Kurt Fleischer, and Alan Barr. Energy constraints on parameterized models. *Computer Graphics*, 21(4):225–232, July 1987. Proc. SIGGRAPH '87.

[19] Andrew Witkin, Michael Gleicher, and William Welch. Interactive dynamics. *Computer Graphics*, 24(2):11–22, March 1990.

[20] Andrew Witkin and Michael Kass. Spacetime constraints. *Computer Graphics*, 22:159–168, 1988.

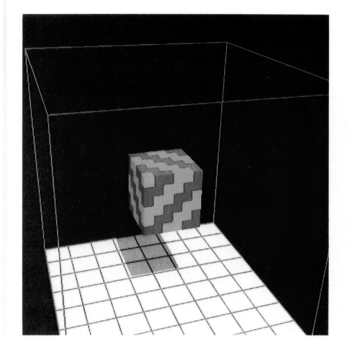

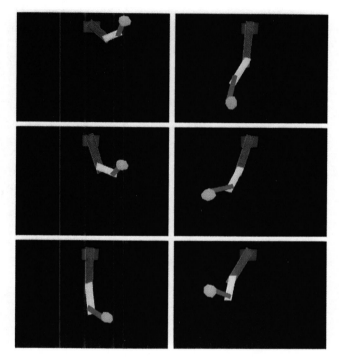

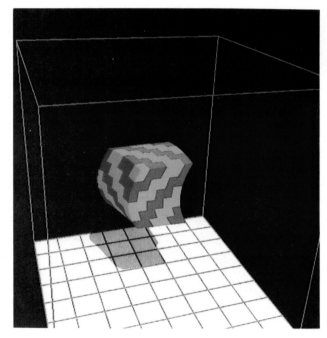

Figure 2: A two-dimensional triple pendulum moving under the influence of gravity. The pendulum, which is nailed in place at the top, is composed of affine-deformable parts connected using attachment constraints. The frames for all sequences are ordered top-to-bottom, then left-to-right.

Figure 1: A three-dimensional second-order deformable object. The object is shown above in its undeformed state. Below it is shown deforming in response to a leftward pull, while its right-hand corners are held in place. This object can bend, whereas an affine body may only stretch and shear.

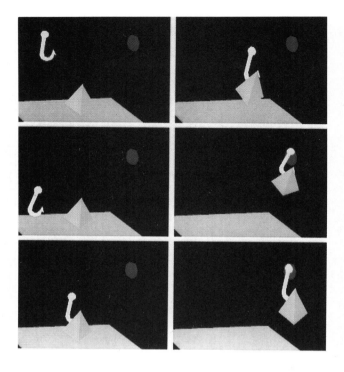

Figure 3: Animation created by chaining motion goals. A sky hook swoops down to grab a pyrmid, then hangs itself up.

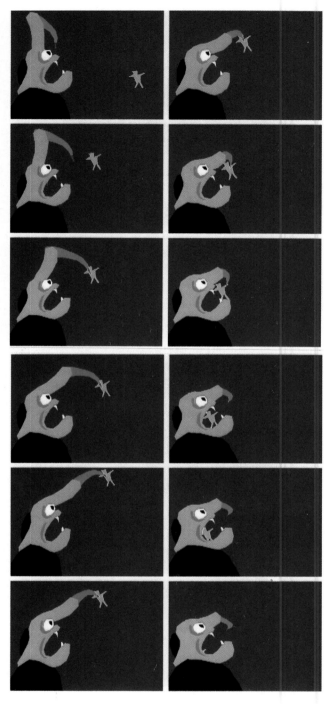

Figure 4: A hinge-horned monster skewers and ingests a small humanoid. This compound behavior is in effect a reflex, triggered by the arrival of suitable prey, which executes successfully over a wide range of initial conditions.

Strength Guided Motion

Philip Lee, Susanna Wei, Jianmin Zhao, and Norman I. Badler

Computer and Information Science
University of Pennsylvania
Philadelphia, PA 19104-6389

Abstract

A methodology and algorithm are presented that generate motions imitating the way humans complete a lifting task under various loading conditions. The path taken depends on "natural" parameters: the figure geometry, the given load, the final destination, and, especially, the *strength model* of the agent. Additional user controllable parameters of the motion are the *comfort* of the action and the *perceived exertion* of the agent. The algorithm uses this information to incrementally compute a motion path of the end-effector moving the load. It is therefore instantaneously adaptable to changing force, loading, and strength conditions. Various strategies are used to model human behavior (such as reducing moment, pull back, add additional joints, and jerk) that compute the driving torques as the situation changes. The strength model dictates acceptable kinematic postures. The resulting algorithm offers torque control without the tedious user expression of driving forces under a dynamics model. The algorithm runs in near-realtime and offers an agent-dependent toolkit for fast path prediction. Examples are presented for various lifting tasks, including one- and two-handed lifts, and raising the body from a seated posture.

1 Introduction

Realistic articulated figure animation is a long-sought goal of computer graphics researchers. While progress in modeling and image generation has been remarkable, many animation schemes still rely on human skill and creativity to effect natural-looking motion. As recent efforts have examined physically-based models to achieve plausibility and accuracy of synthetic models, attempts at realistic human motion have just begun to trace their origins back to biomechanical principles [42, 12, 30]. We believe that human motion models are going to be hybrids of many motion and path generation techniques. The goal is to find effective combinations that provide realistic motion behaviors while simultaneously offering the animator/user reasonable and intuitive control mechanisms. Often described as "task level animation" [48, 41, 15, 4], the idea is to find parametric procedures that implement various *basic* human activities such as grasping, reaching, lifting, walking, and so on. Presumably the list is finite: other behaviors are derived from the sequential or parallel execution of such tasks, combined with appropriate transitions for smooth action.

One of our research goals is to provide task-level control algorithms for human figures [6, 49, 36, 5]. Tasks we are primarily interested in include: multiple constrained reach, view, and object manipulation by an end-effector. The latter is the one we will discuss here; in particular, we examine the problem of *moving a load to a specified position in space*. The resulting motion is dictated by the geometry and is strongly influenced by the *strength* and *comfort* of the agent. Such problems have application in the ergonomic design and evaluation of workplaces for human operators, and maintenance facilities for service personnel.

2 Background

Torques may be used to physically simulate motions of a figure. Typically the joint responses are conditioned by springs and dampers so that responses to external forces can be computed. Such dynamic animations have been studied by many researchers [17, 16, 1, 25, 43, 44, 20, 22, 34, 7]. Solving the dynamic equations, an initial value problem, is computationally expensive, especially if the joints are stiff [1]. Moreover, such motions are annoyingly difficult to control by an animator unless free-swinging motions are in fact desired. The resulting motions appear to drive a hapless mannequin or puppet by external forces such as gravity and collision reactions. When the torques are derived from a spring or vibration model, convincing motions of worms, snakes, and other flexible objects may be simulated [32, 35], but this cannot be the same mechanism used for normal articulated figure motion. Kinematic and inverse kinematic approaches are easier to manipulate and may create the right "look," but suffer from potentially unrealistic motion (velocity, torque) in the body joints. These problems have been addressed as boundary value problems with objective functions. The trajectories are then solved by global optimization approaches [45, 10] or control theory [11], but their methods presume complete knowledge of the driving conditions and overall constraints. Relatively successful animation of locomotion has been achieved by hydrid approaches combining kinematic and dynamic constraints [17, 16, 12].

In robotics, the emphasis is to accomplish a motion within constraints and optimize with respect to some criteria, *i.e.* time, torque, energy, and obstacles [9, 23, 27, 28, 31, 40]. Bioengineers are curious to determine if human motion conforms to some optimality criterion, such as energy [8, 14, 46, 47]. Human motion over its entire range of motion is not optimal with respect to a single criteria.

Despite these diverse approaches to the human motion problem, none has been successful at specifying a task by describing a load and a placement goal, and then completing the task in a realistic (though possibly suboptimal) manner. There has been work on generating a path between two endpoints [37, 26, 39], but the usual solution incorporates constraints and a single objective function that is optimized.

3   Our Approach

We offer a solution which blends kinematic, dynamic and biomechanical information when planning and executing a path. The task is described by the starting position, the load (weight) that needs to be transported, and a goal position for the load. Some simple additional parameters help select from the wide range of possible paths by invoking biomechanical and performance constraints in a natural fashion. *Thus a path is determined from a general model rather than provided by the animator.* In addition, the algorithm has the ability to adapt to changing forces that are required to complete a task. The basic premise of the method is that a person tends to operate within a *comfort region* which is defined by *available strength*. This is even more probable when the person has to move a heavy object.

We support the general principle that constraints predict motion. We considered applying the constraints which would be similar to those that a human encounters when moving. Human motion is known to be diverse, and therefore, no single type of path or strategy is applicable for all cases. To address this, we developed a toolkit of motion generators which produces characteristic motions and a corresponding toolkit of transition identifiers which point to the appropriate motion generator for any situation. The toolkits are the foundation of our human simulation system which is fast enough to allow interactive animation of tasks. The constraints for this system should be intuitive so that manipulation of constraint parameters generate the expected results. Finally, the constraint parameters should be easy to modify, allowing the animator some flexibility and creativity in producing a desired motion.

We assume that a person tends to operate within a comfort region dictated by muscular strength, especially when moving a heavy object. When a person has to accomplish a given task, say lifting a box or cup, he starts from some initial posture and then plans the direction for his hand to move. This planning is based on the person's perception of his strength, comfort range, and the importance of staying along a particular path. After a direction is determined, he tries to move in that direction for a short distance with joint rates that maintain the body's discomfort level below a particular threshold. Once the position is reached another direction is selected by balancing the need to finish the task as directly as possible with restrictions derived from the body's limitations. Again, joint rates can be determined once a new direction is established.

4   Problem Specification

The objective is to find the trajectories, both joint and end-effector, that a human-like linkage would traverse to complete a task (Figure 1) . The task can be specified as a force that has to be overcome or imparted to reach a goal position over an entire path. The task specification can be generalized to describe a complicated task by letting the force be a function of body position, hand position, time, or other factors. In general, task specification can be represented by a *force trajectory*. In addition to task specification by a force trajectory, human motion is guided by many constraints that limit the joint and end-effector trajectories. Constraints that will guide this work are *comfort level*, *perceived exertion*, and *strength*.

Comfort level is defined in a mechanical sense. It is found by calculating, over the entire body, the maximum torque ratio: current torque divided by the maximum torque at each individual joint for the current joint position and velocity. In general when humans move they try to maintain their effort below a particular discomfort level. Therefore, it is desirable to dictate a motion that minimizes the maximum torque ratio of a body in order to maximize the comfort level.

Perceived exertion is a variable used to indicate the expected level of difficulty in completing a task. It depends on the perception of the amount of strength required (an implicit function of the force trajectory) and the amount of strength available. If perceived exertion is low then the comfort level is not expected to be exceeded for the paths "likely" to be taken to satisfy a task, especially for a path that travels a straight line between the initial body position and the goal. However, if the perceived exertion is high, then the end-effector path needs to deviate from a straight path in order to abide by the comfort constraint. Perceived exertion is represented by a cone which is defined by the maximum deviation angle of a path from its current position.

The implementation of *strength* constraints is discussed in the next section.

5   Strength Model

Ultimately, the shape of an end-effector's motion is derived from the body's resource—strength: the maximum achievable joint torque. Strength information (maximum torques) is defined as muscle group strengths and is stored on a joint degree of freedom (DOF) basis. Modeling strength in terms of muscle group strength allows different people to possess different strength capacities in different muscle

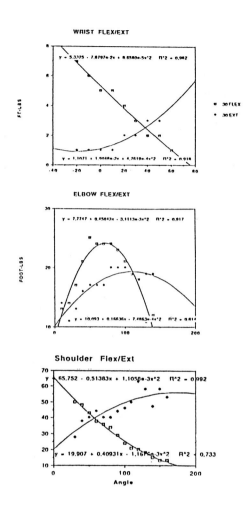

Figure 1: Person performing a lifting task. Sample strength curves shown at the top.

groups. Thus, the difference between two people such as a dancer and a pianist can be readily modeled. Each DOF of a joint has two joint movements which are associated with two different muscle groups. For example, an elbow is modeled to have one DOF. It can only rotate around one axis; its rotational movements are flexion and extension which correspond to the flexor and extensor muscle groups.

Each muscle group strength is modeled as a function of body position, anthropometry, gender, handedness, fatigue, and other strength parameters [2, 29, 33, 3, 24, 13, 21]. In terms of body position, we chose a more generalized model that takes effects of adjacent joint angles into consideration [38].

In our strength model, there are two strength curves to represent the two muscle group strengths at each DOF. The strength information is maintained in *SASS* (Spreadsheet Anthropometry Scaling System) [19] which is a spreadsheet-like system that allows flexible interactive access to all anthropometric variables needed to size a human figure. Strength information of specific individuals or percentiles within a population may be obtained through *SASS*. Figure 1 shows extension and flexion strength curves for shoulder, elbow, and wrist, respectively [18].

6   System Architecture

The generation and control of motion consists of three components (Figure 2):

1. Condition Monitor which monitors the state of a body and suggests motion strategies.

2. Path Planning Scheme (PPS) which plans the direction that an end-effector will move.

3. Rate Control Process (RCP) which determines the joint rates for motion.

The *condition monitor* reports on the current state of a body: current position, maximum strength for a current position, current joint torques, etc. It then suggests motion strategies to the *path planning scheme* which determines an end-effector's direction of travel. The amount of motion of the end-effector in the suggested direction of travel can be arbitrarily set. The rate of travel, constrained by torque, for a path interval can then be computed by the *rate control process*. After the joint rates are resolved and new joint positions are found, these procedures are repeated until the entire joint path is mapped out in a manner that satisfies the specified task. This system architecture is an iterative process which allows changes to the parameters at any time through other external processes. Possible situations to alter any of the parameters are dropping or changing the mass of a load, redirecting the goal, or encountering an obstacle. This is different from the global nature of optimal control-based algorithms. We handle similar global considerations through an external process [30].

6.1   Condition Monitor

The condition monitor gathers information about the current state of a body, assembles the information, and suggests a motion strategy for the next procedure to process. The motion strategies are a function of the constraint parameters: comfort, perceived exertion, and strength. Each

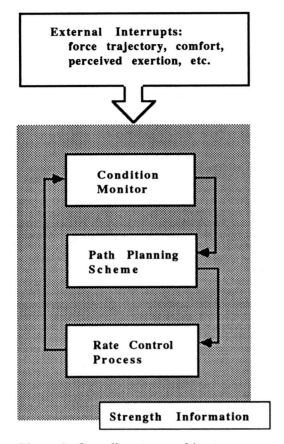

Figure 2: Overall system architecture.

motion strategy, based on the constraints, concentrates on a separate fundamental aspect of motion. The strategies can be divided into those that represent indirect joint control and those that represent direct joint control. For indirect joint control strategies, the end-effector's need to reach a goal is more important than joint considerations; and for direct joint control, joint considerations are more important than reaching a goal. We can also interpret the strategies as particular optimization problems. The condition monitor is the highest level of the three procedures in predicting a path.

6.2   Path Planning Scheme

The path planning scheme, guided by the condition monitor, determines the direction to move. In general, the output of any system is bounded by its headroom[1]. In the case when there is much strength in a system, a situation where indirect joint control applies, the headroom can be used to suggest incremental joint displacements, $d\theta$. A larger headroom allows a larger displacement. The mapping between the cartesian displacement and the joint displacement is

$$dx = \mathbf{J} d\theta \qquad (1)$$

---
[1]The available range of a variable within a constraint.

256

where $\mathbf{J}$ is a $3 \times n$ matrix and n is the number of joint displacements. If the headroom for each joint, which is represented by a weighting vector $\mathbf{w}$, is proportional to $d\theta$, then

$$d\hat{\mathbf{x}} = \mathbf{J}\mathbf{w} \qquad (2)$$

where $d\hat{\mathbf{x}}$ is a normalized direction of reach. $d\hat{\mathbf{x}}$ is then compared to a cone, which represents a set of feasible directions to travel and is derived from perceived exertion. If $d\hat{\mathbf{x}}$ is within the cone then the direction of motion should be $d\hat{\mathbf{x}}$, otherwise the direction can be $d\hat{\mathbf{x}}$ projected onto the cone.

When the system is relatively weak, the suggested direction of motion must not violate the strength constraints. The decision process should shift importance from one strategy where the desirability to reach a goal is a major component of determining a suggested motion to an alternative strategy of avoiding positions where the joints are greatly strained. This leads to schemes where direct joint control is imperative to avoid positions where joints are strained. The methods for PPS are discussed in the Appendix.

6.3   Rate Control Process

The rate control process, the most basic of the three procedures, resolves the speed with which a body moves along a prescribed end-effector path. This requires the use of dynamics, especially when the motion is fast. However, the incorporation of dynamics is difficult. When torques are specified to drive a motion (direct dynamics), control is a problem; when the driving forces are derived by kinematic specification (inverse dynamics), the forces are useful for only a short time interval and they may violate the body's torque capacity; and finally, when the forces optimize a particular function between two sets of positional constraints (boundary value problem), the method presumes that the optimization criteria is valid for the body's entire range of motion.

Dynamics equations can be interpreted as constraint equations solving for joint trajectories if they satisfy the conditions imposed by specific end-effector path and torque limits. The dynamics equations can be reformulated so that they provide a mapping between an end-effector path and a binding torque constraint. A binding torque constraint is the maximum torque allowed to drive a body with maximum end-effector acceleration without the end-effector deviating from the prescribed path. A greater torque would cause excessive inertial force and therefore, undesirable path deviation. It is evident from the derivation of the reformulated dynamics equations (see Appendix), which were originally derived to solve for path completion in minimum time [9], that joint trajectories can be found from the acceleration of an end-effector. In addition to finding the trajectories, the reformulated dynamic equations implicitly determine the force functions (joint torques) to guide an end-effector along a specified path.

Torque limits are established by the current comfort constraint. The comfort level variable, cl, determines the torque limit at each joint by a simple relation:

$$cl = \frac{\tau_{c,i}}{\tau(\theta)_{max,i}} \qquad (3)$$

where $\tau_{c,i}$ is the torque limit for a particular joint, i. The value $\tau(\theta)_{max,i}$, containing the maximum torque for the joint's current position, is obtained by examining the strength curves. When the value of cl becomes greater than one, there is no more strength to accomplish a task and therefore the attempt to complete a task should cease. Comfort level can be adjusted to achieve a desired motion. It influences both the rate of task completion and the direction of travel.

7 Motion Strategies

This is a catalogue of human motion strategies that are evaluated in the condition monitor and are executed in PPS. The strategies are given in the order of increasing discomfort. The modeling of these strategies is discussed in the Appendix.

7.1 Available Torque

When a person moves, the tendency is to move the stronger joint. This is much like the forces due to a spring or other types of potential forces. A stronger spring, based on the spring's stiffness coefficient, would yield a larger displacement per unit time than a weaker spring. Similarly, for a human, the amount of displacement for a joint depends not only on the strength that a joint is capable of, but mainly on the amount of strength that is currently available. The amount of strength available, which is based on the difference between the current required torque to support a particular position and the *effective maximum strength*, which is defined as the maximum strength factored by comfort, is called *torque availability*. If torque availability is low, motion should not be encouraged. Conversely, if the torque availability is high, the joint should do more of the work. Torque availability is the driving factor for a joint to move and to redistribute the joint torques so that the comfort level is more uniform.

7.2 Reducing Moment

As a joint approaches its effective maximum strength, the joint should move in a manner that avoids further stress on that joint while trying to reach a goal. A path towards the goal is still possible as long as the maximum strength is not surpassed for any of the joints. As the body gets more stressed it should attempt to reduce the moment caused by a force trajectory by reducing the distance normal to the force trajectory's point of application. In addition, a reduction in moment increases the torque availability of (at least) the joint that is rapidly approaching its maximum strength. The reduction in the total moment involves examining the moments on a joint by joint basis. At each joint a virtual displacement is given to determine if that displacement provides sufficient moment reduction to continue moving in that direction. This strategy assumes that the body has enough effective strength to allow its joints to move to positions where the overall stress level of the body is smaller than if the joints were only guided by kinematic demands.

7.3 Pull Back

The two previous strategies depend on the current torque to be less than the maximum strength. In these cases, maneuverability in torque space is high and therefore, an end-effector can still consider moving toward a goal without exceeding any joint's maximum strength.

However, when a particular joint reaches its maximum strength, then that joint can no longer advance toward a goal from the current configuration. The Pull Back strategy proposes that the end-effector approach the goal from another configuration. In an effort to determine another approach to the goal, the constraint of moving toward a goal within a restricted path deviation can be relaxed. The emphasis of the strategy is one where the joints dictate an improved path in terms of torques. This can be accomplished by increasing the *ultimate available torque* – the difference of maximum strength to current torque – for a set of *weak joints* – joints that are between the joint which has no ultimate available strength and an end-effector.

In general, the joint with the least amount of ultimate available torque will reverse direction and cause the end-effector to pull back (move away from its goal). The idea is to increase the overall comfort level. When the joints form a configuration that has a greater level of comfort, there might be enough strength to complete the task. Then the governing strategy could return to Reducing Moment, which allows the end-effector to proceed toward the goal.

The Pull Back strategy leads to a posture of *stable configuration*. A stable configuration is a posture that a set of joints should form so that it can withstand large forces, such as those caused when changing from a near-static situation to one that is dynamic.

7.4 Added Joint, Recoil, and Jerk

When the three strategies, Available Torque, Reducing Moment, and Pull Back have been exhausted and an agent still cannot complete a task, it is obvious that the *active joints* – the joints that were initially assigned to the task – cannot supply sufficient strength. When this occurs it should be determined if the task should be aborted or if there are other means of acquiring additional strength. One mode of acquiring more strength is to add a joint to the set of active joints. This assumes that the added joint is much stronger than any of the active joints.

Another mode to consider is to use the added joint to jerk – apply with maximum force – the set of active joints. Jerk reduces the forces necessary to complete a task for the set of active joints. Before jerking is initiated, a stable configuration should be formed by the active joints. After a stable configuration has been formed and the added joint has jerked, the active joints can then proceed to reach their goal since the required torques have decreased. A third possibility is to recoil another set of joints and then jerk with the recoiled set of joints in order to reduce the forces needed by the set of active joints to complete a task. For example, a weight lifter sometimes recoils his legs and then pushs off to reduce the force required in his arms.

8 Binding Constraints

The human motion path determination process has been uncoupled into two binding (active) constraints: comfort and perceived exertion. In the most primitive process of our system (RCP), which involves dynamics, the two constraining parameters must be binding to determine the joint rates.

However, at higher levels of control (such as PPS) it is not necessary for both of them to be binding simultaneously. In fact, as the torque levels change the applicability of a particular constraint to predict motion also changes. Here we present a model that relates the comfort level to the constraints. Also the strategies that bound a comfort level are given.

High Comfort. The perceived exertion constraint is not active but the comfort constraint is because any changes in acceleration (not necessarily large) may cause a joint to exceed the comfort constraint. In general, the force trajectory associated with a motion of high comfort is negligible, but dynamics is important because of the relatively large inertial effects of the body. This group is bounded by motions that are categorized by *zero jerk* condition (see efforts by Girard [16]) and Available Torque.

Regular Comfort. The end-effector can advance toward the goal. Perceived exertion and comfort are loosely constraining and dynamics should be evaluated. Available Torque and Reducing Moment bounds this comfort level.

Discomfort. At this point the comfort level for one or more joints are surpassed. The perceived exertion constraint needs to be changed so that a larger path deviation is allowed. Motion should have slowed down considerably, therefore dynamics is not important and, most likely, is not meaningful. This group is formed by Reducing Moment and Pull Back.

Intolerable Discomfort Many of the joints' comfort levels have been exceeded and there may be other joints which could be approaching their ultimate available torque. In such a situation, strategies can be combined. The pool of strategies are Added Joint, Pull Back, Recoil, and Jerk. Perceived exertion is relaxed and depending on the combination of the strategies, dynamics might be important.

9 Results

The strategies for Available Torque, Reducing Moment, Pull Back, and Added Joint are developed. The following figures (Figures 3 to 6) show the paths that were produced from these algorithms. The task is to pick-and-place an increasingly heavy load from various initial positions to a goal which is located above the body's head. The strength information can be obtained through SASS.

In Figure 3, there are two curves which outline the path of the hand. The right curve is for a task that involves lifting a 10 lb. object; the left curve is for a 20 lb. object. For the right curve, because the object is relatively light, a fast motion is predicted and the solution resembles a minimum time path. For the left curve, the heavier weight draws the

Figure 3: Lifting a 20 lb. and 10 lb. object. Figure 4: Lifting a 30 lb. and 20 lb. object.

 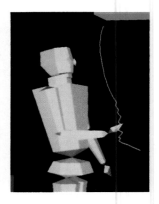

Figure 5: Pull Back   Figure 6: Added Joint

hand closer to the body. This path is rough because it is at the boundary of a solution determined by Available Torque and Reducing Moment. In Figure 4, the right curve is for the 20 lb. lift, and the left curve is for a lift of 30 lb. Once again the algorithm predicted that a heavier object would bring the hand closer to the body.

Figure 5 shows the body with a heavier load (35 lb.). The body immediately executes Pull Back. In this case, the body pulls back to a region of high comfort and therefore the approach to the goal is smooth, without the rough path evident in the previous figures. In Figure 6, the joint chain, initially composed of the joints between the hand and the shoulder, is allowed to extend to the waist. The algorithm decides that it is better to distribute the weight with more joints. Figure 6 shows the advantage of including the waist in the set of active joints.

These algorithms can be applied to any type of task, as long as it is force based. Figure 7 shows a body rising from a chair. A force trajectory is used to represent the body weight. Figure 7 shows the body leaning forward to balance his weight (a consequence of Reducing Moment) to reach a goal, which can be pre-assigned to the position of

Accurate Rendering Technique
Based on Colorimetric Conception

Atsushi Takagi[†], Hitoshi Takaoka[†], Tetsuya Oshima[††] and Yoshinori Ogata[†]

[†]System Engineering Dept. Design Div.
[††]Development Dept. No. 1 Information Systems Div. No. 1
Toyota Motor Corporation
1, Toyota-cho, Toyota, 471 Japan
Tel 0565(28)2121

actual car   resulting image

ABSTRACT

We have developed a rendering technique to generate realistic images meeting designers' requirements by strictly analyzing various physical phenomena relevant to the appearance of actual objects.

We have numerically compared the results of the calculations using this technique with colorimetry values. As a result, both values were virtually equal, so we have been able to confirm the effectiveness of the established technique.

Application of this technique to car design, which has not been realized to a large extent because of severe requests for realism, will make it possible to evaluate styles and colors on a graphics display before making a clay model.

CR Categories and Subject Descriptors : I.3.3 [Computer Graphics] : Picture/Image Generation − display algorithms, viewing algorithms ; **I.3.7 [Computer Graphics]** : Three-Dimensional Graphics and Realism − color, shading, shadowing, and texturing.

General Terms : Algorithms.
Additional Key Words and Phrases : rendering, ray tracing

1 INTRODUCTION

With the advancement of shape modeling techniques to deal with free-form surfaces, CAD was in practical use for vehicle style design since the beginning of the 1980's[1]. In this type of CAD, the mathematical model constructed inside the computer is usually converted into a clay model by a NC-milling machine for three-dimensional evaluation.

Meanwhile, application of the rendering technique has remarkably advanced in recent years making it possible to evaluate shapes and colors on a graphics display before making a physical clay model.

However, because colors and shapes are more strictly evaluated by designers, the requirements for practical use of Computer Graphics (CG) for car design are very severe.

The requirements are summarized below.

Requirement 1 : The image generated should have realism equivalent to photos so that you feel that an actual car has been reproduced.
Requirement 2 : It should be possible to check shapes, material, and color.
Requirement 3 : It should be possible to check shapes and colors at various simulated places and times under various simulated weather conditions.

Recent rendering models are roughly classified into either the ray tracing method or the radiosity method.

The ray tracing method has been widely used since T.Whitted introduced it[2], and various methods have been developed by improving the ray tracing method[3],[4],[5]. Kajiya increased the efficiency of stochastic ray tracing by using a monte carlo approach he called "path tracing"[6]. Then, the calculation method was also improved[7]. The radiosity method was developed to express delicate continuous tone which could not be expressed by the ray tracing method. Initially, some reflection models were developed in which an object and its environment were limited to the uniform diffuser[8],[9]. Then some methods allowing specular objects were proposed[10], and the calculation method was also improved[11],[12]. However, these methods are far from the realism that designers require. Moreover, verification of colorimetry is not performed in these methods. And it will be difficult to satisfy the above requirements **1** through **3**.

This paper proposes a rendering technique that meets the above requirements **1** through **3**. To satisfy the requirements, we systematized the factors relevant to realism by going back to the starting point and observing an actual car.

That is:
(1) Light source : Direct sunlight and sky light.
(2) Material : Reflectance expressing the property of an object.

(3) Color   : Color of an object as it is perceived by the human eye.
(4) Complexity : Complexity inherent in the object.

We arranged physical phenomena to meet requirements **1** through **3** on the above systematized factors (1) through (4) and converted them into an algorithm.

As the result of applying the algorithm to the ray tracing and making reproductive calculation of the actual scene whose brightness and chromaticity were already known through previous measurements, the values were almost equal. From this verification, we could confirm the model's effectiveness.

The following are the techniques established through the research.

[1] A reflection model system adopting luminous quantities.
[2] Technique to accurately handle a light source by dividing it into direct sunlight and sky light, control them, and handle optional weather conditions.
[3] Accurate expression of material.

We could meet requirements **1** through **3** by applying the above techniques. Therefore, shapes and colors can be evaluated through CG.

2 ANALYSIS OF REALISM

2.1 Realism analysis using an actual car

To develop a rendering technique to generate realism equivalent to photos, we examined factors relevant to reality. Therefore, we placed an actual object outside, analyzed the features of each portion's appearance, and estimated the phenomena of the factors. We show the results of this analysis of realism in Fig.2.1 and Table 2.1

Figure 2.1 (a) and (b) show the actual car used for analyzing

realism and Table 2.1 shows the summary of the results of the analysis. Consequently, we could evaluate each item based on four realism criteria – light source, material, color, and complexity.

< Light source >

The outdoor light source included two types – direct sunlight and sky light. However, light from other than from these two types is concentrated from various directions on the surface of an object placed outdoors, such as the light from the ground which reflects direct sunlight and sky light. Conventionally, the influence of sky light and ground light have not been frequently discussed. We examined the influence of sky light and ground light. We found that sky light and ground light should both be considered. For example, 'color under bumper (Table 2.1 ③)' or 'density of shade (Table 2.1 ⑤)'

We concluded that the following should be precisely calculated.

(1) Direct sunlight   : Spectral composition of all weather conditions.
(2) Sky light   : Spectral composition of all weather conditions.
(3) Ground light   : This can be calculated with direct sunlight and sky light accurately.

< Material >

To specify the reflection characteristic of various materials, we measured the reflectance of each material and examined whether or not the calculation results based on the measurement coincided with the change of the actual object's brightness. As a result, we found that use of measured data was by far superior to modeling reflectance in order to accurately express materials. The reflectance to express materials is considered in terms of goniophotometric luminosity; diffusional direction or specular direction. Moreover, the material of transparent objects is expressed by transmissivity.

Therefore, it is necessary to precisely perform the following.

(a) under a clear sky

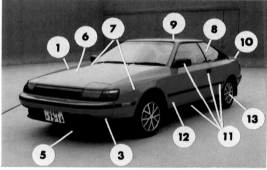

(b) under a cloudy sky

Fig. 2.1 Analysis of realism using an actual car

Table 2.1 Features of an actual car's appearance and their factors   ○ : shows that the item is a main factor

features of appearance	light source			material			color	comp-lexity	others
	direct sunlight	sky light	ground light	diffuse reflection	specular reflection	trans-mission			
① base color of painted surface	○			○			○		
② brightness of highlight	○				○		○		
③ color under bumper		○	○	○			○		
④ clear shade		○					○		
⑤ density of shade		○					○	○	
⑥ reflection of sky light		○			○		○		
⑦ reflection of background					○		○		
⑧ glass feeling					○	○	○		
⑨ brightness of edge							○		sheen , diffraction
⑩ blur							○		lense effect
⑪ parts	○	○	○	○	○		○	○	
⑫ parting line							○	○	
⑬ wheel	○	○	○	○	○		○	○	

(1) Reflectance of diffusion area : High-precision measurement.
(2) Reflectance of specular reflection area : Classify objects into those following the Fresnel formula and those not following the formula to measure reflectance. The latter needs to be measured.
(3) Transmissivity: Consider it for transparent objects like glass. For colored glass, measure spectrum absorption. We examined the influence of sky light and ground light by changing the inclination of surface.

< Color >
The light reflected on or transmitted through an object enters the human eye as spectrum distribution. The color human eyes "perceive" in this case is the sense caused by stimulated ocular cells. Physically, it can be said that ocular cells are receivers weighted by light wavelengths. Therefore, to accurately display the same colors as those that humans perceive on a CRT, it is necessary to reproduce colors by considering the characteristics of the human eye. Many studies on the above have already been reported[13].

< Complexity >
To correctly recognize an object a human sees, the object should be provided with some details. A human usually sees and touches various objects and memorizes the complexity of each object as knowledge. Visual meaning is determined by the association of empirical perception under various experiences. In the case of a car, for example, a human can imagine that it has tires with wheels, door handles, windows, and so on. To make the object appear more realistic on CG, the object should be provided with familiar details, such as side mirrors, license plate, etc.

Complexity is needed not only for the object to be expressed but also for the peripheral background. This is also found in the display examples of the literature[5] which increases realism as a whole by providing the background reflected on an object with complexity.

3 RENDERING MODEL

In this section, the reflection model expression, which is the fundamental model for rendering, is first established. Next, the light source and material which are important factors for realism are modeled, and then they are integrated into the reflection model.

3.1 Reflection model expression

< other work >
The conventional expression of object surface reflection is as follows[8],[9],

$$I(\lambda) = \varepsilon(\lambda) + \int_{\Omega} \rho(\lambda) L(\lambda) \cos\theta \, d\omega. \qquad 3.1$$

where,
λ : Wavelength
$I(\lambda)$: Reflected light going in a certain direction
$\varepsilon(\lambda)$: Light emitting from an object going toward the direction of the reflection
$\rho(\lambda)$: Reflectance of the object's surface
$L(\lambda)$: Incident light
θ : Incident angle
$d\omega$: Differential solid angle of incident light
Ω : Solid angle of the entire incident light
(See Fig. 3.1)

Though this is an excellent expression for a global illumination, it is not clear on the following points.
(1) $\rho(\lambda)$ is not clearly defined. Because there are several different types of object surface reflectance, it is necessary to clarify which type to apply.
(2) $L(\lambda)$ is not minutely analyzed.
(3) Because the unit of each value is not clear, comparison with the actual value cannot be made. Therefore, it is difficult to verify the actual data.

< Our approach >
We have solved the problems described in the above Items (1) through (3) and propose the following expression for practical use.

$$I(\lambda) = \varepsilon(\lambda) + \frac{1}{\pi}\int_{\Omega} \beta(\lambda) L(\lambda) \cos\theta \, d\omega \quad (W \cdot sr^{-1} \cdot nm^{-1} \cdot m^{-2}) \qquad 3.2$$

Where, λ is the wavelength having unit (nm). $I(\lambda)$, $\varepsilon(\lambda)$, and $L(\lambda)$ have the same definition as that of expression (3.1). Each of them is the spectral radiance having each unit $(W \cdot sr^{-1} \cdot nm^{-1} \cdot m^{-2})$. Ω, θ, and ω have the same definition. $\beta(\lambda)$ is the spectral radiance factor of object surface. Actually, however, the spectral reflectance factor $R(\lambda)$ having unit (1) realizing colorimetry is used.
Where,
$R(\lambda)$: spectral reflectance factor (1) from $L(\lambda)$ to $I(\lambda)$

The coefficient $1/\pi$ before the integral sign appears because of using the spectral radiance factor $\beta(\lambda)$ as the reflectance. This expression includes the following to solve the problems (1) through (3).
[1] All units are clarified and the measured value $\beta(\lambda)$ or $R(\lambda)$ is used as $\rho(\lambda)$.
[2] Especially the direct sunlight and sky light are precisely calculated for $L(\lambda)$.

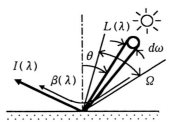

Fig. 3.1 Incident light $L(\lambda)$ and reflected light $I(\lambda)$

This paper advances by omitting $\varepsilon(\lambda)$ for convenience sake. That is,

$$I(\lambda) = \frac{1}{\pi}\int_{\Omega} \beta(\lambda) L(\lambda) \cos\theta \, d\omega \quad (W \cdot sr^{-1} \cdot nm^{-1} \cdot m^{-2}). \qquad 3.3$$

To clarify the expression (3.3), separate the incident light $L(\lambda)$ into specular reflected light, direct sunlight, and other light sources.

$$\Omega = \Omega_R + \Omega_S + \Omega_G \qquad (sr) \qquad 3.4$$

Where,
Ω_R : Solid angle of the area in the direction of specular reflection
Ω_S : Solid angle of the area in the direction of main light source
Ω_G : Solid angle of the area other than the above
The above expression is illustrated in Fig. 3.2.

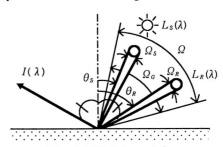

Fig. 3.2 Division of Ω

Where each value is defined as follows:
$L_R(\lambda)$: Spectral radiance of the light from the direction of specular reflection
$L_S(\lambda)$: Spectral radiance of main light source (direct sunlight)
θ_R : Incident angle (rad) of $L_R(\lambda)$
θ_S : Incident angle of $L_S(\lambda)$
$\beta_R(\lambda)$: Spectral radiance factor (1) from $L_R(\lambda)$ to $I(\lambda)$
$\beta_S(\lambda)$: Spectral radiance factor (1) from $L_S(\lambda)$ to $I(\lambda)$
$d\omega_R$: Differential solid angle (sr) of $L_R(\lambda)$

$\Delta\omega_s$: Solid angle of $L_s(\lambda)$

Therefore, the reflected light $I(\lambda)$ is obtained from the expression (3.3) as follows:

$$I(\lambda) = \frac{1}{\pi} \int_{\varrho_R + \varrho_S + \varrho_G} \beta(\lambda) L(\lambda) \cos\theta \, d\omega$$
$$= f(\lambda) L_R(\lambda) + \frac{1}{\pi}\beta_S(\lambda) L_S(\lambda) \cos\theta_S \cdot \Delta\omega_S + G(\lambda). \quad 3.5$$

However, assume $f(\lambda)$ and $G(\lambda)$ are as follows :

$$f(\lambda) \equiv \frac{I(\lambda)}{I_R(\lambda)} = \beta_R(\lambda) \cos\theta_R \, d\omega_R. \qquad 3.6$$

$$G(\lambda) \equiv \frac{1}{\pi}\int_{\varrho_G} \beta(\lambda) L(\lambda) \cos\theta \, d\omega. \qquad 3.7$$

For normal paint surfaces, because $f(\lambda)$ can be approximated by the Fresnel factor f which is independent of wavelength[14], the expression (3.5) can be rewritten as follows:

$$I(\lambda) = f \cdot L_R(\lambda) + \frac{1}{\pi}\beta_S(\lambda) L_S(\lambda) \cos\theta_S \cdot \Delta\omega_S + G(\lambda). \quad 3.8$$

3.2 Light source

3.2.1 Direct sunlight

Because direct sunlight has been ambiguously considered so far, it has been used only as a parallel light source with high luminance. Habu et al.[15] insist that direct sunlight depends on the latitude, season, hour, air contamination, and amount of steam at the arrival point and has the characteristic in which the variation depends on the wavelength. Therefore, because it is assumed that direct sunlight influences the appearance of an object, we decided to rigorously consider direct sunlight.

The spectral radiance $L_s(\lambda)$ of sunlight on the ground surface is expressed by the spectral irradiance $E_m(\lambda)$ $(W \cdot nm^{-1} \cdot m^{-2})$ on the ground surface and its solid angle $\Delta\omega_s$ (sr) as the following expression.

$$L_s(\lambda) = E_m(\lambda)/\Delta\omega_s \quad (W \cdot sr^{-1} \cdot nm^{-1} \cdot m^{-2}) \quad 3.9$$

Moreover, $E_m(\lambda)$ is expressed according to the Beer-Bouguer-Lambert's law as follows[16]:

$$E_m(\lambda) = E_0(\lambda) \cdot e^{-\{C_R(\lambda)+C_M(\lambda)+C_{oz}(\lambda)\}m} \cdot \tau_0(\lambda) \cdot \tau_w(\lambda)$$
$$(W \cdot nm^{-1} \cdot m^{-2}). \quad 3.10$$

Where,

$\Delta\omega_s$: Solid angle when viewing the sun from the ground surface [17]

m : Air mass[18]

$E_0(\lambda)$: Spectral irradiance out of atmosphere[19]. In this case, use CIMO－VII (1981)[20].

$C_R(\lambda)$: Attenuation factor according to Rayleigh diffusion of air molecules[21],[22]

$$C_R(\lambda) = 0.00864 \, \lambda^{-(3.916 + 0.074\lambda + 0.050/\lambda)} \quad (\lambda:\mu m) \quad 3.11$$

$C_M(\lambda)$: Attenuation factor according to diffusion of aerosol[23]

$$C_M(\lambda) = \beta\lambda^{-\alpha} \quad (\lambda:\mu m) \quad 3.12$$

The factors α and β are obtained through measurement[24].

$C_{oz}(\lambda)$: Absorption coefficient due to absorption of ozone[25]

$\tau_0(\lambda)$: Attenuation factor according to oxygen molecules in the atmosphere[26]

$\tau_w(\lambda)$: Attenuation factor according to water vapor in the atmosphere[27],[28],[29]

Among the above values, $\tau_0(\lambda)$ and $\tau_w(\lambda)$ are omitted because they are very weak in visible wavelength, and their influence is small.

3.2.2. Sky light
< Other work >

Our purpose for sky light integration is to clarify spectral distribution and luminance at each point in the sky under any weather condition. Many research studies have been made about luminance so far[30]. For spectral distribution, however, no decisive research has been made. This is because the logical analysis of spectral distribution is difficult since sky light is generated through complex processes such as dissipation of direct sunlight due to air, aerosol, and clouds or repetitive reflection of it on the ground. The following are examples of relevant research. Nakamae et al.(1980) simulated object appearance with CG under clear sky and overcast sky using the CIE standard clear sky light luminance expression[31]. R.V. Klassen(1987) simulated refraction, diffusion, and absorption due to air molecules and aerosol to express the color of sky light through CG[32]. Sekine(1989) analytically calculated spectral distribution at each point of clear sky[33]. In these research studies, however, spectral distribution at each point in the sky under any weather condition was not obtained.

< Our approach >

We proposed a method to obtain spectral distribution at any point in the sky under any weather condition using the empirical formula obtained through measurement.

[1] Classification of sky light

We clarified the sky that we handled. In general, the sky can be classified into the following three types[34].

    <1> Clear sky   : Sky free from clouds

    <2> Intermediate homogeneous sky : Sky in which weather homogeneously changes between clear and overcast skies without clouds scattered in the sky

    <3> Overcast sky : Sky covered with clouds so thick that the sun cannot be seen

In the intermediate sky expressing the intermediate state between clear and overcast skies, clouds are actually scattered. In this section, however, we use the intermediate homogeneous sky in Item <2> for convenience sake. Also in this section. we deal with Items <1> through <3> in order to meet (Requirement 3).

[2] Calculation of spectral distribution at any point of sky light.

The method proposed by us uses the fact that sky light luminance has a certain correlation with color temperature(See Fig. 3.5). The spectral distribution at any point of sky light is obtained as shown in Fig. 3.3. The process to determine spectral distribution of sky light, turbidity factor T_{ul}, and atmospheric dirtiness are described in Item 3.2.3.

The calculation for processes <A>, <B>, and <C> in Fig. 3.3 is defined as follows:

Process <A> (Calculation of sky light luminance distribution)

The luminance distribution at each point in the sky can be obtained by inputting the sun altitude γ_s, turbidity factor T_{ul}, and atmospheric dirtiness. The following luminance expressions are proposed corresponding to the skies <1>, <2>, and <3> classified

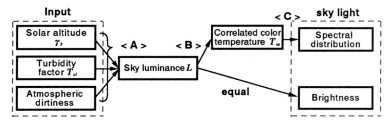

Fig. 3.3 Process to determine spectral distribution of sky light

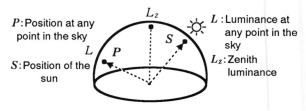

Fig. 3.4 Symbols in the sky

in Item [1].
<1> CIE standard clear sky light luminance function[35].
<2> Intermediate homogeneous sky light luminance function[36].
<3> CIE standard overcast sky light luminance function[37].

The above expressions in Items <1> and <3> are specified as international standards, which express only clear sky and overcast sky respectively. The luminance at each point of the sky is expressed as the ratio to the zenith luminance L_z (cd/m^2). Though the expression in Item <2> is not recognized as an international standard yet, it is shown in the 1988 CIE Technical Report in detail[30]. It is possible to continuously change the luminance at each point of the sky between clear and overcast using the turbidity factor T_{ul} as a parameter. Items <1> through <3> are expressed in the following form respectively.

<1> $L/L_z = f_1(P, S)$ [35]   (1)   3.13
$L_z = g_1(T_{ul}, \gamma_s)$ (cd/m^2)   3.14

<2> $L = f_2(P, S, T_{ul})$ [36]   (cd/m^2)   3.15

<3> $L/L_z = f_3(P, S)$ [37]   (1)   3.16
$L_z = g_2(\gamma_s)$ (cd/m^2)   3.17

Process <B> (Conversion of luminance into correlated color temperature)

When assuming the luminance at any point in the sky as L (cd/m^2) and the correlated color temperature corresponding to the above luminance as T_{cp}(K), the relationship between L and Tcp is shown by the expression below,

$$T_{cp} = \frac{1.1985 \times 10^8}{L^{1.2}} + 6500 \qquad (K). \qquad 3.18$$

The above expression is based on our measurements. That is, we regressively obtained it from the results of examining the relationship between the luminance at any point in the sky and color temperature at any hour and spot in Japan. We found that there is a strong link between them(See Fig. 3.5.).

Process <C> (Conversion of correlated color temperature into spectral distribution)

A method is needed to convert correlated color temperature into spectral distribution using measured data. However, because the method is not determined at present, we used the CIE synthesized daylight expression proposed by Judd, MacAdam, Wyszecki[38].

3.2.3 Weather simulation

As stated in **Requirement 3**, a car body's surface color is evaluated by assuming its appearance at various places and under various weather conditions, because the surface may not look good under a cloudy sky though it looks good under a clear sky.

For the existing CG, most research is made for the rendering of appearance under a clear sky with direct sunlight, and does not include the idea of a rigorously rendered appearance depending on weather condition. We proposed a method to render the appearance of objects under any weather condition. For this, we first considered the spectral distribution and intensity of direct sunlight and skylight which are the main outdoor light sources by defining the factors which determine weather and using the factors as input data.

[1] Factors to simulate weather
It is considered that the following four factors change weather.
(1) Position (Latitude and longitude on the earth).
(2) Date and hour (Hour based on universal time).
(3) Weather simulation factors.
They are the values defined by meteorology.
<1> Atmospheric transmittance: P, P_v.
<2> Coefficient of turbidity α, β, water vapor content, oxygen content, and ozone content.
<3> Turbidity factor: T, T_{ul}.
(4) Atmospheric dirtiness.
This is the parameter to indicate how the atmosphere is contaminated due to artificial factors, though this is not minutely studied at present. For sky light, however, there is the method to indicate the condition of the sky on contaminated industrial areas by correcting the sky light luminance distribution[30].

[2] Calculation for direct sunlight and sky light.
(1) Direct sunlight.
For direct sunlight, $E_m(\lambda)$ in the expression (3.10) can be obtained using the factors described in Item[1] to obtain the direct sunlight value $L_s(\lambda)$ as a light source using the expression (3.9).
(2) Sky light.
For sky light, it is first necessary to know the Luminance distribution of any weather condition. In this case, we use the intermediate homogeneous sky light Luminance function in the expression (3.15). This can also be obtained using the factors described in Item[1].
P, P_v, T, and T_{ul} can be obtained with $E_m(\lambda)$ and air mass m [30].

3.3   Material

To express realism, a rigorous definition of materials as well as light sources are needed. Because the modality of reflection or transmission when light hits an object depends on the object, it is very important for expressing appearance of various materials to accurately check these physical phenomena. Reflection or transmission produced when light hits an object is generally classified into the following four types from ① through ④.

① Diffuse reflection

Most existing research mathematically models the diffusion reflection according to Lambert's law[39],[40]. However, it is difficult to use these model expressions because they include several parameters to delicately change the material, and the parameters must be adjusted through trial and error in order to express a proposed material. Therefore, the model expressions are rarely applied to the requirement to accurately render the materials of existing objects.

Prof. Minato has established the method to specify the diffuse reflection of objects by measuring the spectral reflectance factor showing the diffuse reflection[41]. By using the reflectance obtained through measurement as the reflectance $\beta(\lambda)$ in the expression (3.3), the material of an actual object can accurately be rendered without setting parameters.

The spectral reflectance factor $R(\lambda)$ is measured by changing the angle α(gonio-angle) on the basis of the specular reflection direction as shown in Fig.3.7. Figure 3.8 shows the equipment used to measure $R(\alpha, \lambda)$.

The results of measuring $R(\alpha, \lambda)$ for paint are shown in Fig. 3.9. The material can be decided according to the shape of the

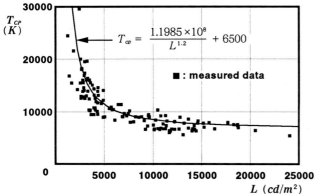

Fig. 3.5 Measured data and approximate formula

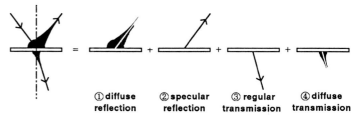

① diffuse reflection   ② specular reflection   ③ regular transmission   ④ diffuse transmission

Fig. 3.6 Classification of reflection and transmission

graph. Therefore, various materials can be created by controlling and changing the graphic shape.

We further developed the method of Minato et al. in order to accurately perform the coloring calculations for any weather condition. That is, we devised the method to calculate $G(\lambda)$ in the expression (3.7) depending on the material. $G(\lambda)$ is an important term to determine the brightness depending on background light.

For example, because $R(\alpha,\lambda)$ of a solid paint surface can be considered as a homogeneous diffusion surface taking an almost constant value when α goes beyond the ranges of $10° \leqq \alpha \leqq 20°$, it is possible to integrate only ω by removing $R(\alpha,\lambda)$ from the integral terms.

Meanwhile, because the change rate of $R(\alpha,\lambda)$ to α is large for a metallic paint surface, it is necessary to accurately calculate $G(\lambda)$ for ω. Especially under a cloudy sky light without direct sunlight, it is not permitted to simply approximate $G(\lambda)$ because the weight of $G(\lambda)$ is large in the coloring calculation expression (3.5). Moreover, because the area of small α (about $0° \leqq \alpha \leqq 30°$) where $R(\alpha,\lambda)$ steeply changes and greatly influences the appearance of objects under a cloudy sky, it is necessary to accurately measure the area.

② Specular reflection

Specular reflection is the factor to determine the reflecting degree of lustrous objects, which is an important factor contributing to realism. Therefore, it is necessary to strictly consider the specular reflection as well as the diffuse reflection. The specular reflection is expressed as the specular reflectance. Because the specular reflection depends on the material, it should be determined for each material.

The specular reflection of a pure glass surface producing no diffuse reflection follows Fresnel's formula. However, it is difficult to formulate the specular reflection because the materials, some paint surfaces, metal surfaces, resin surfaces, and lustrous rubber surfaces considered in this section show characteristics different from Fresnel's formula. Therefore, it is most effective to obtain the specular reflectance through measurement.

For specular reflectance, the influence of light polarization is easily overlooked. However, specular reflectance also depends on the polarized-light condition of incident light. Therefore, to be exact, it is necessary to consider the specular reflectance including the influence of polarized light. For example, blue sky light in clear sky is clearly polarized. Therefore, when considering the reflection of the above light, the above concept is necessary.

We define the extended Fresnel's formula capable of considering the polarization characteristics of incident light.

That is,

$$f = \frac{p r_s^2 + s r_p^2}{s + p}. \qquad 3.19$$

Where, r_s and r_p represent the amplitude reflectance of Fresnel's s-wave and p-wave respectively, and s and p represent the energy ratio between s-wave and p-wave components of incident light respectively.

Only when incident light is natural light, s equals p and the expression (3.19) is expressed as the following formula which has widely been used.

$$f = \frac{1}{2}(r_s^2 + r_p^2) \qquad 3.20$$

③ Regular transmission

For objects to transmit light like glass, it is necessary to obtain regular transmittance through measurement. When assuming regular transmittance as t, as is generally known, t can be expressed as $t = 1 - f$ using the specular reflectance f.

In addition, because the transmitted light is attenuated inside the glass, the color seen through the glass depends on the glass. Therefore, attenuation of transmitted light should also be considered.

If light $L(\lambda)$ $(W \cdot sr^{-1} \cdot nm^{-1} \cdot m^{-2})$ enters chromatic or achromatic glass with the incident angle of θ_1, the transmitted light $T(\lambda, l)$ when the light $L(\lambda)$ advances by the distance $l\,(m)$ through the glass is expressed as following :

$$T(\lambda, l) = L(\lambda) \cdot t \cdot e^{-C(\lambda) \cdot l} \qquad (W \cdot sr^{-1} \cdot nm^{-1} \cdot m^{-2}). \qquad 3.21$$

Where, $C(\lambda)$ represents the absorption coefficient of glass. $C(\lambda)$ can be obtained through measurement with the equipment shown in Fig. 3.8.

④ Diffuse transmission

Though the glass to diffuse-transmit light is rarely used for cars, it is widely used in the world, in which frosted glass is a typical example. To express a material like this, it is necessary to strictly consider diffuse transmission[11].

3.4 Background-synthesizing technique

It is important for enhancing realism to give complexity not only to a car but also to its background. Background pictures have frequently been used for background in order to produce realism[42]. However, though the following conditions are necessary to balance with a display object, they have rarely been executed so far.

(1) Coincidence of perspective between background and display object
(2) Coincidence of illumination conditions between background and display object

For these conditions, measurement is needed as well as background photography. Item(1) shows the condition related to shape, which is not technically difficult. Item(2) is important

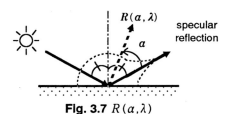

Fig. 3.7 $R(\alpha,\lambda)$

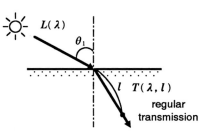

Fig. 3.10 $T(\lambda,l)$

Fig. 3 8 Gonio-spectro photometer

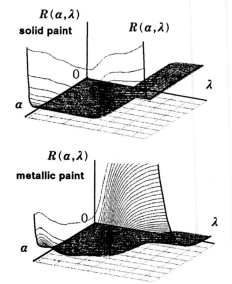

Fig. 3.9 Configuration of $R(\alpha,\lambda)$

because the background and display object are seen as if they are put under the same light source. To satisfy the condition in Item(2), the following conditions <1> and <2> should also be satisfied.

<1> Each luminance of the background displayed on a CRT should be proportional to the corresponding luminance of the actual background.

<2> The reference of brightness between the display object and background should be matched.

To realize Item<1>, it is necessary to consider the characteristics of the film used to photograph the background, scanner to take in the film as picture images, and monitor. However, this is the subject for further research at present. Item<2> is not technically difficult.

4 RESULT

The images generated by the rendering model proposed by us are shown. The computer system used was the COMPUTING SURFACE made by MEIKO Co.,Ltd., which has 256 processors(T800). These generated images have a resolution of 1,280 by 1,024 pixels. The configuration data used was prepared by the TOYOTA Styling CAD System and each surface was Bézier surface of degree three, and the calculation was executed on Bézier surface directly.

The images were generated entirely by applying our algorithm to the ray tracing, and the antialiasing method was not used .

4.1 Verification of calculation model through experiments

We show the effectiveness of the rendering model we proposed by comparing the calculation results using the model with measured values. The following shows a verification experiment made by using an actual car outdoors under a clear sky as an example of the comparison .

< Experiment data >
(1) Data: At 11 : 28 on October 20 in 1989 (Friday)
(2) Location: Toyota-city, Aichi-prefecture, Japan at $35°$ 2'55.07" North and $137°$ 9'45.26" East
(3) Meteorological conditions: Weather : Clear sky (No clouds), Atmospheric transmittance $P = 0.722$, Coefficient of turbidity $\alpha = 0.957$, $\beta = 0.113$
(4) Sun altitude γ_s : $44.35°$ (Air mass $m = 1.442$)
(5) Measuring instruments : Precision pyrheliometer (Model MS − 52 made by Eko Co.,Ltd.), Sun-photo meter (Model MS − 110 made by Eko Co.,Ltd.), Luminance meter (MINOLTA CS − 100)
(6) Actual car used : '86-type TOYOTA CELICA

<Results>
Verification was made by comparing calculation results with measured values at six points of A,B,C,D,E and F as shown in Fig. 4.1. Comparison items used the chromaticity (x,y) and luminance Y (Fig.4.2). As a result, the values were almost

squared. From this verification, we could confirm the model's effectiveness.

4.2 The images resulting from our method

Pictures 1 through 5 show the results on display. Table 4.1 shows calculation time and resolution. Picture 1 shows variation of view point. Pictures 2, 3 show variation of material. Picture 4 shows simulation of different weather conditions. Picture 5 shows other examples.

5 CONCLUSION AND FUTURE WORK

We have developed a rendering technique to generate realistic images meeting designers' requirements by rigorously considering the light source and material and including them in the reflection model expression.

We have compared the results of the calculations using this technique with measurements of actual cars in order to confirm the model's effectiveness. As a result, the values were virtually equal. From this verification, we have been able to confirm the model's effectiveness.

This technique makes it possible to :
(1) Generate an image as if it is an actual object.
(2) Render any material and color.
(3) Render the appearance at any place and time under any weather conditions.

We need to make meteorological observations at many places in the world, such as Tokyo, London, Los Angeles, etc., to check the appearance of cars under various weather conditions.

Further research is needed to improve the background -synthesizing technique.

6 ACKNOWLEDGEMENT

We'd like to express special thanks to Prof. Sachie Minato, Kinki University, for the valuable practical and theoretical advice he provided in the development of this research. We also thank Messrs. Habu and Nakahara of Electrotechnical Laboratory who advised us about direct sunlight, and Prof. Oki of Meijo University who advised us about sky light .

Finally, we express our thanks to Mr. Nagasaka, the head of the System Engineering Dept., Design Div., who proposed and actively supported this research project, and the staff of Engineering Dept. and the Development dept. No.1 Information Systems Div. No. 1.

Table 4.1 Elapsed time & resolution

Fig.	1 ~ 4	5 (a) , (b)	5 (c)
elapsed time	8 min.	30 min.	35 min.
resolution	640 × 512	1280 × 1024	

Fig. 4.1 Measured points A, B,C, D, E, F

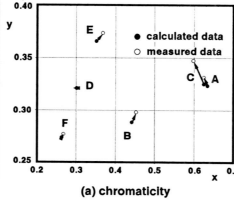

(a) chromaticity

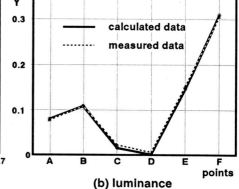

(b) luminance

Fig. 4.2 Comparison of (a) chromaticity and (b) luminance

Variations of view point
PICTURE 1

solid paint   metallic paint

Variation of the material
PICTURE 2

paint No.1   paint No.2

Simulation of the subtle
differences between similar
materials
PICTURE 3

on a clear day   on a cloudy day

Simulation of different
types of weather conditions
PICTURE 4

PICTURE 5
a) ~ c)
EXAMPLES

**a) Magnification of
(PICTURE 4 right)**

b) Two -Tone

**c) For checking
exterior color**

REFERENCE

[1] Higashi,M., I.,Kohzen, J.,Nagasaka, "An Interactive CAD System for Construction of Shapes with High-Quality Surface", E.A.Warman(ed) Computer Applications in Production and Engineering, (North-Holland,1983), P.371 – 390

[2] Whitted,Turner, "An Improved Illumination Model for Shaded Display", Communication of The ACM, VOL.23, No.6,June 1980, pp.343 – 349.

[3] Hall,Ray A., and Donald P. Greenberg, "A Testbed for Realistic Image Synthesis", IEEE CG&A, Vol.3, No.8, November 1983, pp.10 – 20.

[4] Amanatides,John, "Ray Tracing with Cones", Computer Graphics (Proceedings SIGGRAPH '84), Vol.18, No.3, July 1984, pp.129 – 135.

[5] Cook,R.L., T.,Porter, and L.,Carpenter,"Distributed Ray Tracing", Computer Graphics (Proceedings SIGGRAPH '84), Vol.18, No.3, July 1984, pp.137 – 145.

[6] Kajiya,James T.,"The Rendering Equation", Computer Graphics (Proceedings SIGGRAPH '86), Vol.20, No.4, August 1986, pp.143 – 150

[7] Ward,Gregory J.,Francis M. Rubinstein,Robert D. Clear,"A Ray Tracing Solution for Diffuse Interreflection", Computer Graphics (Proceedings SIGGRAPH '88), Vol.22, No.4, August 88 1988, pp.85 – 92

[8] Cohen,Michel F.,Donald P. Greenberg, "THE HEMI-CUBE : A Radiosity Solution for Complex Environments", Computer Graphics (Proceedings SIGGRAPH '85), Vol.19, No.3, July 1985, pp.31 – 40

[9] Hall,Roy A.,"A Characterization of Illumination Models and Shading Techniques",The Visual Computer Vol.2, No.5,(September 1986), pp.268 – 277

[10] Immel,David S., Michel F. Cohen, Donald P. Greenberg,"A Radiosity Method for Non-Diffuse Environments", Computer Graphics (Proceedings SIGGRAPH '86), Vol.20, No.4, August 1986, pp.133 – 142

[11] Wallance,John R.,Michel F. Cohen, Donald P. Greenberg,"A Two -Pass Solution to The Rendering Equation: A Synthesis of Ray Tracing and Radiosity Methods", Computer Graphics (Proceedings SIGGRAPH '87), Vol.21, No.4, July 1987,pp.311 – 320

[12] Cohen,Michel F.,Shenchang Eric Chen,John R.Wallance, Donald P. Greenberg, "A Progressive Refinement Approach to Fast Radiosity Image Generation",Computer Graphics (Proceedings SIGGRAPH '89), Vol.22, No.4, August 88 1988, pp.75 – 84

[13] For example, Hall,Roy A., "Illumination and Color in Computer Generated Imagery",Springer-Verlag, 1988

[14] Baba,Goroh, Hidejiroh,Mori, "The Measurements of Object Colors Which Give Metal-Like-Feeling", Proceedings of The 6th Joint Conference on Color Technology, 1989, November, pp.131 – 134

[15] Habu,Mitsuhiro, Mamoru,Suzuki, Takehiko,Nagasaka, "Measurement of The Solar Spectral Irradiance at Tanashi, Tokyo(1)",Researches of The Electrotechnical Laboratory No.812 ,February,1981

[16] Habu Mitsuhiro, Mamoru,Suzuki, "Measurement of The Solar Spectral Irradiance at Tanashi, Tokyo",J. Illum. Engng. Inst. Jpn. Vol.68,No.2 ,1984 ,pp.83 – 89

[17] For example, R.M.L. Baker and M.W.Makemson,"An Introduction to Astrodynamics ",Academic Press,1960

[18] Kasten,F.,"A rch. Meteor. Geophys. Bioklio, Ser. B.",Vol.14,p.14, 1966

[19] Shibata,kazuo, et. al.,"Spectral Distribution and measurement of Solar Energy",Gakkai Shuppan Center, JAPAN ,p.22 ,1987

[20] WMO – No.590 , "Commission for Instruments and Methods of Observation Abridged Final Report of The Eighth Session", October 1981, pp.8 – 11

[21] Fröhlich,C., G.E.Shaw, "New Determination of Rayleigh Scattering in The Terrestrial Atmosphere", Appl. Optics, Vol.19, 1980 , pp.1773 – 1775

[22] Young,A.T.,"Revised Depolarization Corrections For Atmospheric Extinction ", Appl. Optics, Vol.19, 1980, pp.3427 – 3428

[23] For example, Iqbal,Muhammad, "An Introduction To Solar Radiation", The University of British Columbia, 1983, Academic Press, Chap.6.6

[24] Nakahara,Kanji, Naomasa,Yui, "Method for Outdoor Calibration of Reference Solar Cells", Researches of The Electrotechnical Laboratory No.842 , May, 1984

[25] E.C.Y.Inn, Y.,Tanaka,"Absorption Coefficient of Ozone in The Ultraviolet and Visible Regions", J. Opt. Soc. Am., Vol.43, No.10, 1953, pp.870 – 873

[26] T.G.ADIKS,YU.S. Georgiyevskiy ,M.S. Malkevich and N.S.Filippova, "Atmospheric Transmission in The 0.76 μm O_2 Band ", Izv., Atmospheric and Oceanic Physics, Vol.8, No.4, 1972, pp.369 – 381

[27] P.Koepke, H.Quenzel, "Water Vapor : Spectral Transmission at Wavelengths Between $0.7\mu m$ and $1\mu m$", Applied Optics, Vol.17, No.13, July 1978, pp.2114 – 2118

[28] Gates,David M., "Near Infrared Atmospheric Transmission to Solar Radiation", J. Opt. Soc. Am. Vol.50, No.12, December 1960 , pp.1299 – 1304

[29] Gates,David M.,Walter J. Harrop, "Infrared Transmission of The Atmosphere to Solar Radiation", Applied Optics,Vol.2, No.9 , September 1963, pp.887 – 898

[30] Division 3 , TC 3.09, Average Sky as A Standard CIE Technical Report, "Luminance Distributions of Various Reference Skies", Complete Draft, March 1988

[31] Nishita,Tomoyuki, Eihachiro,Nakamae, "Continuous Tone Representation of Three-Dimensional Objects Illuminated by Sky Light", Computer Graphics (Proceedings SIGGRAPH '86), Vol.20,No.4, August 1986, pp.125 – 132

[32] Klassen, R. V., "Modeling The Effect of The Atmosphere on Light", ACM Transactions on Graphics, Vol.6, No.3, July 1987, pp.215 – 237

[33] Sekine,Seishi, "Spectral Distributions of Clear Sky Light and Their Chromaticities", J. Illum. Engng. Inst. Jpn. Vol.73, No.2, 1989, pp.39 – 45

[34] Sekine,Seishi, "Optical Characteristics of The Turbid Atmosphere", J. Illum. Engng. Inst. Jpn. Vol.71, No.6, 1987, pp.333 – 338

[35] CIE : Publication TC 4.2, No.22, "Standardization of Luminance Distribution on clear skies", 1973

[36] Kittler,Richard, "Luminance Models of Homogeneous Sky for Design and Energy Performance Predictions", Proc. 2. Int. Daylight Conf., Long Beach, Nov. 1986

[37] Natural Daylight. Official Recommendations, Compte Rendu CIE 13e Session 1955, (Paris : The Commision, Vol.2, 1955), Committee(E-3.2), P. II , 1955

[38] Judd, D. B., MacAdam, D. L., Wyszecki, G., J. Opt. Soc. Am., Vol.54, 1964, p.1031

[39] Phong,Bui Tuong, "Illumination for Computer Generated Pictures", Communications of The ACM, Vol.18, pp.311 – 317, 1975

[40] Cook,Robert,L., "A Reflectance Model for Computer Graphics", Computer Graphics (Proceedings SIGGRAPH '81), Vol.15, No.3, August 1981, pp.307 – 316

[41] Minato,Sachie, "Color and Gloss", J. of Color Science Association of Japan, Vol.4, No.1, 1979, pp.29 – 30

[42] Hall,Roy A., "Hybrid Techniques for Rapid Image Synthesis", Image Rendering Trics, SIGGRAPH '86 Course Notes, Vol.16, 1986

A Model for Anisotropic Reflection

Pierre Poulin and Alain Fournier

Department of Computer Science
University of Toronto
Toronto, Ontario, Canada M5S 1A4

Currently:
Department of Computer Science
University of British Columbia
Vancouver, BC, Canada V6T 1W5
{poulin|fournier}@cs.ubc.edu

Abstract

A reflection and refraction model for anisotropic surfaces is introduced. The anisotropy is simulated by small cylinders (added or subtracted) distributed on the anisotropic surface. Different levels of anisotropy are achieved by varying the distance between each cylinder and/or rising the cylinders more or less from the surface. Multidirectional anisotropy is modelled by orienting groups of cylinders in different direction. The intensity of the reflected light is computed by determining the visible and illuminated portion of the cylinders, taking self-blocking into account. We present two techniques to compute this in practice. In one the intensity is computed by sampling the surface of the cylinders. The other is an analytic solution. In the case of the diffuse component, the solution is exact. In the case of the specular component, an approximation is developed using a Chebyshev polynomial approximation of the specular term, and integrating the polynomial.

This model can be implemented easily within most rendering system, given a suitable mechanism to define and alter surface tangents. The effectiveness of the model and the visual importance of anisotropy are illustrated with some pictures.

CR Categories and Subject Descriptors: I.3.7 [Computer Graphics]: Three-Dimensional Graphics and Realism.
General Terms: Algorithms.
Additional Key Words and Phrases: Shadowing, surface mapping, Chebyshev polynomials, hair rendering, scientific visualization.

1 Introduction

Many objects in nature are visually very complex. Crow, as quoted in [13], suggested having different levels of geometric models to capture this complexity. However, as the representation of an object requires the addition of smaller

geometric models to define smaller details, the extra cost of modelling and rendering these details can become very high. Moreover such an object representation would be prone to aliasing problems.

To overcome these problems, approximations to some geometric models have been proposed. If we note D_g the level of the geometry at which objects are usually defined (i.e. polygons or parametric surfaces), then displacement and bump mappings [4] [16] approximate what the geometric model D_{g+1} would define at a higher resolution or magnification. As the details become smaller, even surface mapping becomes highly subject to aliasing problems. At this geometric level, D_{g+2}, the details cannot be seen individually and appear only because of the way they modulate the light reflected off them. This is the reason why these details must be captured by local reflection models.

Traditionally, reflection models have been divided into two components: *diffuse* and *specular* [24] [3] [8] [2]. The diffuse component takes into account the light that interreflects onto elements of a same surface and is reemitted equally in all directions. To model the specular reflection, Torrance and Sparrow [24] assume that the surface is made of highly reflective microscopic facets distributed in v-grooves. If the facets are randomly distributed over the surface, shadowing and masking functions can be statistically estimated, and, for a given distribution of slopes of the facets, the light reflected in a particular direction can be approximated.[1] This type of surface is qualified as *isotropic* because the reflected light intensity at a given point is independent of the surface orientation along its normal at this point.

Many surfaces, however, cannot be modelled by a random isotropic distribution of facets. If an element of such surfaces is rotated around its normal while the light and viewer directions remain unchanged, the light intensity reflected to the viewer will vary. These surfaces are called *anisotropic*. Surfaces made of fur or burnished metal are examples where there is a strong correlation between the orientations of facets and the orientation of the surface. Brennan et al. [6] measured several natural surfaces and showed that surfaces like clouds, forests, oceans and even sand exhibit anisotropy. Anisotropy can be caused by a collection of strongly oriented elements, such as hair in fur or blades

---

[1] All the reflection models discussed in this paper ignore the wavelength. In the facets model, this means that the size of the facets is assumed much greater than the wavelength of the light source.

of grass in a meadow, or by the selected action of an external force. Many natural factors can contribute to preferred orientations of the facets like the wind, the sun's position for the orientation of leaves or the shape of the underwater terrain for waves. Since anisotropy is so prevalent, and our visual system use it as a cue for orientation and depth, a wide range of anisotropic surfaces needs to be accurately rendered to obtain more realistic images.

Moreover, the use of anisotropy is not restricted to the production of realistic images. With the recent emphasis on scientific visualization techniques, more and more information needs to be communicated to the viewers from a single image. The shape, colour, texture, opacity and surface roughness are some properties that can carry information. Anisotropy adds a new dimension to the information transmitted. For instance, a simple vector field over a surface can be associated to a given orientation of the facets on this surface, freeing colour or texture for other information.

This paper first briefly surveys and discusses current anisotropic reflection models. The model based on cylinders is then presented in detail, with its parameters and solutions for the reflected light. Finally images illustrating applications of anisotropy in computer graphics are presented and commented.

2 Previous Work

Kajiya [13] attempted to compute analytically the reflected intensity from a continuous surface. He bases his approach on the general Kirchhoff solution for scattering of electromagnetic waves [1] [2]. For given incident and reflected directions, the intensity reflected by a surface is computed. However, the method has its restrictions. For instance, the Kirchhoff solution is valid only if self-shadowing and multiple scattering are negligible. Even if this limitation is not considered, the size of the surface required (Fresnel zones) by the Kirchhoff solution and the stationary phase method used to approximate the integral [5] introduce new problems that are dependent of each surface type.

Cabral et al. [7] go down to the facet level. Facets are created from a height field and the reflection off each facet is studied, including the blocking factor for incident and reflected light. This method, which can be qualified as *brute force*, is computationally expensive. The computation of the blocking factor is done via a modification of Max's method for the self-shadowing of bump maps [16]. This method can seriously alias the shadows for surfaces which exhibit high frequency behaviour.

In these two approaches, the reflection intensities are computed once and kept in tables; interpolation is used for fast rendering. However, a new table needs to be computed each time another type of surface is being rendered, which involves a few hours of CPU time ($\approx$ 12 hours on an IBM4341 for Kajiya's and around the same time for Cabral's on a VAX 11/785).

In Phong's reflection model, the distribution of the specular intensity is symmetric around the reflection direction. Ohira [29] defines it as elliptic with the intention to simulate the reflection from scratches-like surfaces. However, the definition of the ellipse has no physical motivation and can lead, according to Yokoi et al., to "unnatural images". Takagi et al. [29] extend this idea of an ellipsoid to the reflection model of Torrance and Sparrow [24]. For a surface covered with scratches, the distribution of the normals of the facets can be approximated by an ellipsoid elongated in the preferred orientation of the scratches. For given light and viewer directions, the bisector between these two directions is computed. Then the intensity reflected specularly

to the viewer is considered directly proportional to the ratio of facets with their normal in this bisector direction. These last two models are only valid for "scratched" surfaces with negligible self-shadowing and multiple scattering.

Miller [17] introduced the use of cylinders to simulate anisotropy. When projecting a cylinder onto the viewing screen, only half of it is visible. The intensities at equal intervals of this projected cylinder are computed and averaged. Later, at the rendering stage, if scratches are oriented in the direction of one cylinder, the computed intensity is used to simulate the effect of the anisotropy of the surface.

Miller also adapts the *reflectance sphere* [28] for faster rendering. However, the technique inherits the limitations of the reflectance sphere. Thus, light sources are expected to be far from all the objects in a scene. The projection of the cylinder onto the viewing screen is also restricted to perspective rendering of a scene and therefore, unsuitable for a rendering technique like ray tracing. Another disadvantage is that each cylinder is treated individually, which obliges Miller to neglect the self-shadowing and the inter-reflection of one cylinder onto its neighbours. Therefore in Miller's model, for a given orientation of a cylinder, the same intensity will be computed, whatever the orientation of the surface normal.

3 Cylindrical Scratches

The model proposed here builds on the concept of Miller's cylinders. Scratches are represented by a large number of adjacent small cylinders. The intensity reflected by all the cylinders in one direction is approximated by the reflection off only a single cylinder. This approximation is accurate if many cylinders cover every sampled region of the surface. Moreover, since the cylinders have a very small radius in comparison to their length, the intensity reflected off a cylinder can be approximated by the reflection off only one cross section of this cylinder.

Consider the hierarchy of geometric models discussed previously. At the geometric level D_{g+2}, the details cannot be seen individually and are captured by the reflection model. Including our anisotropic reflection model corresponds to inserting two new geometric levels between the mapping (displacement or bump) and the isotropic reflection model, now identified as D_{g+4}. The isotropic reflection model D_{g+4}, like the facets model of Torrance and Sparrow, characterizes the surface nature of each cylinder. A group of adjacent cylinders oriented in one direction defines the D_{g+3} level while a set of groups of adjacent cylinders represents the D_{g+2} level. Figure 1 illustrates the interaction between these various levels.

To orient the cylinders, surface frame bundles (to use the terminology of [13]) need to be established. One axis is the normal at the surface, N. Another axis is the tangent to the surface, T (thus perpendicular to the normal). This tangent allows the specification of the orientation of the cylinders on the surface. The last axis defined is the binormal, B, formed by the cross product $T \times N$. The cross section of the cylinder of interest thus lies on the plane NB.

Since the normals are already defined for most of the surfaces used in computer graphics, the extra information required for introducing anisotropy is simply a tangent at each point of the surface. Many techniques have been developed to map textures [11] and perturbations of normals [4] onto objects; these techniques can easily be extended to map tangents onto objects.

The cylinders are too small to be seen individually. For each cylinder, the viewer position is so far away relative to the cylinder's radius that its direction can be assumed to be

5 Images

On Image Ia and Ib, twelve spheres with different levels of anisotropy are rendered. A directional light source is used and all the spheres are projected orthogonally onto the screen in order to keep a constant viewing direction. The anisotropy over the spheres is defined by longitudinal scratches; on some spheres the position of one of the two poles is clearly visible as a black region.

Image Ia shows spheres with the anisotropy simulated by positive cylinders. From left to right and top to bottom, the first sphere has a $d = 0.0001$ and $h = 0$. This is practically undistinguishable from an isotropic reflection model. On the next sphere, d is increased to 0.5; the highlight starts forming a ring. The highest anisotropy produced by the cylindrical model is shown on the next sphere where $d = 2.0$ while h is still 0. Note how the highlight ring is clearly defined and how dark regions appear, due to the shadowing between cylinders. On the next sphere (second row), d is raised to 5.0, leaving a floor of length 3.0 between the cylinders. Note how the isotropic highlight reappears due to this floor region while the highlight ring becomes dimmer because the cylinders occupy a smaller region (proportionally to the floor). The floor is raised to $h = 0.86$ on the next sphere, and most of the dark regions disappear. Finally, the cylinders are spaced by only 2.0 with the same $h = 0.86$. The shadowing effect, while less pronounced on this last sphere, still makes the highlight ring dimmer.

On Image Ib, negative cylinders are used, with the same values for d and h. Most of the spheres are quite similar to the ones with positive cylinders, but notice how the self-shadowing effect is more pronounced on the third sphere (with $d = 2$ and $h = 0$).

The anisotropy on a surface also influences the way the environment is reflected onto it. Image II shows four views of the same highly reflective sphere above the unavoidable checkerboard. The surface is not specular so that highlights do not complicate the picture. A directional light source points down on the sphere. On the top left corner, we used a perfect mirror-like reflection. By adding high frequency bumps onto the surface, we get the image on the top right corner; it just adds some noise to the reflection. On the bottom left corner, the surface is given longitudinal anisotropy, and on the bottom right corner the surface exhibits latitudinal anisotropy. Note how the red squares are stretched horizontally on the left while on the right the reflected squares are stretched vertically.

Images III and IV show some objects which we normally associate with anisotropy. In Image III, the objects have been created by sweeping a spline curve, and the triangles produced have their tangents approximated via the same technique than used for the surface normals. In Image IV, the sound system has many anisotropic knobs abd other parts, The hanging cloth on the right is modelled as an isotropic surface. The motifs on the cube in the foreground were created using a 3D texture which provides the various orientations for the surface tangents.

6 Conclusion

We presented an anisotropic reflection model based on covering the surface with groups of microscopic cylinders. Anisotropy is caused by the directional distribution of the normals along the cylinders. Multidirectional anisotropy can be achieved by defining groups of cylinders oriented in specific directions and given specific weights. Two parameters, the distance between cylinders and the height of the floor, provide qualitative and quantitative control over the anisotropy. These parameters can easily be tuned to simulate a specific surface or to produce the desired effect. Slightly different effects can also be produced by "negative" cylinders.

The model takes into account hiding and shadowing between cylinders. The reflected intensity can be determined from regular samples (as seen by the viewer) along the cylinders surface which are then averaged. The sampling angles can also be used to obtain the colour reflected/refracted to the viewer via the anisotropic surface. An analytic solution to the diffuse intensity over the cylinders was developed, as well as an approximation to the specular intensity using Chebyshev polynomials. The Chebyshev approximation can also be used to solve similar problems encountered by Saito et al. [21] for the reflection off rounded edges and Kajiya and Kay [15] for the rendering of fur. It has also been used to solve the specular reflection off a surface lit by a linear light source [19].

There are several related problems yet to solve. One such problem concerns the trade-off between the accuracy of the Chebyshev approximation and the degree of the resulting polynomial. It might be possible to reduce the degree of the polynomial with a more careful study of the maximal difference between the curves such that, for a given display system, no observer could distinguish between the two resulting intensities.

The Chebyshev approximation can also be used to estimate the inter-reflection between cylinders. In the current model the inter-reflection is ignored, but it would be interesting to see if inter-reflection improves the realism of the model enough to justify the extra processing.

The authors also believe this model can be used to provide an additional tool for visualizing information on data like orientation of simple vector fields. However in order to obtain understandable results, some motion must be applied to the surface or to the light source. At the current stage of our implementation we are quite far from real-time motion.

7 Acknowledgement

The authors would like to thank Avi Naiman, Andrew Woo, Mikio Shinya, Peter Cahoon and especially John Buchanan for their help. We also thank Frederic Taillefer for the drapery model used in Image IV. The authors are grateful to NSERC, which provided an operating Grant and a Graduate Scholarship, to Ontario ITRC for their financial support, and to the generous support of the University of British Columbia where the final phase of this work took place.

Appendix

A Model of Negative Cylinders

A negative cylinder is a cylinder subtracted from the surface. The mathematics involved with this type of cylinder are simpler because a negative cylinder cannot be hidden from the viewer by another negative cylinder. Thus, only the self-shadowing and self-hiding have to be considered. The same parameters d and h are used to control the anisotropy, however the floor is pushed downwards by a distance h instead upwards from the surface in the case of positive cylinders.

For negative cylinders, the angles are measured from the surface plane and they represent the opposite of what they did for the positive cylinders[5] (see figure 7, 8 and 9). The

---

[5] The main reason of this redefinition is to generate simpler mathematical expressions.

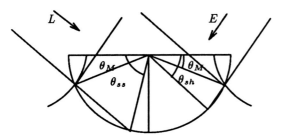

Figure 7: Some Variables for the Negative Cylinders

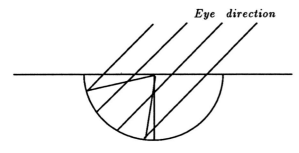

Figure 8: Regular Sampling from the Viewer

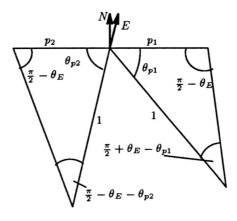

Figure 9: Finding the Sampling Angles θ_p

variation of the normals is then within $[\theta_M, \pi - \theta_M]$, where θ_M is given by

$$\theta_M = \min(\phi_d, \phi_h)$$

and $\phi_h = \sin^{-1}(h)$

$$\phi_d = \begin{cases} \cos^{-1}(d/2) & \text{if } d < 2 \\ 0 & \text{otherwise} \end{cases}$$

The angles at which the self-shadowing θ_{ss} and the self-hiding θ_{sh} stop are then respectively

$$\theta_{ss} = \max(2\theta_L - \theta_M, \theta_M)$$
$$\theta_{sh} = \max(2\theta_E - \theta_M, \theta_M)$$

Simplifications also occur because the floor is always completely visible and illuminated. The sampling angles are computed as

$$\theta_{p1} = \frac{\pi}{2} + \theta_E - \sin^{-1}(p_1 \cos \theta_E)$$
$$\theta_{p2} = \frac{\pi}{2} - \theta_E - \sin^{-1}(p_1 \cos \theta_E)$$

It is worthwhile to note that the analytic solution for the diffuse term as well as the Chebyshev approximation for the specular term are the same as for positive cylinders.

B Chebyshev Approximation

Pseudo-code is provided to compute the Chebyshev polynomials approximating the function $\cos^n \phi$, where $\phi \in [0, x_M]$. The array $a[0..D(a)]$ will contain the coefficients of the polynomial approximating the curve. For more information on the properties of the Chebyshev polynomials for approximation, consult [20].

$D(a)$ is the degree of the polynomial approximation

Approximate $(n, D(a), a[])$
x_M : $\cos^{-1} 0.0039^{\frac{1}{n}}$
for $i = 0$ to $D(a)$
   $sum = 0;$
   for $k = 0$ to $D(a)$
      $x_{cheby} = \cos(k\pi/D(a))$
      $x = x_M \times (x_{cheby} + 1)/2$
      if $(k = 0$ or $k = D(a))$
         $sum = sum + 0.5 \cos^n(x) \times \text{Cheby}(i, x_{cheby})$
      else
         $sum = sum + \cos^n(x) \times \text{Cheby}(i, x_{cheby})$
   endfor
   $b[i] = 2/D(a) \times sum$
endfor
for $i = 0$ to $D(a)$
   if $(i = 0$ or $i = D(a))$
      $a[i] = 0.5 b[i] \times \text{Cheby}(i, x_{cheby})$
   else
      $a[i] = b[i] \times \text{Cheby}(i, x_{cheby})$
   endfor

Cheby $(degree, x)$
   if $(degree = 0)$ return (1)
   if $(degree = 1)$ return (x)
   return $(2x \, \text{Cheby}(degree - 1, x) - \text{Cheby}(degree - 2, x))$

References

[1] Bass, F. G. and Fuks, I. M., *Wave Scattering from Statistically Rough Surfaces*. Pergamon Press Ltd., 1979.

[2] Beckmann, P., Spizzichino A., *The scattering of electromagnetic waves from rough surfaces*. Artech House, Inc., 2nd ed., 1987.

[3] Blinn, J., Models of Light Reflection for Computer Synthesized Pictures. Proceedings of SIGGRAPH'77, In *Computer Graphics* 11, 2 (July 1977), 192-198.

[4] Blinn, J., Simulation of wrinkled surfaces. Proceedings of SIGGRAPH'78, In *Computer Graphics* 12, 3 (August 1978), 286-292.

[5] Born, M. and Wolf, E., *Principles of Optics*. Pergamon, Oxford, 1975.

[6] Brennan, B., Bandeen, W., Anisotropic Reflectance Characteristics of Natural Earth Surfaces. *Applied Optics* 9, 2, (February 1970).

[7] Cabral, B., Max, N., Springmeyer, R., Bidirectional Reflection Functions from Surface Bump Maps. Proceedings of SIGGRAPH'87, In *Computer Graphics* 21, 4 (July 1987), 273-281.

[8] Cook, R., Torrance, K., A Reflectance Model for Computer Graphics. Proceedings of SIGGRAPH'81, In *Computer Graphics* 15, 3 (August 1981), 307-316.

[9] Fournier, A., Fiume, E., Ouellette, M. and Chee, C., FIAT: Light Driven Global Illumination. DGP Technical Memo DGP89-1, Dynamic Graphics Project, University of Toronto, 1989.

[10] Gouraud, H., Continuous Shading of Curved Surfaces. *IEEE Transactions on Computers* 20, 6 (June 1971), 623-628.

[11] Heckbert, P., Survey of Texture Mapping. *IEEE Computer Graphics and Applications*, 6, 11 (November 1986), 56-67.

[12] Immel, D., Cohen, M. and Greenberg, D., A Radiosity Method for Non-Diffuse Environments. Proceedings of SIGGRAPH'86, In *Computer Graphics* 20, 4 (August 1986), 143-150.

[13] Kajiya, J., Anisotropic Reflection Models. Proceedings of SIGGRAPH'85, In *Computer Graphics* 19, 3 (July 1985), 15-21.

[14] Kajiya, J., The Rendering Equation. Proceedings of SIGGRAPH'86, In *Computer Graphics* 20, 4 (August 1986), 143-150.

[15] Kajiya, J. and Kay, T., Rendering Fur with Three Dimensional Textures. Proceedings of SIGGRAPH'89, In *Computer Graphics* 23, 3 (July 1989), 271-280.

[16] Max, N., Horizon mapping: shadows for bump-mapped surfaces. *The Visual Computer*, Vol. 4, 1988, 109-117.

[17] Miller, G., From Wire-Frames to Furry Animals, Proceedings of *Graphics Interface '88*, 1988, 138-145.

[18] Phong, B., Illumination for Computer Generated Pictures. *Communications of the ACM* 18, 6, (June 1975), 311-317.

[19] Poulin, P. and Amanatides, J., Shading and Shadowing with Linear Light Sources. Proceedings of *Eurographics 90*, (September 1990).

[20] Ralston, A., *A First Course in Numerical Analysis*. McGraw-Hill, 1965.

[21] Saito, T., Shinya, M., Takahashi, T., "Highlighting Rounded Edges", Proceedings of CG International 89. In *New Advances in Computer Graphics* 1989, 613-629.

[22] Sillion, F. and Puech, C., A General Two-Pass Method Integrating Specular and Diffuse Reflection. Proceedings of SIGGRAPH'89, In *Computer Graphics* 23, 3 (July 1989), 335-344.

[23] Torrance, K., Sparrow, E., Polarization, Directional Distribution, and Off-Specular Peak Phenomena in Light Reflected from Roughened Surfaces. *J.Opt.Soc.Am.* 56, 7, 1966.

[24] Torrance, K., Sparrow, E., Theory for Off-Specular Reflection from Roughened Surfaces. *J.Opt.Soc.Am.* 57, 9, 1967, 1105-1114.

[25] Trowbridge, T., Reitz, K., Average Irregularity Representation of a Roughened Surfaces for Ray Reflection. *J.Opt.Soc.Am.* 65, 3, 1967.

[26] Watanabe, Y., Suenaga, Y., Hair Animation in Backlight. Proceedings of CG International 89. In *New Advances in Computer Graphics* 1989, 691-700.

[27] Whitted, T., An Improved Illumination Model for Shaded Display. *Communications of the ACM* 23, 6, (June 1980), 343-349.

[28] Williams, L., Pyramidal Parametrics. Proceedings of SIGGRAPH'83, In *Computer Graphics* 17, 3 (July 1983), 1-11.

[29] Yokoi, S., Toriwaki, J., *Computer Science and Technologies, Ch. 3.7 Realistic Expression of Solids with Feeling of Materials*, JARECT, Vol. 18, Ohmsha Ltd., 1988.

Image III: Kitchen scene

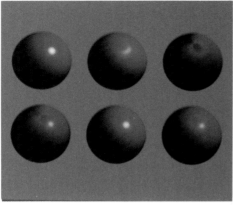

Image Ia: Varying d and h (Positive cylinders)   Image Ib: Varying d and h (Negative cylinders)

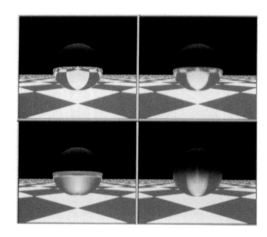

Image II: Reflection (isotropic, scattered, longitudinal, latitudinal)

Image IV: Sound Design

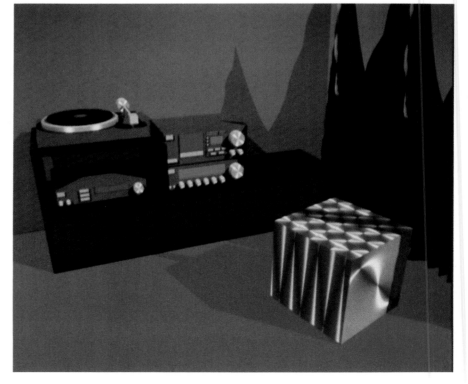

Building Block Shaders

Gregory D. Abram and Turner Whitted

Numerical Design Ltd.
Chapel Hill, NC

Abstract

This paper describes an implementation of Cook's "shade trees" in which shaders are described as networks of modules, building blocks, whose connections can be defined interactively.

The high level interface to the shaders is a graphical editor which permits users to construct complex shaders by connecting shading elements in a network, in effect a graphical shading language. A low level interface to the shaders is also provided. In the low level interface, shading elements are programmed in a standard programming language and compiled into modules which can linked either at run time or compile time.

Each link in the shading network represents a subroutine call. In essence, execution of the network is analogous to the execution of an interpreted language.

CR Categories and Subject Descriptors: I.3.3 [**Computer Graphics**]: Picture/Image Generations - Display Algorithms; I.3.6 [**Computer Graphics**] Methodology and Techniques - interactive techniques; I.3.7 [**Computer Graphics**] Three-dimensional Graphics and Realism - Color, shading, shadowing, and texture.

Additional Key Words and Phrases: shade trees, visual programming.

Access to Shaders

The realism seen in synthetic images is largely due to the advanced techniques now available for simulating the effects of illumination and reflection, collectively called shading. However, access to the best of these techniques has generally been limited to programmers. In this paper we describe a method that provides interactive access to shading techniques for non-programmers.

Currently available commercial rendering systems provide a level of access that is too high to provide needed flexibility, *i.e.* monolithic shading procedures, or too low to be convenient, *i.e.* shading languages. Our approach is to provide an intermediate level of access which is flexible and yet interactive. In this intermediate level interface, shaders are assembled from building block modules by defining the connections between modules.

This paper defines the building block elements, the range of effects that can be achieved with collections of building blocks, and the interface for editing shaders.

Evolution

When shaded display was in its infancy, the simple Lambert law shader was the only function available. A typical rendering program operated on a single primitive surface type, used a single algorithm for determining visibility, and used a hard-wired shader. As better shading models were developed, a common strategy was to hard-wire the best available shader and obtain a wide range of appearances by varying the shading parameters. Shading parameters include coefficients to determine the amount of diffuse reflection, specular reflection, surface shininess, etc.

The amount of control that a user can gain over a shader is extended tremendously through the addition of tables which modify the shading function. Texture maps which tabulate the color, ambient light (environment maps), displacement, or normal perturbation (bump maps) of a surface are the best known examples. In fact, anywhere that a coefficient is used in a shading calculation is a point at which a tabulated array of coefficients can add flexibility to the shader.

Designers of most modern rendering packages recognize the need for more flexibility in the shader. One way to provide this is to make several built-in lighting models available to the user [10], [12]. This provides coarse control of appearance using shader selection and fine control with shader parameters. It also provides efficiency since slower shaders are only used when the surface type calls for it.

Cook's "shade trees" [2] are collections of shading components arranged as a tree. Intermediate shading results are propagated up the tree until the root returns a final shade value. Because of their flexibility shade trees are a wonderfully convenient conceptual model for "do-it-yourself" shader construction.

The key to retaining flexibility in a shading network is the careful selection of built-in functions. Classes of shading functions are distinguished by the scope of their operation. Global operators are those which are able to modify the global variables, generally as a side effect. Local operators produce a result which is assigned to a local variable of some other module. Pipe fitting modules are connection elements which glue other modules together.

As an example of the use of the built-in functions, figure 2 shows a solid textured and bump mapped torus shaded with fog. The elements from which the shader is assembled are shown as a tree in figure 3. Note that *marble* and *plastic* are included as built-ins instead of describing them in terms of their components. (See [7] and [2] for a discussion of the components of each one.) The decision to include such moderately high level functions is based partly on efficiency considerations, partly on convenience in the user interface, but mostly on user expectations [5]. Obviously both the high level functions and their components can be included in the collection of available functions at the cost of some code replication.

Structural and Implementation Details

Each building block component carries one or more "tabs" which define points of connection. Networks are constructed by linking tabs together. Tabs are typed STUFFBEFORE, STUFFDURING, or STUFFAFTER to identify when the child process attached to the tab is to be executed relative to the execution of the parent process. STUFFBEFORE and STUFFAFTER processes are executed automatically with no explicit intervention from the parent process; STUFFDURING processes are called explicitly by the parent.

This implementation of shade trees differs from the traditional model by its explicit control over the order of execution of shading modules, and by the inclusion of connection managers in each module.

Associated with each tab may be the address of a parameter of the parent. If is exists, the the child will overwrite the default value of the corresponding parameter. For example, color is a parameter of the *plastic* process which carries an externally visible tab of type STUFFBEFORE. If a texture map is attached to the color tab of *plastic* then the sampling process of the texture map automatically overwrites the color parameter of *plastic*.

The tabs on shading elements indicate points of connection, but not necessarily data flow. A tab connected to a child function causes the child function to be executed, but the result can be a side effect with no data actually passing from child to parent.

Conceptually, constant parameter values are merely procedures which return constants. However our implementation distinguishes constants from functions for efficiency's sake.

The external representation of each module is an ASCII string containing/name value pairs in the format

```
                name=value
```
for constant parameters and
```
                name@value
```
in the case where value is the name of a function.

We have discovered in the course of using these modules that the *concatenation* operation is extremely common. It is an implicit part of every built-in function through the addition of *before* and *after* tabs. In the actual implementation the *concatenation* element would be missing from figure 3 and *bump map* and *fog* would be attached to the *before* and *after* tabs of the *plastic* module.

The ASCII string which represents the network in figure 3 is:

```
refl1:  plastic before@txtr2 after@atmos color@txtr1 \
        diffuse=CONST1 specular=CONST2
txtr1:  marble freq=FREQUENCY ampl=AMPLITUDE
txtr2:  bump_map name=FILENAME
atmos:  fog
```

At run time the ASCII string is decoded, procedures which are not in memory are loaded, and name/value pairs are converted to pointers.

Programmer/User Interface

Most turnkey rendering applications contain a mechanism for interactively setting shading parameters and previewing the results. While not exactly providing WYSIWYG rendering, they provide a very effective editor for shading effects. There is a clear advantage to retaining this interactivity for more complex shading functions described above.

For networks constructed from built in building block modules, the interface is simply a connection editor. While more elaborate systems such as ConMan [3] and AVS [8] incorporate both a connection editor and a connection manager, our shaders have their connection manager built in. Consequently the connection editor is a very simple piece of code which provides a point-and-click interface for constructing an ASCII description of networks. Figure 4 shows the connection editor and shading previewer. In the window labeled "Shade Tree Editor" a shading network is being constructed from built-in components. To test the effect of this network, a user hits the "Try It" button. A pre-scan-converted sphere is shaded using the newly defined shader in the window labeled "Appearance View."

The user selects a tab at which to extend the tree by clicking on the label for the tab. In the figure the "fileName" tab of the texture sampler is highlighted by a thin box, indicating that it has been selected. The user then pops up a menu of modules, including file names and constants, which is attached to the selected tab. The layout of the schematic of the tree is handled automatically by the editor. Unlike all of the diagrams in this paper, the editor extends the tree from left to right.

The important feature of this style of interaction is the quick feedback provided by the shading preview. This overcomes an argument that shading networks are too complicated for non-programmers to use. Our experience has been that users don't really have to understand the inner workings of the shader functions as long as they can tinker with various combinations and quickly see the effect of their tinkering.

One problem with this graphical shading language is the potential for type mis-matching. When an input tab of one module is

Shading Languages

The unlimited flexibility of a general purpose language permits the introduction of user defined functions, including textures [6], [7]. Common programming practice completely blurs the distinction between tabular and computed shading elements. It is important in building state of the art rendering systems to allow equal access to both types of functions.

The logical extension of this recent development is to provide complete user access to the shading function. One way to accomplish this is to write each shader as a custom coded function. With specialized shading languages to support component shading functions, this approach can be made relatively convenient.

The shade tree conceptual model provides an ideal basis for shading languages. The trees are defined as programs in a shading language which is compiled to produce the actual shader code. This technique has been refined and generalized and its details are described as part of the RenderMan(TM) interface specification [9], [4].

Although languages support extreme flexibility, they generally lack an effective interactive user interface. While this is no impediment to programmers, it keeps typical users from gaining full access to the shading features.

A graphical language, on the other hand, is a natural user interface for specifying shading networks whose underlying structure can be made apparent to the user. The remainder of this paper describes the implementation of the components of such shading networks.

Rendering Model

To a certain extent the nature of the building blocks is influenced by the structure of our rendering model. The most important feature of the model is that shaders stand alone, only loosely tied to other elements of the rendering system. As illustrated in figure 1, modules act on geometry and properties at a point and return values valid at that point.

The operation of the shader is independent of whether geometry at the point is produced by a ray tracer, a z-buffer routine, or some other rendering routine. (For example, the shaders have been used effectively with a volume rendering package [11].) In essence, other rendering code is a funnel to provide the shader with geometry and property data on a point-by-point basis.

Given the need for complex shading it is natural to break shaders into smaller components. These components can then be assembled into complete shading networks using a building block approach.

If the component blocks are provided at too low a level, the networks will be tedious to assemble and the subroutine calling overhead will cause performance to suffer. If the blocks are too large, users will suffer from a loss of flexibility. The major design challenges of building block shaders are first, to provide a comprehensive set of primitive functions at an appropriate level, and second, to build an efficient apparatus that supports the construction and execution of a shading network.

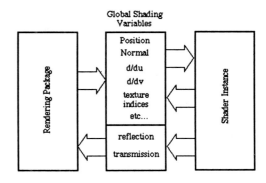

Figure 1. Connection of a shader to the rest of the renderer.

Figure 2. Grooved marble foggy donut.

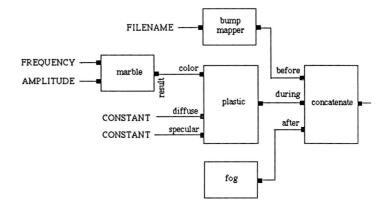

Figure 3. Shading network for figure 2.

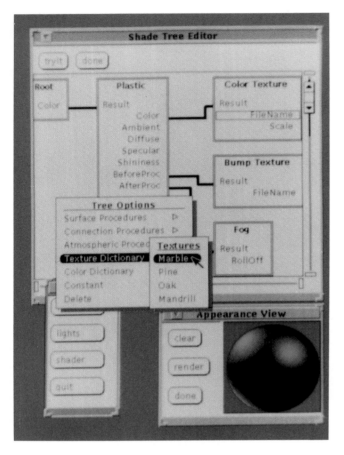

Figure 4. Editor for shading networks.

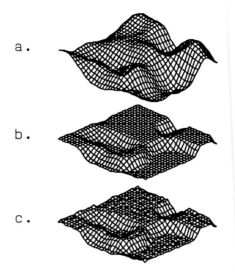

Figure 5. Steps of a stucco height generator.

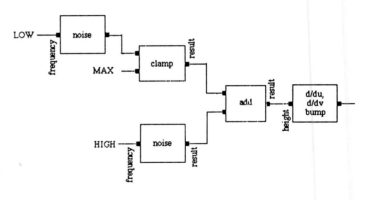

Figure 6. A stucco height generator shader process.

connected to the output tab of another, it is the responsibility of the connection editor to test the types of each tab and disallow connections when the types do not match. We have considered, but not implemented, the automatic insertion of type coercion filters to expand the allowable range of connections. The connection managers in the shading modules do no type checking, relying instead on that done by the editor.

Since extremely complicated shade trees are easy to build with the editor, the user is given an option of collapsing some subtrees into tables to permit faster execution. The shading network can easily be evaluated at every sample point in a regular grid to create a tabulated function. In many cases a user may wish to build and preview elaborate shade trees and then, for the sake of efficiency, select whole subtrees to be used to create a table.

Examples

The first example illustrates the use of the building-block approach to construct a pseudo-stucco bump-mapper. In examining the exterior walls of our building, we decided that a good approximation of the stucco surface might be made by taking a height field generated via a low-frequency noise function, clamping it to simulate troweling, and then adding a lower amplitude but higher frequency noise to roughen the height field. This

process is illustrated below in figures 5a, the low frequency height field, 5b, the clamped result, and 5c, the final height field after adding the high frequency noise.

The stucco model can be implemented, as shown in figure 6, using four building block components: two instances of a noise generator (with different coefficients to produce the low and high frequency results), a truncation process and an adder. Together they form a stucco height field generator which, given the (u,v) coordinates of a point, produce the height of the stucco over the surface at that point. This compound process is then attached to a differentiator, which samples the surface at three points (u,v), (u,v+delta) and (u+delta,v) to produce directional derivatives. The differentiator then calls a built-in utility to apply these directional derivatives to the normal vector.

After settling on this approach to stucco, a single stucco bump-mapping process was created and used as a component of the shader applied to the walls in figure 7.

In the last example (figure 8), the can labels consist of gold overlaid on a textured plastic surface. The select process uses a specialized texture map to determine whether the given point lies in the gold or plastic regions of the label. One of two subtrees is executed, one producing the gold detail via a Cook/Torrance metal shader and one producing the plastic appearance. A single texture map containing the universal price code (and otherwise transparent) is attached to the metal shader to show the UPC overlaying the gold. The plastic surface has two texture maps applied over a base of white: the first transparent except for the blue stripes and the second, the universal price code. The resulting tree is shown in figure 9.

In each of the two examples the building block approach provided the flexibility needed to produce images with a degree of realism that could not be achieved with simpler shaders.

Summary

The usefulness of a building block shader depends both on the ease with which elements are connected and the care with which built-in elements are designed. This paper contrasts the higher level building block approach with the general purpose language approach and gives examples that illustrate how blocks are connected. The approach outlined in this paper is a graphical shading language which is interpreted rather than compiled.

Acknowledgements

We thank Greg Gilley, NDL's R+ Rendering Library Project Manager, and Lee Westover, the guinea pig user, for their technical contributions to the R+ shaders, and Dana Smith for his editorial contributions.

Figure 8. Two Cola-Cola cans.

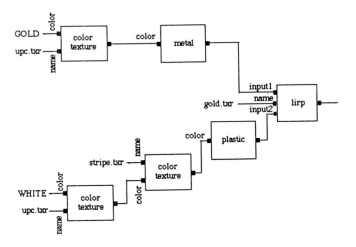

Figure 9. The Cola-Cola can shader.

Figure 7. A tower with stucco walls.

References

[1]   Abram, Gregory D., Lee Westover, and Turner Whitted "Accelerated Rendering," Proceedings of AusGraph '88 (July 1988).

[2]   Cook, Robert L. "Shade Trees," *Computer Graphics*, Vol. 18, No. 3, (July 1984), pp. 223-231.

[3]   Haeberli, Paul, "ConMan: A Visual Programming Language for Interactive Graphics," *Computer Graphics*, Vol. 22, No. 4, (July 1988), pp. 103-111.

[4]   Hanrahan, Pat, and Jim Lawson, "A Language for Shading and Lighting Calculations," these proceedings.

[5]   Nadas, Tom, and Alain Fournier, "GRAPE: An Environment to Build Display Processes," *Computer Graphics*, Vol. 21, No. 4 (July 1987), pp. 75-84.

[6]   Peachey, Darwyn R., "Solid Texturing of Complex Surfaces," *Computer Graphics*, Vol. 19, No. 3 (July 1985), pp. 279-286.

[7]   Perlin, Ken, "An Image Synthesizer," *Computer Graphics*, Vol. 19, No. 3 (July 1985), pp. 287-296.

[8]   Upson, Craig, Thomas Faulhaber, Jr., David Kamins, David Laidlaw, David Schlegel, Jeffrey Vroom, Robert Gurwitz, and Andries van Dam, "The Application Visualization System: A Computation Environment for Scientific Visualization," *IEEE Computer Graphics and Applications*, Vol. 9, No. 4 (July 1989), pp. 30-42.

[9]   Upstill, Steve, *The RenderMan Companion* Addison-Wesley, (Reading, Massachusetts), 1989.

[10]   Verbeck, Channing, James Michener, Andries van Dam, and David Laidlaw, "Extending PHIGS for Lighting and Shading - PHIGS+," July 1987.

[11]   Westover, Lee, "Footprint Evaluation for Volume Rendering," these proceedings.

[12]   Whitted, Turner and David Weimer, "A Software Test-bed for the Development of 3-D Raster Graphics Systems," *ACM Transactions on Graphics*, Vol. 1, No. 1 (January 1982), pp. 43-58.

A Language for Shading and Lighting Calculations

Pat Hanrahan* and Jim Lawson†

*Princeton University

†Pixar

Abstract

A shading language provides a means to extend the shading and lighting formulae used by a rendering system. This paper discusses the design of a new shading language based on previous work of Cook and Perlin. This language has various types of shaders for light sources and surface reflectances, point and color data types, control flow constructs that support the casting of outgoing and the integration of incident light, a clearly specified interface to the rendering system using global state variables, and a host of useful built-in functions. The design issues and their impact on the implementation are also discussed.

CR Categories: I.3.3 [Computer Graphics] Picture/Image Generation- Display algorithms; I.3.5 [Computer Graphics] Three-Dimensional Graphics and Realism - Color, shading, shadowing and texture.

Additional Keywords and Phrases: Shading language, little language, illumination, lighting, rendering

1. Introduction

The appearance of objects in computer generated imagery, whether they be realistic or artistic looking, depends both on their shape and shading. The shape of an object arises from the geometry of its surfaces and their position with respect to the camera. The shade or color of an object depends on its illumination environment and its optical properties. In this paper the term *shading* refers to the combination of light, shade (as in shadows), texture and color that determine the appearance of an object. Many remarkable pictures can be created with objects having a simple shape and complex shading. A well-designed, modular rendering program provides clean interfaces between the geometric processing, which involves transformation, hidden surface removal, etc., and the optical processing, which involves the propagating and filtering of light. This paper describes a language for programming shading computations, and hence, extending the types of materials and light sources available to a rendering system. In Bentley's terminology it would be called a "little" language[3], since, because it is based on a simple subset of C, it easy to parse and implement, but, because it has many high-level features that customize it for shading and lighting calculations, it is easy to use.

Two major aspects of shading are the specification of surface reflectance and light source distribution functions. The earliest surface reflectance models have terms for ambient, diffuse and specular reflection. More recent research has added anisotropic scattering terms[14, 16, 21] and made explicit wavelength and polarization effects. Although not nearly as well publicized, many improvements have also been made in light source description. The earliest light source models consisted of distant or point light sources. Verbeck and Greenberg[29] introduced a general framework for describing light sources which includes attaching them to geometric primitives and specifying their intensity distribution as a function of direction and wavelength.

Light sources and surface reflectance functions are inherently *local processes*. However, many lighting effects arise because light rays traveling from light to surface are blocked by intervening surfaces or because light arriving at a surface comes indirectly via another surface. Turner Whitted termed these effects *global illumination processes*. Kajiya introduced the general light transport equation, which he aptly termed the *rendering equation*, and showed how all these techniques are tied together[15]. Most recent research in shading and lighting calculations is now being focussed on making these global illumination algorithms efficient. Note that global and local illumination processes are independent aspects of the general illumination process.

In parallel to the development of specific shading models is the development of shading systems. Most current systems implement a single parameterized shading model. There are several problems with this approach. First, there is little agreement on what this shading model should be. Almost every rendering system written has used a slightly different shading model. Second, it seems unlikely that a single parameterized model could ever be sufficient. As mentioned earlier, the development of shading models is an active area of research and new material models are continually being developed. Shading also involves many *tricks*, one major example being texture mapping, and the use of rendering tricks is completely open ended. Furthermore, the surface reflectance models of simple and composite materials are phenomenologically based and not derivable from first principles. Shading models that capture the effects of applying varnish or lacquer to wood, or of adding an additional flap to a stage light, are much better expressed procedurally than as mathematical formulae. Another problem with this single parameterized model approach, is that simple shading formula carry the overhead of the most complicated case. This overhead makes it more difficult for users to control, and more time consuming for the rendering system to compute.

Because of these difficulties with the single shading model approach, several systems have been described that provide greater flexibility and extensibility. Whitted proposed that the rendering system have a collection of built-in shaders accessible via a shader dispatch table[31]. Presumably, the interface to these shaders was well-defined so that experienced hackers with access to the source code could extend the system. Cook developed a model which separated the conceptually independent tasks of light source specification, surface reflectance, and atmospheric effects[6]. The user could control each of these shading processes independently by giving a sequence of expressions which were read in, parsed, and executed at run-time by the rendering system. Perlin's image synthesizer carried this idea further by providing a full language including conditional and looping constructs, function and procedure definitions, and a full set of arithmetic and logical operators[24]. But Perlin abandoned the distinction between the shading processes proposed by Cook, and instead introduced a "pixel stream" model. In the pixel stream model, shading is a postprocess which occurs after visible surface calculations. Unfortunately, this makes his language hard to use within the context of a radiosity or ray-tracing program, where much of the shading calculation is independent of surface visibility.

In this paper, a new language is described which incorporates features of both Cook's and Perlin's systems. The goals in the design of the new language were to:

- Develop an abstract shading model based on ray optics suitable for both global and local illumination models. It should also be abstract in the sense of being independent of a specific algorithm or implementation in either hardware or software.

- Define the interface between the rendering program and the shading modules. All the information that might logically be available to a built-in shading module should be made available to the user of the shading language.

- Provide a high-level language which is easy to use. It should have features – point and color types and operators, integration statements, built-in functions – that allow shading calculations to be expressed naturally and succinctly.

A detailed description of the shading language grammar is available in the RenderMan interface specification[1], and many examples of its use are contained in Upstill[28]. The intent of this paper is to point out the features of the new language beyond those described by Perlin and Cook. The design of the new language also raised many subtle design and implementation issues whose resolution required a combination of graphics and systems perspectives. The alternatives that were considered, and the factors that influenced the choices that were made are discussed. Finally, we discuss some of the more interesting parts of the implementation, particularly those aspects where a combination of techniques drawn from graphics, systems and compiler theory were used to improve performance.

2. Model of the Shading Process

Kajiya has pointed out that the rendering process can be modeled as a integral equation representing the transport of light through the environment[15].

$$i(x, x')=v(x, x') [l(x, x') + \int r(x, x', x'') i(x', x'') dx'']$$

The solution, $i(x, x')$, is the intensity of light at x which comes from x'. The integral computes the amount of light reflected from a surface at x' as a function of the surface bidirectional reflectance function $r(x, x', x'')$ and the incoming light intensity distribution $i(x', x'')$. The term $l(x, x')$ gives the amount of light emitted by light sources at x' in the direction towards x. The sum of these

two terms is the amount of light initially traveling from x' to x, but not all that light makes it to x: some of it may be scattered or blocked by an intervening material. The term $v(x, x')$ gives the percentage of light that makes it from x' to x.

The shading language allows procedures, called shaders, to be written that compute the various terms in the above equation. Shaders implement the local processes involved in shading; all the global processes used in solving the rendering equation are controlled by the renderer. The three major types of shaders are:

- *Light Source Shaders.* A light source shader calculates the term $l(x, x')$, the color and intensity of light emitted from a particular point on a light source in a particular direction.

- *Surface Reflectance Shaders.* A surface reflectance shader calculates the integral of the bidirectional reflectance function $r(x, x', x'')$ with the incoming light distribution $i(x', x'')$.

- *Volume or Atmosphere Shaders.* Volume shaders compute the term $v(x, x')$. Only scattering effects need be computed; the effects of light rays intersecting other surfaces are handled by the renderer.

A surface shader shades an infinitesimal surface element given the incoming light distribution and all the local properties of the surface element. A surface shader assumes nothing about how this incoming light distribution was calculated, or whether the incoming light came directly from light sources or indirectly via other surfaces. A surface shader can be bound to any geometric primitive. The rendering program is responsible for evaluating the geometry, and provides enough information to characterize the infinitesimal surface element. Similarly, when a light source shader computes the emitted light, it makes no assumptions about what surfaces that light may fall on, or whether the light will be blocked before it reaches the surface. A light source shader also makes no assumptions about whether it is bound to a geometric primitive to form an area light.

Kajiya has shown how standard rendering techniques can be viewed as approximate solutions of the rendering equation. The simplest approximation assumes that light is scattered only once. A ray is emitted from a light source, reflected by a surface, and modulated on its way towards the eye. This is often referred to as local shading, in contrast to global shading, because no information about other objects is used when shading an object. This shading model is what is used by most real-time graphics hardware and is easily accommodated by the shading language. Whitted's ray tracing algorithm[30] considers these direct transport paths, plus light transported from surfaces intersected by reflected and refracted rays. This can also be accommodated by the shading language by recursively calling light source and surface shaders.

To summarize, the abstraction used by the shading language provides a way of specifying all the local interactions of light, without assuming how the rendering program solves the light transport equation. Thus, shaders written in the shading language can be used by many different types of rendering algorithms.

3. Language Features

The shading language is modeled after C[17], much like many other programming languages developed under UNIX. The specification of the syntax and grammar is available in the specification[1] and examples of its use are described in a recent book[28]. In the following sections the novel features of the shading language are discussed. The emphasis is on the high-level design issues that influenced each feature, and the implementation problems that they posed. The features discussed include the semantics of the color and point data types, the meta types

Pixels are traversed down the leading edge and then horizontally to the trailing edge

Figure 3.

Sub-pixel Vertex Positioning

Faster CPUs allow delaying the conversion from floating point space to fixed point space, aiding precision. Bresenham vector and polygon edge-walking algorithms [Bresenham65] initialized using integer vertexes do not solve the crucially important consistency problem of double-hitting or missing pixels along the shared boundary of abutting triangles [Lathrop90], and cause visually distressing temporal aliasing in animated vectors. We chose to initialize these algorithms using floating-point arithmetic, effectively positioning vertexes between pixels.

For consistency between collinear vectors and edges, we derive the two Bresenham increments from the floating point slope alone, with final precision equivalent to the ratio of two 16-bit integers. We normalize all Bresenham constants values to preserve precision in the integer hardware. As all Bresenham vector generators are founded upon DIV and MOD arithmetic, setting the two hardware increment registers is a simple matter. However, setting the initial error term is not as straightforward, and choosing the correct starting pixel is problematic.

Three principles guided our thinking:

Fidelity Rule: Collinear line segments which overlap select the same pixels (within that overlap). Note that pixel selection being independent of traversal direction is an instance of the Fidelity Rule.

Connected Rule: Start and end pixels of consecutive vectors, or shared polygon vertex pixels, are identical or adjacent. So what is connected in floating point space remains visually connected in screen space.

Extent Rule: When chosen pixels are projected onto either axis, all lie within the projection of the true line segment.

Unfortunately, it is impossible to satisfy all three rules simultaneously, or even to choose the same rules for vectors and triangle edges. For polygons, we satisfy the Connected rule only in the Y dimension. For vectors, on the other hand, we were unwilling to sacrifice the Connected Rule, lest we have unsightly gaps. Instead, we give up the Extent Rule, as necessary, to connect polyline segments.

Once we have identified the first pixel, we are free to calculate the initial data values for that pixel center, such as color/Z/alpha for triangles or the initial error term for vectors. We note in passing that our solution for vectors is appropriate for anti-aliased vectors. It largely solves the problems of abutting triangles and quivering or ratchety vector motion, producing more aesthetically pleasing results. The complexity of this method lies in the floating point software initialization; the hardware is only a common 16-bit integer Bresenham vector and edge walker.

COLOR/Z/ALPHA SYNTHESIS FEATURES

We were less successful in minimizing the hardware to synthesize data values. The decision to synthesize one pixel at a time, coupled with our performance goals, forced a pixel drawing rate of 27.5 ns. To complete pixels at this rate required parallelism.

The difficulty was compounded by each rendering feature needing its own idiosyncratic hardware.

Color Synthesis

Most 3-D rendering employs linear interpolation of color and Z values across an area. Our linear interpolation uses a 28-bit data path. For colors and alpha values, the 28 bits are divided into 1 clamping bit, 8 color bits, and 19 color fraction bits. A full-screen trapezoid requires only 12 fraction bits to remain accurate (within .5) during linear interpolation. The 28-bit width was chosen to support 16-bit Z buffering and quadratic interpolation. Of course, this precision is only of value when the color and depth information are calculated accurately for the initial pixel center. A procedure for this is presented in [Lathrop90].

Pixel addresses and data, although generated one-at-a-time, are pipelined. Trapezoid traversal requires three different color increments, one for horizontal and two for the Bresenham edge-walking. For linear interpolation, we keep only two color derivative registers, since the edge increments differ by exactly a horizontal increment. Since all derivative and initial value calculation is done in software, the hardware need handle only the interpolation itself.

Z Synthesis

For Z buffering, Z values of 16, 24, and 32 bits can be kept in the frame buffer. The 28-bit interpolator provides 16-bit Z values with 12 fraction bits. By duplicating the computation in two chips, one per Z byte, no carries need propagate between them. 24 and 32-bit Z-buffering use 44-bit arithmetic; propagating carries make them slightly slower.

Quadratic Interpolation

Originally we implemented quadratic interpolation to reduce the perceived Mach bands at polygon boundaries which are caused by discontinuous color derivatives [Mach59]. For a more current and detailed discussion, as well as reprints of English translations, see [Ratliff65]. We expected quadratic to come quite a bit closer than linear to preventing this problem. We saw it as between Gouraud and true Phong shading, equivalent in computational complexity to "Fast Phong" shading [Bishop86]. Indeed, by combining quadratic interpolation with an exponentiation table as a texture map, we can directly implement Bishop's "Fast Phong" algorithm.

Quadratic hardware is also useful in accelerating the product of two linear polygon functions. Examples include depth-cued shading (as in the PHIGS model) where a linear shading intensity is multiplied by a linear depth function, or variable transparency, where the linear shading intensity is multiplied by a linear transparency function. This approach succeeds because the linear functions are combined as part of the setup done with high precision in the CPU.

Additionally, initial experiments suggested second-order interpolation would reduce highlight aliasing compared to linear interpolation. Figure 4 shows a curved surface rendered with no color interpolation, linear color interpolation, and quadratic interpolation. Note with quadratic interpolation the boundaries of the highlights are curved.

Quadratic interpolation is set up by fitting a second-order surface to six points: a triangle's vertexes and side midpoints. Six lighting calculations are performed, and the simultaneous equations are solved to give the color derivatives. The hardware then

Flat   Linear   Quadratic

Figure 4.

interpolates by forward differences, requiring three second-derivative registers, each 28-bits wide [Kirk88]. 28 bits is not sufficient precision for full-screen traversal, so software limits the size of quadratic patches. Care must be taken during setup to ensure that overflow is minimized during interpolation. Software limits the second derivative values, although final color values can be clamped to 0 and 255 rather than wrapping.

Alpha Buffering

Alpha buffering is available in all drawing operations for the appearance of transparency or for anti-aliased matting. 8-bit alpha fractions, encoding opacity in units of 1/255, can be multiplied with interpolated or frame buffer pixel values for blending into the frame buffer. In most cases, the blending formula is fixed during the entire drawing operation. One case, the "Z-buffer" blend, selects dynamically between OVER and REVERSE-OVER [Porter84] based on the Z comparison result at each pixel. The hardware cost was four parallel modulo-255 multipliers, one each for alpha, red, green, and blue, plus their data paths.

Texture Mapping

Texture mapping patterns polygons by mapping images onto them. In our implementation, the image must reside in the frame buffer. We interpolate the frame buffer addresses as we traverse the destination polygon. We were able to reuse the color interpolators to synthesize texture map indexes, so little additional hardware is needed. Thus S and T, the coordinate offsets in the texture map, are treated by both software and hardware just as the other triangle attributes: color, alpha, and Z. Alternating independent reads and writes make poor use of the interleaved frame buffer, so texture mapping is much slower than interpolated color. This tradeoff was accepted to keep texture mapping an inexpensive addition.

Texture Address Synthesis

S and T are synthesized as 10-bit offsets into a 1024x1024 texture map. Fast-changing S or T can undersample the map image and cause severe aliasing artifacts. We avoid this by storing a pyramid

of square texture maps [Williams83]. Pre-processing software is used to prepare texture maps of any power-of-two size from 1024x1024 to 1x1. If the S and T interpolation is quadratic, the hardware uses their first derivatives to dynamically select which pyramid level to use:

$$\text{Biggest} = \max\left(\left|\frac{\partial S}{\partial X}\right|, \left|\frac{\partial S}{\partial Y}\right|, \left|\frac{\partial T}{\partial X}\right|, \left|\frac{\partial T}{\partial Y}\right|\right)$$

$$\text{Level} = \text{TRUNC}\left(\log_2\left(\text{Biggest}\right)\right)$$

The size range can also be clamped to limits, for use with smaller texture maps. Smaller and more filtered maps are chosen for object horizons or distant objects. For simplicity, we do not interpolate either between pixels or between maps, and the maps are always square. Consequently, horizons blur more than necessary.

Texture Perspective Approximation

In addition to dynamically selecting filtered maps for anti-aliasing, quadratic interpolation serves another purpose. Linear interpolation of texture indexes does not account for the foreshortening caused by perspective division [Heckbert86]. While some static views may appear reasonable, animation immediately exposes the error. Heckbert points out that for proper appearance it is necessary to perform a divide per pixel to properly generate the S and T values. We have combined a quadratic perspective compensation composed with the linear texture mapping function.

A linear perspective approximation is a poor fit for the inverse of this rational function; a quadratic approximation is much more successful, giving a reasonable appearance except in extreme perspective. Figure 5 shows a graph comparing the perspective warping of a textured span at 45 degrees to the line-of-sight using linear, quadratic, and the correct function. The span extents from the origin to $X = 40$, $Z = 40$, and the eyepoint is back at $X = 0$, $Z = -40$. The span's perspective screen projection covers 20 pixels. In this fairly severe test, quadratic is accurate to 2.6% (less than half a pixel), whereas linear deviates by 17.1%.

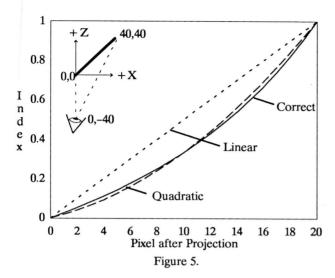

Figure 5.

Quadratic

Figure 6.

Figure 6. shows a cube with a texture map interpolated linearly and interpolated quadratically. The cube is constructed from only two large triangles per side.

Texture Illumination

Illumination can be factored in by reusing the alpha buffering multipliers to multiply the sampled texture color with a interpolated darkening function. Either monochrome or RGB illumination can be modeled. When texture mapping, alpha buffering, and Z buffering are used simultaneously, the visual cues from all three techniques combine well. See Figure 7.

Dithering

Dithering allows a 40-plane frame buffer to do interactive 3-D rendering. By allocating only 12 bits per image (4 bits each of red, green, blue), double-buffered drawing with a 16-bit Z buffer fits into 40 planes. However, 4 bits per color component results in severe color banding. A simple 2x2 ordered dither [Floyd75] can correct this by providing the visual impression of 64 shades of each color component, yet it requires only a few gates and imposes no speed penalty. See the split-screen comparison in Figure 8. The 2x2 pattern is small enough to be invisible on a monitor. Dithering can also be used with other pixel formats. Used with 24-bit color, it provides the appearance of 30 bit color without the added cost of a deeper image memory or higher-precision DACs.

FRAME BUFFER

The frame buffer is the heart of any raster graphics device. Its size determines screen resolution, its depth determines display quality and features, and its organization strongly affects performance. Although we would have preferred to integrate the frame buffer into main memory, the 318 Mbytes/sec. drawing bandwidth and the 437 Mbytes/sec. video requirement were achievable only with a specialized implementation. It is integrated into virtual memory.

Interleaving

We use horizontal 6:1 interleaving to achieve 27.5 ns. sequential pixel writing while individual RAM cycles take 165 ns. to complete. All interleaving requires the ability to control multiple concurrent RAM cycles. We further implemented dynamic cycle selection to maximize RAM throughput. The six RAM banks can perform different cycle types at the same time, such as a full "row/column" cycle in one bank while a page-mode cycle is done in another. While many gates are required to manage six variable cycles concurrently, it greatly improves the bandwidth of the frame buffer and is less expensive than adding more RAMs. We stagger alternate scanlines by 3 pixels, providing a 26% improvement in random vector drawing to achieving 1.1 million 10-pixel vectors per second,

Mixed VRAMs and DRAMs

One way to minimize the frame buffer cost was to use a mix of VRAMs and DRAMs. We used 1 megabit RAMs with similar timing. The DRAMs can hold Z values, alpha values, and off-screen images such as texture maps, pop-up menus, and tile patterns.

By using 1 Megabit VRAMs in the image memory, we are able to fit a competitive 40-plane 3-D graphics subsystem on only one

Figure 7.

Figure 8.

board. Committing to these VRAMs was a major risk, since they had to be chosen several years before production chips became available. To reduce that risk, we chose to use only the basic features and cycles common to all potential vendors. This means omitting "block write," where 16 pixels are cleared by a single cycle, and not using any on-RAM ALU.

CONCLUSIONS

We built a competitive high-end graphics workstation, the DN10000VS, using a holistic approach which emphasized integration and simplification of the graphics hardware. Integration meant improving the CPU for graphics and then making it shoulder more of the load. This proved to be successful, with a considerable increase in performance for both graphics and customer code. Simplification is successful in the control logic and in address synthesis, avoiding the painful ordeal

of microcode, but was not tractable for the frame buffer. Color synthesis is also not simplified; instead, we succumbed to the temptation to add several advanced rendering features, such as alpha buffering and texture mapping.

Multiprocessing proves to be a flexible way of scaling performance, for graphics as well as for applications. It improves a wide breadth of rendering methods and options since it is orthogonal to coding and CPU improvements; as such it contrasts sharply with many hardware accelerators which target a narrow and inextensible set of operations.

In hindsight, the hardware/software boundary was a bit too low. Calculating the color/Z/alpha differentials, adjusting the initial pixel value, and subpixel Bresenham addressing setup in hardware all would have improved the system balance. The 80-plane configuration has the untapped potential of twice the 40-plane bandwidth. Casting features in raw hardware without the possibility of microcode workarounds forced far more extensive simulation and many sleepless nights. Nonetheless, compared with the level of effort microcode entails, and its dangerous invitation to defer facing design complexity until coding time, we believe our approach superior for today's technology.

Finally, the holistic approach unravelled at the frame buffer and color synthesis logic, where raw bandwidth and sophisticated synthesis methods required expensive hardware. This is not a fundamental flaw with the approach but rather the recognition that at the fringes of any system are specialized tasks which defy integration.

ACKNOWLEDGEMENTS

We would like to thank all members of DN10000VS project and in particular the FANG design team, who worked together to make this effort succeed. We were assisted considerably by our anonymous reviewers, and by Victor Odryna and Casey Dowdell, who offered much constructive criticism. We truly appreciate Dr. William Ackerman's tireless efforts to achieve multiprocessing success. And we especially thank Dr. Terence Lindgren, who helped mightily in the presentation of these ideas, offering many insights into subpixel address synthesis and texture perspective approximation.

REFERENCES

Akeley, Kurt, T. Jermoluk, "High-Performance Polygon Rendering," *Computer Graphics*, Vol. 22, No. 4, August 1988, pp. 239–246.

Apgar, Brian, B. Bersack, A. Mammen, "A Display System for the Stellar Graphics Supercomputer Model GS1000," *Computer Graphics*, Vol. 22, No. 4, August 1988, pp. 255–262.

Apollo Computer, "Series 10000 Technical Reference Library: Volume 1 – Processors and Instruction Set," Order No. 0011720–A00, Apollo Computer Inc. 1988.

Bishop, Gary, D. Weimer, "Fast Phong Shading," *Computer Graphics*, Vol. 20, No. 4, July 1986, pp. 103–106.

Bresenham, Jack, "Algorithm for Computer Control of a Digital Plotter," *IBM Systems Journal* 4,1, 1965, pp. 25–30.

Deering, Michael, S. Winner, B. Schediwy, C. Duffy, N. Hunt, "The Triangle Processor and Normal Vector Shader: A

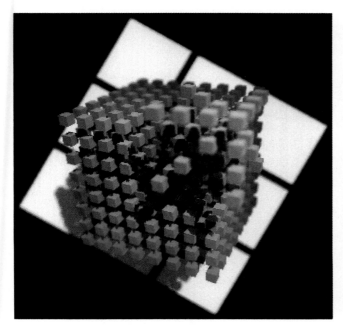

Figure 9. Depth of field image generated by accumulating 23 images.

Figure 10. Soft shadows generated by accumulating 23 images.

series of images are integrated to create correct penumbra. Figure 10 shows the result of illuminating a scene with one light, and accumulating 23 images.

4.4 Doing it all

We have shown how the accumulation buffer provides solutions to the problems of spatial aliasing, motion-blur, depth of field, and penumbra. However, in each of the examples above only one problem was solved independently. For example, the motion-blur, depth of field, and penumbra images all demonstrate artifacts of spatial aliasing.

It is possible to solve all four problems at once. Figure 11 shows an image that demonstrates antialiasing, motion blur, depth of field, and soft shadows. It was created by using all the techniques described above simultaneously. To create this image 66 crude images were integrated. As these images were drawn, the subpixel offset was altered as the geometry was moved in equal steps. In addition, the projection matrix used to draw the images was modified to create depth of field, and the light source was sampled at different points to create soft shadows.

5. Discussion

Many other sampling problems are supported by the hardware architecture described here.

The Accumulation Buffer may be used to support anisotropic reflection models [Kajiya 85]. To do this, surface normals are distributed as images are accumulated. In addition, the Accumulation Buffer can be used to filter texture maps and environment maps. To do this, standard mip-mapping [Williams 83] is done, but no interpolation is performed to filter textures in x and y. As images are accumulated, texture maps are filtered along with the scene geometry. In this way, eight texture accesses can be replaced by one texture map access to improve drawing performance.

Alternate low cost implementations of the Accumulation Buffer can be created by reducing the number of bits in the drawing and the Accumulation Buffers. In such a system 4 bits are provided for each R, G, B and Alpha in the drawing buffer, and 8 bits are provided for each R, G, B and alpha in the Accumulation Buffer. High quality images are generated by dithering images into the 4 bit per component frame buffer and accumulating up to 16 images in the 8 bit per component accumulator. By carefully selecting a different 4 by 4 dither matrix on each pass, most dithering artifacts can be removed from the accumulated images.

Figure 11. Antialiased image with motion blur, depth of field, and soft shadows generated by accumulating 66 images.

Figure 12. Environment mapped image with motion blur, and depth of field generated by accumulating 24 images.

6. Conclusion

The Accumulation Buffer meets our antialiasing requirements of compatibility, high quality, and a smooth tradeoff between performance and quality:

Figure 12 shows a more complex scene generated using the Accumulation Buffer.

1. *Compatibility.* Both the spectacular polygon performance and the accurate Point Sampling of modern workstation graphics systems are leveraged by the multi-pass Accumulation Buffer algorithm. Use of the Accumulation Buffer is independent of all other framebuffer algorithms - it simply improves the quality of any image that can be generated.

2. *High Quality.* There is no practical limit to the image quality that can be obtained with the accumulation buffer. If more than 256 samples are desired, a *weight* less than 1.0 can be used to avoid overflow. Because each sample is computed exactly, both in terms of parameter interpolation and depth buffering, only the number of samples taken limits image quality.

3. *Smooth performance/quality tradeoff.* Performance and quality trade off smoothly as the number of samples per pixel is increased from 1. Because the Accumulation Buffer hardware is separate from the normal rendering hardware, the performance of that hardware is not compromised.

These attributes, in addition to simplicity, elegance, and general purpose application, make the Accumulation Buffer a desirable architectural enhancement to a workstation graphics system.[1]

7. Acknowedgements

We thank the entire VGX graphics group at Silicon Graphics for supporting this work, and appreciate the comments of the reviewers.

---

1. Some aspects of this work are patent pending.

8. Appendix A

The following function is used to specify a simple perspective projection in the SGI Graphics Library.

```
window(left,right,bottom,top,near,far)
float left, right, bottom, top, near, far;
{
    float Xdelta, Ydelta, Zdelta;
    float matrix[4][4];

    Xdelta = right - left;
    Ydelta = top - bottom;
    Zdelta = far - near;
    matrix[0][0] = (2.0*near)/Xdelta;
    matrix[0][1] = 0.0;
    matrix[0][2] = 0.0;
    matrix[0][3] = 0.0;
    matrix[1][0] = 0.0;
    matrix[1][1] = (2.0*near)/Ydelta;
    matrix[1][2] = 0.0;
    matrix[1][3] = 0.0;
    matrix[2][0] = (right+left)/Xdelta;
    matrix[2][1] = (top+bottom)/Ydelta;
    matrix[2][2] = -(far+near)/Zdelta;
    matrix[2][3] = -1.0;
    matrix[3][0] = 0.0;
    matrix[3][1] = 0.0;
    matrix[3][2] = -(2.0*far*near)/Zdelta;
    matrix[3][3] = 0.0;
    loadmatrix(matrix);
}
```

The **window** command above creates a projection matrix that specifies the position and size of the rectangular viewing frustum in the near clipping plane, and the location of the far clipping plane. All objects contained within this volume are projected in perspective onto the screen area of the current viewport.

Subpixwindow, below, duplicates the functionality of **window,** and includes parameters that specify a subpixel offset in screen x and screen y. This function supports subpixel positioning for antialiasing.

```
subpixwindow(left,right,bottom,top,near,far,pixdx,pixdy)
float left, right, bottom, top, near, far, pixdx, pixdy;
{
    short vx1, vx2, vy1, vy2;
    float xwsize, ywsize, dx, dy;
    int xpixels, ypixels;

    getviewport(&vx1,&vx2,&vy1,&vy2);
    xpixels = vx2-vx1+1;
    ypixels = vy2-vy1+1;
    xwsize = right-left;
    ywsize = top-bottom;
    dx = -pixdx*xwsize/xpixels;
    dy = -pixdy*ywsize/ypixels;
    window(left+dx,right+dx,bottom+dy,top+dy,near,far);
}
```

First the pixel size of the viewport is determined. Then delta x and delta y values that incorporate the subpixel offset are calculated. Finally the projection matrix is set using the **window** function.

9. Appendix B

The **genwindow** function below extends the functionality of **subpixwindow** to support depth of field.

```
genwindow(left,right,bottom,top,near,far,pixdx,pixdy,
                            lensdx,lensdy,focalplane)
float left, right, bottom, top, near, far, pixdx, pixdy;
float lensdx, lensdy, focalplane;
{
    short vx1, vx2, vy1, vy2;
    float xwsize, ywsize, dx, dy;
    int xpixels, ypixels;

    getviewport(&vx1,&vx2,&vy1,&vy2);
    xpixels = vx2-vx1+1;
    ypixels = vy2-vy1+1;
    xwsize = right-left;
    ywsize = top-bottom;
    dx = -(pixdx*xwsize/xpixels + lensdx*near/focalplane);
    dy = -(pixdy*ywsize/ypixels + lensdy*near/focalplane);
    window(left+dx,right+dx,bottom+dy,top+dy,near,far);
    translate(-lensdx,-lensdy,0.0);
}
```

First the pixel size of the viewport is determined. Delta x and delta y values that incorporate the subpixel offset are calculated. The projection is then sheared to change the viewpoint position based on the lens x and y offsets, and set using the **window** function. Finally the projection is translated to insure that objects in the focal plane remain stationary.

10. References

1. [Akeley 88] Kurt Akeley, and Tom Jermoluk, "High-Performance Polygon Rendering", Computer Graphics, 1988.

2. [Apgar 88] Brian Apgar, et al., "A Display System for the Stellar Graphics Supercomputer Model GS1000", Computer Graphics, 1988.

3. [Brotman 84] Lynne Shapiro Brotman and Norman I. Badler, "Generating Soft Shadows with a Depth Buffer Algorithm", IEEE CG+A October, 1984.

4. [Carpenter 84] Loren Carpenter, "The A-buffer, an Antialiased Hidden Surface Method" Computer Graphics, 1984.

5. [Cook 84] Robert L. Cook et al., "Distributed Ray Tracing", Computer Graphics, 1984.

6. [Cook 86] Robert L. Cook, "Stochastic Sampling in Computer Graphics", ACM Transactions on Graphics, January, 1986

7. [Deering 88] Michael Deering, et al., "The Triangle Processor and Normal Vector Shader: A VLSI System for High Performance Graphics", Computer Graphics, 1988.

8. [Dippe 85] Mark A. Z. Dippe' and Erlin Henry World, "Antialiasing Through Stochastic Sampling", Computer Graphics, 1985.

9. [E&S 87] Evans and Sutherland, PS 390 Marketing Brochure, 1987.

10. [Fuchs 85] Henry Fuchs, et al., "Fast Spheres, Shadows, Texture, Transparencies, and Image Enhancements in Pixel-Planes", Computer Graphics, 1985.

11. [Goldfeather 86] Jack Goldfeather, et al., "Fast Constructive-Solid Geometry Display in the Pixel-Powers Graphics System", Computer Graphics, 1986.

12. [Heckbert 86] Paul S. Heckbert, "Filtering by Repeated Integration", Computer Graphics, 1986.

13. [Kajiya 85], James T. Kajiya, "Anisotropic Reflection Models", Computer Graphics, 1985.

14. [Kajiya 86] James T. Kajiya, "The Rendering Equation" Computer Graphics, 1986.

15. [Mammen 89] Abraham Mammen, "Transparency and Antialiasing Algorithms Implemented with the Virtual Pixel Maps Technique", IEEE CG+A, July 1989.

16. [Max 85] Max, Nelson L., and Douglas M. Lerner, "A Two-and-a-Half-D Motion Blur Algorithm", Computer Graphics, 1985.

17. [Potmesil 82] Potmesil, Michael, and Indranil Chakravarty, "Synthetic Image Generation with a Lens and Aperture Camera Model", ACM Transactions on Graphics, April 1982.

18. [Potmesil 83] Potmesil, Michael and Indranil Chakravarty, "Modeling Motion Blur in Computer Generated Images", Computer Graphics, 1983.

19. [Potmesil 89] Michael Potmesil, and Eric M. Hoffert, "The Pixel Machine: A Parallel Image Computer", Computer Graphics, 1989.

20. [Reeves 87] William T. Reeves, et al., "Rendering Anti-Aliased Shadows with Depth Maps", Computer Graphics, 1987.

21. [SGI 85] Silicon Graphics, "Silicon Graphics 3000 Technical Report", 1985.

22. [Star 89] Star Technologies, "Graphicon 2000 Technical Overview", 1989.

23. [Swanson 86] Roger W. Swanson, and Larry J. Thayer, "A Fast Shaded-Polygon Renderer", Computer Graphics, 1986.

High Speed High Quality Antialiased Vector Generation

Anthony C. Barkans

Hewlett-Packard Company
Graphics Technology Division
Fort Collins, Colorado 80525

ABSTRACT

A vector generation method is described in which a high quality image rendering scheme is coupled with a high speed scan-conversion algorithm.

The rendering scheme consists of two parts. First a pre-filtering method is used to antialias the vectors. Second a compositing technique is used to compose the vectors into the frame-buffer.

The scan-conversion algorithm presented allows a single vector to be scan-converted by a either a single processor or a set of processors running in parallel. When using parallel processors, antialiased vectors may be scan-converted and written to a frame store at the same high speed as aliased vectors. The VLSI technology used to implement this algorithm is capable of drawing over two million high quality antialiased vectors per second.

INTRODUCTION

The procedural description for drawing a vector is quite simple. However, converting the procedural description into a bit-mapped raster image has three problems. The first problem is that scan-conversion processes typically used to digitize vectors into the frame store do not limit frequency components of the rendered line, resulting in visible aliasing artifacts. The second problem is that placing the rendered vector into an image may require blending with existing geometry and that the vectors be arbitrary colors to convey depth information. The third problem with scan-converting vectors is one of performance, measured in vectors per second. Each pixel in every vector must have its color and address presented to the the frame store. This is a time consuming process due to the large number of operations that must take place. In typical implementations, enabling antialiasing results in lower performance. All of these problems must be solved to provide maximum user productivity in applications with vectors.

STATIC VECTOR IMAGES

The most noticeable visual artifacts are due to incorrect filtering applied to the vectors. Shown in Figure 1 are two sets of vectors. The endpoint description of the set on the left is a simple horizontal translation of the endpoint set describing the vectors on the right. Note that the un-filtered vectors on the right appear jaggy, whereas the filtered set of vectors appear smooth along their length.

FIGURE 1: Filtered and Un-filtered Vectors

Applying filtering to vectors does not, by itself, remove all of the visual artifacts. For example, one of the issues in applying filtered vectors to real applications is determining if subpixel positioning of endpoints is required. The grids of both images in Figure 2 are made of chains of short vectors. While both grids use filtered vectors, the image on the left does not use subpixel positioning for the endpoints [1]. The image on the right makes use of subpixel addressing for vector endpoints. Notice that while the vectors on the left are smooth along their length, they appear crooked because the endpoints are moved from their true location.

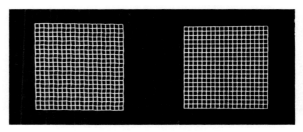

**FIGURE 2: Chains of Vectors
(With-out and With Subpixel Endpoint Locations)**

Another issue is that real applications require vectors with arbitrary color shading be blended into an image that may contain arbitrarily colored geometry. Arbitrarily colored vectors are commonly used to depth cue an image. Figure 3 shows an example of arbitrary color shading applied to vectors blended into a background.

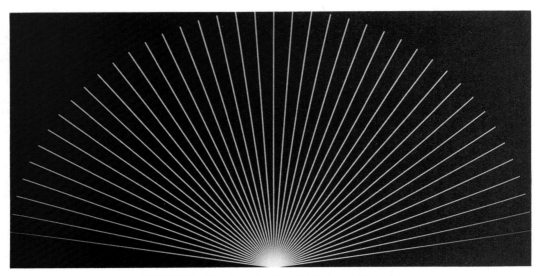

FIGURE 3: Blending Arbitrarily Colored Vectors

The most obvious aliasing artifacts are the jaggies in the minor axis direction. The filtering applied to the vectors in the images shown in Figures 1,2, and 3 has been in the minor axis direction. Aliasing in the major axis direction shows up as endpoint errors. Since endpoints comprise a smaller percentage of the perimeter of an average vector, this artifact is less noticeable to the user. There has been some research into solving this problem [13,9]. These efforts have focused on special cases of one or two isolated endpoints. Unfortunately, isolated vectors are relatively rare in real applications. A general solution for all possible endpoint cases remains an open research issue.

DYNAMIC VECTOR IMAGES

Shown as Figure 4 are two sets of vectors. The endpoint description of the set on the left is a simple horizontal translation of the endpoint set describing the vectors on the right. Both sets of vectors have a slope of 1/200. The set on the left has been filtered.

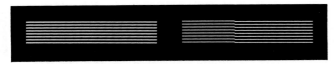

FIGURE 4: Filtered and Un-filtered Vectors

FIGURE 5: Figure 4 Translated Up 1/2 Pixel

The *spatial aliasing* shown by the unfiltered set of vectors in Figure 4 is not the only aliasing problem in computer generated graphics. Another aliasing problem is shown with Figure 5. The image in Figure 5 is the same set of vectors shown in Figure 4 with a vertical translation of 1/2 of a pixel. As the goal of real-time image generation is approached, the images shown in Figure 4 and Figure 5 may be part of a series presented in rapid succession. If these two images are part of a real-time series then the two sets of lines on the left would have the correct apparent motion. That is the set of lines on the left would appear to be slowly moving up. On the other hand, the set of lines on the right would appear to be moving quickly in the horizontal direction. The arrow in Figure 5 points to a step in the set of rendered pixels. This step in Figure 5 is noticeably offset from the equivalent step in Figure 4. It is the motion of these steps that dominate the apparent motion of the un-filtered lines in the real-time series. In other words, the image on the right would appear to be moving at the wrong speed in the wrong direction. This artifact is called *aliasing-induced motion*. A viewer sees the combination of all aliasing artifacts, where the total artifacts are due to both the static spatial aliasing and the aliasing-induced motion. It is important to note that as the goal of real-time generation of complex images is approached, aliasing-induced motion becomes greater and so the total aliasing problem becomes more annoying to the user.

Most of today's vector generation hardware is based on the scan-conversion technique developed by Bresenham [5]. When the algorithm is implemented in hardware it requires a minimum amount of logic and can be executed very quickly, producing a pixel along the major axis at each clock step [18]. The strict application of the technique produces aliased vectors.

Since Bresenham introduced his algorithm, users' expectations of interactive graphics system capabilities have changed. Users now expect vector generation to be fast enough to support complex images with user controlled real-time dynamics. Real-time dynamics has aggravated the aliasing problem since aliasing-induced motion is added to the static frame's spatial aliasing. Fortunately, as users expect more from an interactive graphics system, the speed and density of circuit technology (along with the cost per transistor) has worked in the implementor's favor.

THE FILTERING TECHNIQUE

There have been some attempts to build hardware to render antialiased vectors without filtering the line [15]. However most of the research has focused on using filtering to remove the aliasing artifacts as suggested by Crow [6]. There have been attempts to use hardware to incrementally compute the filter function while rendering [16,11]. The incremental method requires that a simple filter function be used. While these simple filters do provide an improvement in image quality when compared to a non-filtered image, they do not remove all visual artifacts. When the images produced using simple filtering methods are rendered in rapid succession, the aliasing-induced motion is quite noticeable. The computation involved in producing a good filter is too expensive to be done while rendering a vector. An alternative is to pre-compute a set of filter values and store them in a look-up-table, as described by Gupta and Sproull [13]. Computing the filter function takes several minutes on a typical workstation, but once the values are stored in a look-up-table they may be accessed at the hardware clock speed. Since one of the major goals of the implementation was to remove as many visual artifacts as possible, a high quality filter was pre-computed and stored in a look-up-table.

The selection of the filter to store in the look-up-table involves a mathematical analysis [3], supplemented with a subjective assessment [13]. From the mathematical analysis the ideal filter is the SINC function. There are two problems with the practical application of the SINC function to filtering images. The most obvious of these is that the function has an infinite extent. In order to work with look-up-tables the function must be kept local to the region that is being rendered. The other problem is that the function has some negative values. Mathematically, the negative values of the function would require some pixels have a negative contribution to the emitted light, obviously not physically realizable. In order to simulate negative pixels the background may be set to a gray intensity with negative pixels being darker shades of gray. However, requiring a gray background intensity is unacceptable since many users need the image contrast that a black background provides.

A localized function is needed in order to use a pre-computed filter stored in a look-up-table. A lot of work has been done on finding good localized filter functions [19]. One such localized function is generated by multiplying the SINC function by the Hamming Windowing function. The resulting Hamming function is shown on a grid of pixels as Figure 6.

The process of applying the filtering function to the problem of vector antialiasing does not take place in an idealized world. In the mathematical model, the digital to analog converter, the cabling to the CRT, the CRT itself, and the human eye are not accurately accounted for. The implementer is thus forced to use some subjective assessment in fine tuning the filter function.

During the subjective assessment phase for the *Color/Texture Interpolator (CTI) chip* implementation, the function was tuned by turning "knobs" that adjust parameters of the filter function. The first knob selects the mathematical function that forms the basis of the filter. Other "knobs" control the filter volume and filter radius. While turning these knobs it became obvious that a narrow filter, that could be stored as 2 values along the minor axis, could not remove all of the visual artifacts. Widening the filter so that 3 values along the minor axis are used resulted in the best image quality. Subjective assessment was also used to select the physical size and organization of the look-up-table that stores the pre-computed filter function. Choosing a size for the table involves placing limits on the resolution of the table.

During the implementation, it was found that static images alone were insufficient for the assessment. Several test programs were written to animate a sequence of vector images. Two frames from one of the test programs were shown in Figures 4 and 5.

Most often the numerical values that result from the filtering process are thought of as intensity values [16,13,11]. The use of intensity values places limits on the usefulness of the vectors. In many applications an image is desired that shows several colors of vectors, each of which is shaded and/or depth-cued. Other applications may require vectors and polygons in the same image [20]. The limitations imposed by storing intensity values may be removed by using *alpha* values as part of the antialiasing method. The alpha values are used as part of the RGBA image compositing algebra developed by Duff [8]. Elmquist has suggested [9] storing alpha values in the filter look-up-table. Since a general purpose vector generator was desired, the CTI chip has alpha values stored in the filter table.

When using alpha values to antialias a vector, the color at each major axis step is first determined. The three pixels across the minor axis are then each given a separate alpha value. The final color of each pixel is determined by multiplying the major axis step color by the unique alpha value at each pixel and blending it into the frame buffer.

OVERVIEW OF THE HIGH PERFORMANCE VECTOR STEPPING ALGORITHM

In the past, user requirements have made vector speed more important than quality. This is because the productivity of users is directly related to the performance of the system [4]. While users desire high quality rendering, the conventional wisdom [10] is that antialiasing requires time and thus lowers performance. This is based on the fact that for each major axis step an aliased vector requires only one pixel be rendered, whereas a filtered vector is rendered with at least two or, with good filtering, three pixels for each major axis step.

The increase in vector generation speed has allowed users to view complex images with real-time dynamic motion. This increase in vector performance has aggravated the aliasing-

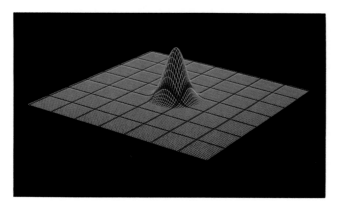

FIGURE 6: The Hamming Function

induced motion artifacts. Therefore, users have begun to demand antialiasing. Unfortunately, there is typically a speed penalty for using the antialiasing feature in the systems that support it [1,11]. Slowing down the frame rate will reduce the aliasing-induced motion, but this is obviously not an optimal solution. Instead, users want the same high frame rate for antialiased images as they get for aliased images.

Vector generation hardware based on Bresenham and digital differential analyzer (DDA) [14] algorithms has been extended to handle antialiased vector generation. One extension is to expand the inner loop to generate filtered pixel values for each major axis step [11,9]. Another approach is to repeatedly draw the line, offsetting the line by one pixel in the minor axis during each pass. The filtering of these vectors is built up during each pass of the line drawing [1]. These solutions result in a performance penalty when antialiasing is enabled. Another problem is if one pixel per clock cycle is produced, there is no guarantee that the frame buffer will be able to perform the random accesses at the required speed. Some frame buffers however, have been architected to eliminate the frame buffer bottleneck [2,12].

As the need for higher performance rendering became apparent, multiple rendering processor architectures were developed. However, the algorithms used to produce antialiased vectors have not taken full advantage of the multiple processors. In all these multiple rendering processor systems, enabling vector antialiasing results in some loss of performance. In one system with an image space subdivision [1] using 20 processors, enabling antialiasing for vector drawing results in a 50% degradation in the vector draw rate. A system using a pipeline of over 1000 primitive processors [7] has been designed. Antialiasing an image with this system requires rendering the frame several times into a 24-bit per color accumulator frame buffer [2,7]. Another system using a pipeline of primitive processors, with support for antialiasing in the individual processors, has been presented [17]. Each processor produces a list of objects that may contribute to the pixel and a filtering stage then produces subpixel coverage maps. In this last system the performance impact of antialiasing is proportional to the image complexity.[1]

In order to fully utilize modern VLSI technology, a parallel algorithm for vector generation was developed. The basis of the algorithm is to efficiently match a hardware implementation to an image space sub-division. In concept, the Bresenham type algorithms automatically step along the major axis and check whether the minor axis should be adjusted. However, the efficient use of multi-processing hardware requires that while each pixel is being processed, the position of the next pixel *for each processor* be determined. This decouples the processors so they can proceed independently. Since this is a more complex algorithm, it requires more logic than the Bresenham algorithm. The additional logic required is relatively easy and cost efficient to implement given modern VLSI technology.

---

1. It should be noted that the antialiasing techniques used in the two systems with pipelines of primitive processors can be applied to both vectors and polygons.

DETAILS OF THE HIGH PERFORMANCE VECTOR STEPPING ALGORITHM

Before presenting the details of the algorithm, the required state information will be described. The state information is received from the configuration pins of the processor and the data packets that are sent to describe each individual vector.

— This implementation supports one, two or four processors, with an image space sub-division along scan lines. The signals S0 - S3 tell a processor which of the scan lines, 0 - 3 (MOD 4), it owns. These signals are directly decoded from the configuration pins of the processor.

— In addition to the S0 - S3 signals, the three configuration bits are used to produce a set of logical signals. These signals are called 4_PP, 2_PP and STEP_CONTROL. The 4_PP signal is asserted if the current processor owns one of every four scan lines in a four processor configuration. The 2_PP signal is asserted if the processor is part of a two processor configuration. STEP_CONTROL is asserted if the current processor is part of a one or two processor configuration.

— The signal Y_MAJOR is asserted if the vector being rendered is Y-major, and not asserted if the vector is X-major. A Y-major vector is one that has a unique Y value for each major axis step of the vector.

— Serpentine mode is a way to specify the output order of the pixels. If the pixels along one scan line are output with incrementing x values, then the pixels for the adjunct scan line are output by decrementing the x values. This ordering is done to improve locality and thus increase throughput into the frame buffer [12]. The SERP signal is set to the value of the sign bit of the slope at the start of each vector. The SERP signal is toggled every time the major axis is stepped.

— The signal MAJ_DEC is asserted if the major axis should be decremented for each major axis step.

— The AA_MODE signal is asserted if the vector is being rendered in antialiased mode. If the signal is not asserted then an aliased vector will be rendered.

— The MIN_1 and MIN_0 signals are the least significant bits of the minor axis position. These are used by the processor to determine the location of its pixels.

— Two signals; MAJ_1 and MAJ_0 are the least significant bits of the major axis position. These are used by the processor to determine the location of its pixels.

Figure 7 is used to show the positions where the pixels for a major axis step may be located. The grid is used to represent pixel locations on the CRT screen. Note that image space is sub-divided along scan lines, such that in a four processor system each processor would be responsible for every fourth scan line. The figure assumes that the current major and minor axis values point to the pixel location shown as 1. For an aliased vector only Pixel 1 would be rendered at the current major axis step. A Y-major antialiased vector would require that the processor responsible for scan line N render the pixels shown as 3, 1 and 5. An X-major antialiased vector would require the pixels shown as 2, 1 and 4 be rendered. In a four processor configuration a different processor would render each of the three pixels required for the major axis step of the X-major antialiased vector.

Real-Time Robot Motion Planning
Using Rasterizing Computer Graphics Hardware

Jed Lengyel*, Mark Reichert*, Bruce R. Donald† and Donald P. Greenberg‡

Abstract

We present a real-time robot motion planner that is fast and complete to a resolution. The technique is guaranteed to find a path if one exists at the resolution, and all paths returned are safe. The planner can handle *any* polyhedral geometry of robot and obstacles, including disjoint and highly concave unions of polyhedra.

The planner uses standard graphics hardware to rasterize configuration space obstacles into a series of bitmap slices, and then uses dynamic programming to create a navigation function (a discrete vector-valued function) and to calculate paths in this rasterized space. The motion paths which the planner produces are minimal with respect to an L_1 (Manhattan) distance metric that includes rotation as well as translation.

Several examples are shown illustrating the competence of the planner at generating planar rotational and translational plans for complex two and three dimensional robots. Dynamic motion sequences, including complicated and non-obvious backtracking solutions, can be executed in real time.

1 Introduction

Motion planning has been regarded as a core algorithmic problem in computational robotics for many years, and many researchers have worked on finding better algorithmic solutions.[Yap85] However, despite the fact that all of the key elements in planning robot motion substantially overlap with computer graphics interests, the problem has not been presented as a computer graphics topic.

The classical formulation of the *Find-Path* or *Piano Mover's* problem is stated as follows: given an arbitrary rigid polyhedral object, P, and polyhedral environment, find a continuous collision-free path taking P from some initial configuration to a desired goal configuration.

---

*Graduate Student, Program of Computer Graphics, Cornell University, Ithaca, N.Y. 14853

†Assistant Professor and Director, Computer Science Robotics Laboratory, Department of Computer Science, 4130 Upson Hall, Cornell University, Ithaca, N.Y. 14853

‡Director, Program of Computer Graphics, Jacob Gould Shurman Professor of Computer Graphics, Cornell University, Ithaca, N.Y. 14853

We view this motion planning process as an algorithmic endeavor analogous to hidden surface removal in computer graphics. First, precise combinatorial solutions exist, but rasterized, approximating techniques (such as z-buffer algorithms) are faster and more effective. Second, such approximation algorithms can be provided with massively parallel, specialized hardware support. Instead of concentrating on more efficient, combinatorially exact algorithms, the end-user is more effectively served by (a) choosing good representations for the geometric constraints, (b) selecting local, isotropic geometric algorithms that are easily parallelizable, and (c) providing or using appropriate hardware support to make the algorithms run very fast.

Our algorithm is based on the configuration space representations that are due to Lozano-Pérez [LPW79], and we use a local, isotropic search algorithm [Don87][Don84] to obtain a very fast motion planning algorithm that runs on standard graphics hardware. Two parts of the local algorithm we present here are very similar to the work of [DT88]. The paths produced have minimal length with respect to an L_1 distance metric imposed on the rasterization which treats translational and rotational movements equally.

In addition to being simple, the algorithm is complete to a resolution (of the rasterization), and while inherently "local", does not suffer from local minima. Many other fast motion planning algorithms, in particular, potential field methods, get "stuck" in local minima and therefore cannot be effectively used to plan paths for complex, concave, or disconnected robots. While these other algorithms run well when the robot is (a) small and convex relative to the environment, or (b) when the space of solutions is "very dense", our planner may be more effective in more complicated cases.

For computer graphics applications, the visual impact of the robot motion is important. Since the motions are time-dependent and complex, real-time graphical playback is desirable to assess the motion sequence, including the complicated back-tracking paths which may be necessary to obtain a solution.

In Section 2 a brief overview of the historical approaches used by the robotics community is presented. Section 3 describes our algorithm in detail. Section 4 presents the results of the implementation for several specific cases. Section 5 presents the conclusions and topics for future research.

2 Background

The *Piano Mover's* problem has been approached in many ways. We present below a brief overview of the two major approaches used by the robotics community, the configuration space and potential field methods, and discuss the advantages and limitations of each method.

2.1 Configuration Space Methods

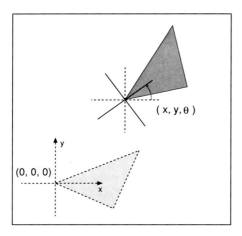

Figure 1: Planar Object.

Consider an object moving in the plane. The object's configuration can be uniquely described by its position in x and y and its orientation in θ. The *configuration space* for such an object is the set of all such possible configurations (x, y, θ) where $(x, y) \in R^2$ (the real plane) and $\theta \in S^1$ (the unit circle). The configuration space for an object moving in the plane is thus $R^2 \times S^1$ (Figure 1). (In robotics terminology, *configuration space* is often abbreviated to *c-space*.)

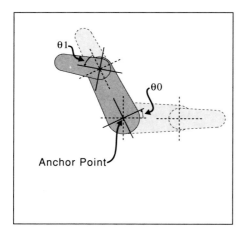

Figure 2: Two-link Arm.

As another example of a configuration space, consider a robot with a two-link arm in the plane anchored at a point. The angle of the base arm θ_0 and the angle of the free arm θ_1 completely determine the configuration of the robot (Figure 2). The configuration space is $S^1 \times S^1$, and a particular configuration is a point $(\theta_0, \theta_1) \in S^1 \times S^1$.

The problem of moving a complex robot through a physical environment can be transformed to the problem of moving a point through a c-space environment. The obstacle constraints in real space are encoded by "enlarged" obstacles in configuration space. If the reference point of the robot is outside of the enlarged c-space obstacles, then the robot itself is outside of the obstacles in the physical workspace. Lozano-Pérez generates the c-space obstacles using a *Minkowski sum* of the robot and the environment. In a

Minkowski sum all the points of one set are offset by the points of another set (Figures 3 and 4). For sets represented by polygons, the Minkowski sum can be thought of as the "convolution" (set sum) of the obstacle polygons by the "negated" robot polygons. This "convolution" can be computed using a convex hull algorithm. This algorithm is suboptimal in the plane[1], and in the case where the generating polygons are convex, Lozano-Pérez gives a method for computing the Minkowski sum in linear $(O(n))$ time. The important ideas of *c-space slices* and *c-space slice projections*, which will be described in more detail later, were also introduced. For a more thorough introduction, we refer the reader to previous papers [Loz80] [LPW79] [Udu77].

Other researchers have used rasterizing techniques in c-space. For example, Lozano-Pérez [Loz87] used a representation of the obstacles derived in [Loz83],[Don87] and encoded them in a bitmap of the c-space. The search algorithm used was not local, isotropic, nor trivially parallelizable, and no hardware support was available.

Dorst and Trovato used a rasterized c-space approach to plan for a two-link arm[DT88]. They described the motion-planning problem in a differential geometry framework, with a metric topology imposed on configuration space and geodesics corresponding to optimal paths. They discretized the c-space and used cost wave propagation and gradient-following to find the optimal paths. The second two parts of the algorithm we present are very similar to their work. Dorst and Trovato do not, however, address the problem of generating the c-space obstacles (the first step in our algorithm.) We also emphasize the hardware context of the algorithm.

Donald described a motion planning algorithm that is a *provably-good approximation* algorithm. It is guaranteed to find a path if one exists at the given resolution and all paths it returns are safe. [See [Don87] for a formal definition of provably-good approximation algorithms.] He also used constraint equations to represent the c-space obstacles, imposed a grid on the c-space, and then used several local "experts" to guide the search through the c-space. This algorithm had the advantage of being complete to a resolution, but a software implementation ran slowly on a sequential machine[2]. We show how a variant of one part of this algorithm runs very fast on modern graphics hardware.

2.2 Potential Field Methods

Potential field methods were first pioneered by Khatib and Le Maitre [KLM78]. The obstacles were represented as zero level surfaces of scalar valued analytic functions, *i.e.* $f(x, y, z) = 0$. A potential field local to each obstacle, whose strength diminishes with the square of the distance from the obstacle, was generated. An arbitrary cutoff value, f_0, was assigned which corresponds to the distance at which the influence of the obstacle is no longer important (Figure 5). The potential field is mathematically described in the following form:

$$P(x, y, z) = \begin{cases} \alpha / f(x, y, z)^2 & f(x, y, z) \le f_0 \\ 0 & f(x, y, z) > f_0 \end{cases}$$

A particle moving in accordance to Newton's laws in such a potential field will never hit the obstacle. Khatib observed that the sum of the gradients is the gradient of the sum; thus adding up the potential fields for many obstacles results in a single function under whose influence the particle cannot hit any obstacle.[Kod89] Since the real object to be maneuvered is not a point mass, Khatib identified a number of "distinguished points" on the object. The potentials of these distinguished points were linearly combined to

---

[1]Note that in general, calculating a convex hull requires time $O(n \log n)$.
[2]Donald used a CADR (MIT-architecture) Lisp machine

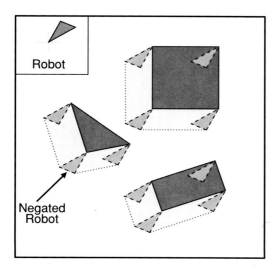

Figure 3: Minkowski Sum of Robot and Obstacles.

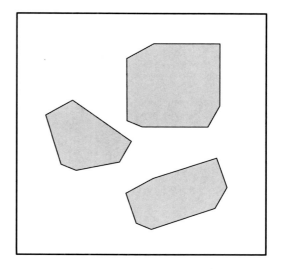

Figure 4: Resultant Polygons from Minkowski Sum.

produce a composite potential on the position and orientation of the rigid body.

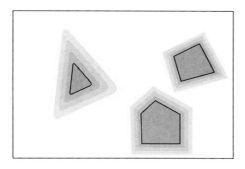

Figure 5: Potential field generated from obstacles. A higher density indicates a higher potential.

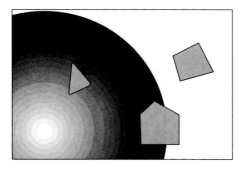

Figure 6: Bitmap potential field generated from goal. A higher density indicates a higher potential.

Potential field techniques have been successful for real-time obstacle avoidance in changing environments, but for motion planning, there are several limitations. One major problem is spurious local minima, especially for concave robots. To escape these local minima, one must resort to randomization techniques or other techniques as described below.

Barraquand and Latombe extended this idea and used bitmaps to represent the obstacles. They generated a separate potential field for a point robot starting from a goal position (Figure 6).[BL89] The potential field is not a function of the euclidean distance to the goal, but is instead a function of the path length to the goal (traveling *around* obstacles, and not "as the crow flies".)

They then used techniques similar to Khatib's to combine point potentials into a single potential field for a more complex body. Although the potential field for a point robot has no local minima, the combined potential field for a more complex robot may have many local minima due to "competition" of the distinguished points. To escape these minima, they described two possible techniques. Both of these techniques search for paths in c-space, with the potential field used as guide for the search.

Their first technique was to "fill" the local minima, which resulted in a planner that is complete to a given resolution. The algorithm we present is similar to this planner, since it also fills c-space and is complete to a resolution.

They suggested that local-minima-filling methods are effective only for low degrees of freedom (due to the memory requirements.)[3] To plan with higher degrees of freedom, they used randomization to get out of the local minima. This planner is capable of planning for robots with a great number of degrees of freedom (as demonstrated with multiple bars linked into chains), but is only probabilistically complete.

3 Algorithm

3.1 Overview

The motion planner presented below is algorithmically based on the grid search method used by Donald [Don87] with the configuration space approach of Lozano-Pérez [Loz80]. It consists of four separate modules.

---

[3]The memory requirements for the planner we present are very similar to those of Barraquand and Latombe's local-minima-filling technique. However, we are aware through personal communication with Tomás Lozano-Pérez , that a complete-to-a-resolution planner that uses techniques similar to the ones we present is being developed on a Connection Machine and appears promising for higher DOF cases.

- The first module allocates a voxel array representation of c-space and rapidly computes c-space obstacles in this array using standard graphics rasterization hardware.

- The second module calculates a c-space navigation function [Kod87] with a dynamic programming technique (expanding wavefront of solutions.) This navigation function is essentially a discrete vector-valued function which, when given the robot's current voxel location in c-space, returns the direction that the robot should move to decrease its distance to the goal.

- The third module determines the shortest path from any voxel start position to the goal if there is a viable solution. Since the navigation function gives the direction to move at every cell, this module can calculate the path quickly, and determine in constant time if a path exists.

- The fourth module produces a real-time kinematic simulation of the robot motion.

Each of these modules is described in more detail below.

3.2   Definitions

The following definitions due to [Loz80] are useful prior to the algorithmic explanations.

A *c-space obstacle*, CO, is a forbidden region of c-space $R^2 \times S^1$.

A *slice*, $CO[\theta_1, \theta_2]$, of CO is CO restricted to an angular interval $[\theta_1, \theta_2]$, i.e. $CO \cap (R^2 \times [\theta_1, \theta_2])$.

A *slice projection* is the projection of $CO[\theta_1, \theta_2]$ onto the "plane" $R^2 \times \{\theta_0\}$ for $\theta_0 = (\theta_1 + \theta_2)/2$.

3.3   Generation of Configuration Space Representation

We calculate the configuration space obstacle polygons by taking the Minkowski sum of the obstacles and the rotated and negated robot as described by Lozano-Pérez [Loz80] (Figure 3). We then use graphics polygon-fill hardware to fill the configuration space obstacle polygons (Figure 4).

When the robot motion is restricted to two degrees of freedom (only translation in the plane) our discrete representation of c-space is a single bitmap with rasterized c-space obstacles. However, when rotation is allowed, the configuration space is represented by a set of bitmaps, where each bitmap is a slice projection representing the configuration space for the angular interval $[\theta_1, \theta_2]$.

While generating a representation of c-space at exactly one orientation is trivial, generation of a conservative, discrete, representation of c-space over some angular interval is more difficult. Our goal is to ensure that, in the bitmap slice representing c-space for the angular interval $[\theta_1, \theta_2]$, no cell is labeled as free if it has a c-space obstacle penetrating it at *any* orientation in $[\theta_1, \theta_2]$. To produce a discrete representation of c-space for the angular interval $[\theta_1, \theta_2]$, we generate n discrete representations of c-space at equally spaced orientations within the interval $[\theta_1, \theta_2]$. The angular increment $\theta = (\theta_2 - \theta_1)/n$. The bitmap slice representation for the angular interval $[\theta_1, \theta_2]$ is the union of all of the sub-intervals. Figure 7 is a pseudo-code implementation of this method.

Note that the bitmap slices are conservative. If any part of an obstacle penetrates a cell, then the whole cell is labeled with "obstacle." This discards some potential paths, but enforces the complete-to-a-resolution property of the planner. If two adjacent cells are labeled as being "free" of obstacles, then the path between them is free, since if there were any obstacle in the way, one or both of the cells would have been labeled with "obstacle," which would contradict the assumption of both cells being "free". Since

movement is allowed only between "free" cells, every path returned is valid (collision-free.)

```
GENERATE C-SPACE()
  For theta = 0 to 2π by 2π/N ( N is # of theta slices)
    Foreach robotPoly in robot polygon list
      For t1 = theta - dtheta to theta + dtheta
        Rotate robotPoly by t1
        Foreach obstaclePoly in environment
          Generate the minkowski sum of
            robotPoly and obstaclePoly
          Fill minkowski polygon with
            obstacle color.
    Read filled polys from frame buffer
    Move bitmap into voxel array.
    Clear frame buffer.
  Return bitmap voxel array
```

Figure 7: Pseudo-code for Generation of Discretized C-Space

3.4   Calculation of Navigation Function

A dynamic programming technique is used to expand a wavefront of solutions from the goal, with a queue to keep track of the current wavefront.[DT88] Each element in the queue holds a position in the rasterized environment and a current length of the path from the goal position. An element is dequeued, its location in the environment is filled with the current length, and then all of its free space neighbors that have not yet been filled are put on the end of the queue with an incremented distance.

This algorithm is essentially isomorphic to the "Bumble Strategy" in Donald's 1984 algorithm [Don84] [Don87], which operated as follows: a search node N on a c-space grid is dequeued, and its c-space grid neighbors are generated. The reachable, unexplored, free-space neighbors are put on the end of the queue. Each new neighbor M contains a backpointer to N, and N's direction from M. This back pointer (and back-direction) corresponds precisely to our navigation function. Note the Bumble Strategy is simply a breadth-first-search (BFS) from the start (or goal.) We regard dynamic programming and BFS as "dual" algorithms in that BFS from the goal yields our dynamic programming algorithm.

```
FILL NAVIGATION FUNCTION(goal location)
  Enqueue goal location with distance = 0
  While queue is not empty
    Dequeue element F
    Label F's location with F's distance
    Enqueue all neighbors of F that are not
      obstacles and that have not yet been
      filled with distance = distance + 1
```

Figure 8: Pseudo-code for Navigation Function Fill

The initial element placed in the queue is the goal node with a path length of zero. The algorithm takes that node out of the queue, fills its location in the rasterized environment with zero, then queues up all of the neighboring nodes with a path length of one. The wavefront continues out like a "brush fire", spreading around the C-space obstacles, in a way similar to flood-fill or seed-fill algorithms used in computer paint programs[Pav81]. Each cell that can be reached from the goal is set just once (Figures 9 and 8.)

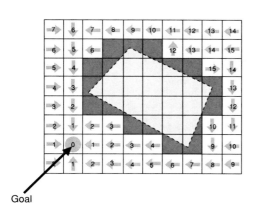

Figure 9: Calculation of Navigation Function.

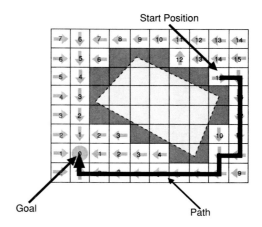

Figure 10: Path Generation.

Note that with the three-degree of freedom case (two translations plus rotation) that the fill expands upward and wraps-around in the theta direction as well as expanding in the x and y directions.

The running time is proportional to the number of free cells in the environment. Complicated scenes which consist of many obstacles have fewer free cells. Thus, paradoxically, more complicated scenes are quicker to fill![4]

3.5 Path Generation

Since the navigation function is generated by a breadth-first search through the rasterized configuration space, it yields the shortest path from the goal to any reachable position in the configuration space (where a "shortest path" is defined to be one passing through a minimal number of voxels.) [See [DT88] for other metrics.] To get closer to the goal from any start position, the robot moves to the lowest-numbered neighboring cell. This corresponds exactly to following the breadth-first search tree to the goal. (We call this process "surfing", since the robot is simply sliding down the "hills" of the potential function.)

If there are multiple cells which have the lowest number, any one can be picked, since each would correspond to a path with the same number of moves needed to reach the goal. Given a choice between a rotation (a move in the theta direction) or a translation (a move in the x or y direction), our algorithm selects the translation option to minimize rotation(Figures 10 and 11.)

By construction, every cell that can be reached from the goal has a neighbor with a lower number than itself (the cell which was queued to label it.) Thus, there are no local minima in the navigation function. The robot can just follow the bread-first search tree to the goal and not worry about getting stuck. The following of the search tree is fast, running in linear time with respect to path length. This path generation technique corresponds precisely to gradient following[DT88][Kod87].

3.6 Display Routines

A program has been implemented which uses standard graphics hardware acceleration to generate dynamic real-time playback of the robot motion, allowing the viewer's position to be interactively modified. Two sequential pre-processing steps are required, the rasterization of c-space and the computation of the navigation function. This discretized configuration space must be recomputed

---

[4]Also observed by [DT88].

```
GENERATE PATH(start location)
  let C = cell corresponding to start location
  let P = NULL
  if C was not reached by fill (label is blank)
    return CANNOT REACH GOAL
  else
    while C is not at goal
      add C to path P
      pick lowest numbered neighbor, L
      let C = L
    return P
```

Figure 11: Pseudo-code for Path Generation (Surfing)

for every change in the obstacle definitions or the robot geometry. The navigation function is recomputed only if there is a change in the goal position. Since the path generation is so fast, this can be computed on-the-fly, and the dynamic sequences of the robot motion can be displayed.

3.7 Use of Hardware

While our algorithm is the slowest possible on serial machines, it is very fast using parallel or specialized hardware.

Each of the above modules can benefit from use of specialized hardware. In our implementation only the first, the generation of the c-space obstacles, and the fourth, the kinematic simulation, use specialized graphics hardware. The second module, the flood-fill, uses a very local operation and is ideal for a distributed computation[BL89]. The third module, the gradient following or bread-first-search-tree following, is essentially a fast serial operation.

4 Examples

The algorithm was tested in several obstacle environments with robots and obstacles of varying shape and convexity. Experimental timings for each of these examples are presented in Table 1. Note that once the preprocessing steps for the configuration space and navigation function are complete, the path-generation algorithm runs almost instantaneously, and real-time motion display is possible.

Problem	Figure	Size	C-space	Fill	Surf	Display
Moving Planar Robot	13b	256x256x120	22.6	44.1	0.11	35.8
Backtracking Planar Robot	13e	256x256x120	*	*	0.11	50.3
Stuck Planar Robot	13f	256x256x120	*	*	0.01	0
Piano (Room1)	14a	192x192x180	26.0	50.2	0.05	27.1
Piano (Room2)	15a	92x92x90	8.1	8.1	0.04	7.2

Table 1: Table of experimental timings. Times are given in seconds. Processing and display was performed on a Hewlett Packard 835 with a Turbo-SRX graphics display. The precalculations whose times marked as "*" for Figures 13e and 13f were already performed for Figure 13b and did not need to be repeated.

4.1 Complex $R^2 \times S^1$

This example illustrates the motion of a complex, concave planar robot. Note the triangular peg obstacles in the upper left-hand corner (Figure 13b.) Since the search algorithm does not rely on a heuristic distance to the goal, backtracking paths are easily found (Figure 13e.) In this example, the robot is not able to turn around until it backtracks all the way to the right side (where the region is devoid of the pegs preventing the turning on the left side).

If the search backwards from the goal (the navigation function) reached the start point, then a path exists from the start to the goal, otherwise one does not exist at the given resolution. With one array reference, it is known whether or not a path can be found from the start configuration to the goal. In Figure 13f, the robot's "head" is stuck between the peg and the wall, and thus the algorithm returns with the result that no path exists.

4.2 $R^2 \times S^1$ motion for 3D robots

Many three-dimensional robots have pieces which are quite distinct vertically. A piano, for example, has small legs and a large main body. By creating two classes of environmental objects, one class of objects which obstruct the legs, and the other which obstruct the body, the algorithm for planar problems can be extended by object space partitioning ($3\frac{1}{2}$D representation.)

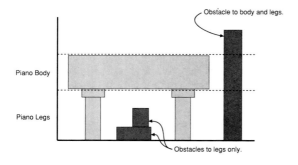

Figure 12: Piano Environment Partitioning.

The rasterization is performed as before, with the exception that the body is now convolved only with the body obstacles, and the legs only with the leg obstacles. The union of the leg and body c-space obstacles is used to create *one* bitmap. Since the leg obstacle is not convolved with the body when generating the c-space obstacles, the piano body can move over it, while the legs maneuver around it (Figure 14a.)

5 Discussion & Conclusion

We have presented a robot motion planner that is fast and, unlike other fast motion planners, is based entirely on complete and provably-good approximation algorithms. The algorithm is based on part of Donald's original algorithm [Don87], which was initially considered to be slow and ineffective for real-time motion planning, but when modified to run on current graphics hardware is actually quite fast.

The planner can handle *any* polyhedral geometry of robot and obstacles, including disjoint and highly concave unions of polyhedra.

The planner is very general and is guaranteed to find a path if one exists at the resolution. In constant ($O(1)$) time, it detects if a path exists from the start location to the goal, or between any two points through the goal (compare [DT88].)

The method is memory intensive, but for many problems the resolutions can be made much lower, especially in the rotational dimension. Storage can also be reduced by eliminating the navigation function value, and only storing a direction at each point, requiring as few as three bits per cell (for the 3DOF case.)

The method is resolution dependent. The higher the resolution, the closer the robot can squeeze by the obstacles. The lower the resolution, the lower the memory requirements.

We believe that we have demonstrated that provably good approximation algorithms for kinematic motion planning can be made to run very fast, if the algorithms are local, isotropic, and can take advantage of special purpose computer graphics hardware for tasks such as rasterization (poly-fill), flood-fill, and gradient-following.

We conjecture that the fastest solutions will involve algorithms similar to ours, that is, characterized by use of

1. Configuration space representations such as [LPW79].

2. Local, geometric, isotropic, parallelizable search algorithms such as [Don87].

3. Appropriate hardware support for geometric computation.

In robotics, and in animation, in addition to kinematic planning and simulation, one also desires to plan robot motions with full dynamics. In recent work, [CDRX88][DX89][DX90] have developed provably good approximation algorithms that generate motions that (1) avoid obstacles, (2) obey dynamic bounds on generalized forces and velocities, (3) respect full Lagrangian rigid body dynamics equations of motion, and (4) are provably close to optimal-time. These algorithms are also grid-based, and currently run very slowly on traditional architectures. We hope that by using techniques similar to those we propose in this paper, that these algorithms can be made to run quickly when modified to exploit appropriate hardware support.

We hope that this paper illustrates the substantial overlap in research areas between the graphics and robotics communities, and fosters collaborative efforts to create more innovative solutions.

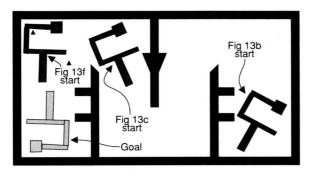

Figure 13a: Key to Robot Positions.

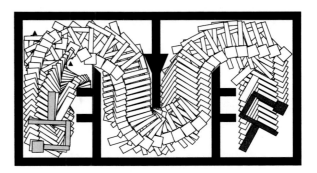

Figure 13b: Moving Planar Robot.

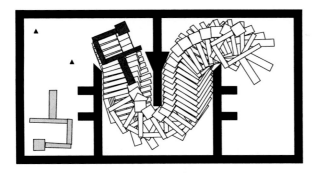

Figure 13c: First Leg of Backtracking.

Figure 13d: Last Leg of Backtracking.

Figure 13e: Backtracking Planar Robot.

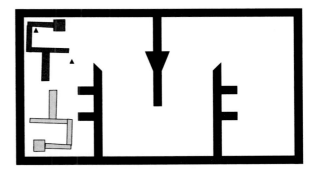

Figure 13f: Trapped Planar Robot.

13a is a key to the start and goal locations of the subsequent figures. In 13b, the robot follows the gradient of the potential function to the goal (which is the same as following the breadth-first search tree.)

In 13c, the robot first moves from the start to the right, since there is not enough room between the pegs on the left to reorient. The robot then has enough room to reorient (the right side is not blocked by the small pegs as on the left.) Finally, in 13d, the robot can squeeze by the small pegs, and obtain the goal position and orientation. 13e shows the entire motion of 13c and 13d. The algorithm is exactly the same as in 13b, simply following the breadth-first search tree. In 13f, no solution exists. Our planner detects this in constant $O(1)$ time.

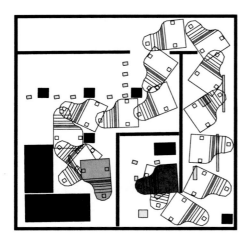

Figure 14a: Moving Piano.

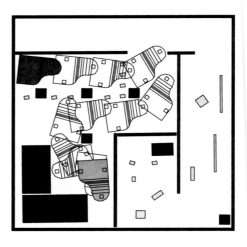

Figure 14b: Moving Piano from Alternate Start.

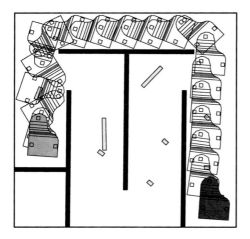

Figure 15a: Piano in Room 2.

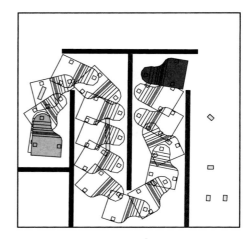

Figure 15b: Piano in Room 2 with Alternate Start.

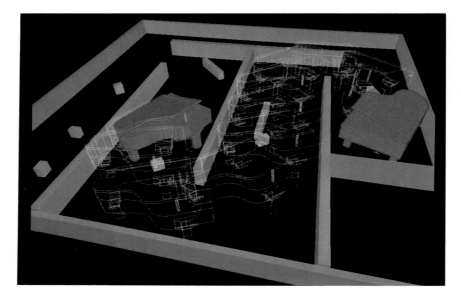

Figure 16: Moving Piano in 3D.

6 Acknowledgements

The authors gratefully acknowledge the National Science Foundation whose two research grants entitled "Interactive Input and Display Techniques" (DCR8203929) and "Visualization for Scientific Computing" (ACS8715478) help support the Program of Computer Graphics. Support for Bruce Donald's robotics research is provided in part by the National Science Foundation under grant No. IRI-8802390 and by a Presidential Young Investigator award, and in part by the Mathematical Sciences Institute. Jed Lengyel is supported by a National Science Foundation Graduate Fellowship. Our interactive graphics computing environment has been substantially enhanced by generous equipment donations from Hewlett-Packard and Digital Equipment Corporation. Thanks to Robotics CS661, and Bruce's teaching assistants Pat Xavier and Russell Brown, for introducing us to the field of robotics (and for assigning Homework 1, which lead directly to this work.) Thanks to Len Wanger for the piano model, to Emil Ghinger for photographic work, to Tim O'Connor for keeping our computers alive and well, to Fran and Ellen for keeping everything else alive and well, to Jim Ferwerda for breathing life into the video system and to Dave Baraff for taking time to show us how to use it. Thanks to Roy Hall for proof-reading drafts of this paper. Special thanks to Wendy, Michele, Rachael, and Iris for their unending patience while this paper was being written.

References

[BL89]   Barraquand, J. and J. Latombe. *Robot Motion Planning: A Distributed Representation Approach*, Report No. STAN-CS-89-1257, Stanford University, Department of Computer Science, May 1989.

[CDRX88]   Canny, J., B. Donald, J. Reif, and P. Xavier. "On the Complexity of Kinodynamic Planning," in 29th Symposium on the Foundations of Computer Science, White Plains NY., 1988.

[Don84]   Donald, B. R. *Motion Planning with Six Degrees of Freedom*, Report No. MIT AI-TR 791, MIT, Artificial Intelligence Laboratory, 1984.

[Don87]   Donald, B. R. "A Search Algorithm for Motion Planning with Six Degrees of Freedom," *Artificial Intelligence*, 31, 1987, pages 295–353.

[DT88]   Dorst, L. and K. Trovato. "Optimal path planning by cost wave propagation in metric configuration space," *Proceedings of SPIE-The International Society for Optical Engineering*, 1007, November 1988, pages 186–197.

[DX89]   Donald, B. and P. Xavier. "A Provably Good Approximation Algorithm for Optimal-Time Trajectory Planning," in IEEE Int. Conf. On Robotics and Automation, Scottsdale, AZ, 1989.

[DX90]   Donald, B. and P. Xavier. "Provably Good Approximation Algorithms for Optimal Kinodynamic Planning for Cartesian Robots and Open Chain Manipulators," in Proceedings of the ACM Symposium on Computational Geometry, Berkeley, CA, 1990.

[KLM78]   Khatib, O. and J. Le Maitre. "Dynamic Control of Manipulators Operating in a Complex Environment," *Proceedings Third International CISM-IFToMM Symposium*, September 1978, pages 267–282.

[Kod87]   Koditschek, D. E. "Exact Robot Navigation by Means of Potential Functions: Some Topological Considerations," *IEEE International Conference on Robotics and Automation*, March 1987.

[Kod89]   Koditschek, D. E. "Planning and Control via Potential Functions," in Lozano-Pérez, T. and O. Khatib, editors, *Robotics Review I*, MIT Press, 1989, pages 349–367.

[Loz80]   Lozano-Pérez, T. *Spatial Planning: A Configuration Space Approach*, A.I. Memo No. 605, Massachusetts Institute of Technology, Artificial Intelligence Laboratory, December 1980.

[Loz83]   Lozano-Pérez, T. "Spatial Planning: A Configuration Space Approach," *IEEE Transactions on Computers*, C-32, 1983, pages 108–120.

[Loz87]   Lozano-Pérez, T. "A Simple Motion Planning Algorithm for General Robot Manipulator," *IEEE Journal of Robotics and Automation*, RA-3(3), 1987, pages 224–238.

[LPW79]   Lozano-Pérez, T. and M. A. Wesley. "An Algorithm for Planning Collison-Free Paths Among Polyhedral Obstacles," *Communications of the ACM*, 22, 1979, pages 560–570.

[Pav81]   Pavlidis, T. "Contour Filling in Raster Graphics," *Proceedings of SIGGRAPH'81 (Dallas, Texas, August 3–7, 1981)*, 1981, pages 29–36.

[Udu77]   Udupa, S. *Collision Detection and Avoidance in Computer Controlled Manipulators*, PhD dissertation, Department of Electrical Engineering, California Institute of Technology, Pasadena, California, 1977.

[Yap85]   Yap, C. K. "Algorithmic Motion Planning," in Schwartz, J. T. and C. K. Yap, editors, *Advances in Robotics*, Lawrence Erlbaum Associates, 1985.

Ray Tracing Trimmed Rational Surface Patches

Tomoyuki Nishita*, Thomas W. Sederberg[†] and Masanori Kakimoto[‡]

*Fukuyama University

[†]Brigham Young University

[‡]Fujitsu Laboratories LTD

Abstract

This paper presents a new algorithm for computing the points at which a ray intersects a rational Bézier surface patch, and also an algorithm for determining if an intersection point lies within a region trimmed by piecewise Bézier curves. Both algorithms are based on a recent innovation known as Bézier clipping, described herein. The intersection algorithm is faster than previous methods for which published performance data allow reliable comparison. It robustly finds all intersections without requiring special preprocessing.

Categories and Subject Descriptors: I.3.3 [Computer Graphics]: Picture/Image Generation; I.3.5 [Computer Graphics]: Computational Geometry and Object Modeling; I.3.7 [Computer Graphics]: Three-Dimensional Graphics and Realism.

General Terms: Algorithms

Additional Key Words and Phrases: Computer graphics, ray tracing, visible surface algorithms, parametric surfaces.

1 INTRODUCTION

The history, theory and capabilities of ray tracing are well documented [3], [5]. This paper deals with the ray tracing of parametric surface patches. Specifically, we present an algorithm for computing all points at which a ray intersects a rational Bézier surface patch of any degree. We also describe an algorithm for determining if a point lies within a trimmed region of the patch. We define a trimmed region to be an area bounded by piecewise (possibly rational) Bézier curves in the parameter plane of the patch.

1.1 Ray-Patch Algorithms

Solutions to the ray/patch intersection problem can be categorized roughly as being based on subdivision, algebraic or numerical techniques.

Subdivision approaches are described by Whitted [19], Rogers [10] and Woodward [20]. These algorithms harness the convex hull property of Bézier surfaces: if the ray does not intersect the convex hull of the control points, it does not intersect the patch. Through recursively subdividing the patch and checking convex hulls, the intersection points can be computed at a linear convergence rate, amounting to a binary search. Whitted's algorithm operates in three dimensions, whereas Rogers and Woodward map the problem to two dimensions.

Numerical solutions to the ray/patch intersection problem include those developed by Toth [18], Sweeney and Bartels [17], and Joy and Bhetanabhotla [4]. Toth's algorithm is based on interval Newton iteration. It works robustly on any parametric surface for which bounds on the surface and its first derivatives can be obtained. Sweeney and Bartels ray trace B-spline surfaces by refining the control mesh using the Oslo algorithm until the mesh closely approximates the surface. The ray intersection is then computed by intersecting the control mesh with the ray, and using that intersection point as a starting point for Newton iteration. Joy and Bhetanabhotla's algorithm uses quasi-Newton optimization to compute the point(s) on the patch nearest the ray, including intersection points.

Kajiya[6] devised an intersection algorithm based on **algebraic** techniques (ie., *resultants*). Kajiya's algorithm reduces the problem of intersecting a bicubic patch with a ray into one of finding the real roots of a degree 18 univariate polynomial.

Our ray/patch intersection algorithm is based on the convex hull property of Bézier curves and surfaces using a technique we refer to as *Bézier clipping*. Traditionally, intersection algorithms (such as curve/curve [13], surface/surface [7], or ray/surface [19]) based on the convex hull property (that is, subdivision based algorithms) perform a linearly converging binary search. Bézier clipping uses the convex hull property in a more powerful manner, by determining parameter ranges which are guaranteed to not include points of intersection. Variations of this concept have proven profitable in algorithms for algebraic curve intersection[12] and planar parametric curve intersection[15]. Bézier clipping has the flavor of a geometrically based interval Newton method, and thus might be categorized as partly a subdivision based algorithm and partly a numerical method.

1.2 Trimmed Patch Algorithms

Previous approaches to the rendering of trimmed patches include adaptive forward differencing [16] and polygonization [9]. Neither of these approaches adapts directly to ray tracing (unless one were to polygonize the patch[9] and then ray trace the polygons). If trimming is caused by a boolean operation involving solid geometric models, rendering can be performed using conventional constructive solid geometry methods[11]. Our algorithm renders trimmed patches defined in a boundary representation, by determining if a point on the patch lies inside or outside a trimmed region. One contribution of this paper is a fast, robust algorithm (based on Bézier clipping) for determining if a ray intersects a collection of trimming curves an even or odd number of times.

1.3 Paper Overview

Section 2 introduces Bézier clipping and applies it to the problem of point classification for trimmed patches. Section 3 describes our ray/patch intersection algorithm, and performance comparisons are presented in section 4.

This paper assumes the reader is familiar with rational Bézier curves and surfaces[2].

The ray/patch intersection algorithm requires patches to be expressed in Bézier form. The point classification algorithm requires trimming curves to be in Bézier form. Conversion from NURBS to Bézier representation is discussed in reference 9.

2 POINT CLASSIFICATION

Figure 1 shows a *trimmed* Bézier surface patch. Its parameter domain (see Figure 2) contains several *trimming curves*, expressed in Bézier (or rational Bézier) form. Regions enclosed by trimming curves are excluded from the patch.

Point classification, in the context of trimmed patch ray tracing, is the problem of determining if a given point S in s, t patch parameter space lies IN the patch, OUT of the patch (in a region enclosed by trimming curves), or ON a trimming curve. If S is a point at which a ray intersects the patch, then S qualifies as a hit if it is IN, and as a miss if it is OUT. If S is ON a trimming curve, it is reported as a hit, but is flagged for possible anti-alias supersampling.

Trimming curves completely enclose an OUT region. This may require linear Bézier curve segments along portions of the patch boundary (as in Figure 2).

Recall a corollary of the Jordan curve theorem: If any ray R in s, t patch parameter space (not to be confused with a "tracing ray" in R^3) emanating from S intersects the collection of trimming curves an even (odd) number of times, then S is IN (OUT of) the patch. Our point classification algorithm amounts to an efficient method of determining that even/odd intersection parity. For this discussion, R points in the positive s direction. In practice, choose the ray in the $\pm s$ or $\pm t$ direction which exits the parameter square in the shortest distance. It might appear that ray/curve tangencies can cause a problem. As discussed in **CASE** B below, this is not a concern.

The algorithm begins by splitting the patch parameter plane into quadrants which meet at S as shown in Figure 3. To determine if R intersects a given Bézier trimming curve an even or odd number of times, we categorize the curve based on which quadrants its control points occupy. For now, assume that no end control point lies on a quadrant boundary (a situation addressed in section 2.2.1).

> **CASE** A: All control points lie on the same side of the line containing R (in quadrants I, II, III, IV, I&II, or III&IV) or "behind" R (in quadrants II&III). The convex hull property of Bézier curves guarantees zero intersections with R.
>
> **CASE** B: All control points lie in quadrants I&IV, but not case A. Since the curve is continuous and obeys the convex hull property, if the curve endpoints lie in the same quadrant, the curve crosses R an even number of times. Otherwise, the curve intersects R an odd number of times. Note that tangencies between the ray and trimming-curve tangencies, even those of high order, do not pose a problem. The only question is whether the curve endpoints straddle the ray.
>
> **CASE** C: All other curves.

If a curve is case A or B no further processing is needed to determine its intersection parity with a ray. For a case C curve, we subdivide it using the de Casteljau algorithm[2] into three Bézier segments in such a way that the two end segments are guaranteed *a priori* to be case A or B. The points at which to subdivide are determined using a technique we call *Bézier clipping*, described

next. Discussion of the point classification algorithm resumes in Section 2.2.

2.1 Bézier Clipping

Figure 4 shows a Bézier curve C and the line L in s, t patch parameter space C is defined by its parametric equation

$$\mathbf{C}(u) = \sum_{i=0}^{n} \mathbf{C}_i B_i^n(u). \tag{1}$$

$\mathbf{C}_i = (s_i, t_i)$ are the Bézier control points and $B_i^n(u) = \binom{n}{i}(1 - u)^{n-i} u^i$ denote the Bernstein basis functions. L is defined by its normalized implicit equation

$$as + bt + c = 0, \quad a^2 + b^2 = 1. \tag{2}$$

The intersection of L and C can be found by substituting equation 1 into equation 2:

$$d(u) = \sum_{i=0}^{n} d_i B_i^n(u) = 0, \quad d_i = a s_i + b t_i + c. \tag{3}$$

Note that $d(u) = 0$ for all values of u at which C intersects L. Also, d_i is the distance from $\mathbf{C}_i$ to L (as shown in Figure 4).

The function $d(u)$ in equation 3 is a polynomial in Bernstein form, and can be represented as an "explicit" (or so-called "non-parametric") Bézier curve[1] as follows:

$$\mathbf{D}(u) = (u, d(u)) = \sum_{i=0}^{n} \mathbf{D}_i B_i^n(u). \tag{4}$$

The Bézier control points $\mathbf{D}_i = (u_i, d_i)$ are evenly spaced in u ($u_i = \frac{i}{n}$). Since $\sum_{i=0}^{n} \frac{i}{n} B_i^n(u) \equiv u[(1 - u) + u]^n \equiv u$, the horizontal coordinate of any point $\mathbf{D}(u)$ is in fact equal to the parameter value u. Figure 5 shows the curve $\mathbf{D}(u)$ which corresponds to the intersection in Figure 4.

Since $\mathbf{D}(u)$ crosses the u-axis at the same u values at which $\mathbf{C}(u)$ intersects L, we can apply the convex hull property of Bézier curves to identify ranges of u for which C does *not* intersect L. Referring again to Figure 5, the convex hull of the $\mathbf{D}_i$ intersects the u axis at points $u = u_{min} = \frac{1}{6}$ and $u = u_{max} = \frac{4}{7}$. Since $\mathbf{D}(u)$ lies inside the convex hull of its control points, we conclude that C does not intersect L in the parameter ranges $0 \leq u < u_{min}$ or $u_{max} < u \leq 1$. Bézier clipping is completed by subdividing C into three segments using the de Casteljau algorithm[2]. Segment 1 is defined over $0 \leq u \leq u_{min}$, segment 2 over $u_{min} \leq u \leq u_{max}$, and segment 3 over $u_{max} \leq u \leq 1$.

2.1.1 Rational Curves

For rational Bézier trimming curves

$$\mathbf{C}(u) = \frac{\sum_{i=0}^{n} w_i \mathbf{C}_i B_i^n(u)}{\sum_{i=0}^{n} w_i B_i^n(u)} \tag{5}$$

with control point coordinates $\mathbf{C}_i = (s_i, t_i)$ and weights w_i, the values of d_i must be modified as follows. Substituting equation 5 into equation 2 and clearing the denominator yields:

$$d(u) = \sum_{i=0}^{n} d_i B_i^n(u) = 0, \quad d_i = w_i(a s_i + b t_i + c).$$

Figure 1: Trimmed Patch

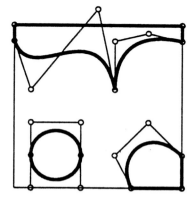

Figure 2: Trimming Curves

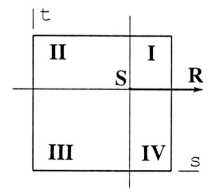

Figure 3: Quadrants

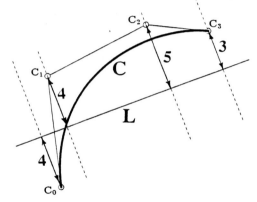

Figure 4: Bézier curve/line intersection

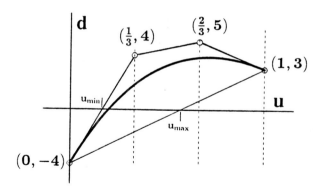

Figure 5: Explicit Bézier curve

Figure 6: Bézier clips per classification

Figure 7: Sample trimmed patch

2.2 Point Classification Algorithm

Returning to the problem of point classification, our goal is to subdivide a case C curve into three segments, such that segments 1 and 3 are assured to be case A or B. This can be accomplished by applying Bézier clipping against either the s quadrant axis ($\mathbf{L} = t - t_r = 0$) or the t quadrant axis ($\mathbf{L} = s - s_r = 0$) where the ray anchor $\mathbf{S} = (s_r, t_r)$. If a case C curve is Bézier clipped against the s quadrant axis, the resulting curve segments 1 and 3 must be case A and segment 2 could be any case. If a case C curve is Bézier clipped against the t quadrant axis, the resulting curve segments 1 and 3 must be case A or B and segment 2 could be any case.

We should clip against the axis which will result in the smallest segment 2. A good heuristic for this is to measure the distance from the curve endpoints to each of the axes. Generally, the larger the distance from an axis, the larger the clip tends to be. Denote $d_s = |d_0| + |d_n|$ for the case when $\mathbf{L}$ is the s quadrant axis, and $d_t = |d_0| + |d_n|$ when $\mathbf{L}$ is the t quadrant axis. Thus, if $d_s > d_t$, it is usually best to clip against $s - s_r = 0$.

The complete point classification algorithm appears as follows. For clarity, we assume that the point is nearest the edge $s = 1$ in the parameter square, so we count intersections of the trimming curves with the ray in the positive s direction. If the distance from the point to one of the trimming curves is less than a tolerance value ON_TOL, the point is declared to be ON a trimming curve. ON_TOL= 10^{-4} is conservative, and was used in producing Figure 7.

```
BEGIN CLASSIFY
INPUT: Trimming curves, Point, ON_TOL
OUTPUT: IN, OUT, or ON
inter = 0;
Push all trimming curves onto a stack;
WHILE Stack not empty
    POP a curve;
    SIZE = largest dimension of the bounding box;
    Determine the case;
    CASE:
```
A No action needed.

B If the curve endpoints $\mathbf{C}_0$ and $\mathbf{C}_n$ are in different quadrants, increment $inter$.

C If SIZE < ON_TOL, report ON and RETURN.

Else if $d_s \geq d_t$, perform Bézier clipping against $\mathbf{L} = s - s_r = 0$. The resulting segments 1 and 3 are guaranteed to be case A, so discard them. Push segment 2.

Else, perform Bézier clipping against $\mathbf{L} = t - t_r = 0$. Push all three segments.

```
    END CASE
END WHILE
If inter is odd, report OUT; else report IN
END CLASSIFY.
```

2.2.1 Implementation

A problem can arise when $\mathbf{R}$ happens to pass through an end control point shared by two trimming curves, because two intersections will be reported when one is often the correct answer. The solution we use is to perturb $\mathbf{S}$ away from $\mathbf{R}$ a sub-pixel distance <ON_TOL. For the same reason, it is important that $d(u_{min}) \neq 0$ and $d(u_{max}) \neq 0$ (in equation 4 and Figure 5) to within floating point precision. Therefore, make the adjustment $u_{min} = 0.99 * u_{min}$ and $u_{max} = 0.99 * u_{max} + 0.01$. Another reason for this adjustment is to avoid infinite loops. Bézier clipping a curve whose endpoint happens to lie on $\mathbf{R}$ (ie., $d_0 = 0$) results in segments 1 and 2 having zero length, and segment 3 is simply the original curve.

2.3 Performance

ON is the classification which is most expensive to compute. Our algorithm can typically compute an ON classification to seven decimal digits accuracy in four Bézier clips. Figure 6 shows the trimmed patch in Figure 1, using color to indicate how many total Bézier clips were used in classifying each ray intersection. The average number of Bézier clips per point to be classified was 1.04 in this example involving ten trimming curves. Figure 7 shows a patch trimmed with precision by eight Bézier curves.

3   RAY-PATCH INTERSECTION

Our algorithm for computing the intersection of a patch with a ray uses the Bézier clipping concept to iteratively clip away regions of the patch which don't intersect the ray.

The most costly single operation in a subdivision-based ray-patch intersection algorithm is de Casteljau subdivision. Typically, subdivision is performed in R^3 for non-rational patches, and in R^4 for rational patches. Woodward[20] (also alluded to by Rogers[10]) shows how the problem can be projected to R^2. This means that the number of arithmetic operations to subdivide a non-rational patch is reduced by 33% (since subdivision is applied only to x, y components, rather than x, y, z) and for a rational patch is reduced by 25% (subdivision in x, y, w rather than in x, y, z, w). Section 3.1 reviews that projection, and further shows how the rational case can be handled by subdividing only *two* components.

Section 3.2 then shows how to apply Bézier clipping to iteratively clip away regions of the projected patch which don't intersect the ray.

3.1   Projection to R^2

A rational Bézier surface patch in Cartesian three space ($\hat{x}, \hat{y}, \hat{z}$) is defined parametrically by

$$\hat{\mathbf{P}}(s, t) = \frac{\sum_{i=0}^{n} \sum_{j=0}^{m} B_i^n(s) B_j^m(t) w_{ij} \hat{\mathbf{P}}_{ij}}{\sum_{i=0}^{n} \sum_{j=0}^{m} B_i^n(s) B_j^m(t) w_{ij}} \quad (6)$$

where $\hat{\mathbf{P}}_{ij} = (\hat{x}_{ij}, \hat{y}_{ij}, \hat{z}_{ij})$ are the Bézier control points with corresponding weights w_{ij}. (The symbols are hatted to later distinguish them from the projected (x, y) coordinate system).

As does Kajiya[6], we define the ray to be the intersection of two planes given by implicit equations

$$a_k \hat{x} + b_k \hat{y} + c_k \hat{z} + e_k = 0, \quad k = 1, 2. \quad (7)$$

We assume that the plane equations are normalized: $a_k^2 + b_k^2 + c_k^2 = 1$. In practice, it is best if the two planes are orthogonal. For primary rays, we use the scan plane and the plane containing the ray, parallel to the screen y axis.

The intersection of plane k and the patch can be represented by substituting equation 6 into equation 7 and clearing the denominator:

$$d^k(s, t) = \sum_{i=0}^{n} \sum_{j=0}^{m} B_i^n(s) B_j^m(t) d_{ij}^k = 0 \quad (8)$$

where

$$d_{ij}^k = w_{ij}(a_k \hat{x}_{ij} + b_k \hat{y}_{ij} + c_k \hat{z}_{ij} + e_k). \quad (9)$$

$\hat{\mathbf{P}}(\hat{s}, \hat{t})$ lies on plane k iff $d^k(\hat{s}, \hat{t}) = 0$.

Note that d_{ij}^k is related to the distance from control point $\hat{\mathbf{P}}_{ij}$ to plane k:

$$d_{ij}^k = w_{ij} \times DISTANCE(\hat{\mathbf{P}}_{ij}, Plane\ k). \quad (10)$$

We can now project the patch to a two dimensional (x, y) coordinate system by taking the projected control point coordinates to be

$$\mathbf{P}_{ij} = (x_{ij}, y_{ij}) = (d_{ij}^1, d_{ij}^2) \qquad (11)$$

from equation 9. The projected patch is defined:

$$\mathbf{P}(s, t) = \sum_{i=0}^{n} \sum_{j=0}^{m} B_i^n(s) B_j^m(t) \mathbf{P}_{ij} \qquad (12)$$

In this projection, plane 1 becomes the y axis, plane 2 becomes the x axis, and the ray projects to the coordinate system origin, $\mathbf{0}$. Figure 8 shows a sample projected patch $\mathbf{P}(s, t)$.

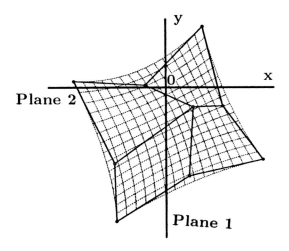

Figure 8: Projected patch $\mathbf{P}$

The ray-patch intersection problem now becomes one of finding

$$\{(s, t) \mid \mathbf{P}(s, t) = \mathbf{0}; \ 0 \leq s, t \leq 1\}. \qquad (13)$$

For a non-rational patch (that is, all $w_{ij} = 1$), $\mathbf{P}$ is a simple orthographic projection of $\hat{\mathbf{P}}$ along the ray. $\mathbf{P}(s, t)$ is always non-rational (all its weights are equal), *even if $\hat{\mathbf{P}}(s, t)$ is rational*.

3.2   BÉZIER CLIPPING $\mathbf{P}$

This section applies Bézier clipping to the problem of finding all solutions to

$$\mathbf{P}(s, t) = \mathbf{0}. \qquad (14)$$

Begin by defining a line $\mathbf{L}_s$ through $\mathbf{0}$ parallel to the vector $\mathbf{V}_0 + \mathbf{V}_1$ as shown in Figure 9. Bézier clipping will be used to identify ranges of the s parameter in which $\mathbf{P}(s, t)$ does not map to $\mathbf{0}$.

If $\mathbf{L}_s$ is defined by its implicit equation

$$ax + by + c = 0, \quad a^2 + b^2 = 1 \qquad (15)$$

then the distance D_{ij} from each control point $\mathbf{P}_{ij} = (x_{ij}, y_{ij})$ to $\mathbf{L}_s$ is

$$D_{ij} = ax_{ij} + by_{ij} + c. \qquad (16)$$

The D_{ij} are shown in Figure 10. Likewise, the distance $D(s, t)$ from $\mathbf{L}_s$ to any point $\mathbf{P}(s, t)$ on the projected patch is

$$D(s, t) = \sum_{i=0}^{n} \sum_{j=0}^{m} B_i^n(s) B_j^m(t) D_{ij} \qquad (17)$$

The function $d(s, t)$ can be represented, in an (s, t, d) coordinate system, as an *explicit* (or so-called *non-parametric*) surface

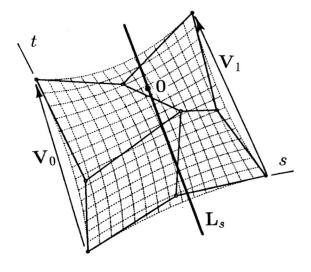

Figure 9: Line $\mathbf{L}_s$

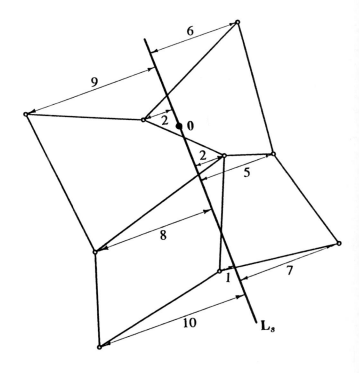

Figure 10: Control point distances

patch[1] whose control points $\mathbf{D}_{ij} = (s_{ij}, t_{ij}, D_{ij})$ are evenly spaced in s and t: $s_{ij} = \frac{i}{n}$, $t_{ij} = \frac{j}{m}$. A point on such a patch has coordinates

$$\mathbf{D}(s,t) = \sum_{i=0}^{n} \sum_{j=0}^{m} B_i^n(s) B_j^m(t) \mathbf{D}_{ij} = (s, t, D(s,t)). \quad (18)$$

The top view of this patch is shown in Figure 11, with control point D coordinates labeled. Compare those values with the distances in Figure 10.

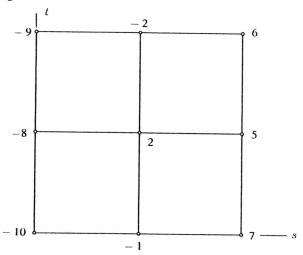

Figure 11: Top view of $\mathbf{D}(s,t)$ patch.

A side view of the $\mathbf{D}(s,t)$ patch, looking down the t axis, is shown in Figure 12. The convex hull of the projected control points

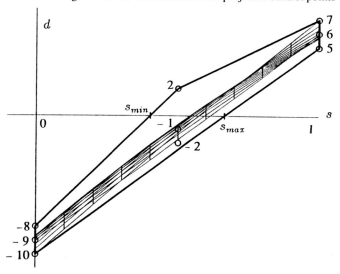

Figure 12: Side view of $\mathbf{D}(s,t)$ patch.

bounds the projection of the $\mathbf{D}(s,t)$ patch. In this example, that convex hull intersects the s axis at points $s_{min} = 2/5$ and $s_{max} = 2/3$. We conclude that $d(s,t) \neq 0$, and therefore $\mathbf{P}(s,t) \neq \mathbf{0}$, for $s < 2/5$ and $s > 2/3$. The de Casteljau subdivision algorithm is applied to clip away those regions, leaving the two dimensional patch in Figure 13.

This process of identifying values s_{min} and s_{max} which bound the solution set, and then subdividing off the regions $s < s_{min}$ and $s > s_{max}$ will be referred to as *Bézier clipping in s*. In an obviously similar manner, we define the process of Bézier clipping in t.

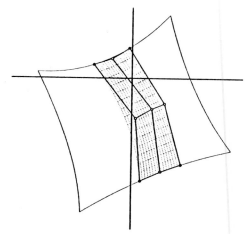

Figure 13: First clip in s.

Our ray-patch intersection algorithm consists of alternately performing Bézier clipping in s and t. Figure 14 shows the patch after Bézier clipping in s, then t, and again in s. The remaining sub-

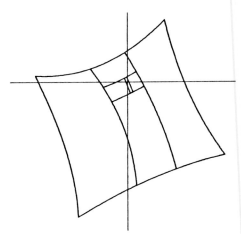

Figure 14: Iterating to the solution.

patch is not yet small enough to satisfy our tolerance conditions. (In this case, let's assume the tolerance value is 10^{-4}. In practice, one should pick a tolerance value which assures sub-pixel accuracy. This is done by finding a bound on the largest first derivative of screen space x or y with respect to parameter space s or t.) However, in computing t_{min}, t_{max} for the next t clip, it turns out that $t_{max} - t_{min} < 10^{-4}$. *Without subdividing in t*, we then compute s_{min}, s_{max} for an s clip, and discover that $s_{max} - s_{min} < 10^{-4}$ also. Thus, in the final step, we compute the intersection to within tolerance without actually subdividing to the clip values. The total number of operations in this typical example is: s_{min}, s_{max} or t_{min}, t_{max} is computed five times, and three pairs of de Casteljau subdivisions are performed.

3.3 No intersection

If a Bézier trim calculation determines $s_{min} > 1$, $s_{max} < 0$, $t_{min} > 1$, or $t_{max} < 0$, the ray does not intersect the patch.

It is possible to have $t_{max} - t_{min} < 10^{-4}$ and $s_{max} - s_{min} < 10^{-4}$, and yet the ray does not intersect the patch. However, this can only occur if $s_{min} = 0$, $s_{max} = 1$, $t_{min} = 0$, or $t_{max} = 1$. Whenever the subpatch lies on the boundary of the original patch, even if the tolerance criteria is satisfied, an additional Bézier clip calculation should be performed to assure that the intersection does lie within the patch boundaries.

3.4 Multiple intersections

If there are multiple intersections, Bézier clipping will not converge to a single value. Therefore, if a Bézier clip fails to reduce the parameter interval width by at least, say, 20%, split the patch in half and resume Bézier clipping on each half. There is little theoretical basis for this value of 20%. Empirically, 20% seems to provide nearly optimal performance in most cases. Execution speed is not highly sensitive to small changes in this 20% value, although for values less than 10%, excessive Bézier clipping can occur and for values greater than 40%, unnecessary binary subdivision can occur.

The case of multiple intersections is illustrated in Figure 15. First, Bézier clipping in s discards regions labelled 1. In attempt-

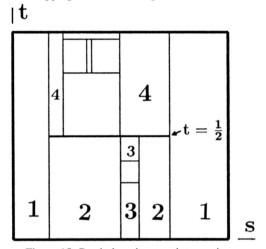

Figure 15: Patch domain - two intersections

ing to clip in t, it turns out that $t_{max} - t_{min} > 0.8$. Therefore, the remaining domain is subdivided in half at $t = 0.5$. A stack data structure is used to store subpatches. We push one of the two subpatches onto the stack, and proceed to process the other subpatch by Bézier clipping in s to eliminate regions 2 and clipping in t to remove regions 3. As in the example in Figure 14, without further subdivision we can compute the intersection which lies between regions 3 to within tolerance.

There remains one subpatch on the stack, which we now pop and begin to process by clipping regions 4. The second intersection is refined in two more Bézier clips, as shown.

3.5 Primary Ray Preprocessing

Bézier clipping can be used to advantage in a preprocessing step applied at the initialization of each scan line. By Bézier clipping **P** against the scan line in both s and t directions, regions of **P** can be discarded which do not intersect any primary ray along the scan line. Figure 16 shows the patch in Figure 8 after Bézier clipping against the scan line (x axis). By performing this preprocess, a savings of up to two subdivisions per primary ray/surface intersection can be realized, and also non-intersecting rays can be detected more often. For example, in applying this preprocessing to rendering the teapot in Figure 17, 86% of the calls to the intersection routine resulted in a hit.

3.6 Implementation

To avoid potential infinite loops due to numerical roundoff, make the adjustment $s_{min} = 0.99 * s_{min}$ and $s_{max} = 0.99 * s_{max} + 0.01$

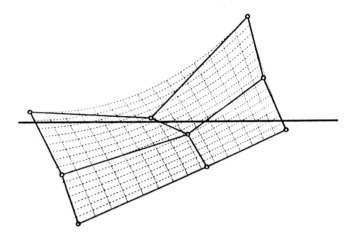

Figure 16: Trimming to the Scan Line.

and similarly for t in computing values at which to Bézier clip.

Other than the ray/patch intersection algorithm, all of the other implementation details are standard. Antialiasing was performed using adaptive supersampling [5], and Murakami's voxel partitioning [8] was implemented. Shadows, reflection and refraction are dealt with in the conventional manner, using our ray-patch intersection algorithm.

4 DISCUSSION

4.1 Examples and Timings

We tested the algorithm on an Iris-4D/70GT workstation and created Figures 17-20 at 500X500 resolution. Each figure caption lists the number of patches in the scene, total CPU time for rendering, (CPU time for rendering a similar scene, not antialiased, with primary rays only), percentage of background pixels, and average number of patch subdivisions per foreground pixel for primary rays. All patches are non-rational bicubics. The chains in Figure 19 were oriented using Free-Form Deformation[14].

4.2 Performance Comparisons

It is difficult to derive precise quantitative comparisons between various ray/patch intersection algorithms. The predominant single expense in most ray-patch intersection algorithms is de Casteljau subdivision. Our intersector spends 45% of its time computing subdivisions. To split a projected two-dimensional bicubic patch in either parameter direction requires 144 floating point operations. All previous subdivision-based algorithms can take advantage of this projection to R^2 (which, as mentioned, saves 33% of subdivision costs for non-rational and 50% for rational patches).

We compared the number of subdivisions per non-background pixel required by our algorithm with the algorithms of Toth[18] and Woodward[20]. To attain three digits accuracy in s, t, Toth reported an average of 19.66 subdivisions for each non-background pixel in his Figure 6 (an example of a single patch in which roughly 30% of non-background pixels involve two ray-patch intersections). We duplicated the patch and viewing parameters for Toth's Figure 6 as nearly as possible, and tested our and Woodward's algorithms. The average number of subdivisions per non-background pixel is listed in Table 1. SUN SPARCstation I CPU times for 120X120 image are shown in parenthesis.

It is difficult to make quantitative comparisons with the other published algorithms. Newton [17] and quasi-Newton [4] itera-

Figure 17: Newell's teapot: 33 patches, 65% background, 5.2 subdivisions/ray, 6.7 cpu min. (3.9 min. primary rays only)

Figure 20: Teapot encased in deformed glass cube: 39 patches, 21.3 cpu min on SUN SPARCstation I

Figure 18: Modified teapot: 2304 patches, 64% background, 4.0 subdivisions/ray, 12.5 cpu min. (8.6 min. primary rays only)

Figure 21: House of mirrors

Figure 19: Chain on patch-work quilt: 4024 patches, 18% background, 5.6 subdivisions/ray, 29.0 cpu min. (17.6 min. primary rays only)

Algorithm	Tolerance	
	2^{-6}	2^{-10}
Our's	8.6	11.4
	(24 sec)	(26 sec)
Woodward	29.2	48.6
	(80 sec)	(116 sec)
Toth	NA	19.6

Table 1: Subdivisions per pixel and (total cpu time)

lis, Minnesota, July 23-27, 1984). In *Computer Graphics 18, 3* (July 1984), 103–108.

[3] DUFF, THOMAS. Compositing 3-D Rendered Images. Proceedings of SIGGRAPH'85 (San Francisco, California, July 22-26,1985). In *Computer Graphics 19, 3* (July 1985), 41–44.

[4] EBERT, DAVID, BOYER, KEITH, AND ROBLE, DOUG. Once a Pawn a Foggy Knight ... [videotape]. In *SIGGRAPH Video Review 54* (November 1989), ACM SIGGRAPH, New York. segment 3.

[5] EBERT, DAVID, EBERT, JULIA, AND BOYER, KEITH. Getting Into Art. [videotape], Department of Computer and Information Science, The Ohio State University, May 1990.

[6] EBERT, DAVID, AND PARENT, RICHARD. Animation of gaseous phenomena using turbulent flow based solid texturing. Tech. Rep. OSU-CISRC-7/89-TR36, Department of Computer and Information Science, The Ohio State University, 2036 Neil Ave, Columbus, Ohio 43210-1277, July 1989.

[7] GARDNER, GEOFFREY. Visual Simulation of Clouds. Proceedings of SIGGRAPH'85 (San Francisco, California, July 22-26,1985). In *Computer Graphics 19, 3* (July 1985), 297–303.

[8] KAJIYA, JAMES, AND KAY, TIMOTHY. Rendering Fur with Three Dimensional Textures. Proceedings of SIGGRAPH'89 (Boston, Massachusetts, July 31-Aug 4,1989). In *Computer Graphics 23,3* (July 1989), 271–280.

[9] KAJIYA, JAMES, AND VON HERZEN, BRIAN. Ray Tracing Volume Densities. Proceedings of SIGGRAPH'84 (Minneapolis, Minnesota, July 23-27,1984). In *Computer Graphics 18,3* (July 1984), 165–174.

[10] KAUFMAN, ARIE. Efficient Algorithms for 3D Scan-Conversion of Parametric Curves, Surfaces, and Volumes. Proceedings of SIGGRAPH'87 (Anaheim, California, July 27-31,1987). In *Computer Graphics 21,4* (July 1987), 171–180.

[11] KLASSEN, R. VICTOR. Modeling the Effect of the Atmosphere on Light. *ACM Transaction on Graphics 6*, 3 (July 1987), 215–237.

[12] LEVOY, MARC. Private Communication, April 1990.

[13] LEVOY, MARC. A Hybrid Ray Tracer for Rendering Polygon and Volume Data. *IEEE Computer Graphics and Applications 10*, 2 (March 1990), 33–40.

[14] MAX, NELSON. Light Diffusion Through Clouds and Haze. *Computer Vision, Graphics, and Image Processing 33* (1986), 280–292.

[15] NISHITA, TOMOYUKI, MIYAWAKI, YASUHIRO, AND NAKAMAE, EIHACHIRO. A Shading Model for Atmospheric Scattering Considering Luminous Intensity Distribution of Light Sources. Proceedings of SIGGRAPH'87 (Anaheim, California, July 27-31,1987). In *Computer Graphics 21,4* (July 1987), 303–310.

[16] PERLIN, KEN. An Image Synthesizer. Proceedings of SIGGRAPH'85 (San Francisco, California, July 22-26,1985). In *Computer Graphics 19,3* (July 1985), 287–296.

[17] PERLIN, KEN, AND HOFFERT, ERIC. Hypertexture. Proceedings of SIGGRAPH'89,(Boston, Massachusetts, July 31-Aug 4,1989). In *Computer Graphics 20,3* (July 1989), 253–262.

[18] RUSHMEIER, HOLLY, AND TORRANCE, KEN. The Zonal Method for Calculating Light Intensities in the Presence of a Participating Medium. Proceedings of SIGGRAPH'87 (Anaheim, California, July 27-31,1987). In *Computer Graphics 21,4* (July 1987), 293–302.

[19] VOSS, RICHARD. Fourier Synthesis of Gaussian Fractals: 1/f noises, landscapes, and flakes. In *SIGGRAPH 83:Tutorial on State of the Art Image Synthesis* (1983), vol. 10, ACM SIGGRAPH.

[20] WILLIS, P.J. Visual Simulation of Atmospheric Haze. *Computer Graphics Forum 6* (1987), 35–42.

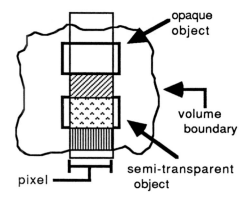

Figure 1: Volume element creation. Shaded areas are the three volume elements.

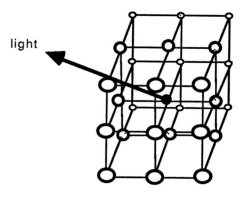

Figure 2: Shadow table Calculation.

Figure 3: The modern pioneer in an art gallery.

Figure 4: A representative image from "Once a Pawn a Foggy Knight...".

Figure 5: A representative image from "Getting Into Art."

Figure 6: Steam rising from a glass. The 6 images are every 30 frames.

Figure 7: Scenes of fog rolling in. The first 6 are every 80 frames. The last 3 are every 40 frames.

Figure 8: Steam rising from a glass. (a) has no shadowing (b) has shadowing of the gas onto the glass. (c) has table-based volume shadowing and self-shadowing. (d) has shadow-traced volume shadowing and self-shadowing.

Footprint Evaluation for Volume Rendering

Lee Westover

Numerical Design Limited

The University of North Carolina at Chapel Hill

ABSTRACT

This paper presents a forward mapping rendering algorithm to display regular volumetric grids that may not have the same spacings in the three grid directions. It takes advantage of the fact that convolution can be thought of as distributing energy from input samples into space. The renderer calculates an image plane footprint for each data sample and uses the footprint to spread the sample's energy onto the image plane. A result of the technique is that the forward mapping algorithm can support perspective without excessive cost, and support adaptive resampling of the three-dimensional data set during image generation.

KEYWORDS: 3D Image, Volume Rendering, Reconstruction, Algorithms.

INTRODUCTION

Volume rendering is the direct display of data sampled in three dimensions. There are two principle approaches to volume rendering: backward mapping algorithms that map the image plane onto the data by shooting rays from pixels into the data space, and forward mapping algorithms that map the data onto the image plane.

---

* Author's current address:

      Sun Microsystems Inc
      PO Box 13447
      Research Triangle Park NC
      27709

This distinction principly manifests itself in how and when reconstruction of the three-dimensional signal is done. Convolution can be thought of as either generating an output sample from many input samples or as spreading one input sample to many output samples. Backward mapping algorithms typically reconstruct the signal at a point in space by looking at that point's nearest data samples and performing some type of interpolation. Forward mapping algorithms differ in that they incrementally reconstruct the original signal by spreading each data sample's energy into space.

Forward mapping algorithms are important because they are easily made parallel. Since each data sample only needs to know about a small surrounding neighborhood of other samples, shading and transforming can be done in parallel for sub-sections of the data. With today's parallel machines having limited local memory, this data distribution gets around the backward mapping problem of having the entire data set at each node.

The reconstruction step is the most complicated part of the algorithm. The renderer must determine the screen space contribution of each sample point to the final image. A brute force method would perform a one-dimensional integration of the reconstruction kernel for every pixel for every input sample. If the renderer can calculate the screen space extent of the kernel, the number of integrations reduces to the number of samples times the number of pixels that fall within the extent. However, this is still an enormous number of integrations.

In an orthographic view, the footprint of the projected reconstruction kernel for any sample is a constant except for a screen space offset. This allows the renderer to build a footprint function table once and use the table for all samples. Since the table is discrete, the renderer builds it on a fine grid to prevent artifacts. Even with this modification, the renderer must perform N^2 integrations of the kernel where N is the number of grid cells in each table dimension.

This paper presents an algorithm that allows the renderer to use a pre-computed footprint function table to build the view-transformed footprint table for a particular view. This pre-computed table is called the generic footprint table because the renderer uses it to calculate the view-transformed table for any particular view. The renderer needs to calculate two things to build the view-transformed table. First, the renderer computes the screen space extent of the projection of the reconstruction kernel. Second, the renderer computes a mapping of this extent to the extent that surrounds the pre-integrated footprint table. Then for each cell in the grid of the view-transformed table, the renderer maps the cell to the generic table and samples the generic table to find the cell's value. Once the renderer builds the view-transformed table, it can use the table for all input samples. The renderer centers the table at the sample's projected screen location and samples the table at the center of each pixel that falls within the table's extent.

PREVIOUS WORK

Researchers have investigated the volume rendering problem in the last few years and these algorithms can be divided along many lines. Blinn [2], Kajiya [7], VanHook [14], Levoy [9] and Sabella [12] describe methods of ray tracing volume densities with algorithms that map pixels onto the data by shooting rays into the data. Frieder [4], Lenz [8], Drebin [3], and Westover [15] use compositing techniques that map the data onto the image plane. Lorensen [10], Upson [13], and Gallagher [7] have investigated various methods of fitting surfaces into each data cell and then rendering the volume as surfaces.

Another distinction between algorithms is whether the original signal is reconstructed and shaded at points of interest or whether the original data samples are shaded and then the shaded volume is reconstructed to form an image. Since shading is typically a non-linear process, interpolating the shaded volume can be problematic due to the high frequencies introduced by the shading model. On the other hand, this method only shades true data samples. Interpolating first, then shading, introduces new data samples into the data set, but shading happens at exact query samples. An enhancement to the algorithm presented in this paper can support either approach.

Footprint determination has much in common with texture map sampling. It is, however, almost the exact opposite problem. In texture mapping, a pixel is mapped into texture space and then all texture samples that lie within the mapped pixel's footprint are weighted and accumulated to form the single texture color [6]. In volume rendering, the footprint is used to spread a single samples contribution onto every pixel that lies within the

mapped voxel's footprint. In both cases, the mapping of a sample from one space into a second space forms an elliptical footprint in the second space.

RENDERING ALGORITHM

The algorithm discussed in this paper is a forward mapping algorithm that shades at input samples, and reconstructs a final image from the shaded volume. This work differs from the original algorithm, described in Westover [15], in four ways. First, the initial algorithm combined the reconstruction step and the visibility step at each voxel. The new algorithm performs reconstruction for all samples in a sheet, where a sheet is defined as a plane through the data that is most parallel to the image plane. Each voxel in a sheet is added to a sheet cash. When all the voxels on a sheet are processed, the sheet is matted into the working image. Second, the algorithm now uses a generalized shading model, Abram [1], that supports many shading techniques including the one from the original algorithm. Third, many of the details of how footprints are calculated and used has changed, as described below. Forth, the new footprint method will allow the algorithm to support both perspective and adaptive refinement.

The algorithm consists of four main parts: transforming, shading, reconstruction, and visibility. For the algorithm to run in parallel, it is critical that each step in the process uses only local information. The renderer processes a sample by transforming the sample from input $<i,j,k>$ grid space to $<x,y,z>$ screen space. It then shades the sample using some shading rule that uses local information. The shaded sample is a $<x,y,z,red,green,blue,\alpha>$ tuple. Next the renderer determines the portion of the image the sample can affect and adds the sample's contribution to the sheet accumulator. The determination of the footprint function, the sampling of the footprint function, and the spreading of the sample's contribution is called splatting. The efficient determination of the effect and an efficient application of the footprint function is the topic of this paper. When all the samples that lie in a sheet are processed, the renderer mattes the sheet accumulator to the working image using a compositing operator [11]. Once all samples are processed, the working image becomes the final image.

FOOTPRINT FUNCTION

The volume reconstruction equation for a regular array of density values is:

$$signal_{3D} =$$

$$\iiint h_V(u-x, v-y, w-z)\, \rho(x,y,z) \sum \delta(x,y,z)\, du\, dv\, dw$$

where $h_V()$ denotes the volume reconstruction kernel, ρ denotes the density function, $\sum \delta$ denotes the comb function, and u,v,w are the coordinates of the kernel.

Moving the summation outside the integral and evaluating the integral at point $<x, y, z>$ results in:

$$signal_{3D}(x,y,z) = \sum_{D \in Vol} h_V(x-D_x, y-D_y, z-D_z) \, \rho(D)$$

where D ranges over the input samples that lie within the range for which the kernel, $h_V()$ is non-zero, and $D_x, D_y,$ and D_z are the screen space coordinates of the sample $<D>$.

Instead of considering how multiple samples contribute to a point, consider how a sample can contribute to many points in space. The contribution at a point $<x, y, z>$ by a data sample $<D>$ is:

$$contribution_D(x,y,z) = h_V(x-D_x, y-D_y, z-D_z) \, \rho(D)$$

Therefore, the renderer can treat each data sample individually and spread its contributions to the output samples.

The total contribution at a given $<x,y>$ location is the sum of the contribution along a ray through the kernel that is perpendicular to the screen with its origin at $<x,y>$. The sum is calculated as the integral along z of the ray. Projecting the sample onto the image plane at pixel $<x,y>$ is:

$$contribution_D(x,y) = \int_{-\infty}^{\infty} h_V(x-D_x, y-D_y, w) \, \rho(D) \, dw$$

For a given sample, ρ is a constant and since ρ is independent of w, ρ can be moved outside the integral:

$$contribution_D(x,y) = \rho(D) \int_{-\infty}^{\infty} h_V(x-D_x, y-D_y, w) \, dw$$

Notice that the integral is independent of the sample's density. Since it only depends on the sample's $<x, y>$ projected location, the function footprint is defined:

$$footprint(x,y) = \int_{-\infty}^{\infty} h_V(x,y,w) \, dw$$

where $<x,y>$ denotes the displacement of an image sample from the center of the shaded sample's image plane projection.

METHOD

For orthographic views, the footprint of each sample is the same except for a screen space offset. Therefore, the renderer needs only to calculate the footprint function once for each view of the data set. Once the footprint is known, the renderer can sample the footprint function at each pixel that lies within the footprint's extent and contribute the appropriate amount to the pixel. The weight at each pixel is:

$$weight(x,y)_D = footprint(x-D_x, y-D_y)$$

where $<D_x, D_y>$ denotes the sample's image plane projection and $<x,y>$ denote the pixel's image plane location.

Sampling the footprint function involves an integration. Many kernels are difficult to integrate analytically and the renderer must use discrete methods. Since the renderer does not want to integrate this function many times for each sample, it builds a table on a fine grid and then performs table look-ups to evaluate the function. The renderer needs to determine two things to build the footprint table for a particular view. First, it calculates the screen space extent of the projection of the kernel, which in an orthographics view is constant for each input sample. All pixels that lie within the extent may be affected by the given sample. Second, the renderer calculates a mapping from the view-transformed extent to an extent that surrounds the projection of a generic kernel. The generic kernel table is calculated by a pre-processing program that runs once for a given kernel.

Since the pre-processor runs once, it does not matter how long it takes to compute the integration of the kernel. By using a pre-computed generic table, the renderer can easily change reconstruction kernels by reloading the generic table from disk.

Once the renderer builds the view-transformed table, the table is used by the renderer for each sample, by centering the table at each sample's projected screen position and calculating the screen space extent of the kernel by offsetting the extent of the projected kernel. For each pixel in the extent, the renderer samples the table to determine the amount of contribution for the pixel. The renderer builds the view-transformed footprint table on a grid that has many samples per pixel. Without oversampling rendering artifacts will occur.

Building the Generic Footprint Table

The method assumes that the extent of the reconstruction kernel is a sphere. If the extent is not a sphere, the preprocessor bounds the kernel by a sphere. For efficiency reasons, the bounding sphere should be as tight as possible. A loose fitting sphere will cause the pre-processor to build a generic table that has many zero entries, which causes the renderer to visit many pixels that are not affected by a given sample. For a spherical kernel, the radius of the sphere is equal to the width of the reconstruction kernel. This sphere, called the unit region sphere, defines the region a sample can affect. Within this region, on a discrete grid, the pre-processor integrates the kernel along the z direction and stores the result in a table. This table is called the generic footprint table. During image generation, the renderer determines the extent of the projection of the view-transformed region sphere. In addition, the renderer determines a mapping of each point in that extent onto the extent surrounding the unit region sphere in order to build the view-transformed footprint table. The projection of the unit region sphere on the image plane is a circle. The mapping from view-transformed extent to generic extent is then a mapping from the projection of the view-transformed region to a circle.

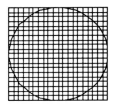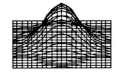

Figure 2. Generic Footprint Function Table

EXTENTS AND MAPPINGS

There are two basic cases for determining extents and mappings: the unit sphere maps to a sphere after applying the viewing transform, or the unit sphere maps to an ellipsoid. The result is a sphere when the input volume has equal spacings in each of the grid directions and the viewing transform has only uniform scaling. The result is an ellipsoid when the input volume has non-uniform spacing in each of the grid directions or the viewing transform has non-uniform scaling. Since a sphere is a special case of an ellipsoid, the renderer currently uses the elliptical method described below for all volumes.

Extent and Mapping for Spherical Kernels

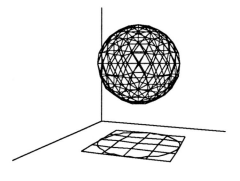

Figure 3. Spherical Kernel

Even when the kernel maps to a sphere, the renderer can not use the generic table directly and must build a view-transformed table. If the grid scale value and the view

scale value are both 1.0, the generic table is used, otherwise the renderer builds a view-transformed. This makes a table access fall exactly at table entries and causes all the interpolations to only occur once.

Extent

Many input volumes have fewer samples per face than the desired number of pixels in the image. This means that the input sampling rate is much smaller than the output sampling rate and each input sample needs to cover many pixels. The renderer calculates the extent of a sample's effect by scaling the unit extent by the grid scale value and the view scale value.

The extent in both the x and y directions is:

$$extent = 2.0*kernel\_width*grid\_scale*view\_scale$$

Mapping

The mapping from scaled extent to unit extent is trivial in the case of a spherical result. The projection of the sphere onto the image plane is a circle. The mapping from one circle to another circle is a scaling by the ratio of the radii of the two circles. The mapping is:

$$mapping = \frac{1.0}{grid\_scale\_factor*view\_scale\_factor}$$

The renderer uses the mapping to map cells of the view-transformed footprint table to the generic footprint table. If the view is simply rotated and the scale factors do not change, the view-transformed footprint table can be used again.

Extent and Mapping for Elliptical Kernels

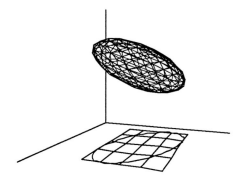

Figure 4. Elliptical Kernel

If the scalings in grid directions are different, the region sphere transforms into a region ellipsoid. The projection of the region ellipsoid is always a screen space ellipse. The extent of a kernel's effect is the extent of the projected ellipse, and the mapping from view-transformed table to generic table is a mapping from the projected ellipse to the unit circle.

Extent

The region ellipsoid is found by transforming the unit region sphere by the grid scale transform and then by the viewing transform. By treating the unit region sphere as a quadric surface, the transformations become matrix multiplications.

Let the original unit sphere be U:

$$U = \begin{bmatrix} 1 & 0 & 0 & 0 \\ 0 & 1 & 0 & 0 \\ 0 & 0 & 1 & 0 \\ 0 & 0 & 0 & -1 \end{bmatrix}$$

and let the grid scale transform be S:

$$S = \begin{bmatrix} S_i & 0 & 0 & 0 \\ 0 & S_j & 0 & 0 \\ 0 & 0 & S_k & 0 \\ 0 & 0 & 0 & 1 \end{bmatrix}$$

and let the viewing transform be V:

$$V = \begin{bmatrix} a & b & c & 0 \\ d & e & f & 0 \\ g & h & i & 0 \\ 0 & 0 & 0 & 1 \end{bmatrix}$$

The grid space region ellipsoid E is:

$$E = S * U$$

To transform the quadric surface the renderer calculates both the inverse viewing transform and its transpose. The resulting screen space ellipsoid R is:

$$R = V^{-1^T} * E * V^{-1}$$

with

$$R = \begin{bmatrix} A & D/2 & E/2 & 0 \\ D/2 & B & F/2 & 0 \\ E/2 & F/2 & C & 0 \\ 0 & 0 & 0 & -K \end{bmatrix}$$

This gives an ellipsoid defined by:

$$Ax^2 + By^2 + Cz^2 + Dxy + Exz + Fyz = K \quad (1)$$

By rearranging terms, completing the square, and solving for x and y, the renderer can calculate the screen space extent of the transformed ellipse. The x extent is:

$$x = \pm \sqrt{\dfrac{K}{A - \dfrac{D^2}{4B} - \dfrac{(E - \dfrac{DF}{2B})^2}{4(C - \dfrac{F^2}{4B})}}}$$

and the y extent is:

$$y = \pm \sqrt{\dfrac{K}{B - \dfrac{D^2}{4A} - \dfrac{(F - \dfrac{DE}{2A})^2}{4(C - \dfrac{E^2}{4A})}}}$$

Mapping

The renderer also needs to calculate the mapping from the projection of the region ellipsoid back to the unit circle. To do this, the renderer first calculates the screen space projection of the region ellipsoid which is an ellipse. To find the ellipse, first rewrite (1) as a quadratic in z. The quadratic is:

$$Cz^2 + (Ex + Fy)z + (Ax^2 + By^2 + Dxy - K) = 0$$

Points on the edge of the projection of R have only one root in this quadratic. There is only one root to the quadratic $aZ^2 + bZ + c = 0$ when $b^2 - 4ac = 0$ or in this case when:

$$(Ex + Fy)^2 - 4C(Ax^2 + By^2 + Dxy - K) = 0$$

Grouping the x^2, the y^2, and the xy terms gives the screen space projection ellipse P:

$$Xx^2 + Yy^2 + Zxy = K \quad (2)$$

where:

$$X = (A - \dfrac{E^2}{4C}) \quad Y = (B - \dfrac{F^2}{4C}) \quad Z = (D - \dfrac{EF}{2C})$$

Once the renderer calculates the screen space ellipse, it can define a transformation that takes points from the screen space ellipse into the unit circle. This is the inverse of the mapping that takes the unit circle into the screen space ellipse. To calculate the second mapping, the renderer needs to calculate two things: the amount to scale along the x axis and the y axis, and the amount of rotation about the view direction.

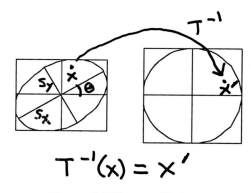

$$T^{-1}(x) = x'$$

Figure 5. Ellipse to Circle Mapping

The renderer finds these values by solving for T such that:

$$P = T * U * T^T$$

writing P as:

$$P = \begin{bmatrix} X & Z & 0 & 0 \\ Z & Y & 0 & 0 \\ 0 & 0 & 1 & 0 \\ 0 & 0 & 0 & -1 \end{bmatrix}$$

and T as:

$$T = \begin{bmatrix} a & b & 0 & 0 \\ c & d & 0 & 0 \\ 0 & 0 & 1 & 0 \\ 0 & 0 & 0 & 1 \end{bmatrix}$$

and U as:

$$U = \begin{bmatrix} 1 & 0 & 0 & 0 \\ 0 & 1 & 0 & 0 \\ 0 & 0 & 1 & 0 \\ 0 & 0 & 0 & -1 \end{bmatrix}$$

and solving for X, Y, and Z:

$$a^2 + b^2 = X \quad (3)$$

$$c^2 + d^2 = Y \quad (4)$$

$$ac + bd = Z \quad (5)$$

This looks like a problem since there are three equations and four unknowns, a, b, c, and d, but T is a matrix that is made up of a scale in the x and y directions followed by a rotation about the z axis. So:

$$a = (S_x)*\cos\theta \quad b = -(S_x)*\sin\theta \quad (6)$$

$$c = (S_y)*\sin\theta \quad d = (S_y)*\cos\theta \quad (7)$$

Plugging (6) and (7) into (3), (4), and (5) and applying some algebraic manipulation brings:

$$\frac{(X-Y)}{Z} = \frac{\cos\theta}{\sin\theta} - \frac{\sin\theta}{\cos\theta}$$

This seems to be a problem when Z is zero but upon investigation of P, when Z is zero, P is a scaling of U, therefore T is simply:

$$a = \sqrt{X} \text{ and } d = \sqrt{Y} \text{ and}$$

$$b = c = 0$$

When Z is non-zero, let:

$$G = \frac{(X-Y)}{Z} \text{ and } w = \frac{\cos\theta}{\sin\theta}$$

then:

$$G = w - \frac{1}{w} \text{ or } w^2 - Gw - 1 = 0$$

using the quadratic formula w is:

$$w = \frac{G \pm \sqrt{G^2 + 4}}{2}$$

Given w, θ is $arctan(\frac{1.0}{w})$. This gives both $\sin\theta$ and $\cos\theta$ and allows the renderer to solve for S_x and S_y using (6) and (7). S_x and S_y are undefined in the above equations when $\theta = 45$ degrees. When this occurs, the renderer cheats and rotates the view an additional 0.01 degrees about the view direction. This allows the renderer to calculate S_x and S_y with little if any effect on the image.

With θ, S_x, and S_y the renderer builds T by multiplying the identity matrix by a scale matrix of S_x and S_y, followed by a z rotation matrix of θ. The mapping from P into U is then the inverse of $T : T^{-1}$.

The renderer uses T^{-1} to map cells of the view-transformed footprint table to the generic footprint table.

TABLE SIZES AND KERNELS

There are three parameters that can change in building footprint tables: the size of the tables, how the tables are accessed, and the table's underlying kernel.

There is a space versus quality tradeoff between the size of the footprint tables and the resultant artifacts in the images. Image 1 shows this tradeoff on an elliptical projection. Each picture in image 1 is of a single sample point scaled 120 by 60 by 60. The upper left picture in the image uses a view-transformed footprint table with 5 by 5 entries. The upper right uses a table that is 11 by 11. The lower left uses a table that is 21 by 21. The lower right uses a table that is 101 by 101. Notice how smoothness increases with table size.

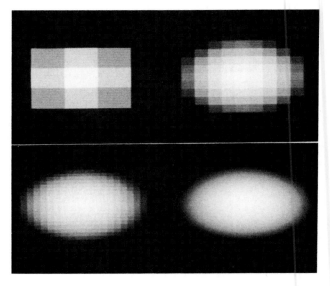

There is a time versus space tradeoff in how the table is sampled. If the footprint table has a lot of entries, then nearest neighbor sampling works fine. If, on the other hand, the table is coarse, then the renderer needs to interpolate samples from the nearest neighbors. Image 2 shows this tradeoff on an elliptical projection. Each picture in image 1 is of a single sample point scaled 120 by 60 by 60. The upper left picture in the image uses a view-transformed footprint table with 5 by 5 entries. The upper right uses a table that is 11 by 11. The lower left uses a table that is 21 by 21. The lower right uses a table that is 101 by 101. In each case, the renderer generates the table value with a bilinear function. Compared to Image 1, the footprint is much smoother on a lot smaller table. However, a reasonable table size is required to avoid bilinear artifacts.

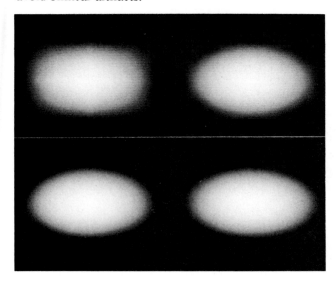

The third thing to change is the kernel itself. The choice of kernel can drastically affect the quality of an image. Image 3 is a single sample as above with four different

kernels. *radius* is the normalized distance from the center of the kernel. The upper left has a cone function modeling the result of the z integration. The upper right has a Gaussian function as the model. The lower left has the first five lobs of a sync function as the model. The lower right has the bilinear function as the model.

Image 4 is a portion of a computed tomography study of a human head. The data is clipped to only show the left eye. The spread of the Gaussian kernel changes in each sub-image. In the upper left the Gaussian is scaled so that its tail stops 25 percent of the way to the next voxel (where 100 percent just touches the next voxel). This scale changes from 25 to 225 percent in steps of 25 percent from left to right and top to bottom. In the first images the kernels are too sharp and do not overlap leaving gaps. In the last images the kernels are very broad and over blur the images. All the images in the following section were generated with a Gaussian kernel with a sigma of 2.5 and a spread of 160 percent.

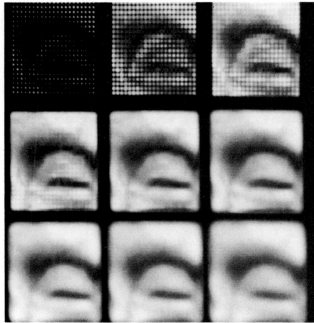

Image 5 shows each of the above kernels operating on a 3 by 3 by 1 grid of constant values. These kernels are approximations to the true z integration of a three-dimensional kernel. The view-transformed table as 10 by 10 entries. The patterns in the upper left image are the result of multiple kernels not summing to one at all points. The patterns in the lower left image are the result of ringing from the sync function at the edges of the sample space. Notice the sharp second order discontinuities at the corners of the image from the bilinear function at the lower right. Superimposed on the images are line drawings of a single scanline's grey value. The green line is when table values were interpolated from nearest neighbors. The red line is when just the single nearest neighbor was used.

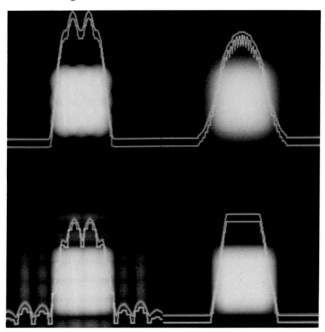

SAMPLE IMAGES

Image 6 is a single sample with an elliptical projection. The four views are of the sample with the volume rotated 0 degrees, 10 degrees, 30 degrees, and 45 degrees about the view direction. The ellipse does not change shape or size as the volume grid is rotated about the z axis.

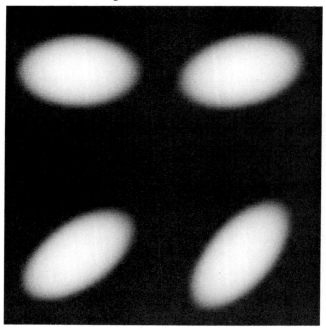

Image 7 is an image of ozone concentrations over the northeast corner of the United States in July 15, 1980. The input grid is 64 by 52 by 32 with very uneven spacing in the z direction compared to the x and y directions. The shading model is the emittance model with color

and opacity based on concentration values. Since the algorithm works back to front, any image (in this case a texture map of state boundaries) can be used as a starting working image. The clouds are colored with blue being low concentration, going to green for intermediate concentration, and finally red where concentration exceeds the government's legal limits.

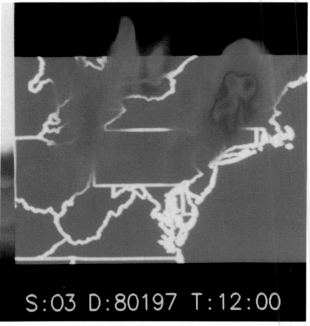

S:03 D:80197 T:12:00

Image 8 is an image generated from the electron density of the p-orbitals of copper chloride. The input grid is 64 by 64 by 64 with even spacing in each grid direction. The viewing transform has only uniform scaling. The shading model is the emittance model with color and opacity based on density value. The underlying data has no surfaces and the image has a cloudy nature.

Image 9 is an isodensity surface from an electron density map of Staphylococcus Aureus ribonuclease. The initial

whose edge is not, in general, straight, as the light gets 'bent' at the specular surface. In case (ii) the shadowing object, embedded in this region of 'bent' light, occludes light rays that are travelling in directions other than the traditional direction, ie. directly from the light.

Case (i) has to be dealt with in the view independent phase. Each ray of the light beam is tested for hits with objects between the specular polygon and the light. If a specular polygon is completely occluded it is passed over. If it is partially obscured we recursively subdivide the specular polygon - processing the smaller ones that can see the light as normal. The subdivision stops when the area of the specular polygon falls below a predefined level. An alternative approach here would be to clip out the silhouette of the obstruction from the beam cross section and to continue to process the remainder similar to Heckbert [8]. We adopt the recursive subdivision strategy - wary of fragmented, non convex polygons that can be produced by recursively clipping.

Case (ii) can be handled in either the view independent or view dependent phase. If it is solved in the former we proceed largely as in case (i) except each ray of the transmitted light beam is tested for hits with objects between the specular surface and the diffuse surface. To solve in the view dependent phase we carry over the rays of the transmitted light beam from the view independent phase as the normals of caustic polygon. A caustic polygon underneath a pixel can only make a contribution to that pixel then, if the rays fired in the direction of its normals hit the specular surface before they hit anything else.

Light - Water Interaction

As stated previously, we confine our application to model a specific subset of first generation specular to diffuse transfer namely the simulation of light - water interaction where the water surface acts as the specular surface. Our principal justification lies in the fact that no computer graphics model of these phenomena has previously been rigorously presented and the results achieved are realistic in terms of rendering, animation and demands made upon the computer - thus extending the class of natural phenomena capable of being effectively simulated.

Strong sunlight incident on water that is gently perturbed, by wind say, will produce familiar sinuous shifting patterns of light on objects beneath the water's surface as they intersect the caustic. Such patterns were studied and painted by Hockney eg [9]. Figure 7 shows two frames taken from an animated sequence showing these effects as viewed underwater when a shaft of light, coming through a window say, is incident on the surface of an indoor pool. These images were generated using an enhanced depth buffer renderer. Note, as predicted in the section on caustics, the sides of the pool, which are roughly tangential to the caustic, are more uniformly lit than the floor, which being roughly normal to the caustic contains the greater variation of light intensities.

As the pattern is driven directly by the water surface, animating the pattern entails animating the water surface. The water surface consists of a polygonal mesh made up of triangles displaced by a height field. The height field is a supersition of a distribution of sine waves of varying frequency and amplitude as used by Max [12] to which the reader is referred since the details of the surface modeling are not essential to the application - more sophisticated water models may easily be substituted. Since, under this model, the wave speed is a function of its frequency and gravity - animating the water surface consists of deciding upon an appropriate frequency/amplitude distribution and fine tuning the time interval over consecutive frames to achieve the desired effect.

Under certain conditions particles or impurities in the water that are within the transmitted beams may become visible by scattering the light - enabling us in effect to see the transmitted light beam as opposed to cross sections through it. As the water surface changes shape regions that previously dispersed the light may now focus it and vice versa - causing the beams themselves to change shape accordingly.

Figure 7. Two frames from an animated underwater caustic sequence.

Figure 8. Two frames from an animated water caustic sequence seen through the water.

If the triangles in the polygonal mesh are sufficiently small, the variation of the refracted rays along an edge of a triangle can be ignored. This approximation enables us to represent the pencil beams as polygonal illumination volumes. These beams are shown in figure 7, and are rendered using a modified version of the light volume rendering technique as proposed by Nishita [13]. As in that paper, assuming uniform particle density, we integrate intensities of the scattered light along segments of rays that lie within the illumination volumes. We also include an additional term in the integration to account for the concentration, or dispersion, of light within the beam.

Figure 8 shows two frames taken from an animated sequence of an outdoor swimming pool seen from above. These images were generated using a standard ray tracer. Strictly speaking, the additional refraction of rays from the diffuse surface, through the water, to the eye means this is an example of specular to diffuse to specular transport. The animation is particularly effective since it is really the combined effect of two separate animations - one imposed on the other. The underwater animating pattern is seen through an animating

water surface. These figures also show the shadow cast by the diving board on the pool - an example of case (i) in the section on shadowing. Figure 9 shows the shadow with the water surface taken away, showing that straight silhouette edges can produce shadows with curved edges.

Since the water surface changes frame for frame, the view independent phase consisting of generating the caustic polygons must be calculated likewise. Since we are considering first generation effects only, it follows that a transmitted beam can only contribute to an image if it is itself within the image. By taking advantage of this, significant improvements in efficiency were obtained by first testing for intersections between the transmitted beam and the viewing frustrum of the image, rejecting those that fall outside.

Finally, we consider a rather subtle example of light - water interaction caused by a meniscus. A pencil partially immersed in water under an overhead light will produce a bifurcated shadow separated by a whitened gap which has been termed the 'shadow-sausage effect' [1]. Both the dry and submerged

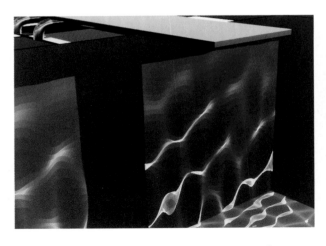 

Figure 9. Pool caustics with water removed.   Figure 10. Caustics from a meniscus.

Fig. 14-1 Example 1

Fig. 14-2 Example 2

Fig. 14-3 Example 3

Fig. 14-4 Example 4

Fig. 14-5 Example 5

Fig. 14-6 Example 6

Fig. 14-7 Example 7

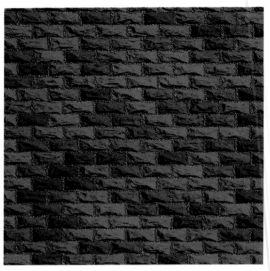

Fig. 14-8 Example 8

Fig. 15 Edo Castle

Fig. 16 Dungeon

No.	L_v	L_h	H	D	V_v	V_h	B_v	B_h	J
1	60	40	20	1.0	0.4	0.4	0.4	0.4	2.0
2	60	40	20	1.1	0.4	0.4	0.4	0.4	2.0
3	60	40	20	1.6	0.4	0.4	0.4	0.4	2.0
4	60	40	20	1.1	0.8	0.8	0.0	0.0	2.0
5	60	60	20	1.1	0.8	0.0	0.4	0.4	2.0
6	60	40	20	1.1	0.8	0.8	0.8	0.8	2.0
7	60	60	60	1.1	0.4	0.4	0.4	0.4	2.0
8	60	25	10	1.05	0.01	0.01	0.0	0.0	3.0

Table 2 Parameter list

(a)

(b)

(c)

(d)

Figure 5: Examples of a road surface under various conditions.

can be considered as an intermediate condition between the 'wet region' and the 'puddle region'. The water surface of a 'drenched region' is not always horizontal and depends on the undulation of the road surface and is a result of surface tension of water. We assume that the normal vector of water surface is determined by the following equation:

$$N_d = \frac{k_p N_p + k_w N_w}{|k_p N_p + k_w N_w|}, \qquad (3)$$

where N_d, N_p, and N_w are the unit normal vectors of a 'drenched region', 'puddle region', and 'wet region', respectively, and k_p and k_w are weights for a 'puddle region' and 'wet region', respectively.

2.3 Examples

Fig. 5 depicts four different scenes for testing animated road surfaces whose conditions change in regard to weather and time; in Fig. (a) a dry road surface taking into account sky light in the morning was rendered. The size of highlight due to specular reflection on the road surface caused by direct sunlight is relatively small and its intensity is not very high. Fig. (b), (c), and (d) show scenes of a road surface just after rain in the daytime, beginning of drying in the evening, and half drying in the morning, respectively. In Fig. (a) the center lines can be seen into the distance, while in Fig. (b) the further the center lines, the less visible they become; it is quite similar to the appearance of real road surfaces. Fig. (b), (c), and (d) show distribution of four classified regions gradually changing with the passage of time, and these figures clearly illustrate that both intensity and size of highlight due to specular reflection are different between a 'dry region' and a 'wet region' because of the difference in their properties of reflection.

Fig. 6 shows the effect of muddy puddles; Fig. (a) shows clear water, while Fig. (b), muddy water. The white sideline in the bed of clear puddles is more visible than that of muddy puddles, especially in the deeper parts.

(a)

(b)

Figure 6: Effect of muddy puddles.

3 Rendering High Intensity Points by Using 2D Filters

Shinya, et al. developed a 2D filter to render streaks of light taking into account only refraction from a cross-screen filter [13] (see Appendix B), but without spectral distributions. It is very important for rendering photo-realistic images to take account of all refraction, diffraction, and spectral distributions, because in the real world not only refraction but also diffraction occurs, and the streaks of light depend upon the wavelength.

3.1 Diffraction due to a pupil (or a diaphragm)

Let's consider an optical image formation system as shown in Fig. 7, and assume that the angle from the incident light to the optical axis of the lens is small, and the angles between the opposite direction of z axis and the ray, which is bent by the optical filter and is projected onto the xz and yz planes, are α and β, respectively.

Among the rays reaching the surface of the pupil (diaphragm) only rays passing through a pupil (diaphragm) arrive at its retina (film plane). The blooming effect around objects with high intensity is a result of the light being diffracted by the pupil. Let's assume that the pupil's diameter is a, then it can be replaced by a slit with width a which is rotated to be perpendicular to each calculation point. As is well known, if rays with wavelength λ pass through the slit with width a, the ratio of rays diffracted toward the diffraction angle θ, $f(\theta)$, is given by the following equation:

$$f(\theta) = \frac{\sin^2 \alpha}{\alpha^2}, \qquad (4)$$

where

$$\alpha = \frac{1}{2} k a \sin \theta, \qquad (5)$$

$$k = \frac{2\pi}{\lambda}. \qquad (6)$$

If the diffraction angle θ is expressed by using α and β,

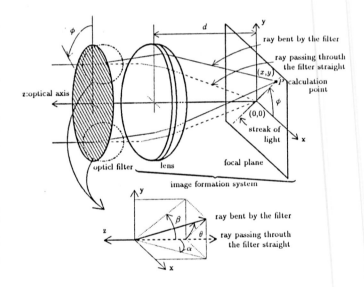

Figure 7: Optical filter and image formation system.

$$\theta = \sqrt{\alpha^2 + \beta^2}. \qquad (7)$$

Due to the pupil the strength of diffracted light depends only upon diffraction angle θ (i.e., the distance between calculation point P and the center of the filter as shown in Fig. 7.) In order to save calculation time and memory, values of the weight function, $f(\theta)$, (strength of diffracted light) for sampled distances are calculated in advance and stored in a look-up table.

Fig. 8 shows an example without filtering, while in Fig. 9 diffraction due to a pupil is taken into account. It was verified that the smaller the pupil diameter, the stronger the effect of diffraction, even though it is not illustrated here.

Figure 8: Image $E_0(x,y)$ without filter.

Figure 9: Effect of diffraction due to a pupil (pupil's diameter is 5 mm).

3.2 A diffraction grating

If rays pass through a diffraction grating consisting of N slits with width a and interval b as shown in Fig. 10, the ratio of rays diffracted toward diffraction angle θ is expressed by

$$f(\theta) = \frac{\sin^2 \alpha}{\alpha^2} \frac{\sin^2(N\beta)}{\sin^2 \beta}, \qquad (8)$$

where

$$\beta = \frac{1}{2} kb \sin \theta, \qquad (9)$$

and α and k are given by Eq. 5 and 6, respectively. Let's assume that the angle of a diffraction grating is set to ϕ as shown in Fig. 7 (the direction of a streak of light is horizontal when angle $\phi = 0$, and vertical when $\phi = \pi/2$.) Diffraction angle θ is expressed by using α and β;

$$\theta = \mid \alpha \cos \phi + \beta \sin \phi \mid . \qquad (10)$$

A streak of light extends only when angle ϕ satisfies the following equation:

$$\alpha \sin \phi - \beta \cos \phi = 0, \qquad (11)$$

while for any other direction,

$$f(\theta) = 0. \qquad (12)$$

One diffraction grating generates one streak of light. In order to generate radial streaks of light, several diffraction gratings with different angle should be used. For example, crisscross streaks of light are generated by using orthogonal diffraction gratings.

If all values of the weight function, $f(\theta)$, are stored in a 2D array, the array is very sparse because non-zero values exist only on streaks of light. In order to save both calculation time and memory, all non-zero values in the region of $y \geq 0$ as shown in Fig. 7 are stored in a look-up table with its x and y coordinates as a result of the symmetrical characteristics of streaks of light.

Fig. 11 shows the effect of diffraction caused by diffraction gratings.

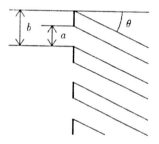

Figure 10: Diffraction grating.

$N_1 = 5$, $a_1 = 1.0$ mm, $b_1 = 1.2$ mm, $\phi_1 = 20°$
$N_2 = 5$, $a_2 = 1.0$ mm, $b_2 = 1.2$ mm, $\phi_2 = 80°$
$N_3 = 5$, $a_3 = 1.0$ mm, $b_3 = 1.3$ mm, $\phi_2 = 140°$

Figure 11: Effect of diffraction caused by diffraction gratings.

number of diffraction gratings = 15

	N	a [mm]	b [mm]	ϕ [°]
average	6	1.0	1.2	0
standard deviation	2	0.3	0.4	10

Figure 12: Effect of diffraction due to eyelashes.

pupil's diameter = 5 [mm]
The same diffraction gratings as those of Fig. 12.

Figure 13: Effect of diffraction due to both pupil and eyelashes.

3.3 Diffraction due to eyelashes

We often observe streaks of light when looking at high intensity objects through a scratched windshield because of diffraction. Eyelashes also cause diffraction effects. In this section we discuss diffraction effects due to eyelashes. Diffraction effect caused by scratches on a windshield could be rendered by using the same idea of the proposed method.

Eyelashes act as a diffraction grating; the width of the slit, a, corresponds to the gap between each eyelash, and the number of the slits, N, the interval of each slit, b, and the angle of the grating, ϕ, also correspond to those of eyelashes.

Note that each eyelash has a different direction, and that their intervals are uneven and also change with the opening of the eyelid. So the parameters, such as the width of the slit, a, the number of the slits, N, the interval of each slit, b, and the angle of the grating, ϕ, should be determined by using random numbers with a certain distribution such as Gaussian distribution. In this paper ϕ is determined by using random numbers whose average and standard deviation are $0°$ and $10 \sim 30°$, respectively, because eyelashes usually grow perpendicular to the skin with some randomness ($10 \sim 30°$). Assuming that the number of eyelashes just in front of the pupil is about $4 \sim 8$, N is determined by using random numbers whose average and standard deviation are 6 and $1 \sim 3$, respectively. In the same way, it is assumed that the average and standard deviation of a are 1.0 mm and $0.1 \sim 0.3$ mm, and those of b are 1.2 mm and $0.1 \sim 0.3$ mm.

One diffraction grating generates only one streak of light. One observes usually $6 \sim 20$ streaks of light with the naked eye, so $6 \sim 20$ sets of diffraction grating are prepared and combined.

Fig. 12 shows the effect of diffraction due to only eyelashes and Fig. 13 demonstrates the effects of both pupil and eyelashes.

3.4 Filtering with spectral distribution

It is clear from Eq. 4 and 8 that intensity and color distribution of diffracted light strongly depend upon the wavelength of the light. Fig. 14 shows from top to bottom diffracted light calculated with only three primary wavelengths, R, G, and B, and every 10nm, 20nm, 40nm, and 80nm over the range of visible light. It is evident from this figure that calculation with more than every 20 nm is inadequate and calculation with only three primary wavelengths yields enormous error. Basically, intensity of diffracted light should be calculated for an entire scene using the whole wavelength of visible light, and then the intensity should be used for filtering; the calculation cost is quite expensive.

The following facts are highly relevant in tiding over this difficulty; streaks of light are caused by only high intensity object, and spectral distributions strongly depend upon light sources. For instance, diffracted light is greatly different as shown in Fig. 15; from top to bottom, the light source with even spectral intensity all over visible light, an automobile head light (a mini-halogen lamp), a street lamp (a multi-halogen lamp), and a lamp for parking lots (a high pressure natrium lamp). In this paper an image $E_0(x, y)$, not taking into account any optical filter, is calculated by using three primary colors, R, G, and B, and the type of the light source causing high intensity is stored for every pixel with such high intensity. Only these pixels are filtered by taking into account spectral distributions corresponding to the light sources stored beforehand.

In Fig. 11, 12, and 13 light sources with the same kind of those in Fig. 15 and the spectral distribution by calculating diffracted light with every 10 nm were used. Fig. 16 also shows the effect of diffraction under foggy conditions.

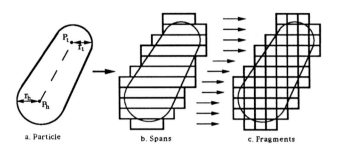

Figure 3: Particle Dicing.

First, each particle processor determines the number of scan lines that the particle will occupy and the particle is diced into spans. Multiple span processors are allocated for each particle processor, and the particle information is sent to them.

Then, each span processor similarly determines the number of fragments it will occupy, allocates fragment processors and sends the particle information to them.

When particles are diced into fragments, there are often more total fragments than will fit into Connection Machine memory. To compensate for this, the image is rendered in subsections or patches. The size of each patch is adjusted such that all the fragments in that patch will fit into memory at once.

The patch height is chosen before allocating span processors such that the number of span processors will not exceed a limit. Likewise, for that horizontal section of the image, patch widths are chosen such that the number of fragment processors will not exceed a limit for each patch.

It is also desirable to fill as many fragment processors as possible up to the limit since empty processors sit idle while the others compute. The processor usage "efficiency" for a given patch size is the total number of data elements (spans or fragments) within the patch divided by the maximum number permitted. The false position method [17] is used to search for patch widths and heights that result in an efficient use of span and fragment processors.

After the fragment processors are set for a given patch size, the color, opacity and depth of that fragment are calculated by finding the closest point to the fragment on the line between the head and tail of the particle. The particle radii, depths, colors and opacities are interpolated between the head and tail to give values at that point. The final fragment opacity is set as a function of the interpolated opacity, the interpolated radius, and the distance from the center of the particle.

Spatial anti-aliasing of particles is performed by ramping the opacity to zero near the edges of the particle. Radii below one pixel are clamped to one pixel and the opacity is lowered to compensate to prevent aliasing due to sub-pixel sized particles. Coverage-masks or multiple samples per pixel were not used because unlike polygons whose edges often touch each other to make a continuous surface, the edges of particles usually do not line up.

4.2 Sorting Fragments and Calculating Transparency

After the color, opacity and depth are calculated for all the fragments in the image patch being rendered, the fragments

are reordered within the CM to make all the fragments covering the same pixel adjacent to each other. They are also sorted within the pixel groups by depth.

The parallel operator *scan* operates on values in 1D arrays of processors. It allows each processor to receive the sum (or product) of all the values in the preceding processors. A segmented scan can be performed on groups of processors to prevent the results from spreading beyond the group. Local sums and products can be efficiently calculated for groups of processors of variable sizes.

Within each pixel group *scan with multiply* is applied to the fragment's transparencies from front to back to determine the total pixel contribution of each fragment. Then, *scan with add* is applied to each color component and the opacity, each scaled by the fragment's pixel contribution. The last processor in each pixel group receives the final pixel color and opacity.

The pixel colors are then sent to processors in the 2D image patch virtual processor set. Each virtual processor representing one pixel of the image patch being rendered receives the final color and opacity from the fragments covering it, if any. Background color is added if necessary, and the patch is finally output to a frame buffer or file.

4.3 Mixing with Other Data Types

A recent addition to this system allows particles to be mixed with other renderable data types such as polygons. The fragments of both particles and polygons are depth sorted together and rendered simultaneously. This permits any number of layers of particles and polygonal objects to move in front of and behind each other with correct hidden surfaces. This can be preferable to rendering the different data types separately and then compositing the images together afterwards.

5 Results

The animated film *Particle Dreams* [24] was created entirely using the animation and rendering tools described above. It contains orbiting fire, an explosion, a snow storm, a crashing head, and a waterfall. These tools are also being used in a commercial production environment to create "burning logos," galaxies, and other effects.

5.1 Snow and Wind

A snow storm was created using white snowflake particles, spirals, and vortices. Some snowflakes were created and dropped above the field of view at each iteration. They were given an initial velocity and spiral axis straight down but with some random variation, and were bounced off the plane of the ground with zero bounce and high friction, so that once they hit, they stuck. [Figure 6a.]

Gravity and air friction were not considered because the air friction damping and gravity would have canceled out at a steady critical velocity.

Gusts of wind were made by moving pairs of vortices across the field of view. A gust procedure was built from two vortex operations so that gusts could be moved between given start and end positions. Gusts were choreographed and tested until the desired swirling effects were achieved.

Finally, "splat" shapes were created by duplicating particles into several particles when they hit a vertical plane.

Figure 4: Water.

5.2 Falling Water

A waterfall was simulated by applying gravity to blue particles and bouncing them off obstacles made of planes and spheres.

Some water droplet particles were created on each iteration randomly within an area at the top of the waterfall. When particles flowed over the last edge at the bottom of the waterfall they were recycled back to the top of the waterfall. Around 60K particles were used for this animation.

Splashes were achieved by placing spherical rocks of different sizes in the path of the flow. The droplets were bounced off the rocks with friction and resilience that varied randomly within a range. When a bounce was detected, the particles were turned from blue to white and then faded slowly back to blue as they fell to the next rock. The variety of blue to white particles gave the waterfall a sparkling quality without any actual lighting calculations.

Motion blur was exaggerated in this sequence: the shutter speed was slightly more than the entire frame duration to give the flow a smoother look.

5.3 Fire

Fire simulation is a more complex effect that can be created using these tools. Extensions to the utilities described above allow arbitrary polygonal objects to be burned.

First, a large number of particles are created with their initial positions located on the surface of the object. This is done by triangulating the polygons of the object and creating some particles randomly within each triangle. To give an even distribution, the number created in each triangle is proportional to the triangle's area. The particles' initial velocities and spiral axes are set to directions between the object's surface normal and the up-most surface tangent vector to cause the fire particles to hug the surface somewhat before curling up.

Second, several groupings of the particles are created, and parameters of color and motion are set to be the same or nearly the same within the groups. Particles are grouped in small regions with similar colors, so different regions of the surface emit different colored flames as if some regions are hotter than others. The particles are also grouped into flickers. Each particle in a flicker group is given a similar spiral axes, initial velocity, start time, and life duration, but with slight variation, so that each flicker had some coherency and was perceived as a unit, rather than each particle being independently random.

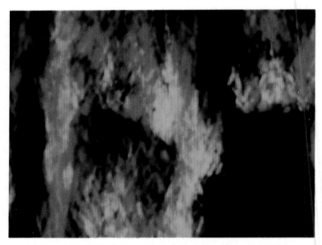

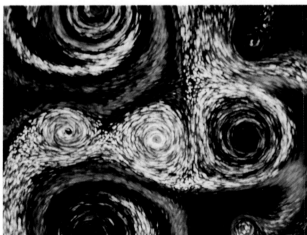

Figure 5: (a) Burning Letters, (b) Vortex Field.

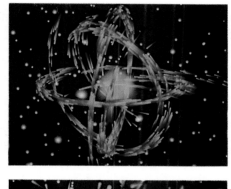

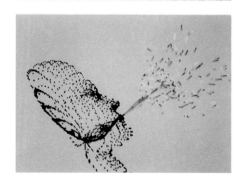

Figure 7: *Left*
(a) Orbiting Fire.
(b) Explosion.

Figure 6
(a) Snowstorm with vortex gust.
(b) Self Breathing Head.
(c) Inverted Tornado.

Figure 8: Waterfall.

The fire particles leave the surface and spiral upward while changing color. After they fade and die, they are recreated again at the initial position on the surface to start another cycle. The spiral axis slowly rotates to prevent duplicate motion, and the flickers have slightly different frequencies to create a pseudo-random rhythm that natural fire can have.

6 Conclusion

Some general tools for animating and rendering particle systems are implemented that permit both kinematic and dynamic control of particles. They are used to create effects that would probably be difficult to achieve using traditional techniques, but there are still many potential additions to this set of particle system utilities.

Future work in this area might include operations that cause particles to influence each other: N-body types of simulations might be used for galaxy simulations, more natural fluid motion, or collision avoidance. In the current implementation particles ignore each other and only follow global rules, sometimes resulting in interpenetration.

More efficient collision detection of surfaces would be beneficial. Currently every particle is tested against every surface element. The ability to create procedural motion for more complex objects (other than particles) including rigid body dynamic simulations would also be desirable.

It would be interesting to compare the parallel speed of particle rendering with that of a serial computer. This was not done because of the unique parallel software implementation. Rendering speed is approximately proportional to the number of processors, and inversely proportional to the number and sizes of the particles. Frame times commonly vary from several seconds to several minutes.

Since data parallel computers have potential for growth in both the speed of processors and the number of processors, they should become more powerful and more available in the future. Techniques that permit computer animation of complex structure and motion automatically and can utilize data parallelism, such as those presented here, may soon be more frequently used.

7 Acknowledgments

Thanks to Lew Tucker for continuing support. Thanks to all the folks at Whitney/Demos Productions for a unique learning experience. Thanks to Thinking Machines Corporation for building Connection Machines computers and being generous. Thanks to Jim Salem, Brewster Kahle, Gary Oberbrunner, and Peter Schroeder for discussions and encouragement. Thanks to J.P.Masser, Jeff Mincy, and Cliff Lasser for Starlisp and its support. Thanks to Arlene Chung and Debbie Mahe for layout and figures. And finally, thanks to John Whitney Jr., Jerry Weil, and Optomystic for the environment to put this work to use.

References

[1] Armstrong, W., Green, M., "The Dynamics of Articulated Rigid Bodies for Purposes of Animation," *Proceedings Graphics Interface '85*, pp. 407-415.

[2] Amburn, P., Grant, E., Whitted, T., "Managing Geometric Complexity with Enhanced Procedural Methods," *Computer Graphics*, Vol. 20, No. 4, August 1986.

[3] Barr, A., Barzel, R., "A Modeling System Based on Dynamic Constraints," *Computer Graphics*, Vol. 22, No. 4, 1988, p. 179.

[4] Carpenter, L.C., "The A-buffer, an Anti-aliased Hidden Surface Method," *Computer Graphics*, Vol. 18, No. 3, 1984.

[5] Fournier, A., Reeves, W., "A Simple Model of Ocean Waves," *Computer Graphics*, Vol. 20, No. 4, 1986, pp. 75-84.

[6] Girard, M., Maciejewski, A., "Computational Modeling for the Computer Animation of Legged Figures," *Computer Graphics*, Vol. 19, No. 3, 1985, pp 263-270.

[7] Hahn, J. K., "Realistic Animation of Rigid Bodies" *Computer Graphics*, Vol. 22, No. 4, 1988, p. 299.

[8] Hillis, W. D., *The Connection Machine*, MIT Press, 1985.

[9] Hillis, W. D., "The Connection Machine," *Scientific American*, Vol. 255, No. 6, June 1987.

[10] Lasser, C., Massar, J.P., Mincy, J., Dayton, L., "Starlisp Reference Manual," Thinking Machines Corporation, 1988

[11] Lucasfilm Ltd, *The Adventures of Andre and Wally B.*, (film), August 1984.

[12] Miller, G., "The Motion of Snakes and Worms" *Computer Graphics*, Vol. 22, No. 4, 1988, p. 169.

[13] Oppenheimer, P. "Real time design and animation of fractal plants and trees. *Computer Graphics*, Vol. 20, No. 4, 1986, pp 55-64.

[14] Paramount, *Star Trek II: The Wrath of Kahn*, Genesis Demo, also in SIGGRAPH Video Review 1982, ACM SIGGRAPH, New York.

[15] Peachy, Darwyn R., "Modeling Waves and Surf," *Computer Graphics*, Vol. 20, No. 4, 1986, pp. 65-84.

[16] Platt, J., Barr, A., "Constraint Methods for Flexible Models," *Computer Graphics*, Vol. 22, No. 4, 1988, p. 279.

[17] Press, Flannery, Teukolsky, and Vetterling, *Numerical Recipes*, Cambridge University Press, 1986, p. 248.

[18] Prusinkiewicz, P., Lindenmayer, A., and Hanan, J., "Developmental Models of Herbaceous Plants for Computer Imagery Purposes," *Computer Graphics*, Vol. 22 No. 4, 1988, pp. 141-150.

[19] Reeves, W. T., "Particle Systems — A Technique for Modeling a Class of Fuzzy Objects," *ACM Transactions on Graphics*, Vol. 2, No. 2, April 1983, reprinted in Computer Graphics 1983, pp. 359-376.

[20] Reeves, W. T., and Blau, R. Approximate and probabilistic algorithms for shading and rendering structured particle systems. *Computer Graphics*, Vol. 19, No. 3, 1985, pp 313-322.

[21] Reffye, P., Edelin, C., Francon J., Jaeger, M., Puech, C. "Plant Models Faithful to Botanical Structure and Development," *Computer Graphics* Vol. 22, No. 4, 1988, pp 151-158.

[22] Reynolds, Craig W., "Flocks, Herds and Schools: A Distributed Behavioral Model," *Computer Graphics*, Vol. 21, No. 4, July 1987, pp 25-34.

[23] Simon, H.D., *Scientific Applications of the Connection Machine*, World Scientific Publishing Co., 1988.

[24] Sims, K., *Particle Dreams*, SIGGRAPH Video Review 1988, ACM SIGGRAPH, New York.

[25] Smith, A. R., "Plants, Fractals, and Formal Languages," *Computer Graphics*, Vol. 18, No. 3, pp. 1-10, July 1984.

[26] Studio Base 2, *Systeme Particulier*, Chesnais, Alain, SIGGRAPH Video Review 1987, ACM SIGGRAPH, New York.

[27] Symbolics, *Stanly and Stella in Breaking the Ice*, SIGGRAPH Video Review 1987, ACM SIGGRAPH, New York.

[28] Terzopoulos, D., Fleischer, K., "Modeling Inelastic Deformation: Viscoelasticity, Plasticity, Fracture," *Computer Graphics*, Vol. 22, No. 4, 1988, p. 269.

[29] Thinking Machines Corporation, *Connection Machine Model CM-2 Technical Summary*, technical report, May 1989.

[30] Weil, J., A T & T Bell Labs, *Boom Boom Boom*, SIGGRAPH Video review 1987, ACM SIGGRAPH, New York.

[31] Wilhelms, J. Barsky, B., "Using Dynamic Analysis for the Animation of Articulated Bodies Such as Humans and Robots," *Proceedings Graphics Interface '85*, pp. 97-104.

[32] Wilhelms, J., Moore, M., "Collision Detection and Response for Computer Animation," *Computer Graphics*, Vol. 22, No. 4, 1988, p. 289.

[33] Yaeger, L., Upson, C., "Combining Physical and Visual Simulation – Creation of the Planet Jupiter for the Film 2010," *Computer Graphics*, Vol. 20, No. 4, 1986, pp 85-93.

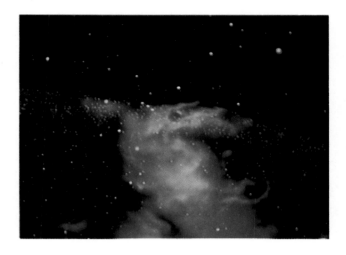

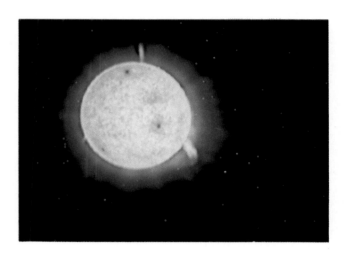

Figure 10: (a) Nebula, (b) Solar flyby. Created by Jerry Weil, Optomytic, for *Earth Day Special 1990*. (Nebula also contains surfaces with color and opacity texture mapping.)

Figure 9: Fire Breathing Dragon. Fire was simulated with particle systems. Dragon by Jerry Weil, Optomystic.

Panels

Grand Challenges of Computational Science

Chair: Larry Smarr, NCSA

Panelists: Gregory McRae, Carnegie Mellon
University
Arthur Freeman, Northwestern
University
David Dixon, E. I. Du Pont De Nemours
Eric Lander, MIT

There has been a massive expansion in the computational infrastructure supporting scientific research in the last five years. Today tens of thousands of researchers have access from their desktop computers to supercomputer centers over the national network. Scientific visualization has arisen as a critical tool of discovery, analysis, and communication; fundamental research problems with economic and scientific impact are being attacked.

Leading researchers discuss how advanced computing and visualization resources are used to advance knowledge on these problems in university, industrial, and governmental research centers. They explain the White House's High Performance Computing Program, a $500 million annual program for computer and technology research and development.

Using Photographic-Quality Images in Desktop Applications

Chair: Jim Rafferty, C-Cube MicroSystems

Panelists: Dan Putman, Adobe Software
Mike Templeman, Aldus Corporation
Andrew Singer, Radius, Inc.

PC technology and applications have advanced significantly, but they are still primitive compared to professional publishing. Ordinary desktop computers cannot use photographic-quality images due to bandwidth constraints; quality is sacrificed because the computer cannot process and manipulate complex images. Today, new technology eliminates these barriers and enables desktop computers to use high-quality, true-color images.

Making photographic-quality images part of ordinary computers enhances and creates a new class of applications. This panel addresses hardware and software advances that remove the technical barriers to 24-bit color images, including compression, printer and board technologies. It discusses new ways to integrate photographic-quality color images into desktop applications.

Interface and New Interactive Systems

Chair: Brenda Laurel, Interactivist

Panelists: David Nagel, Apple Computer, Inc.
Chris Schmandt, MIT Media Lab
Michael Naimark, Independent Media
Artist and Researcher
Douglas Crockford, Lucasfilm Games,
a Division of LucasArts
Entertainment

Developments in theory, technology, the marketplace, and business suggest that we are entering a period of accelerating growth in the variety and pervasiveness of interactive products. Integrated medium technology platforms are emerging in entertainment, design, engineering, manufacturing, and education. Delivery systems range from television screens to bodysuits.

In the world of "traditional" computers, user-interface design has become a discipline with established, sometimes contradictory, theory and design principles. These new interactive technologies underline the need to develop and extend the domain of user-interface design. Panelists identify and discuss key interface issues for new media and technologies.

Special Session: SIGGRAPH Bowl

Co-Chairs: Tomas Porter, Pixar
Pat Hanrahan, Princeton University

Masters: Jim Blinn, California Institute of
Technology
Nick England, Sun Microsystems
Rob Pike, AT&T Bell Labs

Test your knowledge about the history of computer graphics research and the SIGGRAPH conference by participating as a member of the SIGGRAPH Bowl!

A spinoff of the famous televized College Bowl, invited teams representing leading universities and graphics companies will test their knowledge of SIGGRAPH history.

Participants identify quotes from important

SIGGRAPH papers, recognize rendered images and film show animations of past years, and answer trivia questions about events, trends and personalities of past SIGGRAPH conferences.

Multimedia Document Architecture

Chair: Stephen Bulick, U.S. West Advanced Technologies

Panelists: Terry Crowley, Bolt, Berenek, and Newman
Lester Ludwig, Bell Communications Research
Jonathan Rosenberg, Carnegie-Mellon University

Multimedia information systems capable of managing combined text, graphics, still images, audio, and video are leaving the laboratory to enter the mainstream of information technology. An important level of organization for information handled by such systems is the multimedia document, which provides a means for packaging and coordinating related objects of different media types. Furthermore, multimedia document architecture is a fundamental model for representing the structure, content, and presentation characteristics of multimedia documents.

However, most existing architectures are unique — designed specifically for the systems that use them — and do not permit easily exchanged information. This panel addresses some of the current problems associated with multimedia document architectures and important issues of the future.

Beyond Scientific Visualization: Mapping Information

Chair: Donna J. Cox, NCSA

Panelists: Jim Blinn, California Institute of Technology
Richard Ellson, Eastman Kodak Company
Helga M. Leonardt Hendriks, The Leonhardt Language System

The term *scientific visualization* conjures up mental images of molecules reacting or velocity vectors whizzing around. Yet, visualization is migrating beyond the scientific domain because it maps not only numerical, but all data into visual representations.

This panel compares several visualization methodologies and how they have employed advanced computer graphics to map abstract information into meaningful animations and interactive software. Panelists demonstrate how they have organized abstract data or concepts using spatial, quantitative, dynamic, and symbolic techniques to visually communicate maximum information. Examples from linguistics, humanities, education, statistics, engineering, and science are presented.

Interactive Art and Artificial Reality

Chair: Gregory P. Garvey, The New England School of Art and Design/Northeastern University

Panelists: Myron Krueger, Independent Consultant
Ed Tannenbaum, Independent Artist
Don Ritter, Concordia University
Lillian Schwartz, AT&T Labs

This panel focuses on and addresses the distinctions made between computer art, interactive art, artificial, and virtual realities. Panelists consider how the computer, as a symbol-manipulating, all-purpose machine, is a tool that changes the way art is created and experienced. Panelists argue that this view implies interactivity and possibly trivializes static paintbox computer art by changing the viewer's role from passive observer to active participant. Interactivity is discussed as a step toward artificial or virtual realities and a means to define new possibilities in real-time performance.

New Methods, New Artforms: 3D Applications in Sculpture

Chair: Barbara Mones-Hattal, George Mason University

Panelists: Charles Csuri, The Ohio State University
Tony Longson, California State University, Los Angeles
Ken Snelson, Independent Sculptor
Rita Starpattern, Art in Public Places, City of Austin
Sally Webber, Independent Artist

Many artists use computer modeling and animation tools for creating, editing, and presenting sculptural works. Some artists design for the 3D virtual space — others use computers to control 3D output devices to create holograms or other illusory 3D environmental works. Stereolithography and other new technologies offer artists output devices to enhance, extend, and enrich 3D visual communication.

Panelists discuss the effect computers have in the development of new artforms as a result of available new technologies and present their views on potential direction, including collaborative works, interdisciplinary and cross-disciplinary projects, and curriculum revisions in sculpture education.

Hand Tools . . . or Head Tools?

Chair: Robin Baker, Royal College of Art

Panelists: Alison Black, Reading University
Marc Canter, Macromind
Gillian Crampton Smith, Royal College of Art
Bill Verplank, ID 2

Large-firm designers use computers in fields like architecture, where the production aspects of design

California State Lottery —"Decco"

Playing Decco, a woman hallucinates that she's in Cardland. Will she choose Sammy, the desperate Five of Spades? Will he handle rejection?

Ralph Guggenheim
Pixar
3240 Kerner Boulevard
San Rafael, CA 94901 USA

415-236-4000
415-238-0388 (fax)

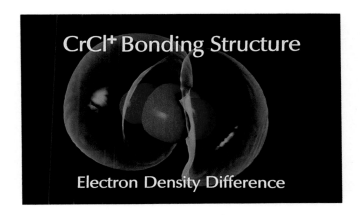

Computational Quantum Chemistry in Catalysis Research

Examples of visualizations of various catalyses involving chromium chloride, magnesium oxide and faujasite clusters.

Dean Geiken
152 Computing Applications Building
605 E. Springfield Avenue
Champaign, IL 61820 USA

217-244-6353
217-244-1987 (fax)

Cuisine Art

A mischievous baby squash takes a whimsical tour through the art museum.

Leoung O'Young
36 Woodycrest Avenue
Toronto, Ontario, Canada M4J 3A7

416-462-3388

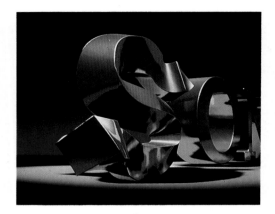

Dancing Sony

The capability of Polygon Pictures' Skelton Coordinate System is demonstrated in its first commercial application.

Toshifumi Kawahara
c/o Polygon Pictures
Bond Street T11
2-2-43 Higashi Shinagawa,
Shinagawa-ku
Tokyo 140 Japan

03-474-4321
03-474-4322 (fax)

Dirty Power

This "power-ful" animation was inspired by the artist's exploration of the oftentimes seductive nature of 3D computer graphics.

Robert Lurye
1231 Georgia
College Station , TX 77840 USA

409-764-7521
409-845-4491 (fax)

Droomfabriek (Dream Factory)

Morphosis uses computer graphics to build a dream factory.

Jeroen Buys
Morphosis b.v.
Rembrandtlaan 24A
3723 BJ Bilthoven, The Netherlands

30-28-72-85
30-28-54-99 (fax)

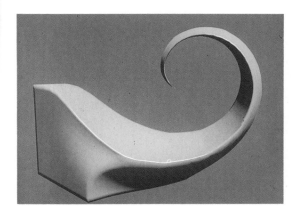

Ductile Flow

Flow patterns are created by iterating non-linear spatial transformations. Polyhedral objects placed in the space follow the flow. Sufficient ductility is provided by adaptive, stochastic subdivision.

Craig Reynolds
Symbolics, Inc.
1401 Westwood Boulevard
Los Angeles, CA 90024 USA

213-478-0681
213-477-1346 (fax)

Entropy

This artful animation, inspired by the Hopi Indian story of creation, explores Darwin's theory of evolution and the issue of entropy.

Robin Noorda
Morphosis b.v.
Rembrandtlaan 24A
3723 BJ Bilthoven, The Netherlands

30-28-72-85
30-28-54-99 (fax)

Fables Géométriques "La Laitière et le Pot au Lait"

La Fontaine's beloved fable of "The Milkmaid and the Jug of Milk" is animated as part of the T.V. series, "Geometric Tales".

Philippe Baudart
Fantome
71 rue Ampère
75017 Paris, France

1-40-53-01-23
1-40-53-02-07 (fax)

Forest Fire Simulation

This realistic visualization of a forest fire is modeled with textured quadric surfaces.

Geoffrey Gardner
MS D12-237
1000 Woodbury Road
Woodbury, NY 11797 USA

516-682-8417
516-682-8022 (fax)

Gas Pipe

The trials and tribulations of a gas pipe.

Phil Hurrell
SVC Television
142 Wardour Street
London W1V 3AU, England

44 71-734-1600
44 71-437-1854 (fax)

The Funtastic World of Hanna-Barbera

The Flintstones meet the Jetsons in this wild flight simulator ride at Universal Studios in Orlando.

Michael Wahrman
deGraf/Wahrman
8936 Keith Avenue
West Hollywood, CA 90069 USA

213-278-2135
213-278-2054 (fax)

The Great "Blue Ouah Ouah"

This loveable character will win his way into your heart.

Philippe Baudart
Fantome
71 rue Ampère
75017 Paris, France

1-40-53-01-23
1-40-53-02-07 (fax)

Grinning Evil Death

A blood-spattered tale of modern-day pest control utilizing 2D animation and 3D graphics.

Mike McKenna
Bob Sabiston
20 Ames Street
E15-023
Cambridge, MA 02139 USA

617-253-0661
617-258-6264 (fax)

I Have Never Seen, But I Know...

All of the creatures and plants in this graceful underwater fantasy were generated and animated by De Leon's Branching Object Generation and Animation System.

Midori Kitagawa De Leon
c/o Visualization Laboratory
College of Architecture
Texas A & M University
College Station, TX 77843-3137 USA

409-845-3465
409-845-4491 (fax)

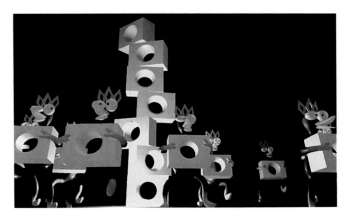

The Hole

The quirky black birds in this artist's first original work are the hole-block builders.

Motonori Sakakibara
Namco Yokohama Mirai Kenkyuto
15-1, Shenei-Cho, Kouhoku-Ku
Yokohama, 223 Japan

045 593 0711
045 592 8086 (fax)

ILM Computer Graphics SIGGRAPH '90 Demo Reel

A demonstration of computer graphics and special effects produced for recent theatric-release motion pictures and commercials.

Nancy St. John
Industrial Light & Magic
P.O. Box 2459
San Rafael, CA 94912 USA

415-258-2000
415-454-4768 (fax)

In Search of Muscular Axis

Polygon Pictures demonstrates their new Skelton Coordinate System which can provide complete mechanism to all types of motion and deformation.

Toshifumi Kawahara
c/o Polygon Pictures
Bond Street T11
2-2-43 Higashi Shinagawa,
Shinagawa-ku
Tokyo 140 Japan

03-474-4321
03-474-4322 (fax)

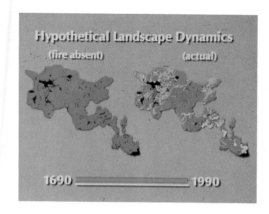

Landscape Dynamics of Yellowstone Park

The historical impact of fire on landscape diversity in Yellowstone Park is demonstrated with graphs from 1690 to 1990.

Colleen Bushell
152 Computing Applications Building
605 E. Springfield Avenue
Champaign, IL 61820 USA

217-244-1987
217-244-1987 (fax)

Life Savers Holes —"Babies"

Are 61 characters made of candy and eight pieces of playground equipment too much for a 30-second spot?

Ralph Guggenheim
Pixar
3240 Kerner Boulevard
San Rafael, CA 94901 USA

415-236-4000
415-238-0388 (fax)

Lava Jr.

John Lasseter's classic film inspires new interpretations.

Randy Bauer
Luxo-Klone Productions
1717 W. Sixth Street, Suite 150
Austin, TX 78703 USA

512-476-0400
512-476-6382 (fax)

Masterplan

Commercial work produced by Morphosis b.v.

Jeroen Buys
Morphosis b.v.
Rembrandtlaan 24A
3734 BJ Bilthoven, The Netherlands

30-28-72-85
30-28-54-99 (fax)

Mathematics! Similarity and the Story of π

Excerpts from several modules of the Mathematics! Project—a series of videotapes to aid in teaching high school mathematics.

Jim Blinn
305 S. Hill Street
Pasadena, CA 91106 USA

818-356-3758
818-356-3763 (fax)

More Bells and Whistles

This data-driven animation of an orchestra uses a MIDI (Musical Instrument Digital Interface) control stream. Software was developed to automate the synchronization of instrument motion based on musical events.

Wayne Lytle
Cornell National Supercomputer Facility
B49 Caldwell Hall
Ithaca, NY 14853 USA

607-255-3985
607-255-0823 (fax)

McDonald's - "Save the Universe"

If all the people in the world came into one McDonald's at the same time, would the earth tilt off its axis wreaking havoc on the universe?

Jon Townley
Metrolight Studios
5724 W. Third Street, Suite 400
Los Angeles, CA 90036 USA

213-932-0400
213-932-8440 (fax)

The Nature

Excerpts from this work produced for Osaka's EXPO '90 dramatically combine live action and computer graphics animation.

Masaaki Taira
3-13-6, Higashi-shinagawa
Shinagawa-ku
Tokyo 140 Japan

03-450-8181
03-471-2607 (fax)

1990 SIGGRAPH Demo Reel

Recent commercial work is highlighted.

Larry Lamb
Lamb & Company, Inc.
1010 South 7th Street
Minneapolis, MN 55445 USA

612-333-8666
612-333-9173 (fax)

The Next Giant Leap

Excerpts from NASA's manned Lunar/Mars Mission Studies.

Gunter Sabionski
NASA/Johnson Space Center
JL4
Houston, TX 77058 USA

713-483-8106
713-483-5200 (fax)

Nissan "Time Machine"

Time Machine is a commercial produced for Japanese television featuring a realistically rendered animated sports car.

Charlie Gibson
Rhythm & Hues, Inc.
910 North Sycamore Avenue
Hollywood, CA 90038 USA

213-851-6500
213-851-5505 (fax)

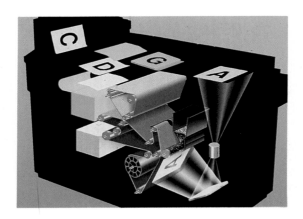

Océ Copy Simulation

An animation that explains how the paper track inside the Océ copier works.

Adriaan Lokman
Morphosis b.v.
Rembrandtlaan 24A
3723 BJ Bilthoven, The Netherlands

30-28-72-85
30-28-54-99 (fax)

Partners

Whimsical animation highlights this commercial piece.

Robin Noorda
Morphosis b.v.
Rembrandtlaan 24A
3723 BJ Bilthoven, The Netherlands

30-28-7285
30-28-54-99 (fax)

Panspermia

Panspermia: The theory that life exists and is distributed throughout the universe in the form of germs or spores.

Karl Sims
Thinking Machines Corporation
245 First Street
Cambridge, MA 02142 USA

617-876-1111
617-876-1823 (fax)

A Passing Shower

Road surfaces, solar penumbra and streaks of light are rendered using novel techniques to produce photo-realistic visual simulation of outdoor scenes.

Eihachiro Nakamae
Faculty of Engineering
Hiroshima University
Saijo-cho, Higashi-Hiroshima 724 Japan

824-22-7111 ext. 3445
824-22-7195 (fax)

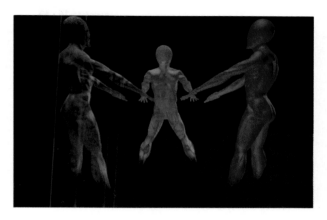

Prebirth

The birth of man as an assembly of three elements: mind, body, flesh, is symbolized using different transparency value and textures.

Osama M. Hashem
220 E. 25th Street, Apt #5A
New York, NY 10010 USA

212-779-1923
212-486-2664 (fax)

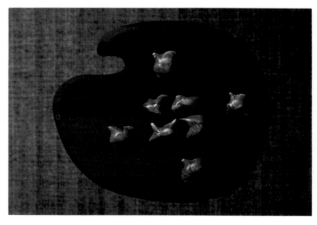

Pigment Promenade

Pigment Promenade proffers playful pals...a whimsical look at paint blobs having fun. Yee-Haw!

Peter Litwinowicz
Apple Computer, Inc.
20705 Valley Green Drive, MS 60W
Cupertino, CA 95014 USA

408-974-1752
408-474-0781 (fax)

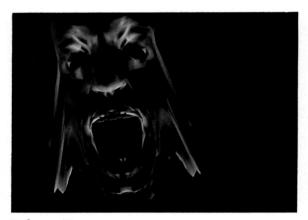

Robocop II

The anti-hero in "Robocop II", a stop motion puppet, recalls his human existence through the use of a computer generated character based on a live actor.

Michael Wahrman
deGraf/Wahrman, Inc.
8936 Keith Avenue
West Hollywood, CA 90069 USA

213-278-2135
213-278-2054 (fax)

A Sequence from the Evolution of Form

The beauty, elegance and content of form is expressed through computer graphics.

William Latham
IBM UK Scientific Centre
St. Clement Street Winchester
Hampshire 5023 9DR United Kingdom

44-962-844-191
44-962-840-094 (fax)

7-Up "Saxaphone"

A fully animated computer generated character interacts with its live-action environment.

Charlie Gibson
Rhythm & Hues, Inc.
910 North Sycamore Avenue
Hollywood, CA 90038 USA

213-851-6500
213-851-5505 (fax)

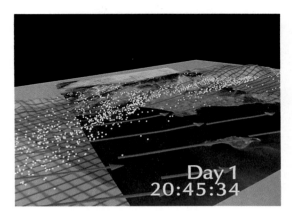

Smog: Visualizing the Components

This visualization shows the results of a numerical model of pollution in the Los Angeles basin.

Colleen Bushell
152 Computing Applications Building
605 E. Springfield Avenue
Champaign, IL 61820 USA

217-244-6830
217-244-1987 (fax)

Splash Dance

This animation illustrates the techniques described in the SIGGRAPH paper, "Rapid Fluid Dynamics for Computer Graphics" in an astounding display of water effects.

Michael Kass
Apple Computer, Inc.
MS 60W
20705 Valley Green Drive
Cupertino, CA 95014 USA

408-974-1754
408-974-0781 (fax)

Solar Crisis Hologram Animation

Waging a desperate battle to divert a devastating solar flare, Earth scientists create an ultra-modern holographic display system in this feature film.

Jamie Dixon
1111 Karlstad Drive
Sunnyvale, CA 94089 USA

408-745-6755
213-823-0433 (fax)

Styro

A dog can't take a walk at night anymore.

Tom Sinnott
676 N. Lasalle Street
Chicago, IL 60610 (USA)

312-440-1875
312-440-1537 (fax)

Sunrise Animation

The use of monochromatic colours and highly controlled lighting effects focuses the viewer on proposed product designs and signage elements.

Semannia Luk Cheung
Design Vision Inc.
479 Wellington Street West
Toronto, Ontario, Canada M5V 1E7

416-585-2020

This Is Not Frank's Planet

The misfit pilots of a small space ship talk their way through a colorful landscape looking for a Mysterious Destination.

Mark Swain
Instructional Media Center
California State University, Chico
Chico, CA 95929-0005 USA

916-895-4421

Think Twice

A double-talking, fully dimensional, two-mouthed blockhead is made possible by Homer and Associates' new "Lip Service" technique.

Peter Conn
Homer & Associates
1420 N. Beachwood Drive
Los Angeles, CA 90028 USA

213-462-4710
213-462-2109 (fax)

NOTES

NOTES